50 STRATEGIES TO ENSURE K–6 LITERACY SUCCESS

Aligning Instruction to the **FIVE PILLARS** of Reading

KIMBERLY A. TYSON

Foreword by Sharon V. Kramer

555 North Morton Street
Bloomington, IN 47404
800.733.6786 (toll free) / 812.336.7700
FAX: 812.336.7790
email: info@SolutionTree.com
SolutionTree.com

Visit **go.SolutionTree.com/literacy/FSK6** to download the free reproducibles in this book. To access the exclusive reproducibles in this book, enter the unique access code found on the inside front cover. Readers with ebooks, please email orders@solutiontree.com to receive access.

Printed in the United States of America

LCCN Control Number: 2025009014

ISBN: 979-8-89374-027-1

Solution Tree
Jeffrey C. Jones, CEO
Edmund M. Ackerman, President

Solution Tree Press
President and Publisher: Douglas M. Rife
Associate Publishers: Todd Brakke and Kendra Slayton
Editorial Director: Laurel Hecker
Art Director: Rian Anderson
Copy Chief: Jessi Finn
Production Editors: Kate St. Ives and Madonna Evans
Copy Editor: Charlotte Jones
Proofreader: Jessica Starr
Text Designer: Laura Cox
Cover Designer: Rian Anderson
Acquisitions Editors: Carol Collins and Hilary Goff
Content Development Specialist: Amy Rubenstein
Associate Editors: Sarah Ludwig and Elijah Oates
Editorial Assistant: Madison Chartier

This book is dedicated to the women who have shaped me, some of whom I've had the privilege of knowing and others whom I've observed from afar.
Strong women. Kind women. Confident women.
Generous women. Spiritual women. Trailblazing women.
Thank you for serving as role models that have inspired confidence over my life and career.

Acknowledgments

This book would not have been written were it not for the many educators with whom I have had the pleasure to work, collaborate, and support over the years—administrators, principals, teachers, and instructional coaches. Each of you serves a distinct and important role. The dedication shown for your students academically, emotionally, and socially every single day inspires me. Each time I sat down to write, you were at the forefront of my mind.

Deep appreciation and respect is due to my Solution Tree friends and colleagues. First, a sincere thank you to Jeff Jones, Douglas Rife, and the editorial advisory board for giving this book the green light. Next, enormous appreciation goes to Hilary Goff, who was never too busy to listen to the quandaries that arose along my writing journey. Additionally, your expert guidance and timely feedback helped shape this literacy resource. Claudia Wheatley, thank you for being my friend and always providing just the right nudge at just the right time. Sharon Kramer, it has been a privilege to support your work as you strengthen teachers who need your deep expertise most.

Thank you to Dr. Lyndsi Smith, principal of Pettit Park Elementary Technology Academy, who contributed to this manuscript during early conversations about the content and specifically lending her expertise to the Leader's Lens elements. Additionally, thank you to the teachers in Kokomo School District, Indiana, for sharing images and stories of how you support literacy learning that inspired this book. May you continue to greatly impact students' ability to learn and achieve at high levels.

A sincere thank you to each of the professional educators who generously gave your time to serve as reviewers. Finally, thank you to each talented member of the Press who edited and designed this manuscript in order to make the final product shine.

Thank you to my dear friends and family for checking in while I was absent writing in my office for many months, for always asking about progress made, and for kindly listening to my response.

Solution Tree Press would like to thank the following reviewers:

Lindsey Bingley
Literacy and Numeracy Strategist
Foothills Academy Society
Calgary, Alberta, Canada

John D. Ewald
Education Consultant
Frederick, Maryland

Shauna Koopmans
Instructor, School of Arts and Education
Red Deer Polytechnic
Red Deer, Alberta, Canada

Luke Spielman
Principal
Park View Middle School
Mukwonago, Wisconsin

Sarah Svendsen
Pre-Kindergarten Teacher
Pine Crest School
Boca Raton, Florida

Rachel Swearengin
Fifth-Grade Teacher
Manchester Park Elementary
Lenexa, Kansas

Visit **go.SolutionTree.com/literacy/FSK6** to download the free reproducibles in this book. To access the exclusive reproducibles in this book, enter the unique access code found on the inside front cover. Readers with ebooks, please email orders@solutiontree.com to receive access.

Table of Contents

About the Author

Kimberly A. Tyson, PhD, or "Dr. Kimberly," as she is known by many, has served as a classroom teacher, college administrator and instructor, reading clinician, and literacy consultant across the United States in classrooms ranging from preschool to twelfth grade. When teaching elementary students and serving in clinical settings, she became keenly interested in how children learn to read and, in particular, in strategies that support emerging and struggling readers. She honed that interest when working with striving, struggling, and illiterate adults in reading clinics.

Kimberly contributes literacy insights at Dr. Kimberly's Literacy Blog (www.drkimberlytyson.com). She has written classroom curriculum and language arts sections of standardized assessments and chaired the Elementary Reading National Evaluation Preparation Committee for Pearson Education. Kimberly is a past president of several professional organizations and actively participates in contributing to the profession.

Over the years, she has joined with teachers, principals, and administrators to improve literacy in readers of all ages. Through The Literacy Lens Audit®, a research-based literacy audit she developed, Kimberly guided literacy leaders in assessing and improving curriculum, instruction, environment, and student achievement across schools and districts. In addition, Kimberly has worked with educational organizations, such as the I-READ Department of Education literacy improvement program, and educational service centers. She has also supported statewide literacy initiatives.

Kimberly discovered her love of word learning and vocabulary when working with middle and high school students in several initiatives within Kansas City Public Schools. Since then, vocabulary improvement has been the focus of much of her work and is captured in *Blended Vocabulary for K–12 Classrooms: Harnessing the Power of Digital*

Tools and Direct Instruction. Kimberly earned her doctorate from the University of Missouri–Kansas City.

To learn more about Kimberly's work, visit www.drkimberlytyson.com or follow her @tysonkimberly on X and Instagram @tysonkimberlya.

Foreword

by Sharon V. Kramer

What if there was just one resource that contained relevant, easy to understand information and strategies to deeply implement the five pillars of reading? No more searching online or through a myriad of publications, or completing modules or courses for an entire semester or year, to ensure quality reading instruction is truly happening daily in every classroom in all elementary schools. Fortunately, there is one resource that answers many questions and contains more than fifty strategies that work in every setting—*Fifty Strategies to Ensure K–6 Literacy Success* is a practical, easy-to-read guide with a user-friendly structure. It bridges the gap between literacy research (specifically the National Reading Panel's findings on the five pillars) and practical, evidence-based classroom strategies.

This book is timely, given the current focus on the science of reading (embodied in the five pillars) in schools, districts, and state departments of education. It emerges as an essential resource in this current educational climate, specifically designed to address a critical gap in existing literacy materials. While numerous publications adeptly explain the foundational five pillars and their supporting research, many fall short in providing clear, actionable, and evidence-based classroom strategies that busy educators can readily implement.

Kimberly A. Tyson masterfully builds important background knowledge while infusing implementation strategies so that every reader understands the why and how of phonemic awareness, phonics, fluency, vocabulary, and comprehension. Her extensive experience as a classroom teacher, reading clinician, and national literacy consultant is evident in every word. Kimberly offers a unique perspective because she has been a student of quality reading instruction for years, even authoring *Blended Vocabulary for K–12 Classrooms: Harnessing the Power of Digital Tools and Direct Instruction,* and has utilized all these strategies to ensure students become confident readers. As a national literacy consultant, Tyson has supported thousands of educators across varied socioeconomic and geographic contexts—from urban and rural schools to affluent and low-income communities—helping them implement evidence-based literacy practices. This blend of practical "what works" and theoretical "why it works" from an individual who has navigated both realms significantly enhances the book's authority and applicability for educators.

Readers of this book will be delighted to find that the author consistently moves beyond the rhetoric surrounding the science of reading to offer specific steps to bring these generalities to life. Tyson provides the tools and strategies with real-life examples that make a true difference. Her conversational approach and inclusion of classroom examples make the strategies more meaningful and encourage the reader to move forward with confidence.

One of the most impressive attributes of this book is the inclusion of not only teachers but instructional coaches and school leaders in the process. Examples and strategies for coaches are embedded in each chapter, as well as a Leader's Lens that can be used to support and monitor the progress of both students and teachers with the idea that growing readers is everyones' job. This builds a culture where everyone is responsible for every student's learning.

Too often educators see the five pillars as separate entities that must be addressed. This book supports educators in understanding and implementing each of the five pillars as interconnected components of a comprehensive literacy program. Tyson demonstrates how each pillar is a necessary part of the whole as each one is explored and discussed. This alignment of the pillars fosters a deeper understanding of the reading process that allows educators to address the needs of all learners, hence the approach to learning to read is diagnostic and precise rather than random and scattered. The core philosophy underpinning this book is the cultivation of intentionality in every aspect of literacy education. Intentional instruction is purposeful teacher decision making, grounded in evidence-based practices, learning targets, and continuous assessment data, that is responsive to individual student needs. This focus ensures its applicability to diverse learners, including struggling readers and English learners, by providing differentiated and explicit instructional approaches. The strategies offered are designed to be adaptable and sensitive to the varied linguistic, socioeconomic, and developmental needs of all K–6 learners, promoting a pedagogical approach rooted in genuine inclusivity.

Fifty Strategies to Ensure K–6 Literacy Success fosters a common language and research-based understanding among educators, promoting collaborative efforts in improving literacy outcomes. Each chapter contains an explanation of the important vocabulary related to the pillar. Clarity always precedes competence in any undertaking. As educators collaborate to build shared knowledge of each pillar and connect them one to the other, more students learn more. The true mission of any school or district is learning for *all*. It has never been more evident than now that literacy is key to ensure we reach all students. In fact, most would agree that there can rarely be improvement without literacy improvement.

As the author suggests, this book is not meant to be read cover to cover. The power of this work is that each chapter can be read in any order. We all have professional books on our shelves that have never been read. It is not that the books are not well-written or important, it is a matter of time. This is a book that is so meaningful to the everyday work of educators that it should never be on a shelf. Its repeated emphasis on collaborative learning and structured next steps indicates that this book is not merely a resource for individual teachers, but a tool for building collective efficacy within a school. It provides a framework for professional learning communities, fostering a culture where educators learn from each other, which leads to consistent, high-quality reading instruction. I encourage readers to actively engage with the book's content. Become students of the content to enhance your instructional practices and, ultimately, ensure K–6 literacy success.

This book represents a comprehensive and accessible blueprint for implementing the five pillars of effective reading instruction. It is a resource that reflects a deep and abiding commitment to the field of K–6 literacy education. Ultimately, the future of society depends on the collective effort of educators to ensure every student achieves reading success. *Fifty Strategies to Ensure K–6 Literacy Success* stands as an indispensable partner in that noble and vital endeavor.

Introduction

I was a young, novice kindergarten teacher fresh out of college in the 1980s. At 21, my first teaching position was in a laboratory school where I welcomed 32(!) kindergarten students. Many of my students were from well-educated families whose parents were professors at the university associated with the elementary school where I taught.

I was eager to do my best as I taught a room brimming with energetic young students. Similar to many beginning teachers, I spent hours combing the curriculum, trying to be a step ahead of my lesson plans. Letters, sounds, and read alouds were a large and important part of each day's literacy routines. I recall that most of my students were able to read to some degree at the end of the school year, but I had little idea why. I was perplexed as to why some students learned to read so easily while others struggled. And I had little idea how to help my struggling readers.

I became increasingly curious about how children learn to read. I soon became engrossed in a master's degree program in reading where I served as a graduate assistant in a reading clinic. During those two years, I soaked in everything I could from my classes, professors, and the clinical work with struggling readers of all ages, including adults. From these experiences, I became hooked on developing my knowledge and skills in order to help often-frustrated students become able readers.

Unexpectedly, I went directly into a doctoral program where I was privileged to learn from several influencers in the field of reading and literacy. Anthony Manzo (1969; Manzo & Casale, 1985; Manzo, Manzo & Thomas, 2006), one of the early leaders in content area literacy, taught me a great deal about how we assess, diagnose, and support students to become literate, lifelong learners.

Over the years, I've had a continuing interest in literacy, primarily early literacy. Working in shifting roles and serving as a literacy consultant with teachers and leaders,

I continually think about what skills, knowledge, and strategies teachers need to help their students become readers and deepen their literacy skills.

The *five pillars of reading*, (1) phonemic awareness, (2) phonics, (3) fluency, (4) vocabulary, and (5) comprehension, as identified by the National Reading Panel (NRP), had an impact on federal legislation and literacy initiatives in the early 2000s (National Institute of Child Health and Human Development [NICHD], 2000a). Interestingly, the impact of the NRP report and findings continues today. When the five essential pillars were first identified in the year 2000, many teachers and administrators were unfamiliar with the specific components. At that time, I helped thousands of teachers serving in urban and rural settings, affluent settings, and schools with students from impoverished families. I watched teachers grow their skills and confidence around the five pillars. They began making intentional, evidence-based decisions about how best to implement phonemic awareness, phonics, fluency, vocabulary, and comprehension in their classrooms.

With the COVID-19 pandemic came the rise of the science of reading (SoR), 21st century style, which once again brought the five pillars to the forefront in elementary classrooms in particular. In the fall of 2022, returning from a work trip, I drafted the outline for the book you are about to read. And then it sat. Every once in a while, I'd reread it and put it away. In January 2024, I reviewed the outline again and let it take shape in my mind. It seemed like the right time to bring my experiences, research, and strategies for the five pillars to life.

About This Book

The science of reading has been adopted in thirty-eight states (Schwartz, 2024b) and is rapidly moving across the United States. The main tenet, that research should inform reading practices, is here to stay. The five pillars of reading impact elementary teachers, in particular, as they plan and deliver literacy instruction.

As I reviewed resources, I found numerous books that addressed the pillars. Most provide a sound explanation of each pillar and supporting research. However, none of the resources take an in-depth approach that not only provides important background information but also includes clear, easy-to-follow, evidence-based classroom strategies to support K–6 students.

Fifty Strategies to Ensure K–6 Literacy Success: Aligning Instruction to the Five Pillars of Reading addresses this gap and sets itself apart from other books of similar topics in that it is heavy on practicality and includes fifty strategies (with ten additional strategies accessible online only at **go.SolutionTree.com/literacy/FSK6**). My goal in writing this book is to equip teachers, coaches, and principals to understand the *what, why,* and *how* to implement the five pillars in elementary classrooms to benefit students' literacy learning.

What You Can Expect From This Book

As I developed *Fifty Strategies to Ensure K–6 Literacy Success*, teachers, coaches, and principals were front of mind. I continually thought about the question, What is essential for you to know when implementing the essential pillars to support students' literacy growth? The five pillars serve as fundamental building blocks for equipping students for lifelong reading success. As a lifelong educator, I firmly believe that understanding the what, why, and how as you refine your classroom instructional practice is time well spent.

You may serve as a teacher, instructional coach, principal, curriculum director, or district administrator as you read this book. Each of your roles is important as you strive to implement the science of reading and best first instruction in classrooms. My overarching goal is to provide a common language and research-based understanding about how each pillar impacts students as they develop and deepen their literacy skills. That knowledge provides a foundation to engage with and explore ways to deeply implement the five pillars best suited to meet the needs of learners in each unique classroom.

Read, explore, implement. Begin the conversation in your school about how the pillars and the strategies can best meet the needs of your students. Reach out to me to join a book chat. Take the next step to forward evidence-based literacy learning in your setting.

Structure and Features

This book is structured as a how-to guide, and its features focus on implementing the five pillars in the classroom. Given its length, this resource is not intended to be read cover to cover in a sitting or two. It is organized, instead, to facilitate the ability to dip in and out of chapters to best support your current instructional needs. For example, you may wish to better understand the science of reading and how to design your classroom environment to best support literacy for students, which is explored in chapter 1. Or, you may be an early educator teaching emergent readers who need strategies for teaching phonemic awareness and phonics, which are found in chapters 2 and 3. If you're an intermediate teacher, you may choose to focus on how to best teach vocabulary and comprehension, both of which are unpacked in chapters 5 and 6. Regardless of how you choose to read and digest the content, use this book as a tool and resource to support reading instruction.

While this book includes a great deal of content and features, no book can be everything to everyone. For example, while the five pillars are the focus of this resource, there are other contributors to reading success, one of which is motivation. Motivation can be addressed through social interaction and by providing reading choice through classroom libraries, for example. Additionally, I don't address how to organize your instruction within the literacy block—other resources do that well, such as *Literacy in a PLC at Work®: Guiding Teams to Get Going and Get Better in Grades K–6 Reading* (Maeker & Heller, 2023). And, while there are computer-assisted programs that have merit, this book does not include an extensive review of those programs. Rather, use the guidelines presented to determine whether your computer-assisted programs are good tools for student practice and review. Finally, this book is primarily focused on how to implement evidence-based literacy strategies that support each pillar, which includes best first instruction and strategies suitable for small-group instruction and support for struggling readers and English learners.

In chapter 1, I begin by providing a historical perspective on how literacy instruction has shifted and evolved since the early 1900s, along with a thorough description of the science of reading and its impact on K–12 education. Additionally, you'll find five strategies specific to intentional instruction and establishing a literacy-rich environment to support teaching and literacy learning.

Chapter 2 details phonemic awareness, the first of the five pillars of reading. I have included the challenges of teaching phonemic awareness as well as the characteristics of effective instruction along with nine instructional strategies.

Chapter 3 takes a deep dive into phonics as a building block for fluency and comprehension. You can explore seven strategies that will support students as they connect sounds and symbols.

Chapter 4 explores fluency as the bridge to comprehension. You'll find eleven strategies to support modeled, paired, and repeated reading.

The fourth pillar, vocabulary, is unpacked in chapter 5 and includes ten direct and indirect word learning strategies.

Comprehension—the heart of reading—culminates the five pillars of reading and is explored in chapter 6. Eight before-, during-, and after-reading strategies support your students as they read and comprehend fiction, nonfiction, and informational texts.

Each chapter is organized around three questions: (1) What is it (the pillar)?, (2) Why is it (the pillar) important?, and (3) What works in the classroom? I've used this framework to organize professional learning for educators for many years, and I've found that it is straightforward and useful in helping research make sense in the classroom, where it matters. Naturally, the *what works* portion is always the heart of the presentation, and it is the heart of this resource.

Each chapter includes challenges specific to teaching that pillar. They will help you think strategically about the factors that influence why a student may be having difficulty with acquiring phonics skills, for example. Or, they will help you decide what to do when students lack the vocabulary necessary for reading and comprehending. For each pillar, you'll find characteristics of effective instruction related to it. These high-level elements provide a broader picture of that pillar and will support your instruction.

At the beginning of each chapter, you'll find key vocabulary highlighted in a text box. If you're reading with colleagues, this will help you develop a common vocabulary around literacy, the science of reading, and the pillars.

The strategies are the star of each chapter. Each strategy table includes suggested grade levels, instructional grouping, and tips and considerations along with simple steps summarizing each strategy. They're formatted to provide all the information at a glance.

You'll find recommended resources in the form of book lists in most chapters that will help you learn more, support your students, and grow your professional library.

At the end of each chapter, there are *five key takeaways*. They'll provide a quick highlight to refresh your learning and focus discussion with your grade-level team. You'll also find *five key next steps* to move learning forward as you consider each next step. Here, you'll consider suggestions and plan how you can take next steps toward implementing strategies found within each pillar.

The Leader's Lens included at the close of each chapter provides supervision support and classroom connections (look-fors) for leaders. Each Leader's Lens was designed with input from a practicing elementary principal specifically to help principals and coaches support effective literacy instruction.

Intended Audience

The following educators can benefit from this resource depending on your role and goals for reading this book.

- Teachers
- Collaborative teams
- Principals and district leaders
- Instructional coaches

Those who teach students in K–6 classrooms will benefit most from this book. In each chapter, you will find a clear description of the pillar, why it's important, and what works in the classroom.

Working together as a collaborative team is always recommended since discussion, feedback, and insights from others strengthen our practice. I hope you will engage in a book study as you explore each pillar. At the end of each chapter, you'll find next steps that can guide your conversations and help you plan the actions you will take to deepen literacy instruction in your classrooms and school.

If you are a principal or district leader, you have an important leadership role as your school and district implement the science of reading. This resource provides the *what, why,* and *how* to lead and sustain implementation of the five core literacy practices in elementary classrooms.

If you are an instructional coach, your role is important and challenging as you train and support teachers. This book will help you do both. Divide the book into manageable chunks that can be delivered and discussed in grade-level collaborative meetings, staff meetings, or professional learning days. At the end of each chapter, next steps and the Leader's Lens will give you a lot to consider as you support teachers in implementing the pillars with their students.

How You Can Use This Book

This book is a wealth of information for supporting teachers, coaches, and principals through the implementation of strategies that support the five essential pillars. There are numerous ways you can use this book within your classroom, collaborative team, or school. I suggest the following types of activities as you move forward with best practices in your setting.

- Engage in a whole-faculty or collaborative-team book study to deepen your understanding as you implement evidence-based strategies in your school. Think about using collaborative digital tools to store and share ideas.
- Use the unique access code found on the inside front cover of this book to access the fifty strategies at **go.SolutionTree.com/literacy/FSK6** and print them to use as step-by-step guides and references as you implement the five pillars.
- Become clear on the tenets of the science of reading and the components of structured literacy.
- Engage in discussions about intentional instruction and intentional literacy-rich environments in your classrooms that support students' listening, speaking, reading, and writing growth.
- Have conversations about how to increase book access in your classrooms to support readers of all varied backgrounds, levels, and interests.
- Become clear on the key differences between phonemic awareness, phonological awareness, and phonics. Understanding the differences will serve you well as you help emerging readers acquire early reading skills that positively impact reading and spelling.
- Learn how to integrate phonemic awareness with letters while keeping the focus on sounds.
- Implement high-quality, evidence-based phonics instruction in classrooms as students *learn to read* and *read to learn.*
- Learn about orthographic mapping and how it relates to spelling, decoding, and reading automaticity.

- Grow fluent readers through a plethora of research-based fluency strategies that help students read accurately with appropriate speed and expression to support comprehension.
- View the YouTube videos on my channel (www.youtube.com/@Learng Unlimited) to see students engaged in fluency activities that are evidence-based and fun while building their fluency skills.
- Discuss how to create a culture of word learning that supports vocabulary acquisition across the school day.
- Understand the word gap that some students have as they enter school and, even more importantly, how to address it.
- Create a word-filled classroom that brims with direct and indirect word learning opportunities to enrich and build students' vocabularies so they are better equipped to read, engage, and comprehend text.
- Learn more about theories of comprehension to get clear on your definition of comprehension, which will influence your instruction.
- Equip students to understand varied text types and structures in order to purposefully read and comprehend text.
- Implement strategies to assist students in engaging with text before, during, and after reading.

It's Time to Get Started

To begin, you'll learn about the changing landscape in literacy over recent decades. In addition, you'll think about how intentional instruction and intentional environments support the five pillars of effective reading instruction. I encourage you to spend some time in chapter 1, take current stock, and reflect on how your classroom literacy environment fares in order to consider how it can be enriched to support and extend literacy learning.

One final word specific to the strategies. If I were in your shoes, I might be tempted to move quickly to the strategy figures. Since this book is designed to be a resource in which you can dip in and out to get what you need, begin where it best serves your needs, implement a strategy, reflect, try another one, and so on. However, I think you'll benefit from spending time getting clear on the definition of each pillar (What is it?) and the research behind each pillar (Why is it important?) prior to implementing strategies (What works in the classroom?). Wherever you choose to launch your journey within this book, I trust the strategies, resources, and tools will support your effort to create strong, literate students who are well equipped for lifelong learning.

fifty strategies

Chapter 5

Chapter 6

Key Vocabulary

Literacy and Literacy-Rich Environments

Anchor Chart	A written tool that supports instruction or classroom procedures and "anchors" learning for students
Balanced Literacy	The predominant approach for teaching reading in elementary schools since the late 1990s; it includes common components such as shared reading, guided reading, and independent reading.
Five Pillars of Reading	The core elements of effective reading instruction, as evidenced by research from the National Reading Panel; they include phonemic awareness, phonics, oral reading fluency, vocabulary, and comprehension.
Gradual Release of Responsibility	Refers to scaffolding instruction for students that includes three stages: modeling (typically by the teacher), practicing with students, and the student performing the strategy independently; I refer to this as the show me, help me, let me protocol.
Instructional Strategies	Learning techniques, methods, or processes that a teacher uses during instruction to help improve student learning and outcomes; they typically provide the opportunity to actively engage students as they become more literate, metacognitive learners.
Learning Targets	A statement that describes the knowledge or skills students will gain by the end of a lesson or unit of study; they are often expressed as *I can* statements in student-friendly language.
Literacy-Rich Environment	An environment in which students are surrounded by print-rich materials and have multiple opportunities to engage with language, word learning, and authentic texts for a variety of purposes throughout the day
Models of Reading	Reading models that delineate the complexity of reading and how it develops, creating a picture of how people learn to read
National Reading Panel	A group of scholars—scientists, educators, researchers, administrators, and teacher educators—convened by the National Institute of Child Health and Development to work with the U.S. Department of Education; the NRP's sole purpose was to understand the research and summarize its findings in order to benefit educators and children. The National Reading Panel Report had an impact on federal legislation and literacy initiatives in the early 2000s.
Science of Reading (SoR)	Refers to a comprehensive, interdisciplinary body of evolving research that sheds light on the best research-affirmed practices to better understand how we learn to read, the skills involved, and the brain's connection to reading; the SoR is not a reading program, philosophy, or purchased curriculum.
Sound Walls	A tool to support phonemic awareness, sound-symbol relationships, and phonics instruction
Structured Literacy	An all-encompassing term that refers to instruction that is evidence-based and provides explicit, systematic, engaging, multisensory, and developmentally appropriate instruction
Word Walls	A visual display of words essential to reading, writing, or learning specific content

CHAPTER 1

The Literacy Landscape

Excellent literacy instruction builds a strong foundation for learning and, in turn, equips children to develop their potential, growing into adults who participate fully in their communities and society, enjoying the fullness that continuous learning brings to their lives.

—International Literacy Association

There may be no other educational endeavor that is as vital to our society as learning to read. Reading is a fundamental skill on which the health and welfare of our democratic society lie. In frequent conversations with parents of preschool children, early interest in reading is always a source of pride and anticipation, as it should be, because we all recognize alphabet knowledge as an important first step toward reading.

Learning to read is a complex, multifaceted process. It is a subject that has been studied, dissected, and discussed (sometimes heatedly) for decades to better understand how children acquire the skills necessary to make the sound-symbol connection, a prerequisite to reading words. What we know and understand about the reading process has expanded over time. How we teach students to read and mature as lifelong readers has evolved as well.

In this first chapter, we begin with a look at several well-known models of reading that provide an explanation for how reading develops. Then, we'll take a close look at the history of the National Reading Panel and the influence it has had on reading instruction for nearly twenty-five years. Finally, we'll explore recent developments in the reading landscape.

The Shifting Literacy Landscape

Evidence-based instructional strategies support all readers, including struggling readers and students learning English. I've observed the literacy landscape shift over time, with a focus on reading more independently versus reading with more accountability, teaching whole language versus phonics, and using leveled reading materials versus authentic text.

The following sections provide a context for reading in which I explore three models of reading. Additionally, we'll look at the National Reading Panel and how their findings impact the science of reading, now adopted in legislation in forty states and the District of Columbia (Schwartz, 2024b). Then, we'll move to the importance of high-quality instruction and how intentional instruction is laid out in the science of reading. Finally, we'll look at how an intentional literacy-rich environment supports literacy learning for all students.

Teacher decision making is key. Learn about your students as individuals and readers. Follow the science. Teach with intentionality.

Models of Reading

Models of reading help delineate the complexity of reading and how it develops. They create a picture of how people learn to read. They are, however, not a model of reading instruction. They seek to explain the reading process, not how to teach reading. In other words, models of reading are important because they help us conceptualize reading. While they don't spell out how to teach reading, how we conceptualize reading typically impacts instruction and remediation, material selection, and how we respond to students as readers.

Various models of reading have been developed by educational researchers to explain the reading process. They vary from each other and seek to explain or show the interactions among the many factors involved in the process of reading. Models can be simple, such as the simple view of reading (Gough & Tunmer, 1986), or fairly complex, such as active view of reading (Duke & Cartwright, 2021; Scarborough, 2001). The psycholinguistic model of reading is an early model developed by Ken S. Goodman (1967), an influential whole-language advocate. More recent models include both cognitive and sociocultural factors (Cartwright & Duke, 2019), while others do not. Some models have catchy acronyms, such as direct and inferential mediation (DIME; Ahmed et al., 2016), direct and indirect effects model of reading (DIER; Kim, 2017), and deploying reading in varied environments (DRIVE; Cartwright & Duke, 2019). Each includes elements unique to the researchers' interpretation of how we learn to read. The *double helix theory of teaching* includes elements from these models but is specifically designed to inform teaching (Wyse & Hacking, 2024).

In the following, we'll look closely at three models that have influenced reading instruction over the past forty years. They include the simple view of reading (Gough & Tunmer, 1986), the reading rope (Scarborough, 2001), and the active view of reading model (Duke & Cartwright, 2021). These models reference the five components of reading as delineated by the National Reading Panel (NICHD 2000a, 2000b). The simple view of reading and Scarborough's reading rope are mentioned and pictured repeatedly within science of reading articles and documents, hence the impact on both science and instruction. The most recent model, the active view of reading (Duke & Cartwright, 2021), expands the view of reading and includes elements related to the reader's self-regulation along with bridging process, which includes print concepts, reading fluency, and more. The elements of each model are summarized in table 1.1. Each model has strengths and, of course, limitations. Consider this as I unpack each one.

Table 1.1: Reading Instruction Models

Simple View of Reading (Gough & Tunmer, 1986)	Scarborough's (2001) Reading Rope	Active View of Reading (Duke & Cartwright, 2021)	Five Pillars of Reading (NICHD 2000a, 2000b)
Word recognition	Phonological awareness	Phonological awareness	Phonemic awareness
	Decoding	Alphabetic principle, phonics knowledge, decoding	Phonics
	Sight recognition	Fluency	Fluency
Language comprehension	Vocabulary	Vocabulary knowledge	Vocabulary
	Background knowledge Verbal reasoning Literacy knowledge Language structures	Language comprehension	Comprehension

Source: Adapted from Maeker & Heller, 2023.

The Simple View of Reading

The simple view of reading (SVR; Gough & Tunmer, 1986; Hoover & Gough, 1990) is known as a landmark contribution to the field of reading. Based on the work of Edmund Burke Huey (1908/1968), the SVR is straightforward yet captures the key cognitive activities associated with comprehending print. The simple view posits that reading (R) is the *product* of decoding (D) and language comprehension (C). They express it as: $D \times C = R$.

The simple view does not suggest that reading is a simple process. The researchers (Gough & Tunmer, 1986; Hoover & Gough, 1990) acknowledge that reading is a complex process; however, the model is a simple representation of the components (D × C) as two parts, both equally important. Additionally, decoding (word identification) and language comprehension occur independently and sequentially.

Decoding refers to all the work the reader does with phonics and comprehension, which is influenced by background knowledge and vocabulary that the reader has obtained through experiences, conversations, and read alouds. Philip B. Gough and William E. Tunmer (1986), two prolific educational researchers, also make the case for listening (language) comprehension and its relationship to reading. With emerging readers who cannot yet decode, reading with and to them using a wide variety of text types helps build listening comprehension skills. Today, we more commonly refer to decoding as *word recognition* and listening comprehension as *language comprehension*, which more accurately depicts the science of reading (Duke & Cartwright, 2021).

The SVR has instructional implications for the classroom. For example, if we put too much emphasis on teaching phonics through skill and drill, students may become adept at decoding but may lack sufficient background knowledge and vocabulary to comprehend proficiently. Conversely, if we don't spend enough time teaching phonics, students may not have the necessary skills to decode automatically, which negatively impacts comprehension. However, decoding skills are not enough to make skillful readers. Building background knowledge and vocabulary is essential as well. Along with a sound phonics curriculum, every school should have an intentional plan for building vocabulary and background knowledge through intentional read alouds along with direct and indirect word learning opportunities.

The Reading Rope

As I mentioned previously, reading is a complex and multifaceted process. Hollis S. Scarborough (2001), an American psychologist and literacy expert, sought to clarify and extend our understanding of reading fifteen years after the simple view of reading emerged. Her visual representation of reading as a rope has captured the attention of educators. Scarborough's reading rope, which has bubbled to the surface with the advent of the science of reading, seeks to take the many complexities of reading and help us make sense of them using a visual metaphor of ropes or strands for each element. The story goes that Scarborough twisted together pipe cleaners to represent the many interconnected strands of reading, and thus, the reading rope emerged.

Scarborough divides reading into two major strands: (1) language comprehension and (2) word recognition. Word recognition, the lower strand, is made up of these elements.

- Phonological awareness (sounds)
- Decoding (letters)
- Sight recognition (words)

Language comprehension, the upper strand, includes these elements.

- Background knowledge (facts, concepts, and so on)
- Vocabulary (breadth and depth and so on)
- Language structures (sentences)
- Verbal reasoning (inferences, metaphors, and so on)
- Literacy knowledge (print concepts, genres, and so on)

As students become more proficient readers, language comprehension becomes increasingly strategic, and word recognition becomes increasingly automatic. Additionally, the twisted ropes depict the interconnectedness of the two major components of reading—language comprehension and word recognition—and the interdependency of the subskills listed.

In summary, the reading rope gives educators a much clearer idea of the *what* of reading by including the subskills associated with language comprehension and word recognition. However, the *how* and degree to which each of the strands should be emphasized is not included. As educators, we must support our students to become readers who are both strategic and automatic. The strategies in this book address how you can intentionally implement these strands with your students. When these components intertwine, students become more skilled, accurate, and fluent readers who comprehend well.

The Active View of Reading

In 2021, another influential model of reading emerged to further delineate the complexities and overlapping elements of reading. The active view of reading (AVR) model was developed by respected literacy researchers Nell K. Duke and Kelly B. Cartwright (2021) with the intent of extending the simple view of reading to better align with advances in research over more than thirty-five years since the simple view was published.

The active view of reading model includes the following three key elements based on the science of reading.

1. The causes of reading difficulty beyond word recognition and language comprehension
2. The bridging processes between word recognition and language comprehension
3. The role of self-regulation in reading (Duke & Cartwright, 2021)

The AVR model extends the simple view of reading and overlaps with the reading rope, though there are differences as well. The active view of reading provides a more comprehensive view of reading, particularly with the addition of the reader's self-regulation and the bridging processes between word recognition and language comprehension. Reading fluency is often described as the bridge between decoding and comprehension (see chapter 4, page 133). While fluency is important, other factors impact reading as well; these include print concepts, vocabulary, morphology, and letter-sound-meaning flexibility. These bridging processes have a significant impact (effect size 0.70) on reading.

Duke and Cartwright (2021) posit that the active view of reading has more implications for instruction than the simple view of reading and better reflects the current science of reading. The bridging processes that overlap between word recognition and language comprehension can help you look at factors other than decoding for students who aren't growing as readers. Motivation and engagement, both components of self-regulation, are important reader considerations to keep in mind as you seek to develop active readers. Additionally, we sometimes refer to students who struggle with motivation and engagement as striving readers.

The National Reading Panel

Within the literacy landscape, reading models shape our views and thinking about reading and instruction. Additionally, educational researchers in the field of literacy influence instructional best practices, and researchers don't always agree on research outcomes and their implications. In the early 2000s, the National Reading Panel (NICHD, 2000a, 2000b) was convened to examine the literacy research and summarize their findings on evidence-based effective methods of teaching children to read. The history of the emergence of the National Reading Panel is, in my estimation, interesting. Perhaps that's because I've been involved in literacy and the broader landscape of literacy education for decades. I hope you'll find it interesting, too.

Historians consider 20th and 21st century reading debates similar to those in the 18th and 19th centuries (Balmuth, 2009). In the 20th century, the best-selling book *Why Johnny Can't Read—And What You Can Do About It* by Rudolph Flesch (1955) created quite a stir. Flesch argued that the reason many children were unable to read was because of a lack of phonics instruction. He advocated direct and systematic phonics instruction for early readers. In the 1960s and 1970s, the debate continued over whether phonics instruction should be code- or meaning-focused (Chall, 1967). Code-focused instruction emphasizes the scope and sequence related to teaching phonics, while meaning-focused instruction prioritizes comprehension. In the 1980s, researchers debated whether the reading process was bottom up (reading words from part to whole or decoding) or top down (reading words from whole to part or language comprehension; Gunning, 1996), which relies on schema and background knowledge.

In the late 1980s and 1990s, there was a great debate referred to as the "reading wars," which focused on two groups and schools of thinking. Experts and practitioners were at odds over whether early reading instruction should focus on whole language or basic skills. In the whole-language camp, teachers created a print-rich environment with plenty of books and read alouds to help students value and love reading. They believed that as a result of an immersive environment of oral language and books, students would learn to read without direct phonics instruction (Goodman, 1986). In the other camp, those lined up with basic skills instruction believed that if we explicitly taught students the specific reading skills they needed, then they would become readers.

When the debates began to undermine confidence in public education, the federal government stepped in (Shanahan, 2005). In 1997, Congress tasked the National Institute of Child Health and Development to work with the U.S. Department of Education to determine what research said about reading. They coalesced a group of scholars—scientists, educators, researchers, administrators, and teacher educators—who became known as the National Reading Panel. Over the course of two years, the fourteen-person NRP screened over 100,000 existing research studies for inclusion and examined about 420 to make recommendations regarding the best ways of teaching children to read. The NRP's sole purpose was to understand the research and summarize its findings in order to benefit educators and children.

After two years of study, the group delivered The National Reading Panel Report, weighing in at over 500 pages (NICHD, 2000b). While the report was not received without criticism (Allington, 2002), it has shaped literacy instruction since its publication. This influential report focused primarily on five topics—(1) phonemic awareness, (2) phonics, (3) oral reading fluency, (4) vocabulary, and (5) comprehension. The final, lengthy report was condensed into a broadly disseminated summary, which impacted educational policy and influenced curriculum development and materials. To give an example of the report's impact, results of a national survey given twenty years after the NRP report indicated that 55 percent of K–2 and elementary special education teachers identified all five focus topics from the report correctly, while 78 percent of postsecondary educators got all five elements correct (EdWeek Research Center, 2020).

Outside of its significant impact, the report and its findings deserve merit and consideration because the report was shaped by a diverse group of scholars from a variety of fields and because none of the members had any financial benefit or ties to commercial companies. In addition, there was outside input through five public hearings throughout the process. Finally, strict review criteria were employed, and the "panel drew evidence only from research that provided a great deal of certainty in determining what instructional actions cause higher achievement" and "only drew conclusions based on a high degree of certainty that the findings were correct" (Shanahan, 2005, p. 2). It is important to note that the group did not provide opinions, nor did they have to reach consensus. While over thirty reading-related topics were considered, the list was narrowed to eight (Shanahan, 2003). From the eight topics, the five essential pillars of reading emerged.

The report's findings became part of federal policy and, as a result, Reading First (Institute of Education Sciences, 2008) was formed, which provided funding to struggling schools and prioritized professional development on the five elements of reading, often referred to as the five pillars. Across the United States, professional learning for

K–3 teachers focused on strengthening teachers' knowledge and skills specific to the five pillars of essential reading instruction.

The Science of Reading

Literacy instruction is in the spotlight across the United States and has received a great deal of attention. Since the late 1990s, the predominant approach for teaching reading in elementary schools has been a balanced literacy instructional model. The basic premise of the model was to marry the whole-language approach and phonics instruction to help put an end to the reading wars and support children to become readers. The balanced literacy approach centered on daily instruction following the format of a reading and writing workshop, which included common components such as shared reading and writing, guided reading and writing, and independent reading and writing.

It appears that an explicit and systematic approach to phonics instruction was often lacking to the degree needed for primary students to become proficient readers. When I conducted numerous literacy audits across school districts, I frequently found a lack of systematic phonics instruction to be a common occurrence in schools that subscribed to balanced literacy instruction.

Over the pandemic, kitchen tables became virtual classrooms, giving parents a front-row seat to reading instruction. Some parents realized that their children were not learning to read as well as anticipated and became alarmed by the methods used to teach reading. This led to a resurgence in attention focused on reading instruction, which was popularized by podcasts and articles featured in *The New York Times* (for example, Kristof, 2023) and in other national publications.

One of the most influential podcasts to fuel changes in reading instruction was *Sold a Story: How Teaching Kids to Read Went Wrong* by American Public Media (Hanford, 2022–present). This series, initially published in 2022, features education reporter Emily Hanford and focuses on raising people's awareness regarding current reading instructional practices. Popularity for the series swept the United States. In short, the global pandemic left many marks on the educational landscape; one of these was a resurgence in examining how we research reading and apply research findings to how we teach and learn to read, now referred to as the science of reading. We explore this further in the following sections.

What Is the Science of Reading?

Interestingly, the term *science of reading* is not new to the 21st century. While used in the 18th century in connection to text reading, it was first used referring to pedagogy in the 1830s (Shanahan, 2020). Today, SoR refers to a comprehensive body of research that sheds light on the best, research-affirmed practices to better understand how we learn to read, the skills involved, and the brain's connection to reading. This research base is interdisciplinary and draws from research over the past five decades in cognitive sciences, speech pathology, special education, neuroscience, linguistics, and other areas. Gleaning from multiple fields of research allows us to have a broader sense of what comprises evidence-based reading and writing instruction.

There is one caveat regarding evidence: While there are decades of research about reading processes and reading development, not all of this research has been empirically tested within the context of what works in the classroom. In order to do that, there must be a control group (students who don't receive the method tested) and an experimental group (students who receive the method or treatment). This research is both costly and time-consuming. In sum, though we may understand a specific element of the reading process, it doesn't necessarily mean we understand instructional implications. We have learned much, but researchers and practitioners still have more to learn about which reading and writing elements or strategies work within specific contexts and groups of learners. "Excellent and equitable literacy instruction," as advocated by the International Literacy Association (ILA; 2019, p. 2), depends on our own continued professional learning.

While the science of reading places great emphasis on phonics instruction, it is important to note that it also includes the broader scope of reading components often referred to as the five pillars of reading instruction—phonemic awareness, phonics, reading fluency, vocabulary, and comprehension.

Relative to effective instruction, SoR advocates stress the importance of structured literacy. Structured literacy includes a systematic and explicit approach to instruction that applies to phonemic awareness and phonics (National Early Literacy Panel, 2008; NICHD, 2000b), oral reading fluency (Kuhn & Stahl, 2003; NICHD, 2000b), vocabulary (NICHD, 2000b), and comprehension strategies (NICHD, 2000b). Additionally, diagnostic measures enable the teacher to address students' individual needs to differentiate instruction. Finally, instruction is cumulative and builds on earlier knowledge and skill building.

The science of reading has received attention not only from researchers but also from popular media (Hanford, 2018; Wexler, 2019). At times, it has been contentious and harkens back to the "reading wars" of the 1990s that resulted in the formation of the National Reading Panel producing the National Reading Report, as previously discussed. However, this time, the interest in how to teach early literacy is playing out at the kitchen table, on social media, and in print media rather than solely in academia.

In summary, the science of reading *is* a collection of evolving, interdisciplinary research providing evidence that informs reading and writing instruction; teaching based on the five pillars of reading; and instruction that is both systematic and explicit. It is also important to note that the SoR *is not* a reading program, philosophy, or purchased curriculum.

Next, we'll look at why the science of reading is important and its implications for classroom instruction.

Why Is the Science of Reading Important?

The current iteration of the science of reading has swept across the United States in a few brief years. As of September 2024, forty U.S. states and the District of Columbia have passed laws and policies in support of evidence-based reading instruction in schools (Schwartz, 2024b). Many states include the five pillars of reading in their legislation. Some legislation is wide-ranging and includes specific teacher certifications. Many address issues such as instructional materials, professional development, and specific assessments and interventions.

In many schools and districts, the science of reading has supplanted balanced literacy with a more explicit and systematic instructional model that includes the five pillars, or essential elements of reading. Once again, "getting back to basics," as outlined by the National Reading Panel, has become the norm across many U.S. elementary classrooms (NICHD, 2000a, 2000b). The science of reading has led to renewed emphasis on evidence-based instructional practices, which is a good thing. Right? The broad answer is "Yes, of course." However, there are lessons to be learned from previous literacy efforts, namely the Reading First initiative from the early 2000s, which included the five pillars as its foundation (Armbruster, Lehr, & Osborne, 2009).

As previously stated, the SoR emphasizes the five pillars of reading, which is backed by research (NICHD, 2000b). Additionally, the call for explicit and systematic phonics instruction has been stated repeatedly and benefits students, especially struggling readers and English learners. However, these were also integral to Reading First, which was implemented in kindergarten to third grade in 5,880 schools (Gamse, Bloom, Kemple, & Jacob, 2008). At that time, schools that received funds were mandated to teach explicit and systematic phonics and the five foundational pillars of reading. A large quasi-experimental study found several statistically significant outcomes. These included time spent on teaching the five essential components, the use of highly explicit instruction in grades 1 and 2, and the amount of professional development in reading (Gamse et al., 2008). However, this massive emphasis on pedagogy did not bring the results we had hoped for, and it did not improve students' reading comprehension (Gamse et al., 2008), the hallmark of reading.

We should learn lessons from these results. Have no doubt, the five pillars, along with a structured literacy approach, are important to meet the needs of many students to acquire skills and proficiencies necessary to become readers. However, in actuality, there is no single evidence-based approach, curriculum, or strategy that will meet the needs of every student in your classroom.

Students' responses to instruction require instructors to sometimes dig deeper to meet every student's literacy needs. Effective reading instruction must be coupled with teacher decision making based on assessments, both informal and formal, that help us better respond to specific needs of students who aren't making adequate progress. More of the same isn't typically what these students need. Many need a *both-and* approach, explicit and systematic instruction in the five pillars *and* strategies that specifically address skill deficits *along with* time spent in authentic text in order to fine-tune instruction for these students.

Another pedagogical *both-and* is called for as well. We need to improve *both* phonics instruction *and* build background knowledge, vocabulary, and comprehension at the same time. It is a disservice to emerging readers to "skill and drill" phonemic awareness and phonics skills until they reach perfection. We must integrate ample amounts of oral language and meaningful conversation to increase vocabulary (see chapter 5), read alouds so that students hear fluent reading (see chapter 4), and reading from high-quality fiction and nonfiction to build story grammar and comprehension (see chapter 6). Intermediate students must be reading from diverse, challenging texts and apply strategic reader behaviors (see chapter 6) that will lead to better comprehension.

Applying the vast amount of empirical evidence about "what works" in the classroom is the key to making certain that all students become proficient readers. And, as research findings shift and evolve, our instructional practices should reflect new learning and evidence.

What Works in the Classroom?

The NRP (NICHD, 2000b) examined research focused on children in grades K–12. According to Timothy Shanahan (2003), a member of the NRP, the "NRP report marks a watershed in the application of research to practice and policy" (p. 654). In their final report, the NRP identified five pillars as the core of effective reading instruction, which include phonemic awareness, phonics, oral reading fluency, vocabulary, and comprehension. While order was not important, the research was clear on the value of each of these elements in the larger picture of teaching children to read. The panel also made clear that each component should be taught as interconnected to the other pillars as part of a comprehension literacy program (NICHD, 2000b). The findings of the panel, including the five pillars of reading instruction, became the source of many curriculum materials for K–12 instruction, particularly students in grades K–6.

While the NRP was organized under President Bill Clinton, it became the basis of the federal No Child Left Behind Act of 2001, which resulted in the Reading First initiative under President George W. Bush. The Reading First program provided funds to low-achieving schools to improve reading instruction for primary grade children focused on the five pillars.

Though the pillars were never gone, so to speak, the science of reading has resurfaced the pillars as a core element of effective reading instruction. On a practical level, I think about the five pillars relative to a target, shown in figure 1.1, used in target sports. During the summers of my master's program, I was a counselor in the Pocono Mountains of Pennsylvania and taught archery to countless summer campers. We talked a lot about keeping your aim steady and to focus on the bull's-eye.

Figure 1.1: Comprehension is the goal for the five dimensions of reading.

The outer rings of the target can be thought of as the varying degrees of proficiency students have relative to phonemic awareness, phonics, fluency, and vocabulary. Through assessment and instruction, our goal is to move students closer and closer to mastery. However, no matter what skill level a student is performing at, we must always keep our eye focused on the bull's-eye, which is comprehension.

Whether you teach early learners or intermediate students, the goal of literacy instruction is always comprehension. Hitting the comprehension bull's-eye takes focus, adjustment, and differentiation. For kindergarten and first-grade students, the focus is language comprehension via read alouds, sounds and symbols, word learning, and conversations about text. As students become readers, we must provide opportunities to build fluency, vocabulary, and background knowledge, all of which support comprehension.

The Importance of High-Quality Reading Instruction

Students deserve high-quality reading instruction. The public and educational shift to the science of reading, which emphasizes instruction based on evidence, attests to the importance of high-quality reading and writing instruction. How well we teach reading can have a long-lasting impact on the lives of students and how well they can fully participate in society. Some students have literacy levels so low they do not receive the full benefit of this participation (Shanahan & Shanahan, 2008).

While vitally important, high-quality literacy instruction can take a great deal of time, but the following practices and considerations for intentional instruction and intentional environments can focus our efforts toward achieving this high-quality instruction.

Intentional Instruction

Intentional instruction is an important element to effectively implement the five pillars of reading instruction. Rather than a lock-step approach, consider each pillar and the interconnectedness among the pillars as you seek to develop strong, capable readers.

What Is Intentional Instruction?

Intentional instruction, to me, implies being purposeful. It embodies teacher decision making based on evidence-based literacy instruction, learning targets, information from assessments, and your students (making small adjustments based on individual student data leads to more intentional outcomes).

Let's apply being intentional to whole-group instruction, which is a mainstay delivery method for core Tier 1 instruction. The key to effective whole-group literacy instruction, according to Wiley Blevins (2024), prolific literacy author and researcher, is to differentiate instruction and modify expectations of learning outcomes for specific students. In his book, *Differentiating Phonics Instruction for Maximum Impact,* he provides many evidence-based strategies and examples of how to intentionally differentiate and adapt grade-level content for students. Response to intervention experts Mike Mattos and colleagues (2025) also address the importance of effective and purposeful grade-level Tier 1 instruction based on standards and learning targets in their work *Taking Action: A Handbook for RTI at Work™*.

For effective whole-group instruction, we can turn to literacy routines we already engage in each day and be more intentional with little additional effort. Read alouds, for example, occur daily in many elementary classrooms. Yet, in *Read Alouds for All Learners*, Molly Ness (2023) recounts that, according to teachers' self-reports, most read alouds are unplanned. Opportunities exist to make your read alouds more purposeful. For example, think about the purpose or goal for the read aloud. Are you reading the book to build background knowledge for a science lesson, or are you reading the picture book to help build vocabulary and word learning? By determining its purpose, your read aloud will immediately become more intentional and focused. I'll provide two examples for how intentionality can shape a read aloud.

In the first example, Ness (2023) provides a simple three-step process that elevates the read aloud to a thoughtful practice with a defined purpose that benefits students. The process includes three simple steps: (1) evaluate, (2) explain, and (3) engage and extend.

1. First, *evaluate* the text for background knowledge needed as well as opportunities for literacy tie-ins and obstacles students might face that would interfere with comprehension.
2. Next, *explain* by incorporating think-alouds to show students how to make meaning from the text and note novel vocabulary words that might need additional instruction.
3. Finally, *engage and extend* the learning by having students actively reflect about the text and provide literacy-rich extensions based on the text.

Another example of how to make the read aloud more intentional and purposeful is anchored word learning (Beck, McKeown, & Kucan, 2013), described fully in chapter 5, which is an ideal choice to capitalize on the elevated vocabulary typically found in picture books. With just a little preplanning, you can highlight and directly teach tier two level words found in the text, which have broad applicability to other texts.

Beyond bringing intentionality to the read aloud through practices like these, there are many other ways to increase purposefulness in literacy instruction. Creating a classroom environment that is filled with language, conversation, and print, for example, is another intentional elevation that increases word learning. In chapter 5, you'll find many ideas and strategies for how to intentionally expose your students to a range of vocabulary through direct and indirect word learning opportunities.

Intentional instruction not only applies to whole-group instruction but also to small-group and individual work to support struggling readers. In chapter 4, you'll find how to intentionally pair your students so that each benefits from time spent in paired reading. To support struggling readers, you'll need to hone instruction based on assessment data to specifically address their needs. An awareness and ability to act in response to the individual learning needs of students is at the heart of intentional instruction.

Why Is Intentional Instruction Important?

As educators, we work diligently to support and encourage our students in their literacy journey. In order to do that well, it requires a level of expertise that is constantly growing and evolving as new research emerges. The science of reading has focused our attention to provide evidence-based instruction. In doing so, advocates have highlighted the need for systematic and explicit instruction. This is sometimes referred to as structured literacy, which is also mentioned numerous times in the NRP's report from which the five pillars emerged (NICHD, 2000b). Intentionality is key, as the following sections detail.

Structured Literacy

Structured literacy is an all-encompassing term that refers to instruction that is evidence based and provides explicit, systematic, engaging, multisensory, and developmentally appropriate instruction. The term originated from the International Dyslexia Association in 2016 (Cowen, 2016), which, as a reading specialist who has served in numerous clinical settings, I don't find surprising. Students who are dyslexic or struggle with learning to read often benefit from a structured approach that is even *more* explicit, systemic, and multisensory than typical. In structured literacy, skills build on one another, and the emphasis is on teaching in a manner that supports students as they develop the skills needed for accurate decoding. Instruction is systemic, cumulative, and diagnostic.

Finally, structured literacy also includes diagnostic literacy instruction, and teachers provide differentiated, individualized instruction based on information gleaned from formal and informal assessments. Teachers must have a repertoire of ongoing assessments that include formal and informal measures. In their book *Literacy in a PLC at Work®: Guiding Teams to Get Going and Get Better in Grades K–6 Reading*, Paula Maeker and Jacqueline Heller (2023) provide an excellent explanation of how assessments and targeted interventions fit into the teaching-assessing-learning cycle. Differentiating instruction to meet individual student needs occurs through a continuous cycle of assessment and teacher judgment, which rounds out the premises of structured literacy. Structured literacy as a form of intentional literacy instruction is important because it provides a systematic and explicit approach to teaching the foundational elements of reading.

Systematic and Explicit Instruction

We hear a lot about *systematic* and *explicit* instruction as related to the science of reading framework. However, these two terms are used in the same sentence and directive so frequently that it's easy to use them interchangeably and view them as synonymous even though they're not. Let's take a moment to look at the differences between them, how this difference plays out in classrooms, and why both are important forms of intentional instruction.

Systematic instruction refers to skills that build from simple to more complex with a cycle of review and repetition. For example, let's look at identifying sounds within the phonemic awareness pillar. The sequence of skill progression is identifying initial sounds, then final sounds, and then medial sounds. Systematic instruction also refers to a clearly defined scope and sequence, which we'll look at more in chapter 3. If you've participated in curriculum mapping, you've likely included or developed a scope and sequence as a part of the process.

Explicit instruction refers to direct instruction rather than an implicit or discovery method. For example, when teaching sounds during phonics instruction, the teacher directly tells students the sound-symbol correspondence, such as how the */f/* sound at the beginning of *fish* is spelled with the letter *f.* Or, when reading aloud, the teacher may quickly define an unusual word for students and then return to reading rather than have them guess what the word means. In sum, systematic and explicit instruction are important because together they provide a format for direct instruction when teaching foundational skills.

What Works in the Classroom?

As teachers, literacy is one of the most important instructional chunks of your day and encompasses ongoing decision making. Intentional instruction includes carefully selecting strategies that support students as they become proficient readers. Additionally, knowing when to shift responsibility from teacher-centered modeling and instruction to student independence requires intentional thought. More about selecting strategies and the gradual release of responsibility is found next.

Strategies Don't Exist in a Vacuum

Strategies, as a term used in education, became "popular in the 1970s to signify the cognitive aspects of information processing" (Afflerbach, Pearson, & Paris, 2008, p. 365). Instructional strategies are learning techniques, methods, or processes that a teacher uses during instruction to help students learn how to consciously implement a plan, adapt their learning, and monitor results to improve their performance in learning (Harris & Hodges, 1995). Readers employ strategies that are deliberate and goal-directed as they become literate, metacognitive learners (Afflerbach et al., 2008). This book is brimming with instructional and organizational strategies, fifty of them. While it may be tempting to flip through the book and select a few strategies for one or two pillars and begin implementing them with your students, I'll offer a few considerations.

Each instructional strategy was carefully selected because of research-based evidence that supports the strategy, and each was specifically included to support one of the five pillars. In each chapter, the information prior to the strategies titled *What is it?* and *Why is it important?* establish the context within which the strategy sits.

Strategies don't exist in a vacuum. In this book, they are seated within and support the five pillars of reading. You'll likely experience more success if you take the time to understand the *what* and *why* behind each strategy. Also, remember that when we try new instructional routines or strategies, it's often rocky initially. Don't give up after one try. Work through being uncomfortable and the awkwardness of trying something new with students. If you implement the strategies alongside your grade-level or collaborative team, you can also benefit from feedback and support from colleagues.

Gradual Release of Responsibility

The concept of scaffolding instruction emerged from Lev S. Vygotzy's (1978) Zone of Proximal Development (ZPD). The ZPD is the range in which the learner is able to perform but only under adult guidance and support or with a peer who has more knowledge or skill (Vygotsky, 1978).

Let's apply this concept to learning new skills such as skiing, riding a bike, or even baking bread. We often accomplish a new skill by learning from someone who is not only adept but also models specific skills. They show or model the steps and provide tips until we feel comfortable to try the skill or process, girded by support. Then, we receive feedback until we can perform the skill independently.

In education, this format of learning based on modeling from a proficient reader (usually the teacher) is called the *gradual release of responsibility* (GRR) framework (Fisher & Frey, 2021; Pearson & Gallagher, 1983). When teaching new skills (automatic actions such as decoding) or strategies (creating a purpose for reading to better comprehend), we must begin with a clear goal or objective and relate that to students so they know what they're supposed to do.

Gradual release includes a three-step process summarized in the following list, as envisioned by P. David Pearson and Margaret C. Gallagher (1983), two prominent literacy researchers.

1. The teacher models the strategy during instruction.
2. The student participates in guided practice with the teacher.
3. The student performs the strategy or skill independently.

I usually describe sequence as *show* me (modeling), *help* me (guided practice), *let* me (independent practice).

Over the years since 1983, we've learned a few things. Douglas Fisher and Nancy Frey (2008, 2021) recommend inserting a fourth step, the collaborative stage. In this stage, students work together, providing support to one another, which seems to be a nod to Vygotsky's model. The collaborative stage may function as the third step in the gradual release sequence, followed by independent practice.

Throughout this book, references to the gradual release of responsibility framework is directly mentioned and often implied. Sometimes, within a strategy table, you'll see a reference to teacher modeling before an explanation of the steps of the specific strategy. Keep in mind that even if it's not directly mentioned, I suggest following the show me, help me, let me protocol.

As frequently occurs when we learn new skills and strategies, gradual release is not always linear, and students may move back and forth between stages (Fisher, 2008). It's not quite as simple or straightforward as show me, help me, let me, and the timeline can sometimes occur in a lesson or two, while other times it takes much longer, particularly with struggling readers who may need more explicit instruction. All are important considerations as you move your students toward independence.

Just as intentional instruction is important as we refine our skills as teachers, an intentional environment is also vital to support students as they become strategic literacy learners.

The Needs of English Learners

While we are still learning how to best support English learners (ELs) in acquiring reading skills, research and observation provide us with some generalizations for instruction. Several recommendations emerge from research that can help guide us in supporting students as they acquire both early reading skills and more advanced skills required for reading challenging informational text.

- What we know about teaching literacy for non-ELs is also the foundation for teaching reading for ELs (Goldenberg, 2020).
- Students need explicit early language development to support beginning English reading development (Saunders, Foorman, & Carlson, 2006). Oral language instruction helps students understand words and the texts used in learning to read.
- ELs need additional instruction in vocabulary development, both in everyday language and academic language (Bailey, 2007; Goldenberg, 2020). Chapter 5 includes strategies for helping students develop everyday words (tier one words) and academic vocabulary (tier two and tier three words).
- ELs who experience difficulty learning to read can benefit from the same type of interventions as non-EL students with more of it (Gersten et al., 2007).
- ELs will most likely need additional time spent in small-group instruction to develop their phonemic awareness skills. Some sounds in English may be difficult to hear and may not exist in their native language.

The Needs of Struggling Readers

When working closely with teachers, one of the most frequent questions asked of me is how to support struggling readers. Intervening early and often is critical at this stage of reading development. As respected researcher Timothy Shanahan (2016b) notes, "Kids who struggle early tend to continue to struggle, and we need to intervene early to interrupt that cycle."

As we know, reading is complex and multifaceted, which is reflected in the AVR model (Duke & Cartwright, 2021), unpacked earlier in this chapter. Work with struggling readers is supported by implementing a continual cycle of assess-instruct-reflect-revise. I experienced much success with the students whom I had the privilege of assisting using this cycle. In my years of clinical work, I found that the more the reader was struggling, the more systematic, explicit, and multisensory I became in my approach. In the following chapters, I'll share the strategies I frequently implemented with struggling readers specific to the five pillars. You'll notice the strategies typically include an instructional protocol that begins with explicit teacher modeling and direction. Over time, the skillful and observant teacher shifts responsibility to the student as they become proficient in the specific skill.

- For phonemic awareness and phonics skills, I routinely used Elkonin boxes (Elkonin, 1963), letter tiles, colored discs (to represent sounds), and rubber bands (to stretch sounds). I also frequently relied on the Orton-Gillingham approach (Gillingham & Stillman, 1960), in which I was certified; it is a strategy developed for struggling readers who need a very explicit and sequential approach to learn phonemic awareness and phonics.
- For fluency, I routinely used the Neurological Impress Method (NIM) and echo reading strategies, outlined in chapter 4. Students also listened to audio texts, such as those included in the fluency chapter, to hear a fluent model reader and to build language comprehension. In addition, students self-selected reading materials of interest to them to keep their motivation high.
- Many struggling readers need a jump start to build their oral and reading vocabulary. Flooding the classroom with words and displaying enthusiasm about word learning is key to addressing word gaps. Direct word learning strategies (see chapter 5) work well, along with lots of informal conversations about words. I also focused on tiered vocabulary, building basic word knowledge (tier one words) for English learners, and words that had high impact across content domains (tier two words), all explained in chapter 5.
- To build metacognitive comprehension strategies, I routinely worked with students to identify and use appropriate before-, during-, and after-reading strategies as outlined in chapter 6. A few of these include activating background knowledge and setting a purpose (before reading), using text structure to support comprehension and rereading when needed (during reading), and summarizing orally and by writing (after reading).

In summary, three generalizations emerge based on the vast work of reading clinicians who support readers in clinical settings (Johnson et al., 2024). A clinical setting differs markedly from the classroom; nevertheless, their insights can help classroom teachers and include the following.

- **Focus reading instruction on the five pillars—both individually and connected to one another:** For example, while a teacher may focus on intensive decoding support with struggling readers, it must be connected to authentic reading and writing as well as vocabulary building and comprehension.

- **Engage in frequent, continuous cycles of assessment and instruction:** In order to best support struggling readers, it is critical to determine specific needs in order to fine-tune instruction. For example, one student may have difficulty identifying final and medial sounds, and another may have challenges with blending and segmenting sounds. Instruction for each of these students would have a very different focus, which impacts instruction, intensity, and practice.
- **Consider affective factors when planning instruction:** My experience when working with striving and struggling readers is that particularly as they advance in grades, their motivation and confidence for reading are zapped. Think about beginning with a reading interest survey and conversation to gain a sense of a student's interests and provide choice in reading materials and writing tasks. Draw from the classroom library and media center to support students in selecting reading materials that support and build their reading identity.

Teacher decision making is key. To best meet the needs of your struggling readers, focus instruction on the five pillars individually and collectively and make intentional, evidence-based decisions based on assessment data as well as student interests and choice.

Intentional Environments

The International Literacy Association (2019) endorses "learning environments that provide opportunity for robust, literacy-rich experiences, interactivity, and exploration of thought" (p. 2). Creating a literacy-rich classroom environment that supports engagement and skill development in listening, speaking, reading, and writing across grade levels and content-area classrooms benefits students. Students gain a great deal from an environment enriched with print and digital media, oral language and conversation that supports early literacy skills, and more advanced reading and writing skill development, particularly regarding nonfiction and informational text (Buckley-Marudas, 2016).

Building a literacy-rich environment requires intention and careful consideration when selecting books and reading materials to build a diverse classroom library. Teachers may also choose posters, anchor charts, and bulletin boards that support and enrich learning. In the following sections, I examine why educators need to intentionally create literacy-rich classrooms and why it's important. I recommend ways to achieve this, whether you teach emerging and early readers or students who read fluently. Effective classroom environments rich with print and digital media support literacy learning in a variety of ways and help keep students motivated in all aspects of literacy.

What Is a Literacy-Rich Environment?

An intentionally literacy-rich classroom is one in which students are surrounded by a print-rich environment and have multiple opportunities to engage with language, word learning, and authentic texts for a variety of purposes throughout the day. From the atmosphere and decor of the room to interactions with peers and teachers, every element of a literacy-rich classroom is designed to motivate students to engage with the elements of literacy.

Literacy-rich environments have a significant impact on what goes on in the classroom, and they set the stage for interactions with language and a wide variety of text genres. To be clear, I'm not referring to beautifully decorated classrooms. While some teachers enjoy designing carefully coordinated classrooms, I'm focused on the elements that support and encourage students to become engaged in literacy learning.

Why Is a Literacy-Rich Environment Important?

An intentionally designed literacy-rich environment, aligned with the science of reading, provides a setting that encourages and bolsters student ability and motivation in speaking, listening, reading, and writing in a variety of authentic ways through print and digital media. A literacy-rich environment extends beyond classrooms to hallways. Reading and writing are among the most important endeavors within schools, and school visitors should clearly understand this through visual displays that support and show evidence of literacy learning.

It's not only important for early literacy but also supports content-specific learning. They're so vital that the International Literacy Association (2019) specifically calls for educators to "develop a literacy learning environment that empowers students and sets them up for the greatest chance of success" (p. 2).

Classrooms that support adolescent literacy development are also characterized by spaces and cultures that promote "connections, interaction, and responsiveness, which lead to student engagement and reflection" (Meltzer, 2001, p. 7). In secondary classrooms, teachers should integrate the skills and strategies that support disciplinary reading and writing (Urquhart & Frazee, 2012). Depending on grade level and the content area, elements of a literacy-rich environment include, but are not limited to, the following.

- Classroom libraries
- Content posters
- Anchor charts
- Learning targets
- Word walls (to support word learning vocabulary and reinforce high-frequency words)

- Sound walls (to support phonemic awareness and phonics)
- Labels
- Computers
- Displays of student work
- Displays of books and information
- Bulletin boards
- Plenty of opportunities to read, write, listen, and speak

As Alan J. Cohen (2020) states, "Your room is your best co-teacher" (p. 40). Unfortunately, many classrooms lack an environment that supports engagement with language, word learning, and opportunities to interact with text across the day. Cold, hard chairs carefully aligned in straight rows do little to encourage student interaction and engagement with each other or with texts. Walls that are barren, except for exit signage, and classrooms that include few books and materials for students to read won't help build strong and engaged readers and writers.

On the other hand, walls cluttered with posters, charts, and too much "stuff" can also create an environment that distracts rather than enhances literacy learning. Classrooms that are coordinated and designed down to the smallest detail—picture zebra-print bulletin boards, zebra-print book bin labels, charts, pencil cases, and so forth—are overloaded with cute, colorful things that don't necessarily enhance learning. While themes can be fun, keep in mind that the primary importance is for classroom environments to support learning and engagement for all students.

Students need access to interesting books and materials, both in print and digitally. Access to these materials helps to celebrate diverse learners and scaffold instruction based on the needs, languages, cultures, and experiences students bring to the classroom. In the following section, I'll share strategies for building a literacy-rich classroom environment that supports reading, writing, and word learning.

Characteristics of a Literacy-Rich Environment

Creating a classroom that supports language development, reading, writing, and engaging with text is doable with a few tips and strategies. The following ideas, tips, and strategies to integrate oral language, environmental print, learning targets, anchor charts, classroom libraries, and other tools will help make your classroom one that promotes, encourages, and extends literacy learning.

Resources to Support a Literacy-Rich Environment

- *It's All About the Books: How to Create Bookrooms and Classroom Libraries That Inspire Readers* by Tammy Mulligan and Clare Landrigan (2018)
- *The Book Whisperer: Awakening the Inner Reader in Every Child* by Donalyn Miller (2009)
- *The Commonsense Guide to Your Classroom Library: Building a Collection That Inspires, Engages, and Challenges Readers* by Donalyn Miller and Colby Sharp (2022)
- *Game Changer! Book Access for All Kids* by Donalyn Miller and Colby Sharp (2018).
- *Leading a Culture of Literacy: How to Ignite and Sustain a Love of Literacy in Your School Community* by Lorraine M. Radice (2024)
- *Spaces and Places: Designing Classrooms for Literacy* by Debbie Diller (2008)

It is vital to build a repertoire of professional resources that expand your thinking about specific topics—in this case, literacy-rich environments. Use the resources in the feature box as a place to begin or grow your personal library to inspire professional growth.

Oral Language

Quiet classrooms have their place; however, students should have ample opportunities to engage in language with their peers and the teacher. Engaging in purposeful oral language can be as simple as morning meetings that take place in many elementary classrooms. Students of all levels benefit from informal discussions of the weather, local events, and cultural events while simultaneously absorbing language and building informal word knowledge. Additionally, oral conversations are an ideal way for students to hear new vocabulary in context and provide an opportunity for students to build schema, or background knowledge, which aids language and reading comprehension.

Another important way to build oral language is by having students respond to reading. Students benefit from talking about what they've read, sometimes referred to as dialogic conversations. Simple tools to guide discussions, as described in chapter 6, can be used with early readers and provide scaffolding, focusing their attention on the text.

Socratic seminars and literature circles (Harvey, 2002) are two structures that support oral language within classrooms. *Socratic seminars*, or discussions meant to deepen understanding of complex text, can be used to encourage in-depth discussion around literature and informational text. The discussion, often begun with open-ended questions, encourages active listening skills and thoughtful dialogue among students. Literature circles, often referred to as book clubs, provide the perfect setting for intermediate students to discuss trade books and novels they have read. Word learning blossoms in a literacy-rich environment that directly and indirectly supports conversations and oral language activities that provide the much-needed context for word learning.

Children need to be seen *and* heard (Reed & Lee, 2020). Talking *with* students and providing opportunities for them to talk *with* one another support expressive language development. The tips and examples in the strategy shown in figure 1.2 will support the intentional use of oral language with your students.

Environmental Print

Environmental print refers to the written language that surrounds students in their classrooms. This includes print on the classroom's walls and other surfaces and such items as commercial and teacher-made charts, motivational and curriculum-related posters, sound walls, word walls, bulletin board displays, and exhibits of student work.

In primary classrooms, alphabet and number charts, along with color and shape charts, are common. Many elementary teachers also have pocket charts filled with letters, onsets and rimes, individual words, sentences, or poems. These elements help encourage early alphabet learning and enable students to form connections between speech, print, and writing.

And now for a brief word of caution. In some classrooms, the amount of print easily borders on "environmental overload" and is often decorative in nature. Monthly calendars, class schedules, seasonal displays, attendance charts, number and shape charts, class rules, job charts, group rotation schedules, lunch menus, and notices pepper bulletin boards and cover sections of the whiteboard (see figure 1.3, page 36) which can be overwhelming as a menagerie of shapes and bright colors. When using a specific element such as a number chart during instruction, distractible or highly visual children will likely have difficulty focusing on it because the amount of environmental print is overwhelming.

Strategy: Oral Language

Literacy-Rich Environment

Grade Level:	Instructional Grouping:	Consider This:
☑ K ☑ 1 ☑ 2 ☑ 3 ☑ 4 ☑ 5 ☑ 6	☑ Whole Group ☑ Small Group ☐ Individual	• Oral language activities don't need to take up much time and can be easily integrated into daily activities. • Oral language skills can be developed in conversations related to content or texts. • Mix up a variety of activities that include phonemic awareness development as well as activities that build content and background knowledge.

What is it? Oral language involves both speaking and listening. It incorporates how words sound, what they mean, and what ideas they communicate.

Why is it important? Oral language lays a necessary foundation that supports word learning and literacy skills. Think about how babies and toddlers begin to learn words. They hear and respond to sounds, words, and directions long before they are able to respond with language. In time, they begin forming sounds and words and responding to directions with their limited vocabulary. In the same way, the use of strategically building oral language skills in the classroom provides time for students to build word learning skills and participate in language skill development.

What works in the classroom?

- **Utilize morning meetings:** Simply engaging in conversations related to personal lives, activities, and events builds social skills and allows students an opportunity to practice and build oral language through meaningful conversation.
- **Employ closing circles:** Ending the day with a brief review of activities and learning targets provides opportunities to tie oral language skills to the curricular focus.
- **Develop conversational tools:** Students benefit from talking about text. Use simple behavioral and conversation tools to provide support for their discussion. Behavior reminders can include "Look at others when you respond" and "Use your quiet voice." Include conversation starters such as "Which character would you want to be friends with and why? or "The biggest surprise for me was when __________." You can also develop questions to support informational text such as "I learned something new about __________" or "I never knew that __________ did __________ in the ocean" or "__________ was a new word to me."
- **Implement literature circles:** Engaging in conversations related to a specific narrative text allows students to develop language skills specific to story grammar, sequencing events, themes in literature, and character development while engaging with their community of readers.
- **Incorporate Socratic seminars:** Participating in higher-level collaborative discussions related to a specific topic (which could come from the theme of a novel or read aloud) allows students the opportunity to form ideas around text and respond to others based on insights from the text. In this way, students deepen their understanding of challenging text from reading and oral discussion.
- **Purposefully use "turn and talk" within lessons:** Partner talk is a small but meaningful way to purposefully provide opportunities at specific times within a lesson for students to connect listening and speaking skills in order to enhance content understanding.

Figure 1.2: Strategy—Oral language.

*Visit **go.SolutionTree.com/literacy/FSK6** and enter the unique access code found on the book's inside front cover to access a reproducible version of this figure.*

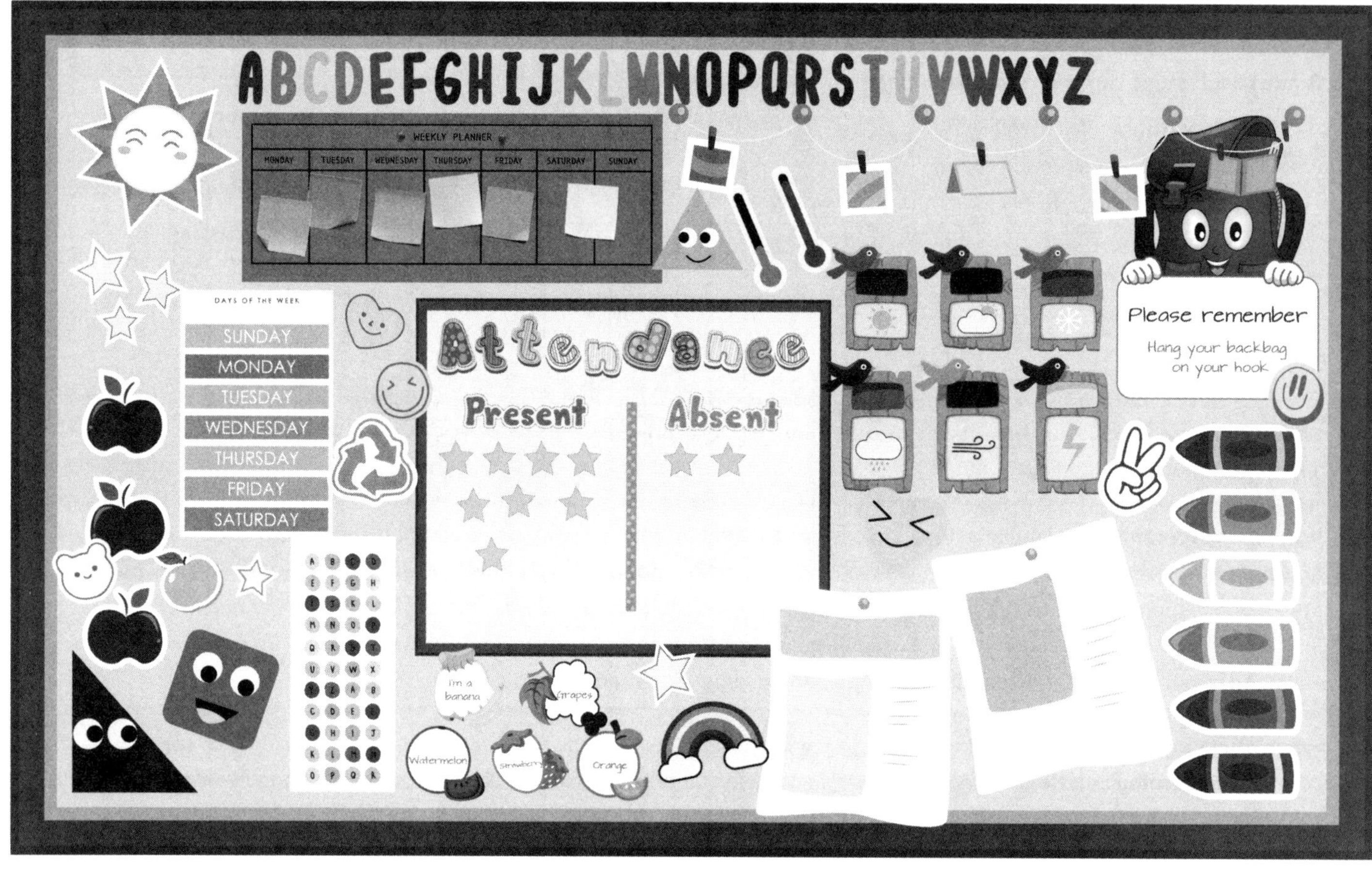

Figure 1.3: Example of environmental overload.

Labels on objects are sometimes found in elementary classrooms as well. Teachers may label areas of the rooms with small signs such as *table*, *sink*, *calendar*, and so on. Labeling, for vocabulary development and reading purposes, is best done *with* students as an instructional activity rather than by the teacher prior to the school year. When co-creating labels, students have the opportunity to connect word learning with print, spelling, and reading. It is important to note that in schools with large English learner and special education populations, labels in classrooms and hallways can benefit intermediate students as well. Labeling is both a fun and purposeful activity when done jointly with students of varied ages and grade levels. Use the strategy in figure 1.4 to implement labeling in your setting.

In short, labels on objects in the classroom and areas throughout the school support emerging readers and English learners. Creating labels with students supports them as they make connections between listening, speaking, writing, and reading.

Strategy: Labeling the Classroom

Literacy-Rich Environment

Grade Level:	Instructional Grouping:	Consider This:
☑ K ☑ 1 ☑ 2 ☑ 3 ☑ 4 ☑ 5 ☑ 6	☑ Whole Group ☑ Small Group ☐ Individual	• Use a thick black or blue marker and thick, bold print with students to create labels that are easily read from across the classroom. • Do not laminate labels, since this creates glare from overhead lights and negatively impacts readability. • Include labels in grades 4–6 if your student population includes English learners. Consider creating labels with students during small-group instruction.

What is it? Labeling the classroom includes labeling objects such as tables, chairs, the sink, the bulletin board, a fish tank, and so forth. It also includes name labels for bins, desks or tables, and the coat rack.

Why is it important? Labeling the classroom enhances literacy learning by creating a print-rich environment for learners. Early readers and English learners benefit from connecting speech to print and spelling while labeling familiar objects around the classroom and, coming full circle, connecting written words to reading.

What works in the classroom?

- **Create and label objects with students:** A primary purpose of labeling is to help students connect speech to print; however, it also builds language and background knowledge. For example, have a conversation with students about fish, tanks, and where they live prior to writing "aquarium" on a label, naming each letter as you write. Then have students join you in reading the word aloud.
- **Label using familiar names:** Names of objects can differ across the United States. For example, in some areas people refer to storage areas as "cabinets" rather than "cupboards." When labeling, use the name most familiar to your students.

- **Connect labeling with phonemic awareness:** Use labeling as an opportunity to support phonemic awareness and phonics for emerging readers. For example, when writing "aquarium," ask students to identify the beginning, middle, and ending sounds. Slide your hand under the word as students blend the sounds to read "aquarium."
- **Consider including pictures with written words or labels:** For early learners, consider including a picture, such as a pencil sharpener, with the written words "pencil sharpener."
- **Label key room elements:** During conversations with students, label items such as the coat rack, bulletin board, window, and so on.
- **Keep labeling across the school year:** Don't feel like you have to label everything in the first week of school. It is far better to create labels over time with students. As new things are added to the classroom, talk about the item or object, and then create the label. Or, as new book themes or genres are added to the classroom library, discuss with students and use the opportunity to create a label for a book bin.

Figure 1.4: Strategy—Labeling the classroom.

continued ▶

- **Revisit and reinforce words on labels:** Labeling isn't meant to be a "once-and-done" activity. Revisit and reread labels during whole- or small-group instruction. At that time, you can tie in phonemic awareness and phonics activities such as clapping syllables, noting spelling, word parts, and blending sounds to read the words on each label.
- **Label objects in multiple languages:** Consider labeling objects in multiple languages to support English learners.

Visit ***go.SolutionTree.com/literacy/FSK6*** *and enter the unique access code found on the book's inside front cover to access a reproducible version of this figure.*

Learning Targets

Learning targets are statements that describe the knowledge and skills students will gain by the end of a lesson or unit of study. Learning targets, learning goals, or targets are terms that are often used interchangeably. It is easy to think of learning targets as answering the question, What will students know and be able to do by the end of a lesson or unit of study? In other words, the knowledge and skills that students need to demonstrate to achieve specific standards become learning targets. For teachers, learning targets provide a clear focus for instruction and assessment. They help you guide students during lessons and provide specific criteria and meaningful information on which to assess progress toward learning goals.

The process of developing learning targets begins with teachers and collaborative teams making meaning of the standards by analyzing each standard to plan instruction and assessment. Katie White (2017), an assessment expert, suggests a straightforward method for determining learning targets (summarized in the following).

1. **Circle the verbs (and other words that indicate what students should do) in the standards:** Verbs include *identify, explain, analyze, show, determine, summarize, list,* and so on. You'll notice that each verb helps the teacher determine an appropriate assessment to determine mastery of that standard.
2. **Underline key concepts, vocabulary words, and contextual information:** Adding this step provides a deeper understanding of what is required within that standard. Vocabulary knowledge, in particular, varies from student to student and especially with English learners. Also consider how the knowledge or skill related to the learning target could be acquired from print, digital, and video sources.

Following this, teachers can develop these into learning targets or student-friendly *I can* statements as recommended by Richard J. Stiggins, Judith A. Arter, Jan Chappuis, and Stephen Chappuis (2004). For example, "I can compare characters and events in a story" is an English language arts target for second-grade students. For fifth-grade students, a learning target specific to mathematics might be, "I can explain patterns when multiplying a number by powers of 10." When learning targets are written in student-friendly language, they provide an important anchor for students to clearly understand the goal of the lesson. Please see figure 1.5 for an illustrated example.

I suggest including learning targets in lesson plans and posting them as *I can* statements on the whiteboard prior to the lesson. Refer to them intentionally at the beginning of each lesson to provide the learning focus for students. You should also refer to learning targets within the lesson and then circle back to recap at the end. Targets can also be included in pacing guides and written in order of skill complexity. Collaborative teams should consider including success criteria for each learning target along with specific assessment tasks that can be used to monitor mastery of each target. In short, identifying learning targets is an important part of planning and accountability for teachers and students within the learning process.

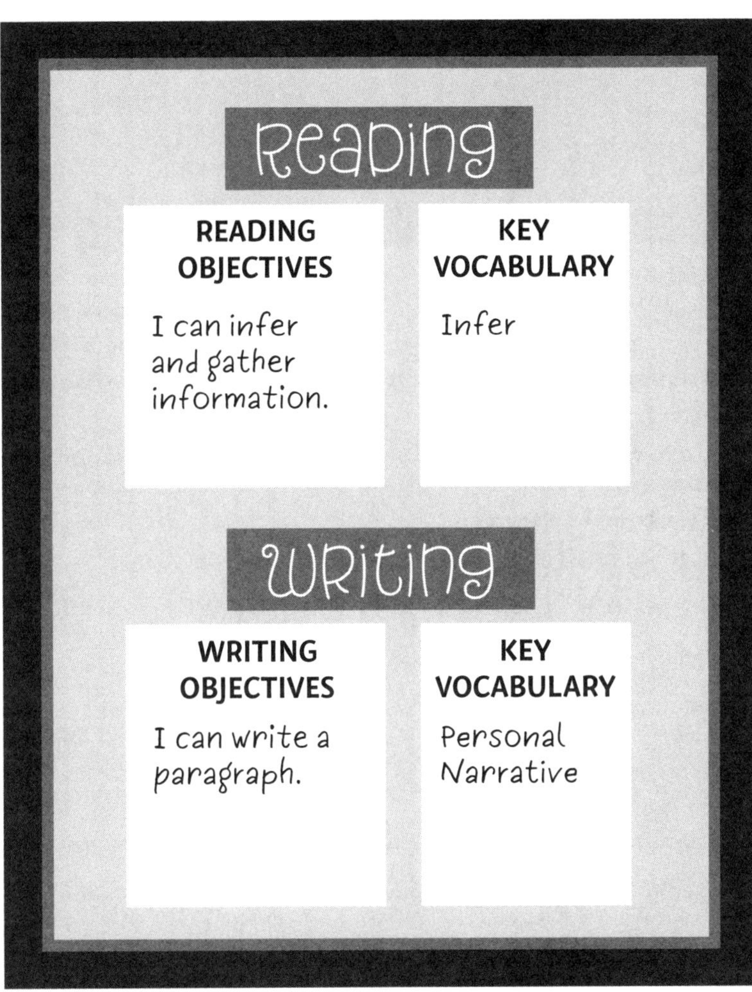

Figure 1.5: Learning targets written as *I can* statements.

There are a variety of ways to create and post learning targets. The strategy and tips in figure 1.6 (page 40) will provide a reference to you and support learning for students.

Learning targets, simple to record and post, support teachers and students by making standards clear. They should be part of a literacy-rich classroom that prepares and supports students as they learn.

Anchor Charts

Anchor charts, either co-developed by teachers with students or commercially produced, are written or image-based charts that support instruction and serve as a reference

Strategy: Learning Targets

Literacy-Rich Environment

Grade Level:	Instructional Grouping:	Consider This:
☑ K ☑ 1 ☑ 2 ☑ 3 ☑ 4 ☑ 5 ☑ 6	☑ Whole Group ☑ Small Group ☐ Individual	• Including learning targets in your lesson plans makes it simple to transfer to a whiteboard or chart paper each day. • Encourage students to state their learning in *I can* language. • Learning targets can be used in small groups while focusing on a specific skill to help anchor the focus.

What is it? A learning target is a statement that describes the knowledge or skills students will gain by the end of a lesson or unit of study. They are often expressed as *I can* statements in student-friendly language.

Why is it important? Learning targets and success criteria provide clarity to both teachers and students. They help teachers engage and guide students in the learning process and provide specific, predetermined goals that teachers can use to assess progression toward success criteria (Dimich et al., 2022).

What works in the classroom?

- Post *I can* statements prior to the lesson on a whiteboard.
- Utilize a consistent place to post learning targets for reading, mathematics, and other content areas.
- Include *I can* statements on rubrics, examples of student work, and assessments.
- Refer to I can statements before each lesson to identify what students should know and be able to do following the lesson.
- Return to *I can* statements in the midst of the lesson and circle back at the end to keep the target in focus.
- Encourage students to create their own learning goals and express them as *I can* statements.
- Examples from the 2023 Indiana Academic Standards include:
    - Grade 1 English Language Arts Standards, 1.RC.4: I can "make and confirm predictions about what will happen next in a story."
    - Grade 3 Mathematics Standards, 3.CA.6: I can "demonstrate fluency with mastery of multiplication facts and corresponding division facts of 0 to 10."
    - Grade 5 Science Standards, 5-PS1-4: I can "conduct an investigation to determine whether the mixing of two or more substances results in new substances."

Source for standards: Indiana Department of Education, 2023b, 2023c, 2023d.

Figure 1.6: Strategy—Learning targets.

*Visit **go.SolutionTree.com/literacy/FSK6** and enter the unique access code found on the book's inside front cover to access a reproducible version of this figure.*

for students. Similarly to labeling the classroom, I think the power of anchor charts is in co-creating them with students. Figure 1.7 shows an example of a co-created anchor chart featuring a timeline of the Middle Ages. Students added labels and key vocabulary integral to the unit of study. When co-created, the teacher and students build ownership of the content, and the anchor chart provides an in-the-moment record of learning, making it more accessible for students to refer to throughout the unit.

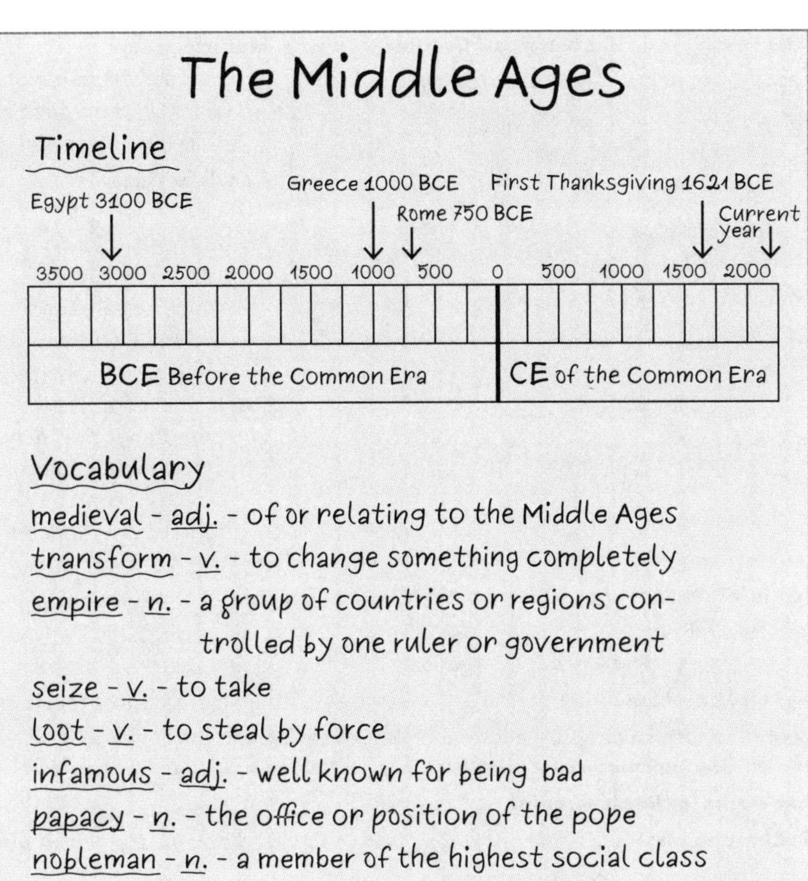

Figure 1.7: Middle Ages anchor chart featuring a timeline and key vocabulary.

Students in all grade levels can benefit from summarizing and recording content in an anchor chart that is written in student-friendly language. Students can also contribute to making the charts. For example, students in the primary grades may contribute by writing a letter when co-creating a "words that start with *A*" chart. In intermediate grades, a student can serve as the recorder and capture the class's thinking on the chart. Remaining students could also contribute by writing vocabulary words on sticky notes and placing them on the anchor chart, for example. By developing anchor charts with students of any grade, they can clearly see the connections between thinking, listening, speaking, writing, and reading.

Anchor charts don't have to be overthought or complicated. The following strategy and tips in figure 1.8 (page 42) will be helpful as you plan and organize content that would be suitable for an anchor chart.

Anchor charts serve as a simple reference point for students to return to content, poems, or classroom rules. I suggest creating them with students for another opportunity to support the connection between reading and writing.

Word Walls and Sound Walls

A word wall, such as seen in figure 1.9 (page 43), is a visual display of words essential to reading, writing, or specific content. When used to support instruction and

Strategy: Anchor Chart

Literacy-Rich Environment

Grade Level:	Instructional Grouping:	Materials:
☑ K ☑ 1 ☑ 2 ☑ 3 ☑ 4 ☑ 5 ☑ 6	☑ Whole Group ☑ Small Group ☐ Individual	• Large chart paper often works best, depending on the size of the group and purpose of the chart. • Use wide-tip, colorful markers. **Consider This:** • Use of color should be strategic. Black will help words stand out, and color choices for other visuals can enhance details and serve as visual aids. • Anchor charts can be used for so many purposes. Examples include directions, procedures, comparing and contrasting information, poems for choral reading, and summarizing content. • Include simple pictures and diagrams to support the text and aid comprehension, especially with early learners. • Once anchor charts have been fully utilized for the lesson or unit, a picture can be taken and added to a binder for students to refer back to if needed.

What is it? An anchor chart is a written tool that supports instruction or classroom procedures and "anchors" learning for students.

Why is it important? Anchor charts can serve as both an instructional tool and one that provides a reference point for students to recall a strategy, content, or procedure used in the classroom.

What works in the classroom?

- **Chart paper:** Have chart paper ready and supported on an easel or the whiteboard. Sticky chart paper also works well to adhere to a wall or whiteboard.
- **Preplan:** Preplan the anchor chart activity by selecting a lesson for which summarizing the content on an anchor chart could serve as a useful reference tool for students.
- **Title the chart:** Some teachers choose to title the chart beforehand. I suggest recording the chart and having students discuss and determine an appropriate title.
- **Record the content:** Consider developing the chart in thirds.
  - On the top third, record the title after the chart is completed. Consider including an *I can* learning statement. For example, "I can tell the difference between fiction and nonfiction books."
  - In the middle third, record the key points related to the topic. In this example, you could create a vertical line in the middle of the chart and record "Fiction Books" on one side and "Nonfiction Books" on the other. Proceed to record the key characteristics of each as you discuss them and provide examples from the classroom library.
  - On the bottom third, consider providing examples. For fiction and nonfiction books, you could record titles or quickly draw books and put a title on the image. This is a good place to get student contributions through sticky notes as well.
- **Recap:** When the chart is complete, recap the content and discuss with students an appropriate title to record on the top third.
- **Display:** You can choose to display the chart on a hanging rack specifically made for charts, or you can display it on a bulletin board or the whiteboard for a few days to make it easy to refer to during a whole-group lesson or small-group instruction. We have seen examples where teachers have a bulletin board or wall that is dedicated to the current focus for reading (as well as a space for writing and math). This would be a great place to place anchor charts (and the learning targets).

Figure 1.8: Strategy—Anchor chart.

Visit ***go.SolutionTree.com/literacy/FSK6*** *and enter the unique access code found on the book's inside front cover to access a reproducible version of this figure.*

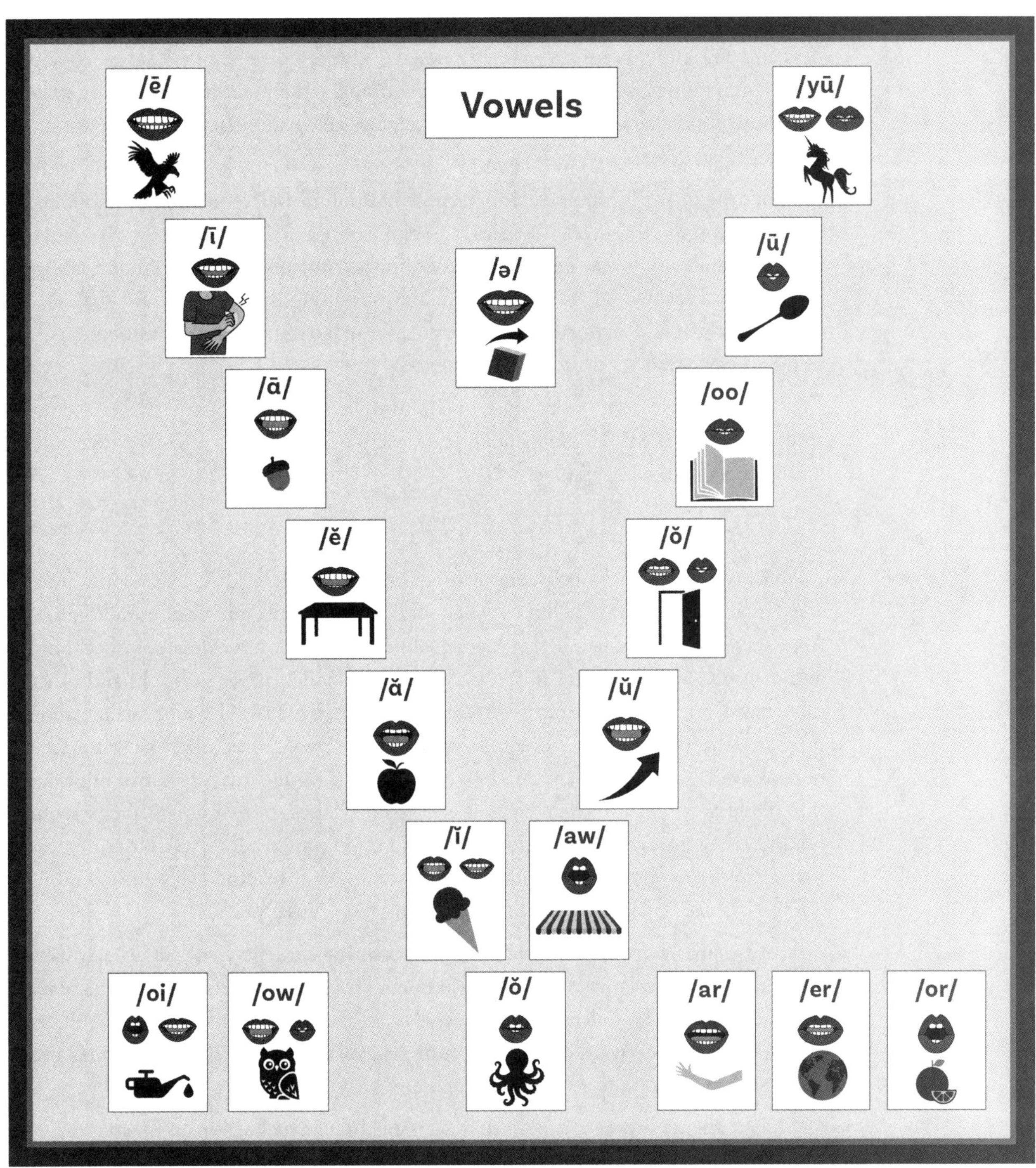

Figure 1.9: Example of sound wall display of vowels along with mouth movements to support emerging readers.

independent writing, a word wall can be an effective device to build word consciousness and aid students in internalizing new vocabulary. In chapter 5 (page 204), I provide the rationale for word walls and how to make them an integral part of classroom instruction and support as students integrate new vocabulary into their writing.

Sound walls are a variation on word walls. A sound wall may look similar to a word wall, but the intent is different. The purpose of a sound wall is to support phonemic awareness, sound-symbol relationships, and phonics instruction. In the primary grades, high-frequency words may be grouped according to initial sounds. For example, alongside the word *mat* would also be a picture of lips forming the */m/* sound. In chapter 2 (page 72), you'll find an organizational strategy to make sound walls a meaningful part of instruction and support for your students.

In short, unless you tie word walls or sound walls directly to instruction and show students how to use them independently, they'll likely just be static displays of words and images taking up wall space.

Classroom Libraries

Students need access to books in print and digital formats (ILA, 2023a) and from a variety of sources—public libraries, school libraries, home, and classroom libraries. Access refers to the availability of high-quality books in homes, classrooms, schools, and community libraries (ILA, 2000). Access to a wide variety of books and other materials, along with opportunities to read them, are the basis of a successful reading program (Routman, 2014; Zemelman et al., 2005). Book access is key since the lack of book availability leads many children not to choose reading for pleasure or information (Holdaway, 1979). When students are provided access to well-designed classroom libraries, they interact more with books, spend more time reading, exhibit more positive attitudes toward reading, and have higher levels of reading achievement (ILA, 2000; National Assessment of Educational Progress [NAEP], 2005).

It is particularly important to work toward ensuring students living in poverty have access to books—and they often don't—at home, in a school, or through a local library (Krashen, 2004; McQuillan, 1998). Access to books is so critical that school libraries can "reduce or even balance the effect of poverty" (Krashen, 2021), a finding also confirmed by Keith Curry Lance and Debra E. Kachel (2018).

While changing a student's access to the school library may be difficult for an individual teacher, and changing access to books in the home or through a local community library may be impossible, teachers have more control over the realm of their classroom. This is why the classroom library can play such an important role in the intentional creation of a literacy-rich environment.

Classroom libraries provide a foundation for developing students' literacy skills while supporting self-selection and wide reading. They are so essential that the National

Council of Teachers of English (2017) highlights the importance of classroom libraries by creating a position statement to reinforce their critical importance to the reading, social, and emotional lives of students:

> Classroom libraries—physical or virtual—play a key role in providing access to books and promoting literacy; they have the potential to increase student motivation, engagement, and achievement and help students become critical thinkers, analytical readers, and informed citizens. As English language arts educators, we know that no book is right for every student, and classroom libraries offer ongoing opportunities for teachers to work with students as individuals to find books that will ignite their love for learning, calm their fears, answer their questions, and improve their lives in any of the multiple ways that only literature can.

Research demonstrates that classroom libraries play a key role in literacy learning (Atwell & Merkel, 2016; Gallagher, 2009; Worthy & Roser, 2010). This is particularly true for economically disadvantaged students. In one large-scale study of over 350 schools and more than 18,000 students from families of limited income, researchers filled classrooms with high-quality books to enhance the literacy and language environment (Neuman, 1999). Results showed the students in spaces with classroom libraries increased their time spent reading by 60 percent compared to a control group. In addition, literacy-related activities more than doubled, and letter knowledge, phonemic awareness, concepts of print and writing, and narrative skills rose more than 20 percent over the control group.

Access also means time—time for students to read books (Krashen, 1997). It is perhaps not surprising that there is a clear relationship between the amount of time children read for fun and reading achievement (Campbell et al., 1996; Krashen, 2004; Taylor et al., 1990). Teachers can provide instruction on essential literacy skills, but if students are not provided access to interesting books they want to read and time to read, they will never reach their full literacy potential (Gambrell, Malloy, & Mazzoni, 2007).

It's important to note that I am not referring to "drop everything and read" time, sometimes referred to as DEAR time. Instead, I am referring to students self-selecting books of interest, which will motivate them to read and also support teacher-student and student-student conversations around text, and the time to explore these books themselves or in concert with their teachers.

Not only is the classroom library the basis for students' solo exploration and connection to books, but a classroom library can also be the perfect venue and source to create a community of readers inside and outside the classroom. These are communities that read consistently, talk about books, and share book suggestions with fellow readers. Donalyn Miller (2009), a former award-winning teacher and consultant, does a stellar job of explaining how to create a vibrant classroom culture grounded in reading for diverse purposes in *A Book Whisperer*. In the book *Leading a Culture of Reading,* Lorraine M. Radice (2024) also suggests making reading visible through "I'm currently reading" posters, making books a part of the daily routine, and beginning lessons or the school day with brief book talks. Another example is to paint a cabinet or similar object using chalk paint on which you record classroom read alouds as shown in figure 1.10. All of these simple but meaningful suggestions help create a community in which reading and literacy are woven into the fabric of the classroom.

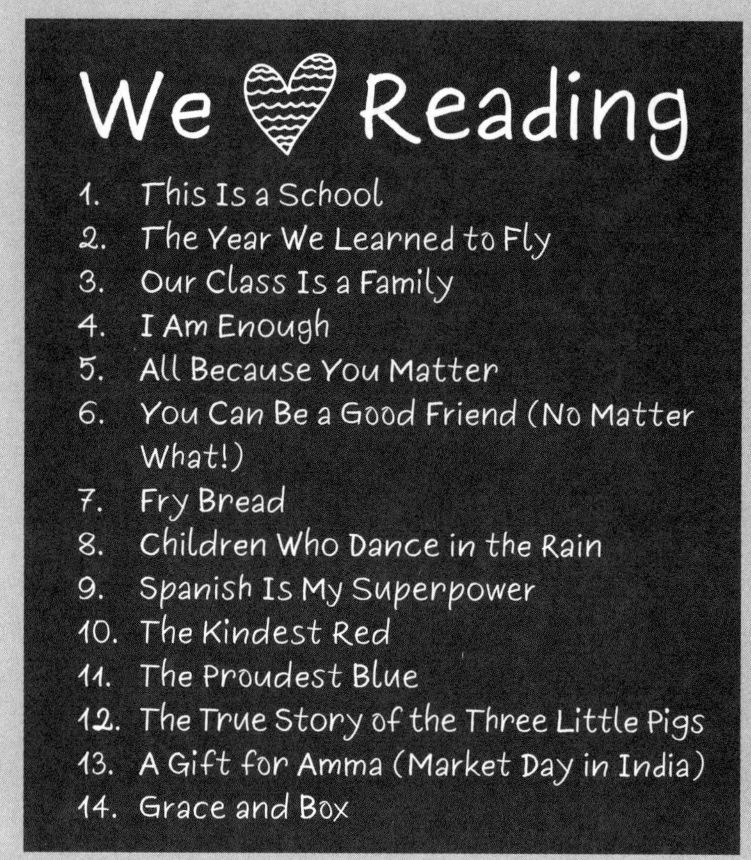

Figure 1.10: Example of creating a community of readers by recording read alouds.

A particular benefit of creating a community of readers is that students are then more prone to build excitement for reading through their interactions with one another. Every classroom includes students ranging from reluctant to avid readers. Reaching reluctant readers, which is always a goal, may be simpler than we sometimes think. Jim Trelease (2006), author of the best-selling *The Read-Aloud Handbook*, suggests that just one positive experience with a book can create a reader. Providing a wide range of books and text types helps to create interest, having students complete a reading interest survey helps guide you when making book suggestions and selecting books to add to your classroom library (Benning, 2014), and, importantly, readers of all types—especially reluctant readers—benefit from talking with classmates about books. Sometimes, the benefits of a reading community can even be put to work beyond the walls of the classroom. Radice (2024) provides many suggestions about how to create a schoolwide community of readers and extend the literacy footprint to engage families and the community through hosting reading community events in online spaces, for example.

The classroom library is only as strong as the selections and diversity within the shelves. Selecting books and digital resources when building your classroom library is important and sometimes not mentioned enough. In developing a classroom library, the goal is for the selections to help build strong and capable readers who can read a wide range of challenging texts. Giving thought to text selection pays dividends in building student engagement, cultural relevance, and continued interest in the classroom library.

Text selection is key, and considerations include the following.

- Select texts that motivate students to read for authentic purposes, build content knowledge, and are complex enough to grow students as readers (Cervetti & Hiebert, 2019; Hiebert, 2013).
- Choose texts with rich, sophisticated themes, which help build language, vocabulary, and world knowledge that support additional reading (Cervetti & Hiebert, 2019).
- Diversify your classroom library to reflect students within your classroom, school, and community. Students need opportunities to read and engage with texts that include characters that look like them and have experiences similar to them (Henderson et al., 2020; Koss & Paciga, 2022). Using diverse texts for instruction and providing access to culturally representative texts impacts literacy achievement and motivation (Fisher & Frey, 2018; Gangi, 2008; Teale & Gambrell, 2007).
- Create text sets that can help build student knowledge around specific topics such as owls, volcanoes, or protecting the environment. Reading related informational texts about a specific subject aids in growing specific vocabulary (Cervetti et al., 2016) and forming connections among ideas gleaned from reading multiple sources (Cervetti et al., 2015). Text sets also provide meaningful opportunities to scaffold challenging text. Instruction can begin with a read aloud and shift to texts that students read independently or in pairs and then discuss with peers.

Students of all ages and grades regularly read both print and digital text. With the massive growth of technology in classrooms (Klein, 2022), most schools include access to both print and digital text, and technology continues to play a larger role in the classroom (Herold, 2022). So how does this play out when thinking about classroom libraries and access to books digitally?

When we think about reading connected text in general, especially for students who are building their reading skills, we must keep our focus on comprehension. In an interview with *Education Week*, Naomi S. Baron (2021), the author of *How We Read Now: Strategic Choices for Print, Screen, and Audio*, states that students generally comprehend better when reading printed text over digital (Schwartz, 2023). In her meta-analysis, which is a summary of results gleaned from many independent research studies, Virginia Clinton (2019) finds that reading digitally had a negative effect overall on reading performance relative to reading print. Additionally, students were more aware of their comprehension when reading printed text compared to reading text on a screen.

Printed text is especially important when thinking about young children who are developing their reading skills. Another meta-analysis looked specifically at thirty-nine studies and compared print and digital reading with young children (Furenes et al., 2021). Results revealed that children understood printed books better than the digital version of those books.

Conversations about the text also differed between digital and printed texts. For example, when parents read printed books with their children, they tend to have conversations related to characters, discussing what might happen next and connecting the story to children's lives. In contrast, when reading digital texts, the conversations focus more on the technology than the story and events. As an example, the child might tap on a tree featured in the story to learn more about the tree's characteristics. Keep in mind that digital texts have some advantages—the ability to tap on a character or object to learn more about those things helps children build their background knowledge. However, this is not the same as comprehending the text narrative, making inferences, and deepening understanding of characters and themes. When contextualizing these findings to classroom libraries, I believe there is a continued and important place for building and maintaining a collection of printed books along with digital resources in classrooms.

In addition to the importance of selecting resources, one should consider the qualities of an effective classroom library. It exists as more than a simple collection of trade books. The classroom library is an integral tool for enhancing students' independent reading and literacy development around the five pillars identified in the science of reading. To be an effective tool, however, it must exemplify the characteristics of a quality classroom library. These characteristics include the following considerations, starting with ample accessible titles, as observed in figure 1.11.

Figure 1.11: A high-quality classroom library includes numerous diverse titles.

- The library should contain a large supply of books ranging from a core collection of about 300–600 titles (Fountas & Pinnell, 1996) or about seven books per student (International Literacy Association, 2000). Additionally, the classroom library should be supplemented by the school library or media center (Huck & Zhang, 2021). While the number of books is important, the quality of the collection is critically important as well. In fact, I'd choose a less robust classroom library that includes more recently published, diverse, and high-quality selections over one that emphasizes volume.
- The library should include new books added routinely to spark interest and old, worn, and tattered books should be discarded periodically.
- A wide variety of genres including fiction, nonfiction, and informational books is key. These should be divided into subgenres, topics, or themes as appropriate.
- The library should offer a fairly equal division of fiction and nonfiction, especially in fourth grade and beyond.
- A wide variety of formats—wordless books, big books, picture books, chapter books, graphic novels, series, hardcovers, paperbacks, and magazines—is important. Genres and selections are dependent on various considerations including the grade level, students' reading levels, and students' interests.
- Current reference books such as age-level appropriate dictionaries, thesauri, almanacs, atlases, and encyclopedias are a must.
- Current books should be included; at least one-third of the books should have been published within the last five years.
- Make sure diverse and culturally relevant books are part of the library, especially those that reflect populations and languages present in the school (Henderson et al., 2020).
- Include multiple copies of hot-off-the-press titles. This is especially true for students in intermediate grades.
- Books spanning a range of complexity, including predictable, easy-to-read books, decodable books, and books of a more challenging nature, should be part of the library.
- Offer books that include a wide range of difficulty spanning at least two grades above and two grades below the designated grade level, although picture books should be included at all levels because they often include more advanced vocabulary.
- Offer text sets that include several titles and genres on a specific topic or theme which can change over time based on student needs, student interests, content coverage, and so on.

- Include books suitable for a book club or partner reads, especially in grade 2 and beyond.
- Make sure to offer mentor texts that the teacher reads aloud and to which students can refer or reread.
- Include materials other than books—magazines, newspapers, comics, audiobooks, writing paper, and art supplies—to encourage children to respond to reading.

Additionally, a classroom library should be inviting with a clearly delineated area out of the traffic flow, such as in figure 1.12. Ideally, there should be enough space to accommodate a variety of storage options, such as bookshelves, tubs, and book racks, along with a means for book displays. It is also helpful to provide a few cushions or bean bags for reading or comfortable furniture with a rug to help separate the area. Finally, materials should be organized according to a logical classification system and clearly labeled with easy-to-read, visible signs. Students must be able to easily find books, authors, and genres that pique their interests (Henderson et al., 2020).

Figure 1.12: Example of comfortable seating to encourage reading in the classroom library.

High-quality classroom libraries don't just happen; they're built. And they don't build or fund themselves. I would be remiss not to mention that many schools and districts do not provide funds to support classroom libraries. In my experience working in schools across the United States, I found that many teachers developed and funded their classroom libraries out-of-pocket. Lyndsi Smith, who contributed to this book, was a classroom teacher and coach and now serves as an elementary principal.

When Lyndsi was a teacher, she experienced a lack of school funds but also wanted to move her classroom library when changing grade levels or schools. In order to do this, she built her library mostly out-of-pocket, which allowed her to own and move books when she changed grade levels.

While it is unfortunate that teachers often pay for books, teachers are remarkably resourceful when building their classroom libraries. For example, some teachers take advantage of Scholastic's warehouse book sales that occur in cities across the United States. These sales include a wide variety of books—many recently published—at low cost. In addition, many teachers save points from classroom book sales and use those to build their collections. Others ask parents to donate books for their child's birthday and place a book placard inside the book with the child's name. Some receive books from teachers who are retiring, although I would caution that many of these collections should be weeded of old, outdated, and tattered books. On learning more about the importance of classroom libraries to support literacy learning, some districts I've worked in began allocating funds to build a core classroom library that permanently remains in the classroom even as teachers moved grade levels.

There are other ways to build your classroom library as well. Perhaps you teach in a school that has moved away from reading programs that include lots of leveled texts. Rather than discarding the leveled texts, they can easily be repurposed and organized by topic within classroom libraries.

Rotating books is another way to keep your library fresh and new. Even though you may have hundreds of books, it doesn't mean they all have to be available at the same time. Consider changing up books to create renewed excitement. Selections can be based on current content units, genre trends, or new book sets. Another way to refresh your classroom library is to rotate or trade books with another grade-level teacher. By doing so, students in both classrooms have access to new titles, series, and genres that can renew their interest in the classroom library.

In addition to building your classroom library, you'll want to keep up with recently published books and book award winners. I suggest joining a few online educator communities to get you started. It's easy to follow communities on X (https://x.com) and BlueSky (https://bsky.social) through their hashtags. Some groups post on both and some on a specific platform. For example, every Monday, teachers and librarians post about what they're reading collected under the hashtag #IMWAYR. Typically, there are images of picture books and trade books with a very brief snippet or review. Another group on BlueSky, #titletalk, meets monthly and engages in an online discussion about books. A few others to check out include #booklove, #kidlitlove, #kidlit, #booktalk, and #shelfietalk. Additionally, I would be remiss not to mention the *Nerdy*

Book Club blog (also on BlueSky @nerdybookclub), which has published lengthier reviews of children's literature for many years.

Instagram (www.instagram.com), a popular social media app, is a great place to find children's book enthusiasts (sometimes referred to as "bookstagrammers") and follow individual or publisher's posts and daily stories. Here are a few that we enjoy following to keep current! Looking for diverse books? Follow @hereweeread and @the consciouskid, accounts that post about books with diverse characters that will quickly find their way to your classroom library. Penguin House posts via @readbrightly and their colorful and informative posts will help you find niche titles to capture your readers. If you're looking for children's books as well as the occasional adult read, then you should follow @littlebooksbigworld, where you'll find recommendations to suit your students and you. Consider following children's authors and poets, too, such as Rebecca Kai Dotlich (@rebeccakaipoet), an author of many children's poetry books, including *Welcome to the Wonder House* (Dotlich & Heard, 2023), which was awarded the Lee Bennett Hopkins Poetry Award.

Every student deserves ready access to books to support independent reading. Classroom libraries should be a vital, growing, and integral part of the literacy-rich environment of every classroom. Dedicating time to organizing, displaying, and carefully curating the classroom library can be a fun and meaningful activity to begin each school year, either alone or with your students (Hawkins, 2021; Mulligan & Landrigan, 2018). Use the following strategy and tips in figure 1.13 to organize and categorize your growing book collection.

Strategy: Organizing a Classroom Library

Literacy-Rich Environment

Grade Level:	**Instructional Grouping:**	**Consider This:**
☑ K ☑ 1 ☑ 2 ☑ 3 ☑ 4 ☑ 5 ☑ 6	☑ Whole Group ☑ Small Group ☐ Individual	• Begin small so you don't get overwhelmed. Keep adding one or two books per student each year. Don't be afraid to search garage sales and resale shops such as Goodwill for books. • Depending on the grade level of students, it can be a great collaborative activity to organize the classroom library with students. • When creating the library space, think about what you enjoy as an adult reader (such as comfort, quality, variety, and organization).

What is it? A classroom library is a collection of books and materials, such as high-interest magazines, that support independent reading, instruction, and read alouds.

Why is it important? A classroom library provides easy access to books and can serve as a hub to motivate kids to read independently and to build a classroom community of readers.

What works in the classroom?

Organizing a classroom library doesn't have to be intimidating. If you begin organizing by selecting a few of the following categories, you'll soon have a well-organized classroom library that students will love to explore.

Categorizing Books

- **Authors:** Organizing books by beloved authors is an easy way for students to find an author that appeals to them and to read all the books by the author, both from the classroom library and supplemented by the school and public library.
- **Genres:** Categorizing books by genres is a simple yet effective way to organize books. You can keep it simple by organizing by fiction, nonfiction, and informational if your selection is limited. However, if your library is sizable, organizing books by specific genres helps students be aware of more genres and assists them when selecting books. Consider genres such as science fiction, mysteries, historical fantasy, historical fiction, realistic fiction, traditional literature, autobiography, poetry, action and adventure, graphic novels, and so on.
- **Themes:** Themes such as friendship, kindness, pets, and cooking are an easy yet meaningful way to organize books.
- **Topics:** Children frequently select books by interest, regardless of book difficulty or level. Selecting subjects such as dinosaurs, energy, holidays around the world, weather, how-to books, and space, for example, helps children find books in their interest.
- **Series:** Organizing books by series is simple and important. Students often become hooked on reading by finding a series or author they enjoy reading and proceed to read the entire collection.

Organizing Books

- **Colored bins:** Using colored bins to hold books of varied genres can help students easily locate books. For example, you could use red bins for fiction picture books, yellow bins for chapter books, blue bins for chapter books in a series, and green bins for nonfiction books.
- **Baskets:** Baskets on shelves or the floor can be a good place to store magazines or newspapers.
- **Shelving:** Ideally, low shelves provide a great space for storing reading materials; display books on top of the shelf to create interest!
- **Labels:** Labeling the book bins or shelves with specific laminated labels helps students locate books more easily. Some teachers even use images of the author for a book series or an image of a planet for science fiction, for example. For younger grades, it often helps to label both the bins and the books for easy book returns.

Figure 1.13: Strategy—Organizing a classroom library.

Visit ***go.SolutionTree.com/literacy/FSK6*** *and enter the unique access code found on the book's inside front cover to access a reproducible version of this figure.*

In summary, classroom libraries provide the easiest, most direct access to books for students. Children need time to read independently every day to become strong and capable readers. It has been established that time spent leisure reading and comprehension are related (Locher & Pfost, 2020; van Bergen et al., 2021). Additional studies exploring the longitudinal effects of print reading habits on the development of reading skills (Torppa et al., 2020; van Bergen et al., 2021) and into adulthood (Locher & Pfost, 2020) also provide empirical support for eyes on self-selected text.

Wrapping It Up

The literacy landscape has shifted to prioritize the science of reading as the predominant framework for reading instruction across the United States. In this chapter, I focused on two key areas—intentional instruction and intentional literacy environments—to demonstrate how both impact literacy learning. School leaders can use the Leader's Lens (figure 1.14) to support teachers moving forward with effective literacy practices. Consider the Five Key Takeaways (page 56) as we shift to focus on the five essential pillars of reading instruction. Think about intentionality as it relates to your instruction and literacy environment as you consider the Five Key Next Steps (page 56).

Leader's Lens

Intentional Instruction and Intentional Literacy Environment

Consider the following supervision supports and classroom connections as you lead or guide teachers in implementing intentional instruction and a literacy-rich classroom environment.

<table>
<tr><th colspan="2">Supervision Supports</th></tr>
<tr><td>Practical Research</td><td>• Do teachers understand the premise behind the science of reading? Can they interpret classroom research specific to elements of literacy and the five essential pillars of reading?
• Do teachers understand the why behind a literacy-rich environment aligned to support intentional instruction through the science of reading?</td></tr>
<tr><td>Professional Development</td><td>• Is there professional development needed to fill in the gaps specific to the science of reading?
• Have a staff discussion regarding intentional instruction and structured literacy.
• How would you support collaborative teams as teachers implement structured literacy specific to the five pillars?
• What is essential professional development specific to the importance and design of literacy-rich environments?</td></tr>
<tr><td>Feedback and Expectations</td><td>• Are you specific with expectations of what classrooms should include to support literacy instruction aligned to the science of reading research?
• Does your feedback support instructional aspects of a literacy-rich environment in ways that advance student learning?</td></tr>
<tr><td>Financial Focus</td><td>• Is there money budgeted to provide high-quality literature for classrooms (including decodable texts and high-interest and engaging texts)?
• Is there money budgeted to support literacy-rich environment materials and items such as sound walls, bean bags, or rugs?</td></tr>
<tr><th colspan="2">Classroom Connections (Look-Fors)</th></tr>
<tr><td>Oral Language</td><td>• Notice the type and frequency of oral language opportunities for students.
• Notice if there are regular opportunities such as turn and talks to practice language, conversation, and deepen content knowledge.</td></tr>
<tr><td>Literacy-Rich Environment</td><td>• Notice the print around the classroom to determine whether it is purposeful or more decorative in nature.</td></tr>
<tr><td>Learning Targets</td><td>• Notice whether lessons include a clear literacy focus.
• Notice whether learning targets are posted and referenced.
• Notice whether learning targets are written in student-friendly language.</td></tr>
<tr><td>Anchor Charts</td><td>• Notice the evidence of co-created charts to anchor learning.
• Notice if anchor charts are referenced during instruction.</td></tr>
<tr><td>Word Walls and Sound Walls</td><td>• Notice evidence via word walls or sound walls that language development and word learning are a priority.</td></tr>
<tr><td>Classroom Libraries</td><td>Is there a designated classroom library?
• If yes:
  • Notice the organization and quality of books and materials to support student access.
  • Notice whether there are a variety of genres represented and the amount of multicultural and diverse books.
  • Notice the amount and percentages of fiction, nonfiction, and informational text.
• If no:
  • Support teachers in developing an understanding of the need for a classroom library and extend resources.
  • Help teachers brainstorm where to begin.</td></tr>
</table>

Figure 1.14: Chapter 1 leader's lens.

Visit ***go.SolutionTree.com/literacy/FSK6*** *for a free reproducible version of this figure.*

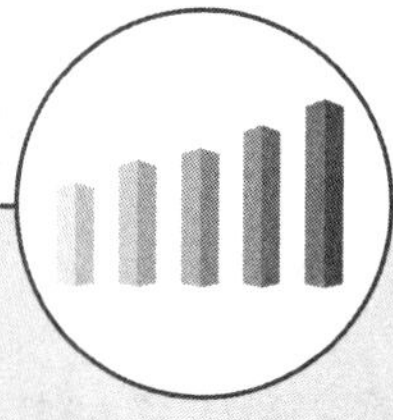

Five Key Takeaways

Consider the following key takeaways individually or discuss them with your collaborative grade-level team.

1. **Models of reading:** Models of reading help delineate the complexity of reading and create a picture of how people learn to read. While they don't spell out how to teach reading, how we conceptualize reading typically impacts instruction and remediation, material selection, and how we respond to students as readers.
2. **The National Reading Panel Report (NICHD, 2000a):** The National Reading Panel was convened in the early 2000s to examine literacy research and summarize their findings on effective evidence-based methods of teaching children to read. The report has been influential on policy and educational practices, including the five pillars of effective instruction—phonemic awareness, phonics, fluency, vocabulary, and comprehension.
3. **Science of reading:** The science of reading refers to a comprehensive body of research that sheds light on the best research-affirmed practices to better understand how we learn to read, the skills involved, and the brain's connection to reading. The research base is interdisciplinary and drawn from research in cognitive sciences, speech pathology, special education, neuroscience, linguistics, and other areas.
4. **Structured literacy:** Structured literacy is an all-encompassing term that refers to instruction that is evidence-based and provides explicit, systematic, engaging, multisensory, and developmentally appropriate instruction based on information collected from formal and informal assessments.
5. **Literacy-rich classrooms:** A literacy-rich classroom, endorsed by the International Literacy Association, is one in which students are surrounded by a print-rich environment and have multiple opportunities to engage with language, word learning, and authentic texts for a variety of purposes throughout the day. From the atmosphere and decor of the room to interactions with peers and teachers, every element of a literacy-rich classroom is designed to motivate students to engage with the elements of literacy.

Five Key Next Steps

Consider the following questions individually or discuss them with your collaborative grade-level team.

1. **Models of reading:** Consider the models of reading. Is there a model that best depicts how you view reading? Does it inform your instruction? If so, how?
2. **Science of reading:** How has the science of reading impacted your instruction? What about teaching using a structured literacy format has shifted your instruction?
3. **Classroom environment:** In what ways is your classroom designed to support all types of literacy, such as oral language, word learning, independent and self-selected reading, and writing?
4. **Literacy-rich environment:** Consider specific elements that are currently in your classroom to support literacy learning. What specific actions could you easily do to enhance your classroom literacy environment? Have you considered having another grade-level collaborative team member do a literacy walkthrough of your classroom and provide feedback about its strengths and next steps to further support literacy learning? In what areas do you feel you might be most in need of feedback?
5. **Classroom library:** How does your classroom library support independent reading? Growing a classroom library can be challenging. Is there a way to work with parents, the librarian or media specialist, or collaborative team members to build your classroom library?

Key Vocabulary

Phonemic Awareness

Alphabet Knowledge	The knowledge of letter names and the ability to identify the sound of letters along with their printed shape
Alphabetic Principle	An understanding of the relationship between letters (graphemes) and sounds (phonemes); these sounds and spelling represent spoken language.
Articulation	The way in which speech sounds are produced; with young children, we often use the term *mouth moves*. Understanding how sounds are produced is an important phonemic awareness skill.
Effect Size	Measures how meaningful the relationship between variables is in a research outcome; effect sizes, reported frequently in research, are useful because we can compare the results of varied studies on the same topic (for example, phonemic awareness, vocabulary, or comprehension). We interpret effect sizes as follows: below 0.20 is negligible, between 0.20 and 0.39 is small, between 0.40 and 0.79 is moderate, and over 0.80 is large.
Grapheme	One or more letters that represent a single phoneme (sound)
Onsets and Rimes	The initial phonological unit in a word (onset), and the letters that follow the initial sound (rime) Example: pan /p/ is the onset; /an/ is the rime. Example: chin /ch/ is the onset; /in/ is the rime.
Meta-Analysis	A report of a single statistical analysis (effect size) that combines the results of multiple research studies that address the same topic or question
Phonemes	The smallest unit of sound within a word; there are forty-four phonemes in the English language.
Phonemic Awareness	The ability to hear, identify, and manipulate individual sounds—phonemes—in spoken words; phonemes are the smallest units of sound in spoken language.
Phonological Awareness	The ability to recognize and manipulate various units of speech sounds, such as syllables, onset-rime, and phonemes
Sound Walls	A speech-to-print tool that provides a visual representation of phonemes
Striving Readers	A term used to describe students in grades 4-12 who may struggle with reading and be reading below grade level; this may include reluctant or unmotivated readers and English learners.
Struggling Readers	A term used to describe readers who experience problems with decoding, comprehension, or both

CHAPTER 2

Phonemic Awareness
Building a Sound Foundation

> If a child memorizes ten words, the child can read only ten words. But if a child learns the sounds of ten letters, the child will be able to read 350 three-sound words, 4,320 four-sound words and 21,650 five-sound words.
>
> —Martin Kozloff

Phonemic awareness is the first of the five pillars of reading identified by the National Reading Panel (NICHD, 2000a). Often referred to as a building block to reading, it is an essential pillar for early literacy instruction because it provides a foundation for phonics. In this chapter, you'll find out how it helps emerging readers recognize that sounds can be heard, identified, and manipulated in spoken words.

We'll begin by exploring the challenges to phonemic awareness instruction and how we can address those challenges through systematic and explicit instruction. Next, we'll look at the elements of effective phonemic awareness instruction and strategies for helping students become proficient at hearing, identifying, and manipulatinig sounds. I recommend integrating instruction and connecting sounds with their letters along with well-chosen read alouds that highlight the selected sound or sounds. By making these direct connections, we help make the implicit explicit. Finally, you'll be equipped with specific strategies for helping struggling readers who need more support as they learn how to isolate, blend, and segment sounds to form words.

What Is Phonemic Awareness?

Phonemic awareness is the ability to hear, identify, and manipulate individual sounds—phonemes—in spoken words. Phonemes are the smallest unit of sound within a word, and there are forty-four of them in the English language. Phonemic awareness is an oral language skill; it's all about hearing and manipulating sounds.

Keep in mind, hearing *sounds* comes first, and then recognizing *symbols* comes second. For example, when students hear the word *pan,* they should be able to hear and identify three distinct sounds (phonemes), as in */p/ /ă/ /n/.* Additionally, if they hear */p/ /ă/ /n/,* they should be able to blend those sounds and say the word *pan.* Additionally, when the */p/* sound is deleted, they hear */ă/ /n/* as the remaining sounds.

Phonemic awareness and the umbrella term *phonological awareness* are distinct terms with distinct differences. They are often confused and used interchangeably (ILA, 2020; Rice et al., 2022; Spear-Swerling et al., 2005; Young, Paige, & Rasinski, 2022). I've also found that not only are these two terms confused, but *phonemic awareness* and *phonics* are also often used incorrectly (Ehri, Nunes, Willows, et al., 2001). It's understandable, since they all begin with *phon-,* the Latin root meaning *sound.* Given this quandary, it is important to begin with the definitions of each term.

Phonological awareness is the ability to distinguish and manipulate units of speech sounds such as syllables, onsets (the part of the word that comes before the vowel), rimes (the part of the word that contains the vowel and any consonants that come after it), and phonemes (Piasta & Hudson, 2022). Phonological awareness is a part of oral language development and includes an awareness of rhymes, words, syllables, alliterations (as in *h*ungry *h*ippo), onsets and rimes, and phonemes. Phonological tasks may include segmenting sentences into words, segmenting words into syllables, or deleting syllables in a word (for example, What is *sunshine* without *shine*?) These tasks are simpler for early readers than tasks requiring phoneme manipulation (Liberman et al., 1974). Because phonemic awareness is a critical early reading skill within phonological awareness, it receives specific attention.

A few additional terms in this chapter and the next are essential to clarify. *Phonemes* are the smallest unit of sound in the pronunciation of words. They are identified by the sound they make (acoustic) and by their articulation (mouth moves). For example, *sat* has three phonemes, */s/ /ă/ /t/. Graphemes* are one or more letters that symbolize a single phoneme or sound. For example, *chop* has three phonemes, */ch/ /ŏ/ /p/.* You can hear three distinct sounds, and the mouth makes three distinct moves.

Phonics, which is discussed at length in chapter 3, is an approach to teaching reading that emphasizes the relationships between *graphemes* (symbols) and *phonemes* (sounds). For example, in phonemic awareness, we ask students, "What sound do you hear at the beginning of *sit*?" And, during phonics instruction, we change the question to "What letter makes the /s/ sound at the beginning of *sit*?" Phonics explicitly connects *sounds* (phonemes) to the corresponding *symbols* (letters or graphemes).

It is important to be able to differentiate between the three terms—phonological awareness, phonemic awareness, and phonics—and how each plays out in the classroom, as shown in figure 2.1, to be able to select appropriate resources and instructional strategies to support each. Additionally, distinguishing the difference between the terms phonemes and graphemes is important as you help students hear and recognize spoken sounds—phonemes—and the letter or letters—graphemes—that represent those sounds. In doing so, we can move forward to explore why phonemic awareness deserves attention as we teach children to read and, indeed, why it is a pillar.

Phono-	What it means...	How it looks in the classroom...
Phonological Awareness	An umbrella term that refers to the ability to distinguish and manipulate units of speech sounds such as syllables, onsets and rimes, and phonemes	Clapping words in a sentence Clapping or tapping syllables in a word Rhyming
Phonemic Awareness	The ability to hear, identify, and manipulate individual sounds—phonemes—which are the smallest units of sound in spoken language	Ability to distinguish individual speech sounds in words. *met* /m/ /ĕ/ /t/ Ability to isolate, blend, and segment sounds Adding, deleting, and replacing phonemes within words
Phonics	An instructional method that teaches letter (grapheme) and sound (phoneme) relationships	Identifying letter names Identifying letter sounds Decoding and encoding

Figure 2.1: Distinguishing between *phono-* words.

Why Is Phonemic Awareness Important?

Phonemic awareness is particularly important to literacy instruction because it is the top predictor, along with letter knowledge, of early reading success during the first two years of school (Cirino, Child, & Macdonald, 2018; NICHD, 2000a; Schatschneider et al., 2004; Share, Jorm, Maclean, & Matthews, 1984). For beginning readers, phonological awareness skills and early reading are highly correlated (Anthony & Francis, 2005; Anthony & Lonigan, 2004; Troia, 2014). In order to provide a foundation for phonics instruction, the NRP recommends explicit, systematic instruction in phonemic awareness. The following sections lead us toward an understanding of the forms this systemic instruction can take and how to implement it, first by further exploring phonemic awareness as part of the foundation of reading, then by examining the challenges in teaching it, and finally by looking at how it can be taught.

Phonemic Awareness as a Building Block to Reading

Phonemic awareness has long been considered important in early literacy development. Students from a wide variety of backgrounds benefit from explicit instruction in foundational literacy skills (D'Angiulli, Siegel, & Hertzman, 2004; Torgesen et al., 2001). The National Reading Panel (NICHD, 2000a) reviewed fifty-two studies on phonemic awareness instruction. In their meta-analysis, the panel reviewed studies that included a control group and an experimental group. The instructional sequence studied focused on phoneme isolation, phoneme identity, phoneme categorization, phoneme blending, phoneme segmentation, and phoneme deleting. The statistic used in the analysis was effect size. Effect size refers to how much the treatment group outperformed the control group. If an effect size is 0, the control group and the experimental group (treatment group) performed the same, meaning that the training had no effect. Further, 0.20 indicates a small change, 0.50 is moderate, and 0.80 is large. Results of the meta-analysis were positive in that the overall effect size for phonemic awareness was 0.86. The result for reading outcomes was 0.53, and the result for spelling was 0.59. These results support the conclusion that phonemic awareness instruction is not only beneficial but also supports students as they apply these skills to reading and spelling.

As a building block to reading, students need to understand that words are made up of sounds (phonemes). So, what makes teaching phonemic awareness challenging? Simply put, phonemic awareness is not a natural skill; we hear and understand speech without being aware of phonemes. When listening, words bump up against other words, and sounds bump up into each other in many words. Listening for distinct words and then for small, discreet sounds can be challenging for some students.

In English, we must teach phonemic awareness because our written system is dependent on understanding the relationship between phonemes and graphemes (letters) in order to read and write. While phonemic awareness is a building block to reading, it *is not* the block. Phonemic awareness should be integrated within the broader context of foundational skills for early literacy (Mesmer, 2020; Shanahan, 2011) that include the following.

- Print concepts
- The alphabetic principle
- Reading aloud daily to support fluency and listening comprehension
- Writing activities such as dictating stories and writing names
- Using precise language to engage students in word learning and vocabulary development

Perfect phonemic awareness skills are not the goal. Instead, think of phonemic awareness as an important piece within the foundation of literacy, which should be taught alongside reading and writing in kindergarten and first-grade classrooms (Ehri et al., 2001).

Challenges of Phonemic Awareness Instruction

Phonemic awareness instruction, though the first pillar, relies on underlying foundational skills being present. When these skills are not well developed, it can make instruction challenging. In the following, I touch on foundational skills that support phonemic awareness, what happens when early learners don't have these skills, and certain situations that can challenge literacy skill acquisition.

- **Concepts of print:** Students who lack "print awareness" or "concepts of print" often don't understand that words within print carry meaning. Further, they do not understand that words make up sentences and sentences make up books which can be read. Although print awareness and phonemic awareness are distinct and separate skills, they interact within reading development. Lacking fundamental concepts of print makes learning phonemic awareness skills challenging.
- **Oral language:** Phonemic awareness requires the ability to break words down into their tiniest parts or individual sounds, known as phonemes. This can be tricky because sounds blend and bump into each other, which is called coarticulation. Coarticulation, coupled with students who have limited experience with oral language, makes developing phonemic awareness even more challenging.
- **Hearing:** Students must be able to hear tiny, individual sounds in order to develop phonemic awareness skills. If students have trouble hearing correctly, they may also have trouble distinguishing between sounds and producing them.
- **English learners:** Students who are learning English often have challenges when learning phonemic awareness. Some sounds in the English language may not be present in their native language, making it difficult to hear and produce them.
- **Not a natural skill:** Prior to developing phonemic awareness skills such as isolating, blending, and segmenting, oral language was only about making meaning. Students must now shift their listening to isolating sounds and putting them back together so they can develop phonics understanding in order to read. In a nutshell, it's a lot of moving parts. And, it's not natural. Consistent instruction and practice are key.

Despite these challenges, the results of the NRP's meta-analysis clearly show that phonemic awareness can be taught (as detailed in the next section), and students benefit because it helps them learn to read and spell (NICHD, 2000a).

Teaching Phonemic Awareness

One of the best things about phonemic awareness instruction is that it doesn't require special materials. Phonemic awareness instruction is brief, cheap, and fun. When I taught kindergarten and first grade, I routinely shared with families that phonemic awareness is an activity you can do with your child in a playful, relaxed manner. For example, when my own children were young and long before they were reading, I frequently drew their attention to sounds in words. As we'd be driving to the pool, I'd say something like, "Oh, look at the beautiful park. What sound do you hear at the beginning of *park*?" To emphasize rhyming and substituting sounds, I would go on to say, "If I changed the sound at the beginning of *park* to */m/* (making the sound, not naming the letter), what is the new word?" And, moving to a more advanced skill, I would go on to say, "What if I dropped the sound */ark/,* what sound is left?" To which one of them would respond, "*/p/*." And, just like that, sound exploring was over and they'd return to excitedly talking about friends they hoped to play with at the pool. No letters and no flash cards were involved; we simply noticed and played with sounds. Such easy, impromptu exploration can happen in the classroom, too—while lining up to go to lunch or recess, while getting supplies out for the day, or when discussing something the students might notice out the window, for example.

In order to read, children need phonemic awareness—to be able to *isolate*, *blend*, and *segment* sounds in words. They must become adept at segmenting words into individual sounds and then taking those sounds and blending them together to make a word. For example, when students hear the word *pet,* they should hear three sounds, */p/ /ĕ/ /t/.* And, they should be able to take the individual sounds, */p/ /ĕ/ /t/*, and blend them together to make the word *pet*. Phonemic awareness activities pay off greatly by developing these vital skills in a way that can be quite natural and accessible for the teacher.

The easiest way to help students detect phonemes is to teach them to monitor their mouth positions (articulation). When their mouth moves to another position, that indicates the next phoneme. Let's use *pot* as an example. Have students pronounce the word *pot* aloud. Tell them to pay attention to how their mouth moves. Ask, "How many sounds do you hear in *pot?* Did you say three? That's correct."

Students can sound out or decode when they can segment a word by hearing individual sounds and then blend them together to read words. The specific skills associated with phonemic awareness are a stronger predictor of later reading skills than broader phonological awareness skills (Melby-Lervåg et al., 2012).

Through phonemic awareness instruction, students also understand how individual and groups of sounds are represented in writing (Rice et al., 2022). There are many strategies we can implement in our classrooms to help students develop those skills, which we'll explore in the What Works in the Classroom? section (page 67).

In the next sections, we'll explore both systematic and explicit instruction and why it's important when teaching phonemic awareness skills. Additionally, I'll introduce an instructional sequence for teaching eight phonemic awareness skills.

Systematic and Explicit Instruction

While impromptu sound and word awareness games can offer great benefits to students, they should be offered in addition to intentional instruction. The National Reading Panel recommends explicit and systematic phonemic awareness instruction as a must-have for early reading success (NICHD, 2000a). Teaching phonemic awareness skills must also be combined with teaching students to apply those skills within words (Ehri et al., 2001). For example, we teach categorization so students detect that words sound different from each other. We practice isolating sounds so students recognize that words are made up of distinct sounds. And, we should practice blending embedded within the context of reading words. According to a meta-analysis (Ehri et al., 2001), when teachers applied blending to reading words, effect sizes for first-grade students were much larger than when blending was taught in isolation from reading. In the following section, we'll discuss using instructional sequences to teach blending along with other key literacy skills.

Phonemic Awareness Instructional Sequence

In this section, I'll introduce an instructional sequence for teaching eight phonemic awareness skills. An instructional sequence, or protocol, presents each subskill in a logical and sequential order that aligns with systematic and explicit instruction. Using the protocol, the teacher models skills, questions, and receives feedback from students in a very explicit and predictable manner. Eight phonemic awareness skills are listed in figure 2.2 (page 66), along with an instructional sequence for each. Listed first are the three skills that have the most impact—(1) isolating, (2) segmenting, and (3) blending. Spend most of your time here, especially with struggling readers. The instructional sequence for each skill is important. In each example, you'll notice I usually have the student verbalize the sounds or words following the initial instruction. That's important; don't skip it. Keep in mind, students don't need to have 100 percent mastery of each of these phonemic awareness skills in order to decode words. And, keep in mind that phonemic awareness should be embedded within the broader scope of literacy, including print awareness, letter recognition, and word learning. Employ read alouds to support phonemic awareness, fluency, and language comprehension as well.

Phonemic awareness, as a building block for phonics and reading, helps students develop a solid understanding of hearing, segmenting, and manipulating individual sounds. In spite of the instructional challenges that exist, about ten hours of systematic and explicit instruction is sufficient for most children to become proficient. In the next section, we'll look at the elements of effective phonemic awareness instruction along with ready-to-implement-tomorrow instructional strategies.

Phonemic Awareness Skill	Instructional Sequence
Phoneme Isolation The ability to isolate and identify specific sounds (phonemes) within words, including the first, middle, or last sound	**T:** "The word is *mat*. Say the word *mat*." **S:** "Mat." **T:** "What sound do you hear at the beginning of *mat*?" **S:** "/m/." **Note:** The initial sound is /m/, the medial (middle) sound is /ă/, and the final sound is /t/. In phonemic awareness, children learn initial sounds first, final sounds next, and medial sounds last. Ask separate questions for each sound, beginning with initial sounds.
Phoneme Blending The ability to hear individual sounds in a word and blend them together to say a word	**T:** "The sounds are /m/ /ă/ /t/. Say the sounds /m/ /ă/ /t/." **S:** "/m/ /ă/ /t/" **T:** "If we say the sounds quickly and blend them, what is the word?" **S:** "Mat."
Phoneme Segmentation The ability to recognize that a word has a specific number of sounds	**T:** "The word is *mat*. Say the word *mat*." **S:** "Mat." **T:** "How many sounds do you hear in *mat*?" **S:** "/m/ /ă/ /t/. Three sounds."
Phoneme Identification The ability to recognize a common sound in different words	**T:** "The words are *mat, milk,* and *move*. Repeat the words *mat, milk,* and *move*." **S:** "*Mat, milk, move.*" **T:** "Tell me the sound you hear that is the same in *mat, milk,* and *move*." **S:** "/m/."
Phoneme Categorization The ability to recognize a word with a different sound in a group of three or four words	**T:** *(Example with a beginning sound)* "The words are *fun, bun,* and *mop*. Which word sounds different from the others?" **S:** "Mop."
Phoneme Addition The ability to add sounds (phonemes) to a given word to produce a new word	**T:** "The word is *up*. Say the word *up*." **S:** "Up." **T:** "Add the sound /p/ to the beginning of *up*, what is the new word?" **S:** "Pup."
Phoneme Deletion The ability to delete initial and final sounds (phonemes) in a given word to produce a new word; this also includes blends such as /pl/ and /st/	**T:** *(Example with a beginning sound)* "The word is *pup*. Say the word *pup*." **S:** "Pup." **T:** "Take away, or delete, the sound /p/ at the beginning of *pup*, what is the new word?" **S:** "Up." **Note:** Continue with an example deleting an ending sound.
Phoneme Substitution The ability to substitute sounds to form new words; substitution includes beginning, medial, and ending sounds	**T:** *(Example with a beginning sound)* "The word is *pot*. Say the word *pot*." **S:** "Pot." **T:** "Change the first sound to /h/ at the beginning of pot, what is the new word?" **S:** "Hot." **Note:** Continue by changing to an ending sound, medial sound, or using words with onsets and rimes or multisyllabic words.

T = teacher
S = student or students

Figure 2.2: Phonemic awareness skills.

What Works in the Classroom?

Phonemic awareness instruction should be age appropriate, playful, and energetic. Thinking about phonemic awareness as more than simply skill instruction means choosing appropriate materials such as chants, songs, rhymes, and word games. Read alouds of poems, alliterative stories, and text, along with sound play, help students become aware of language and sounds outside of skill instruction.

While many teachers engage in these types of activities, intentionality is key. Understanding the why behind your selections of read alouds, sound games, and language exploration will help you achieve your instructional goals, and students will benefit. Partnering with parents is important, too. Invite them to engage in simple phonemic awareness activities at home and send home simple activities or post them on your classroom website to encourage them to support their child's emerging skills. Practicing these skills outside the classroom extends and reinforces their development. In the following sections, I include characteristics of effective phonemic awareness instruction that will bolster your intentionality along with strategies for developing phonemic awareness.

Characteristics of Effective Phonemic Awareness Instruction

Phonemic awareness instruction is effective and transfers to helping students learn to read and spell (NICHD, 2000a), especially struggling readers (Ehri et al., 2001). Based on a meta-analysis of sixteen studies (Erbeli et al., 2024), instruction for emergent readers should take place in small doses on most days. Consistency is key. There are common, evidence-based characteristics (Mesmer & Kambach, 2022) that inform effective phonemic awareness instruction. These characteristics are summarized in table 2.1.

Table 2.1: Characteristics of Effective Phonemic Awareness Instruction

Phonological Awareness	Effective phonemic awareness instruction should be taught as part of the broader picture of phonological awareness, or language sounds (Shanahan, 2008; Yopp & Yopp, 2000). Children must be familiar with rhymes, recognize separate words, syllables, simple onsets (/m/ as in *mop*), and rimes (/ŏp/ as in *mop*). Some students will enter school understanding this, and others will not. Make certain all children are fluent with the broader phonological awareness skills to move to phonemic awareness.
Interactive Read Alouds	Interactive read alouds support phonemic awareness and print concepts, and they are recognized as an important and engaging element to support literacy success (Cunningham & Zibulsky, 2011; Beck & McKeown, 2007; National Early Literacy Panel, 2008). An effective read aloud begins with intentional, well-chosen text selections. Unfortunately, the quality of read alouds in preschool and kindergarten classes varies widely (Kindle, 2011; Massey, Pence, Justice, & Bowles, 2008). Keep intentionality in mind when reading aloud to support phonemic awareness; select from books that include rhyming, alliteration, and playful language.

continued ▶

Shifting From Modeling to Independence	When using instructional sequences that include what the teacher says and how students respond, as outlined in the strategy tables, follow the gradual release of responsibility framework (Pearson & Gallagher, 1983) as previously discussed. The sequence is intentional and shifts students from following a model to becoming independently proficient along the continuum of phonemic awareness skills as shown in figure 2.2 (page 66).
Grade Levels and Grouping	Phonemic awareness benefits children most when taught in kindergarten and first grade as they are learning to read (NICHD, 2000a; Rehfeld, Kirkpatrick, O'Guinn, & Renbarger, 2022). If students do not have alphabetic knowledge, teaching letter knowledge at the same time as phonemic awareness is important so they can transfer phonemic awareness to phonics and decoding. Phonemic awareness skills can be taught and practiced as a whole group, but the research suggests scaffolding instruction by teaching most skills during small-group instruction (NICHD, 2000a) is most effective since students will undoubtedly be at different stages of their phonemic awareness development (Ehri et al., 2001; Williams et al., 2009).
Time Allotment	A meta-analysis of sixteen studies (Erbeli et al., 2024), which included both experimental and control groups of students, revealed that 10.2 hours across the school year is the optimal amount of time for phonemic awareness instruction. After that, there are diminishing returns. While 10.2 isn't a magic number, it's a good marker to keep in mind. Across a typical 180-day school year, that's less than five minutes per day, with some variation depending on individual student's needs (Erbeli et al., 2024). Focusing instruction is critical so that the few minutes each day are well spent.
Focused Instruction	Focus is important when teaching phonemic awareness skills. For example, rather than teaching isolating, categorizing, and deleting sounds in one lesson, it is best to focus on one or two skills rather than too many (Ehri et al., 2001). Based on a meta-analysis, the NRP (NICHD, 2000a) along with Ehri and colleagues (2001), note that focusing on one or two phonemic awareness skills produces stronger skills and greater transfer to reading than focusing on too many. More *is not* always better.
Oral Instruction With Non-Letter Representation	Oral phonemic awareness instruction, accompanied by non-letter tokens or plastic counters, can serve as a useful precursor to letters (Lundberg et al., 1988) This is especially helpful when supporting struggling readers. For example, many non-readers can begin segmenting sounds using Elkonin boxes (Elkonin, 1963; Mesmer & Kambach, 2022). To use Elkonin boxes, students move plastic discs that represent sounds into individual boxes. Visuals and instructional protocols are found later in this chapter (page 84).
Phonemic Awareness Instruction and Phonics	Phonemic awareness, in the sequence of learning to read, precedes phonics. While we know young children can hear and identify sounds in words before they know all twenty-six letters in the alphabet, there is evidence that supports reciprocity between phonemic awareness and phonics (Brady, 2020; Clayton et al., 2020). In other words, phonemic awareness instruction supports phonics; likewise, phonics instruction supports phonemic awareness. When able, connect phonemic awareness instruction with phonics lessons (Bus & IJzendoorn, 1999; NICHD, 2000b; Stalega et al., 2024).

Phonemic Awareness Instruction and Phonics *(continued)*	When considering whether to add letters, a meta-analysis (Ehri et al., 2001) showed that phonemic awareness instruction was more beneficial when taught with letters. Before adding letters to phonemic awareness, keep in mind that the addition of letters adds complexity to the task. If students are not firm in letter-sound matching, stick with blank tokens to represent sounds. Students should first understand that there is a relationship between letters and spoken sounds, known as the alphabetic principle, in order to benefit from the addition of letters. When able, connect phonemic awareness instruction with phonics lessons (Bus & IJzendoorn, 1999; NICHD, 2000b; Stalega et al., 2024) along with reading and writing (Ehri et al., 2001). As students understand that letters represent sounds, printed letters represent anchors for phonemes (Clemens et al., 2021). For example, if the phonics lesson focuses on the beginning sound */f/* as in *fun*, include */f/* examples during phonemic awareness practice. Additionally, integrate read alouds that highlight the initial */f/* sound, such as *Big Frank's Fire Truck*, *The Berenstain Bears Forget Their Manners*, and *A Fish out of Water*. While reading aloud, have children indicate with a thumbs-up each time they hear the initial */f/* sound. All of these integrated activities make the implicit *explicit*. Connect, connect, connect!
English Learners	Research with K-2 students focusing on direct, explicit instruction in phonemic awareness and phonics shows great benefit for English learners (Lesaux & Siegel, 2003; Vaughn, Mathes, Linan-Thompson, & Francis, 2005). Instruction should be language-rich and include modeling, feedback, and a focus on developing vocabulary and word knowledge (Calderón, 2011; Saville-Troike, 1984). English learners should also continue to develop language proficiency in their native language along with English through home, school, and community experience (Manyak, 2007; Moll & Dworin, 1996; Verhoeven, 1994).

Integrating the elements described listed in the table is essential to support emergent readers as they develop and secure their phonemic awareness skills. In the next section, you'll find strategies for implementing purposeful phonemic awareness strategies in your classroom to support students' early reading development.

Strategies to Develop Phonemic Awareness

In the previous sections, we explored essential instructional elements that help guide young students as they develop phonemic awareness. In this section, you'll find simple strategies to build phonemic awareness and phonological awareness with early learners. Many of the strategies in this chapter include phonological awareness skills since some of your students will need these skills in preparation for more specific phonemic awareness skills. Also, while many of these strategies are very brief and playful, they nevertheless reinforce the skills needed in the continuum of literacy skill development. Think *play and practice* rather than *skill and drill.*

Read Alouds for Phonemic Awareness

- *A, My Name is Alice* by Jane Bayer (1984)
- *Each Peach Pear Plum* by Janet and Allen Ahlberg (1978)
- *Llama Llama Red Pajama* by Anna Dewdney (2015)
- *One Wide River to Cross* by Barbara Emberley (1992)
- *Ricky, the Rock That Just Couldn't Rhyme* by Mr. Jay (2023)
- *Six Sleepy Sheep* by Jeffie Ross Gordon (1991)
- *Tikki Tikki Tembo* by Arlene Mosel (2007)

Phonemes and Skill Identification

You'll notice that phonemic awareness strategies include reinforcing and practicing the big three skills—isolating, segmenting, and blending sounds. Students must be proficient at isolating sounds, segmenting sounds, and blending them together to form a word (Ehri, 2020).

When planning instruction, here are a few things to keep in mind.

- Typically, identification tasks such as *"Which one doesn't sound like the other—can, tan, fun?"* are easier for early learners than production tasks such as *"What sounds do you hear in* fish*?"*
- Continuant sounds (for example, */r/*, */m/*, */n/*) are easier to manipulate and hear than stop sounds (for example, */b/ /d/ /t/*).
- Be careful not to elongate sounds. Please don't say */bŭh/* for */b/* or */pŭh/* for */p/*! I've heard well-meaning teachers and parents do this over and over. Instead, quickly stop the initial sound. I understand that it's easy to elongate the sound, but it hinders blending sounds. For example, */buh/ /ă/ /tuh/* becomes a three-syllable word instead of *bat*, a one-syllable word.
- Finally, remember that one sound can be represented by more than one letter. For example, the word *ship* has three sounds, as in */sh/ /ĭ/ /p/*, but four letters. This is especially important to keep in mind when students use plastic discs to represent sounds as in Elkonin boxes (described later in this chapter).

Phonemic awareness skills, generally ranging from simple to more complex, are shown in figure 2.3. Be aware that while these skills range from less to more complex, they are also overlapping in nature (Anthony & Lonigan, 2004).

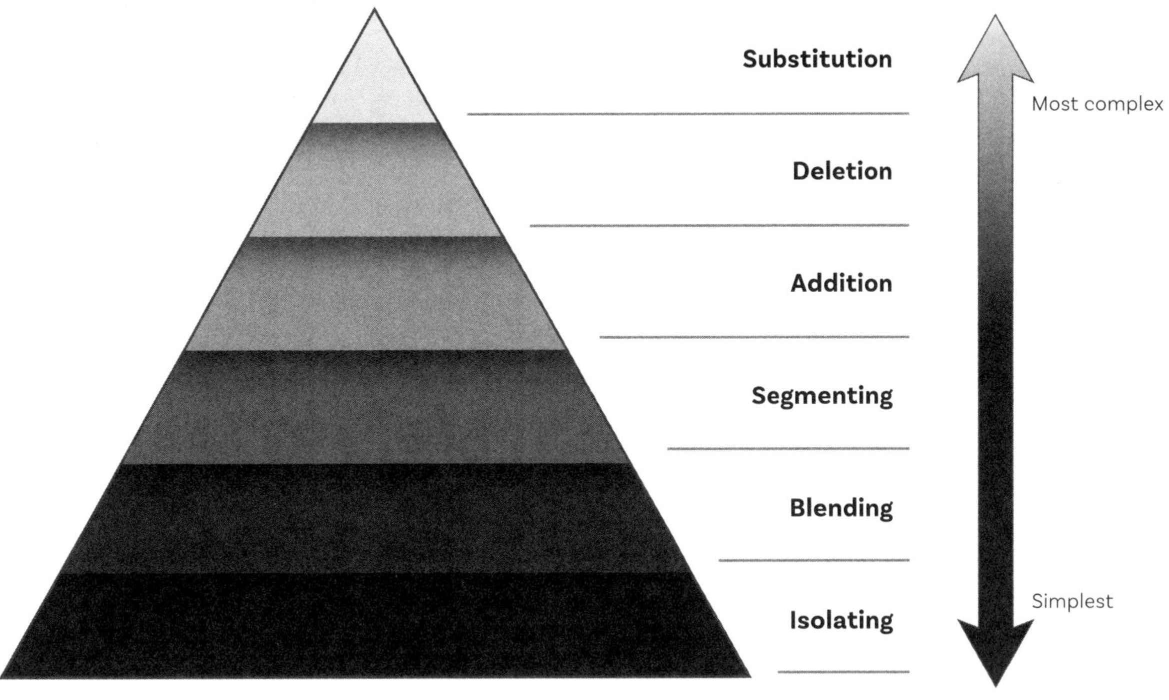

Figure 2.3: Phonemic awareness skills progression.

In this section, we looked at elements of effective instruction, which included grade levels and grouping for instruction, interactive read alouds, and English learners, to name a few. Additionally, I highlighted the importance of focusing on isolating, blending, and segmenting sounds when teaching phonemic awareness. In the next section, you'll find instructional strategies to support students as they develop their skills in isolating, categorizing, blending, substituting, and segmenting sounds. Additionally, you'll find a specific instructional sequence for strategically using Elkonin boxes with students.

Sound Walls

Sound walls are a speech-to-print tool that provide a visual representation of phonemes (see figure 2.4, page 72). They benefit emerging readers as they provide a cue to connect sound, mouth moves (articulatory moves), and print.

Sound walls support students by helping them identify and segment words into phonemes. By monitoring the articulatory gestures associated with phonemes, students benefit in their ability to read and spell (Castiglioni-Spalten & Ehri, 2003). Sound walls are typically organized by initial sounds along with an accompanying image of how the mouth articulates.

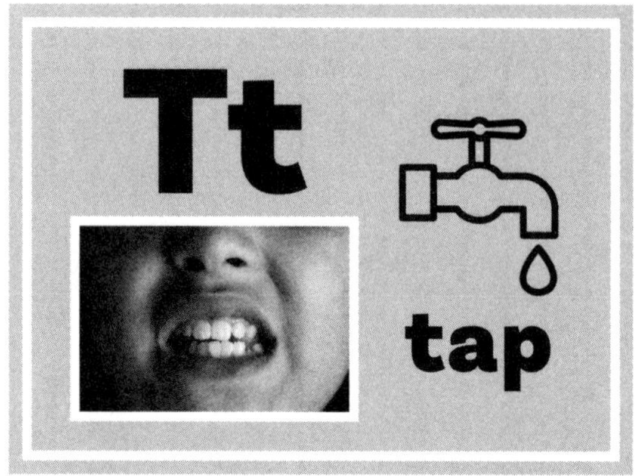

Figure 2.4: Students making mouth moves for *t* and *u*.

While phonemic awareness activities primarily emphasize sounds, sound walls take the emphasis a step further. Some features and characteristics of sound walls include the following.

- Organizing and grouping words by initial sounds matched with an image of a mouth to show the shape the tongue and mouth make when making the sound
- Matching the articulation of sounds (phonemes) to the letters (graphemes) that represent those sounds
- Grouping vowels and consonants separately matched with images of objects alongside the shape of the mouth
- Representing any combination of the forty-four phonemes in English

Please see figure 2.5 for an illustrative example of a sound wall.

There are several ways to make sound walls an effective instructional tool that supports emergent readers. First, create them with students by having them be a part of developing the wall and how sounds are organized. Next, integrate the sound wall into daily instruction and routines. In doing so, you'll keep them from becoming a static decoration but rather an important learning tool that supports phonemic awareness by helping students connect mouth movements, sounds, and letters.

The strategy in figure 2.6 (page 74) provides guidance for using sound walls.

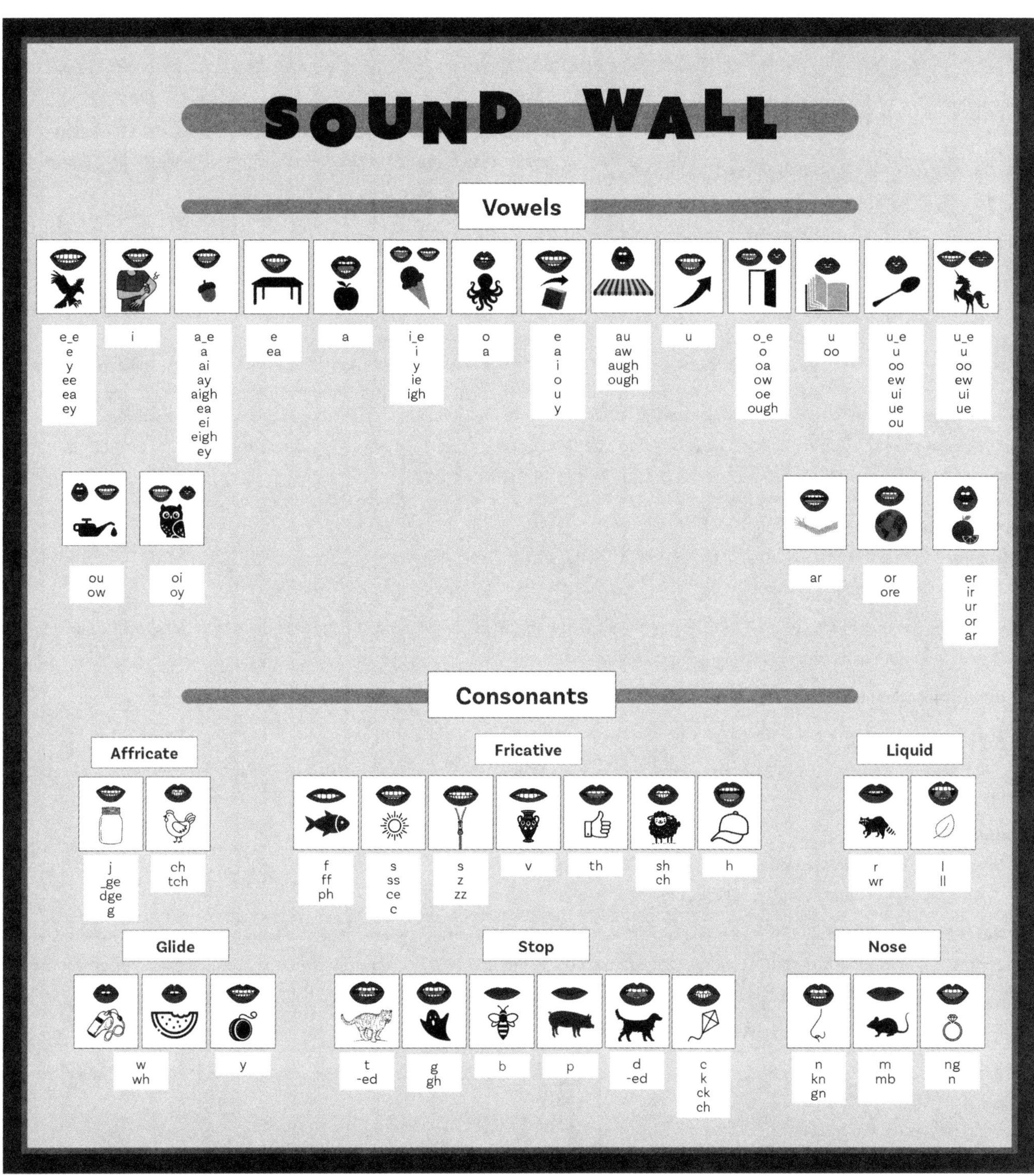

Figure 2.5: Illustrative example of a sound wall.

Strategy: Sound Walls

Pillar: Phonemic Awareness

Grade Level:	Instructional Grouping:	Consider This:
☑ K ☑ 1 ☑ 2 ☐ 3 ☐ 4 ☐ 5 ☐ 6	☑ Whole Group ☑ Small Group ☑ Individual	• Always construct the sound wall with your students. In other words, resist spending time in the summer creating a beautiful sound wall to have ready for the first day of school. • There are no rigid "rules" for how to organize. You'll find what works best for how you use the sound wall with students. Don't overcomplicate the process. • Consider taking pictures of students making the mouth moves to display on your wall.

What is it? A sound wall is a speech-to-print tool that provides a visual representation of phonemes to categorize phonemes.

Why is it important? Sounds walls provide a visual cue that connects sounds, mouth moves, and print for emerging readers as they learn the forty-four sounds that phonemes make in English.

What works in the classroom?

Organizing

- **Arrange:** Arrange common sound patterns and mouth position cards together.
- **Consonants and vowels:** Consider placing consonants separately from vowel sounds. Some teachers refer to and label the vowel section as "vowel alley."
- **Include images:** Place the sound with the letter, image of the mouth move, and an image of a matching object.
- **Small charts:** If you only have a few students who struggle with phonemic awareness, consider making small, laminated charts with students that include sound patterns and mouth positions to use during small-group instruction.

Instruction

- **Integrate phonemic awareness and letters:** When adding a new sound, image, letter, or word, intentionally integrate the sound with the associated letter or letters.
- **Refer to the sound wall:** When reading aloud, as you notice a sound that was recently taught, direct students to the sound wall. When writing during whole-group instruction, refer to the sound wall as you write and spell specific words.
- **Add mirrors:** Consider adding a basket of mirrors near the sound wall so students can practice and observe their mouth moves while referring to the sound cards.
- **Practice:** Use the sound wall to practice one or two specific sounds (less is better) for a bell ringer activity as students are lining up.

Figure 2.6: Strategy—Sound walls.

*Visit **go.SolutionTree.com/literacy/FSK6** and enter the unique access code found on the book's inside front cover to access a reproducible version of this figure.*

Phoneme Isolation

One of the easiest phonemic awareness tasks for students to master is isolation, or the ability to isolate and identify specific sounds within words, including the first, middle, and final sounds. For example, "Say the first sound in *dog,* the final sound in *dog,* and the middle sound in *dog.*" The progression of learning sounds is hearing the initial sound first, final sound next, and medial or middle sounds last when learning to isolate and identify sounds.

Practicing phoneme isolation may be used as a bell ringer activity or as students line up. For example, you could say, "Students at the rocket table, what sound do you hear at the beginning of *map*?" Students respond by making the */m/* sound. "Very good. The rocket table can line up." Go on with, "Students at the planet table, say the sound you hear at the end of *fish.*" Students respond by saying the sound */sh/.* "That's right. The planet table can line up." And so on.

The following two strategies provide games to practice with sounds. Both sound bingo (Klinner, n.d.) and I Spy are fun, gamelike activities to reinforce beginning and ending sounds. See the simple steps in figure 2.7 and figure 2.8 (page 77).

Strategy: Sound Bingo

Pillar: Phonemic Awareness

Grade Level:	**Instructional Grouping:**	**Materials:**
☑ K ☑ 1 ☑ 2 ☐ 3 ☐ 4 ☐ 5 ☐ 6	☑ Whole Group ☑ Small Group ☑ Individual	• You'll need a set of bingo cards for each student with pictures on them. You can easily make these or find them online. (Laminate them to allow for re-use.) • Discs or dry erase markers to mark off images **Consider This:** • Consider the skill level of students and pair students if appropriate. • You can also choose to focus on beginning sounds or ending sounds only or combine both sounds.

What is it? Phoneme isolation is the ability to isolate and identify specific sounds (phonemes) within words, including the first, middle, or last sound.

Why is it important? Being able to isolate individual sounds is a prerequisite skill to segmenting and blending sounds together to make words.

Figure 2.7: Strategy—Sound bingo.

continued ▶

What works in the classroom?

Simple steps

Each student has a bingo card with pictures. Quickly identify any pictures that might be unfamiliar and model how the game works *(show me)*. Then do another example or two together *(help me)*.

T (directions): "Look at the pictures on your card. I'm going to say the sound at the beginning of a picture that may be on your card. If you find a picture that begins with that sound, mark it with your dry erase marker. Let's try one together. The beginning sound is /s/. If you have a picture on your card that begins with /s/, mark it. On my card, I have a picture of a swingset. I hear /s/ at the beginning of *swingset*, so I will mark it with my dry erase marker."

S: (*Students scan their bingo card, look for a picture that begins with the target sound, and cover their picture with a colored disc.*)

T: (*Continue by pronouncing sounds while students look for pictures that begin with the sound and mark their cards. The student who covers five pictures [across, down, or diagonal] calls "sound bingo."*)

S: (*The student who calls "sound bingo" names each picture along with the beginning sound.*)

Variations

- Play the sound game as directed previously and focus only on ending sounds.
- If most students have alphabet understanding, include names of letters *and* sounds.

Visit ***go.SolutionTree.com/literacy/FSK6*** *and enter the unique access code found on the book's inside front cover to access a reproducible version of this figure.*

Phoneme Categorization

In phonemic awareness, categorization is when students identify the word that does not belong with the others in a group of words (three or more). For example, when focusing on initial sounds, the teacher may orally say the words *fish, fan,* and *shark* while directing students to listen for the word that does not have a beginning sound like the others. In turn, students should identify the word *shark* as having a beginning sound different from the other two. The teacher may follow up with, "That's correct. *Shark* begins with the */sh/* sound and *fish* and *fan* begin with the */f/* sound." Students can listen for beginning, middle, or ending sounds. It is a more advanced skill since students must be able to isolate and identify sounds before they can categorize. Please see figure 2.9 (page 78) for an example of a good categorization exercise (Padak & Rasinski, 2008).

Strategy: I Spy

Pillar: Phonemic Awareness

Grade Level:	Instructional Grouping:	Materials:
☑ K ☑ 1 ☐ 2 ☐ 3 ☐ 4 ☐ 5 ☐ 6	☑ Whole Group ☑ Small Group ☑ Individual	• Use a flat basket or tray and place lots of random objects on the tray (for example, scissors, fork, various small toys, pen, marker, paper, crayon, and so on) • The *I Spy* books (series) by Jean Marzollo along with the Spot It! themed games also work well for this phonemic awareness activity.

What is it? Phoneme isolation is the ability to isolate and identify specific sounds (phonemes) within words including the first, middle, and final sound.

Why is it important? Being able to isolate individual sounds is a prerequisite skill to segmenting and blending sounds together to make words. This is a fun, playful activity that helps students practice isolating and identifying phonemes.

What works in the classroom?

Place the tray with objects on the table in front of the students or small group and quickly name the objects.

T: 1. "Today, we are going to play a game called I Spy. I will say a beginning sound and you will find an object on the tray or in your hand that begins with that sound and tell us what it is. Then we'll say the sound and object."

2. (*Model with an object on the tray. Then do another example or two with students.*)
3. (*Begin by naming the objects on the tray and invite each student to take an object and place it in their hand.*)
4. "I spy with my little eye something in ________________'s hand that begins with the /p/ sound."

S: "Pencil."

T: "*Pencil* begins with the /p/ sound. Let's say the name and sound together."

T and S: "Pencil, /p/."

Continue moving around the circle and name the beginning sound of the object in each student's hand. Continue naming initial sounds for objects on the tray; when students respond, repeat the sound and object with students until you've completed all the objects on the tray.

Variations

- If you are working with one to three students, you could use a page from an *I Spy* book and name sounds followed by students finding the object on the page.
- The Spot It! themed game includes round cards with objects pictured on them and would work as well. Each student could take a card or you could hold up a card and name beginning sounds for which students identify the matching image.
- Change it up by having students recognize additional sounds including ending, beginning and ending, and medial sounds.

Figure 2.8: Strategy—I Spy.

*Visit **go.SolutionTree.com/literacy/FSK6** and enter the unique access code found on the book's inside front cover to access a reproducible version of this figure.*

Strategy: Odd Word Out

Pillar: Phonemic Awareness

Grade Level:	**Instructional Grouping:**	**Materials:**
☑ K ☑ 1 ☑ 2 ☐ 3 ☐ 4 ☐ 5 ☐ 6	☑ Whole Group ☑ Small Group ☑ Individual	• Picture cards **Consider This:** • This skill activity can be done orally or with picture cards for which you identify the images for students.

What is it? Odd word out is a gamelike activity in which students identify which image does not belong with the others in a group of words (three or more). You can choose to focus on beginning, middle, or ending sounds.

Why is it important? Being able to isolate and categorize sounds is another way of focusing students on listening carefully and distinguishing between sounds.

What works in the classroom?

Preparation

- In advance, select groups of words (three in each group) with two being similar and one not similar based on sounds.
- You may choose to focus on beginning sounds (most simple) in one lesson, ending sounds (next in progression) in another, and medial sounds (most difficult) in another.

Sequence

Beginning Sounds

Begin by modeling the strategy with a sample set of words (show me). Then do another example or two together (help me).

T: "I'm going to say three words. Listen carefully to the words so that you can tell me which does not sound like the others." (*Let me.*) "The words are *hat*, *mat*, and *pot*. Which word does not belong?"

S: "Pot."

T: "Why does *pot* not belong?"

S: "Because *pot* begins with the /p/ sound." (Or some variation of that.)

(*Complete several more sets of words for a few minutes.*)

Variations

- Depending on the skill level of students, continue with ending sounds and medial sounds using the same sequence. Focus on only one or two (beginning and ending, beginning and medial, and so on) sounds in one session.
- Include cards with the words printed on them. Continue the sequence as previously described.

Figure 2.9: Strategy—Odd word out.

*Visit **go.SolutionTree.com/literacy/FSK6** and enter the unique access code found on the book's inside front cover to access a reproducible version of this figure.*

Phoneme Blending

Blending phonemes is an important skill for early learners, right up there with isolating and segmenting sounds. Students must become proficient at isolating, segmenting, and blending sounds together. The next strategy (figure 2.10) uses the image and actions of a turtle—slow and steady—to reinforce hearing every sound and blending them together to form words (Padak & Rasinski, 2008; Young, Paige, & Rasinski, 2022).

Strategy: Turtle Talk

Pillar: Phonemic Awareness

Grade Level:

- ☑ K
- ☑ 1
- ☐ 2
- ☐ 3
- ☐ 4
- ☐ 5
- ☐ 6

Instructional Grouping:

- ☑ Whole Group
- ☑ Small Group
- ☑ Individual

Materials:

- Wide rubber bands
- Turtle image taped to a popsicle stick

Consider This:

- This strategy is simple to demonstrate for parents and caregivers at a parent night. Another alternative is to record the strategy and upload it to a classroom blog or website for them to view and do at home.
- I've included several variations depending on the skill level of your students. Variations two and three would work well in small groups.
- Some teachers also tape turtle images on popsicle sticks so students can move the turtle along the letters as they stretch the sounds.
- You can also use a wide rubber band to model s-t-r-e-t-ch-i-n-g sounds slowly as you say words during whole and small-group instruction.
- Before each variation, model blending sounds together to form a word and then do a few examples with students.

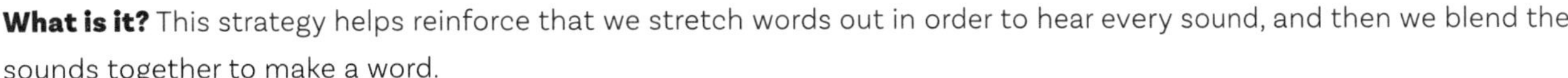

What is it? This strategy helps reinforce that we stretch words out in order to hear every sound, and then we blend the sounds together to make a word.

Why is it important? Students need to hear individual sounds in words, segment those sounds, and blend them together to form words.

What works in the classroom?

Before the Activity

You may wish to read aloud one of the suggested books to make certain that students understand the concept that turtles (tortoises) are known for being slow. Books featuring turtles include *Hi, Harry! The Moving Story of How One Slow Tortoise Slowly Made a Friend* by Martin Waddell (2003), *Let's Go, Slow Moe!* by L. C. Madalyou (2021), or *The Tortoise and the Hare*, a fable by Aesop and adapted and illustrated by Janet Stevens (1984).

Figure 2.10: Strategy—Turtle talk.

continued ▶

Simple Steps

Variation 1: Teacher as the Lead

T: 1. (*Remind students of the turtle analogy and that turtles do everything slowly.*)

2. We're going to stretch sounds in words just like a turtle would do. Listen as I say sounds, and then you'll blend them together to make a word: /f/ . . . /ĭ/ . . . /l/." (*Say each sound very slowly, stretching out the sounds.*)

S: (*The students repeat the word* fill *while stretching the individual sounds.*)

T: "Now blend the sounds together to make a word. Can you name the word?"

S: "Fill."

(*Do several more examples for and with students and pronounce each word.*)

Variation 2: Paired Listeners

T: "This time I would like you to work with a partner. You will think of a word and say the sounds slowly like a turtle. Then, your partner will repeat the word slowly and stretch out the sounds. After that, your partner will blend the sounds together to make a word."

S: (*Students work together in pairs, taking turns stretching sounds and having their partner blend the sounds together and name the word.*)

Variation 3: Matching Sound and Letters

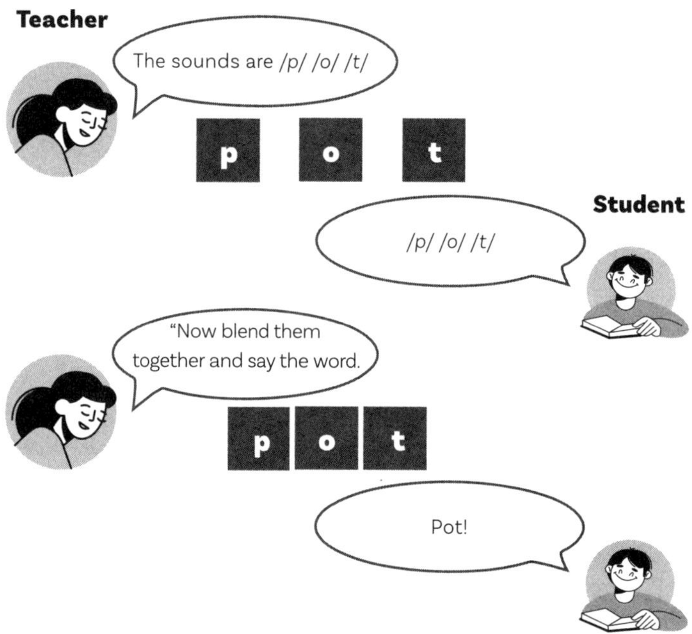

This time, add letters to the activity. I prefer using letter tiles to show how to stretch sounds (move tiles apart) and blend them (move tiles together).

You can also put an image of a turtle on a popsicle stick for young students to manipulate and move their turtles slowly across each letter as they stretch the sounds, or you could use a wide rubber band to stretch sounds as suggested previously.

T: "/p/ . . . /o/ . . . /t/." (*Say each sound very slowly, stretching out the sounds.*) "Now blend them together to make a word. Can you name the word?"

S: "Pot." (*The student can slide the letter tiles together.*)

Visit **go.SolutionTree.com/literacy/FSK6** *and enter the unique access code found on the book's inside front cover to access a reproducible version of this figure.*

Phoneme Substitution

Phoneme substitution is a more advanced phonemic awareness skill because we are asking students to substitute a sound in a word to form a new word. Substituting sounds can occur at the beginning, middle, or ending position in a word. For example, if focusing on ending sounds, the teacher may say the word *big* and ask students, "What word do we have if we change the */g/* at the end of *big* to */t/*?" While phoneme substitution is a more complex skill, students who are proficient at substituting sounds will be ready for the following two strategies. Presto chango (figure 2.11) provides practice in substituting sounds (Padak & Rasinski, 2008).

Substituting sounds is a more advanced phonemic awareness skill on the continuum of phonemic awareness skills that students must develop. The repetitive nature built into presto chango helps students play with sounds and develop proficiency in substituting sounds and letters to make new words.

Strategy: Presto Chango

Pillar: Phonemic Awareness

Grade Level:	Instructional Grouping:	Materials:
☑ K ☑ 1 ☑ 2 ☐ 3 ☐ 4 ☐ 5 ☐ 6	☑ Whole Group ☑ Small Group ☑ Individual	• Letter tiles or whiteboard **Consider This:** • Select several word families before the activity such as */-ot/*, */-ig/*, */-en/*, and so on. • If you are combining this activity with letters, I suggest using letter tiles. Place about ten tiles on the table. Then slide new letter tiles into place to form words and take away letter tiles in words. • I've provided two variations; you can think of more depending on group size and skill levels.

What is it? This activity focuses on word families and is a simple way to have students play with sounds and substitute sounds to make new words.

Why is it important? In the continuum of phonemic awareness skills, substituting sounds is one of the more advanced skills. When children know a word such as *bend*, they can substitute the beginning sound to form many more new words (or nonsense words). They can also substitute middle sounds and ending sounds (rimes) to form new words.

What works in the classroom?

Always have students repeat the word after you initially say it.

Model the Activity (sounds only)

T: 1. Let's begin with the word *hot*. Say the word *hot*. If we take away the */h/* sound, we have */-ŏt/*." *(This can be a listening-only activity, or show this with tiles or on the whiteboard.)*

2. Now if I add the */p/* sound—presto chango—now we have *pot*. Say *pot* with me."
3. *(Provide several more examples, and then invite students to do it with you).*
4. "Now I'd like you to try it."

Figure 2.11: Strategy—Presto chango.

continued ▶

Variation 1 With Letter Tiles

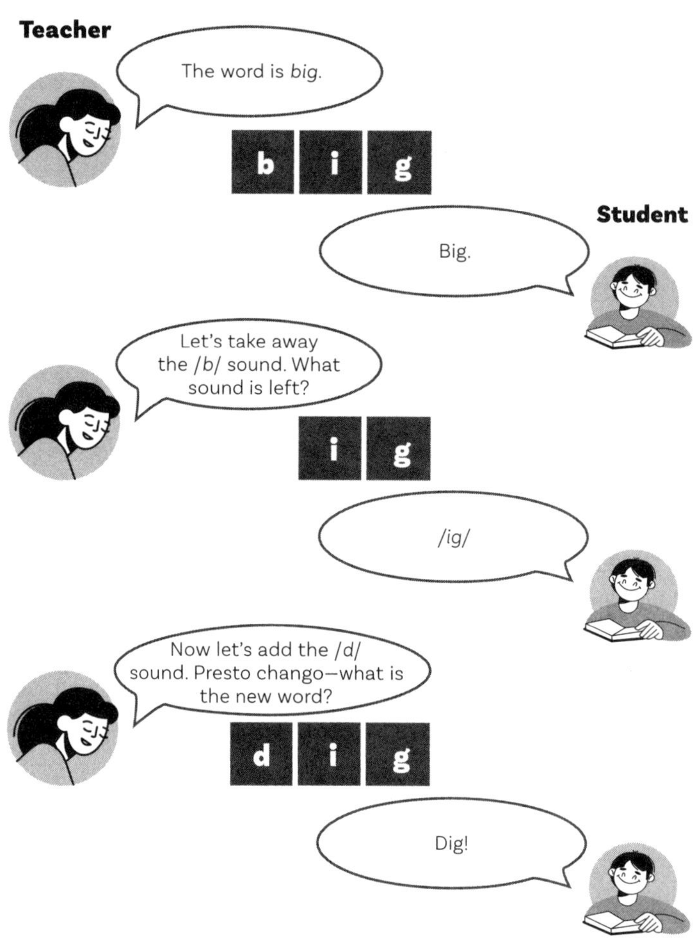

T: The word is *big*. Say the word *big*. Let's take away the /b/ sound. What sound is left?"

S: "/ĭg/"

T: "Now add the /d/ sound. Presto chango—what is the new word?" (*Move hand left to right under the word.*)

S: "Dig."

Variation 2 With Letter Tiles

Place eight to ten letter tiles from which the student can choose to build new words.

T: "The word is *sad*. Take away the /s/ sound. What sound is left?"

S: "/d/."

T: "Add a new letter or sound of your choice. Presto chango—what is the new word?"

S: "Bad, dad, had, mad . . ."

Visit ***go.SolutionTree.com/literacy/FSK6*** *and enter the unique access code found on the book's inside front cover to access a reproducible version of this figure.*

Many students need a good deal of practice as they learn to substitute sounds and letters to make new words. Lucky roll (figure 2.12) provides fun, fast-paced practice in substituting sounds in words (Kung, 2020). It can serve as a fun bell ringer activity or to practice sounds as students make their way to small-group instruction.

Strategy: Lucky Roll

Pillar: Phonemic Awareness

Grade Level:	Instructional Grouping:	Consider This:
☑ K ☑ 1 ☑ 2 ☑ 3 ☐ 4 ☐ 5 ☐ 6	☑ Whole Group ☑ Small Group ☑ Individual	• Place dice in small, clear plastic containers so that students can shake and roll them inside the container and you won't be losing or chasing them. • I suggest introducing this activity during small-group instruction so that you can model the activity and do several more examples with students. • This activity is a great bell ringer activity since there isn't really a sequence to the activity. • Variations of this game work well across multiple skills and subjects.

What is it? Lucky Roll is a phonemic awareness activity that provides practice as students learn to manipulate sounds in words to make new words.

Why is it important? Students need to have the ability to substitute sounds in order to form new words. Substitution is an advanced phonemic awareness skill and includes changing beginning, medial, and ending sounds.

What works in the classroom?

Materials

- Six-sided dice (one die) for this activity.
- Have a set of word cards available, typically one-syllable CVC words such as *cat, pig, mug, top, pet, bun,* and so on.

Model: Demonstrate how to play the game with students by shaking the die several times in the container and completing the task (*show me*). Then have students roll the die a few more times and complete the task associated with the number.

Steps

- **Whole class:** Roll a die, and the students complete the task that corresponds with the number.
- **Small group:** Using a soft die, students can take turns rolling the die and completing the skill associated with the number.

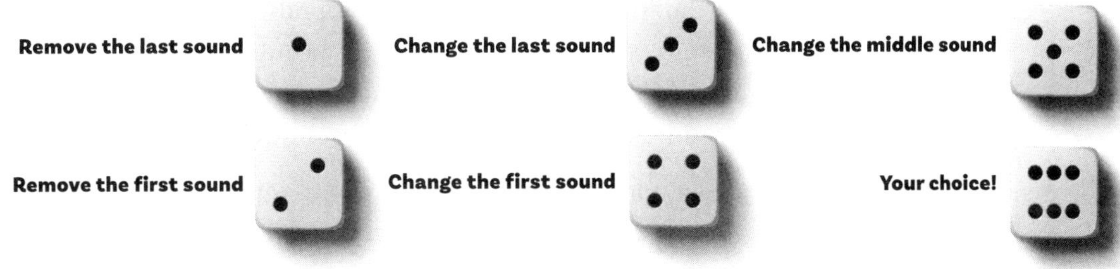

Figure 2.12: Strategy—Lucky roll.

Visit ***go.SolutionTree.com/literacy/FSK6*** *and enter the unique access code found on the book's inside front cover to access a reproducible version of this figure.*

Lucky roll should be one strategy in a repertoire of strategies that provides students with regular practice in playing with and manipulating sounds. Among the strategies shared here, lucky roll is more advanced since students should be proficient with substituting beginning, middle, and final sounds in order to play.

Phoneme Segmentation

Phoneme segmentation is the ability to break words down into individual sounds. For example, children who are able to segment sounds can hear and break the word *hat* into three sounds, */h/ /a/ /t/.* I recommend beginning with two-phoneme words such as *it* or *up* so that students achieve success before moving to words with three sounds like *big* or *hat.*

This simple phonemic awareness activity is playful and fun. It borrows from the tune of "The Farmer in the Dell" to help students hear and segment sounds in words. See the simple instructions in figure 2.13 to start singing and segmenting with your students.

As mentioned previously, teaching phonemic awareness should be playful, energetic, and fun. Singing, reading aloud, and chorally chanting rhymes support phonemic awareness. Singing songs like this helps students have fun while practicing their ability to hear and segment words into specific sounds.

Elkonin Boxes

Elkonin boxes serve as an important means of making the invisible (sounds) visible to students. They can be used in a variety of ways to support phonemic awareness, which are described in the next section. Elkonin boxes, sometimes referred to as "sound boxes" (Elkonin, 1963), are one of my favorite strategies to help early learners focus on individual sounds in words. D. B. Elkonin, a Russian psychologist, developed the boxes to help students have concrete means to identify, segment, and manipulate phonemes. This strategy is explicit, systemic, and multisensory. Over the course of my career, I've used Elkonin boxes routinely with struggling readers. For many, the light bulb went on when using this strategy. Frequently, students began making progress with more advanced phonemic awareness skills and, eventually, reading words and connected text.

Segmenting sounds is one of the more challenging phonemic awareness skills and one that needs a lot of practice. Elkonin boxes serve as a concrete visual representation of sounds. Prior to understanding that letters represent sounds, students can segment words into sounds by moving non-letter, plastic discs into individual boxes for each sound. The steps in figure 2.14 (page 86) are sequential. I've also included in the figure a few variations and more advanced skills as students move through the progression.

Elknonin boxes have been one of my favorite strategies to support students as they develop their phonemic awareness skills specific to segmenting, substituting, and blending sounds. I've found it particularly effective when working with struggling readers and English learners as they build their early reading skills.

Strategy: Singing and Segmenting

Pillar: Phonemic Awareness

Grade Level:

- ☑ K
- ☑ 1
- ☐ 2
- ☐ 3
- ☐ 4
- ☐ 5
- ☐ 6

Instructional Grouping:

- ☑ Whole Group
- ☐ Small Group
- ☐ Individual

Consider This:

While this activity can be done on a whim, I suggest making a list of CVC words and sequentially working through the list as you sing this song.

What is it? This playful activity uses the tune to "The Farmer in the Dell" to reinforce hearing and segmenting sounds in three- and four-sound words, depending on the skill level of students.

Why is it important? Phoneme segmentation is the ability to recognize that a word has a specific number of sounds. A majority of instructional time should be spent isolating, segmenting, and blending sounds together to form words.

What works in the classroom?

Use the tune from "The Farmer in the Dell." If you need a quick refresher, listen to this one from Super Simple Songs on YouTube (www.youtube.com/watch?v=E-krsNziXEw).

Change the lyrics to the following:

Say the sounds you hear,
Oh say the sounds you hear,
Let's sa-ay all the sounds
Oh say the sounds you hear!
[*Insert word*]

Say the word aloud and then students clap their hands with each segmented sound.

Three sounds/claps	**Four sounds/claps**
cup /c/ /u/ /p/	pond /p/ /o/ /n/ /d/
bed /b/ /e/ /d/	stick /s/ /t/ /i/ /ck/
chip /ch/ /i/ /p/	drum /d/ /r/ /u/ /m/

Figure 2.13: Strategy—Singing and segmenting.

*Visit **go.SolutionTree.com/literacy/FSK6** and enter the unique access code found on the book's inside front cover to access a reproducible version of this figure.*

PHONEMIC AWARENESS

Strategy: Elkonin Boxes

Pillar: Phonemic Awareness

Grade Level:	Instructional Grouping:	Materials:
☑ K ☑ 1 ☑ 2 Struggling Readers: ☑ 3 ☑ 4 ☑ 5 ☑ 6	☑ Whole Group ☑ Small Group ☐ Individual	• Small round discs (represent the sounds of letters) • See the template in reproducibles for making your own Elkonin boxes. I suggest using cardstock and laminating them. **Consider This:** This strategy is fairly intense, about five or so minutes is adequate with kindergarten and first-grade students.

What is it? Elkonin boxes help students to form the foundational skills of isolating, identifying, segmenting, and manipulating letters and sounds in words. Elkonin boxes are small, square boxes in which students identify a phoneme by moving a token or disc into a box representing each sound they hear in a word.

Why is it important? Isolating, segmenting, and blending sounds to say words are three critically important skills as students learn to read. Elkonin boxes can help the invisible become visible for struggling readers in particular. They assist students in stretching sounds and identifying initial, medial, and final sounds in words.

What works in the classroom?

The sequence I use may be slightly different from others you have seen. Coming from a clinical setting, the sequence may be more rigid than some. In my professional opinion, following the sequence is critical, especially with struggling readers.

Modeling the Strategy

T: 1. "I'm going to say a word. Then you'll repeat the word after me. As you say the word, think about the sounds you hear. You'll say the word slowly, and as you say each sound, you will move one chip into a sound box for each sound that you hear."

2. *Show Me:* Model several times using a two-sound Elkonin box and a word such as *at*.
3. *Help Me:* Following this, do several more two-sound words with the student.

Words with two sounds: VC

Always begin with a simple word with two sounds (VC) so that the student experiences success.

Place the two-box sound box and two discs on the table in front of the student.

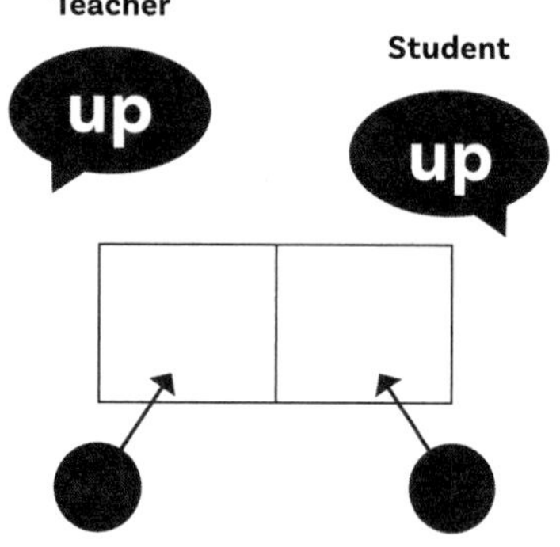

T: "The word is *up*. Say the word *up* slowly."

S: "Up." (*The student says the word* up *slowly.*)

T: "How many sounds do you hear in *up*?"

S: "Two."

T: "Correct. What is the first sound you hear in *up*?"

S: "/ŭ/."

T: "Move the chip to show me where the sound /ŭ/ is in *up*."

S: (*The student moves a disc into the first box for* /ŭ/.)

T: "That's right. What is the next sound you hear in *up*?"

S: "/p/."

T: "Move the chip to show me where the sound /p/ is in *up*."

S: (*The student moves a disc into the second box for /p/.*)

T: "The word is *up*. Say the word *up* with me." (*Slide your finger/hand beneath the discs from left to right as you say* up.)

S and T: "Up." (*Slide your finger/hand beneath the discs from left to right.*)

Note: You can proceed to ask additional questions such as, "What is the first sound you hear in *up*?" and so on. Complete a few additional two-sound words, having the student move discs into the sound box to represent sounds.

Words with three sounds: CVC

Teacher places the three-box sound box and three discs on the table in front of the student.

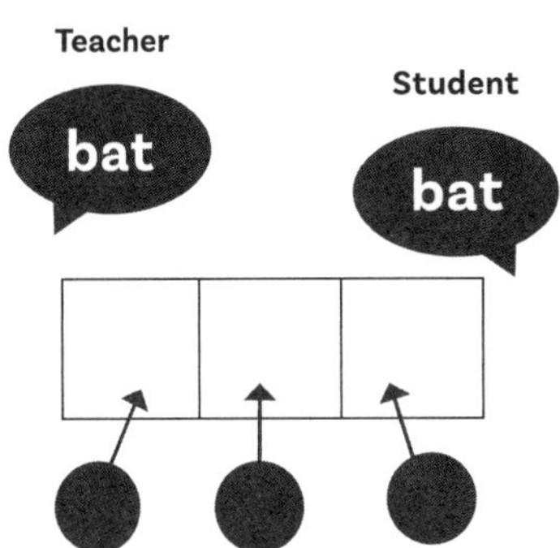

T: "The word is *bat*. Say the word *bat*."

S: "Bat." (*The student says the word* bat *slowly and listens to individual sounds.*)

T: "How many sounds do you hear in *bat*?"

S: "Three."

The sequence continues and the student moves a disc into the first box for /b/, a disc into the second box for /ă/, and one into the third box for /t/.

The sequence continues exactly as previously described for additional CVC words.

Advanced Skills

Digraphs and choosing sound boxes

As the student progresses, place two or three sets of sound boxes in front of the student—one with two boxes, three boxes, and even four boxes, as shown in the image. This forces students to think immediately about how many sounds they hear in the target word and decide how many boxes they will need. See the following sequence for a word with three sounds, with the initial sound being the /ch/ digraph.

Begin the session by placing a two-sound sound box and a three-sound sound box on the table.

T: "The word is *chip*. Say the word *chip* slowly."

S: "Chip." (*The student repeats slowly.*)

T: "How many sounds do you hear?"

S: (*The student says the word* chip *slowly.*) "Three sounds. /ch/ /ĭ/ /p/."

T: "Think about how many sounds you hear in chip. Choose the boxes that you will need and move the chips into the boxes as you say each sound in the word."

S: (*The student chooses the three-sound sound box [take away the two-sound sound box] and moves the chips as they say the sounds* /ch/ /ĭ/ /p/.)

Phoneme addition and deletion

As the student progresses, I introduce adding and deleting sounds.

T: "The word is *sand*. Say the word *sand*."

S: "Sand." (*The student says the word* sand *slowly.*)

T: "How many sounds do you hear?"

Figure 2.14: Strategy—Elkonin boxes.

continued ▶

S: (*The student repeats the word* sand *slowly.*) "Four sounds. /s/ /ă/ /n/ /d/."

T: "Choose the boxes and move the chips into each box for the sounds you hear in *sand.*"

S: (*The student moves the discs into four boxes.*)

T: "The word is *sand.* I'm going to take away the /s/ sound. Take away the first disc. The sounds left are *and.*" (*Say the word* and.)

S: (*The student says the word* and *slowly.*)

T: "How many sounds do you hear now?"

S: "*And,* three."

You can add and delete sounds using different variations such as having the students add or delete tokens.

Note

- If the student makes an incorrect choice, *do not correct them.* Allow the student to move through the choice with the discs. Usually the student will self-correct, which is an important metacognitive behavior.
- You can also ask additional questions such as, "What is the first sound you hear in *chip*?" or "What is the final sound or middle sound you hear in *chip*?"

Visit ***go.SolutionTree.com/literacy/FSK6*** *and enter the unique access code found on the book's inside front cover to access a reproducible version of this figure.*

Wrapping It Up

Because it is an essential foundational pillar for early literacy instruction, implementing consistent phonemic awareness instruction is key to helping young and emergent readers develop literacy skills. Early reading success depends on students' understanding of sounds and letters. There are many fun and varied ways in which to engage students with sounds in words, songs, and authentic text. School leaders can use the Leader's Lens (figure 2.15) to support teachers moving forward with effective literacy practices. Consider the Five Key Takeaways (page 90) as you work to engage in the chapter's strategies. Think about intentionality as it relates to your instruction and literacy environment as you consider the Five Key Next Steps (page 90).

Leader's Lens

Phonemic Awareness

Consider the following supervision supports and classroom connections as you lead and guide teachers through implementing effective phonemic awareness instruction.

Supervision Supports	
Practical Research	• Have you shared current research on the importance of phonemic awareness? • Have you shared materials and resources that support best practices in phonemic awareness instruction?
Professional Development	• What do you consider essential professional development for phonemic awareness? Where would you begin? • How would you support collaborative teams as teachers implement phonemic awareness practices within the literacy block? • Are there phonemic awareness resources to consider purchasing for the professional library?
Feedback and Expectations	• Does my feedback support phonemic awareness that is intentional and explicit? • Am I specific with expectations of what phonemic awareness should look like in the classroom?
Financial Focus	• Is there money budgeted to provide materials that could be used for phonemic awareness instruction?
Classroom Connections (Look-Fors)	
Literacy-Rich Environment	• Notice the use of wall space to support phonemic awareness (sound wall). • Notice the selection of books in the classroom library that support phonemic awareness and alphabet knowledge.
Direct Instruction	Notice the following instructional practices which include: • Defined time for phonemic awareness instruction • A focus on one or two skills per lesson • Instruction that moves from less complex to more complex skills • The majority of time focused on isolating, segmenting, and blending sounds • Instruction that sometimes include letters • Instruction that is differentiated depending on student's proficiency

Figure 2.15: Chapter 2 leader's lens.

*Visit **go.SolutionTree.com/literacy/FSK6** for a free reproducible version of this figure.*

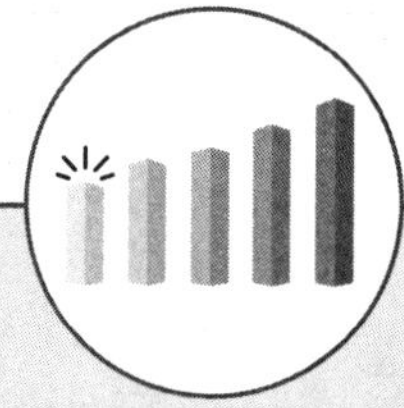

Five Key Takeaways

Consider the following takeaways individually or discuss them with your collaborative grade-level team.

1. **Phonemic awareness:** Phonemic awareness, the first of the five essential pillars, is the ability to hear, identify, and manipulate individual sounds—phonemes—in spoken words. Phonemic awareness is a top predictor of early reading success and benefits students because it helps them learn to read and spell.
2. **Phonemic awareness with letters:** While phonemic awareness typically precedes phonics in terms of skill development, as soon as students understand the alphabetic principle, you can display letters during phonemic awareness instruction. Keep your intention and purpose clear.
3. **Small-group instruction:** Phonemic awareness skills can be taught and practiced as a whole group, but research suggests scaffolding instruction by teaching most skills during small-group instruction (NICHD, 2000a) since children will undoubtedly be at different stages of their phonemic awarenessdevelopment (Ehri et al., 2001).
4. **Grade levels:** Phonemic awareness instruction is integral within the literacy block for kindergarten and first-grade students as well as older, struggling readers. Be systematic, have fun, and watch your students' sound and word awareness grow.
5. **Three impactful phonemic awareness skills:** The three most impactful phonemic awareness skills are isolating, segmenting, and blending. Spend most of your time here, especially with struggling readers.

Five Key Next Steps

Consider the following questions individually or discuss them with your collaborative grade-level team.

1. **Key definitions:** Think about the definitions of *phonemic awareness, phonological awareness, phonics, phonemes,* and *graphemes.* Are you and your collaborative team clear on each definition? If not, check out the key vocabulary section at the beginning of the chapter.
2. **Phonemic awareness instruction:** Think about your current phonemic awareness instruction. Is it explicit and systematic? Playful and fun? Consider the materials you use for teaching phonemic awareness. Is there variety? Do you use read alouds, chants, and songs to reinforce sounds and rhymes in addition to specific skill instruction?
3. **Phonemic awareness and letters:** What did you think about combining letters with phonemic awareness instruction? Do you do that during your lessons? Are you able to keep your focus on phonemic awareness rather than phonics?
4. **Phonemic awareness strategies:** Think about the strategies included for phonemic awareness skill development. Are there any specific strategies you want to try? Share with your grade-level team and discuss which ones they've implemented with their students.
5. **Integrating phonemic awareness:** Phonemic awareness should be embedded within print awareness, letter recognition, and word learning, along with fluency and comprehension through read alouds. Implement regular routines to integrate phonemic awareness with other literacy skills. Share with your grade-level collaborative team how you do this in whole- and small-group instruction.

Key Vocabulary

Phonics

Analytic Phonics	An approach to reading that emphasizes larger sound units when decoding; this approach uses word families or known words as analogies to figure out unknown words.
Connected Text	Multiple sentences that are related to one another (National Center on Improving Literacy, n.d.)
Decodable Text	Texts written using letter-sound correspondence that students have learned and provide practice for early readers to apply their growing phonics skills
Decoding	The ability to apply knowledge of letter-sound relationships to translate a word from print to speech
Digraphs	A combination of two letters representing a single sound; examples include *ph*, *sh*, and *ch*.
Diphthongs	A sound formed by two vowels in a single syllable; examples include *ai*, *ou*, and *oi*.
Encoding	The ability to hear and segment words into individual sounds (phonemes)
Explicit Instruction	Refers to how the teacher delivers instruction, in this case, directly
Homographs	Words that look the same but sound different such as *wind* as in the wind blows and *wind* as in wind up a toy
Homonyms	Words that sound *or* look the same but have different meanings, such as *right* and *write*
Homophones	Words that sound the same but have different meanings, such as *bear* and *bare* or *to*, *two*, and *too*
Orthographic Mapping	Refers to the process in which the brain permanently connects sounds, spelling, and meaning, which provides quick retrieval of words and reading automaticity, important for comprehension
Phonics	Refers to an instructional method that teaches the connection between symbols (graphemes) and sounds (phonemes)
Phonological Processing	Refers to the automatic mental processing of speech codes that occurs during speaking, listening, reading, and spelling (Ashby et al., 2023)
Predictable Text	A type of controlled text that includes repeated phrases or sentences on each page, with one new word that changes in the refrain
Synthetic Phonics	An approach to decoding in which the reader converts letters into sounds and blends those sounds to form a word; sometimes we think of this approach as whole-to-part-to-whole.
Systematic Instruction	An instructional sequence that organizes skills into a logical sequence that makes clear letter-sound relationships, larger units of sound/letter combinations (onsets and rimes), and spelling patterns (*ea*, *ie*, *oa*, *ou*)
Word Building	A phonics strategy in which students practice and apply their knowledge of letters and sounds outside of connected text by building and manipulating letters to form words

CHAPTER 3

Phonics
Making the Sound-Symbol Match

> At one magical instant in your early childhood, the page of a book—that string of confused, alien ciphers—shivered into meaning. Words spoke to you, gave up their secrets; at that moment, whole universes opened. You became, irrevocably, a reader.
>
> —Alberto Manguel

In early reading instruction, phonics receives a great deal of attention, and the science of reading has pushed phonics instruction to the forefront. While this position is well-deserved, keep in mind that phonemic awareness and phonics are symbiotic in nature. They each support the other when teaching children to read. Phonics instruction alone, as previously mentioned, will not ensure students become proficient readers.

This chapter is brimming with key vocabulary, discussion on the challenges of phonics instruction, and instructional tips and strategies. We'll take a look at phonics as a building block to fluency and comprehension along with systemic and explicit instructional approaches, including considering the four generalizations for phonics instruction. Finally, we'll briefly look at texts types and how they impact instructional approaches as well as instructional strategies specific to phonics instruction.

What Is Phonics?

Phonics refers to an instructional method that teaches the connection between symbols (graphemes) and sounds (phonemes), which moves students forward on their path to reading. Students learn letter-sound correspondence, or the symbol-sound match, and how to use this knowledge to decode printed words. They, in turn, use their understanding to read and spell words (Harris & Hodges, 1995).

Understanding phonics, or how letters and sounds work within English, is an essential element in learning how to read. Although English is more complex than some languages, it is still more regular and systematic than not, and phonics helps us decode or read words. A simple explanation of decoding is the ability to transform graphemes (symbols) into the corresponding phonemes (sounds) in order to blend and pronounce words. When learning to read, students must understand the major grapheme-phoneme relationships and how to use this to decode and spell words. Phonics also refers to reading-spelling skills that students acquire through instruction.

Why Is Phonics Important?

Learning to read is not as simple as *learning the sounds + learning the alphabet = decoding.* For some, this may be true, but for many students, it is not that straightforward. In its simplest form, reading requires students to make the sound-symbol connection in order to decode or read words. More accurately, learning to read is a complex cognitive process. In order for readers to engage in understanding what they read, they must have the ability to decode. If young readers are unable to decode words, they cannot access meaning independently. Understanding phonics is the key to unlocking reading.

Phonics as a Building Block to Fluency and Comprehension

As a building block to phonics, students must first have a good grasp of phonemic awareness, print concepts, and the alphabetic principle. As a reminder, *phonemic awareness* is the ability to hear, identify, and manipulate individual sounds—phonemes—in spoken words. *Print concepts* include understanding book orientation, that print runs left to right, and that words are made up of groups of letters with each separated by a space. *Alphabetic awareness* is the understanding that the twenty-six letters of the alphabet represent speech sounds. These concepts sound simple, but for children with little exposure to printed material in their lives, they can be new. While most kindergarten students move from acquiring phonemic awareness skills to connecting sounds with their corresponding letters, not all will make this shift. This shift may be delayed due to a lack of foundational skills discussed later in this chapter in the challenges section where instructional suggestions are also presented.

Reading aloud provides the perfect opportunity to teach these concepts in a natural manner by talking about and demonstrating features of books with students. This includes showing the front and back cover, title page, and page numbers; pointing to words as you read; and showing that we read from left to right and top to bottom.

Talking about print helps students gain an understanding that print is made up of words with spaces in between and that sentences end with punctuation marks. Additionally, words—made up of letters—can be read and carry meaning. Finally, students must grasp the alphabetic principle. Students acquire many of these early literacy concepts through systematic and explicit instruction along with an ample amount of modeling oral reading and writing.

Similar to phonemic awareness serving as a building block to phonics, phonics is a building block to reading fluency and comprehension. The end goal, or target, is comprehension. Reading completes the listening, speaking, writing, and reading continuum. Put another way, what we hear and say can be written as words, and words can be read. Keeping this continuum in mind helps us teach phonemic awareness and phonics as connected to the broader picture of literacy rather than as discrete skills existing in a vacuum.

While phonics instruction is critical, it is one essential part of a comprehensive reading program in kindergarten to third grade. It is not the whole program. Phonics is situated within a broader array of skills acquired through direct instruction in reading and writing, ample practice, and motivation specific to reading and writing activities.

Challenges of Phonics Instruction

Phonics instruction can be challenging for a variety of reasons, which are summarized in this section. Again, the foundational skills summarized next make a difference in how easily students respond to phonics instruction.

- **Lack of the concepts of print:** Students should be fully aware of the concepts of print as they learn phonics. Unfortunately, some students enter schools with little to no print awareness or understanding that print carries meaning. These concepts include the alphabetic principle; directionality of text in English (left to right and top to bottom); book features; the connection between listening, speaking, writing, and reading; the fact that print carries meaning; and the way that words are separated by spaces and punctuation marks. Understanding concepts of print lays the groundwork for students making the sound-symbol connection.
- **Limited phonemic awareness:** Students who have limited phonemic awareness and phonological skills will experience challenges learning phonics. Those students who can isolate, blend, and segment sounds will more readily shift to connecting sounds with letters. For students who are not progressing as anticipated, I suggest assessing their phonemic awareness subskills and spending time teaching and practicing the three most impactful skills—isolating, segmenting, and blending. If they do not yet understand

the alphabetic principle, use Elkonin boxes with plastic tokens to help students practice hearing and manipulating distinct sounds in words. You can find a full description and protocol in chapter 2 (page 84). For students who are not able to segment spoken CVCs into phonemes, I suggest modeling how to use a mirror so they can pay attention to their mouth positions and movements.

- **Many confusing words:** We can all agree that there are a lot of confusing words in English that make it challenging to teach phonics. For starters, there are words that sound the same but have different meanings, such as *bear* and *bare* (homophones). To make it a little more challenging, there are words that sound *and* look the same but have different meanings, such as *to, too,* and *two* (homonyms). Finally, there are words that look the same but sound different, such as *wind* as in the wind blows and *wind* as in wind up a toy (homographs). Let's just say it's confusing for many students and particularly for English learners.
- **Lack of scope and sequence:** It may seem outrageous, but I've been in more than a handful of school districts that did not have a phonics curriculum that included a detailed scope and sequence. A thorough scope and sequence are necessary for teachers as they strive to teach phonemic awareness and phonics in an explicit and systematic manner. The instructional sequence is designed to present skills from less to more complex and typically includes a robust cycle of repetition and cumulative practice. Additionally, a scope and sequence support collaborative teams as they align learning targets, instruction, assessment, and interventions.

Phonics Can Be Taught

Phonics skills can be taught, and systematic and explicit approaches are preferred. However, teaching phonics includes more than just an explicit approach. A comprehensive approach to phonics instruction also includes a scope and sequence, assessments, and intentional instructional routines such as those included in the Strategies to Develop Phonics Skills section (page 109). All grade-level teachers and paraprofessionals should be aware of how to best teach phonics skills in whole-group and small-group instruction.

In order to benefit most from systematic and explicit phonics instruction, students' letter-sound knowledge should be automatic. In the next section, see how key evidence-based practices support you as you guide students in learning the alphabet—the code to reading.

Alphabet Knowledge

Understanding the alphabetic principle, that there are systematic and predictable relationships between phonemes and graphemes, is critical in order for students to become proficient at reading and spelling. Alphabet recognition is an important part of understanding these relationships.

In addition to understanding the stages that students move through, literacy researchers Cindy D. Jones and D. Ray Reutzel (2012) compiled the following advantages for alphabet recognition based on their research with kindergarten students across two years. These advantages are not only interesting but also useful as you think about instruction and observe your students' skills. You'll no doubt recognize how these advantages can influence alphabet instruction.

- **Own-name advantage:** Young children first learn letter names and sounds that occur in their first name, particularly the first initial (for example, *t* as in *Taylor* and *c* as in *Corbin*). This is largely due to exposure to their first name and frequent practice writing their name (Treiman & Broderick, 1998).
- **Alphabet order advantage:** Children learn letters at the beginning of the alphabet and the end of the alphabet before learning the letters in the middle (McBride-Chang, 1999). This is likely due to exposure in children's books, songs, and instruction as well as the way that human memory functions. We typically remember items at the beginning and end of a list with better accuracy than the middle of the list (Sternberg, 2006). (Now you'll reformat your grocery list!)
- **Letter-frequency advantage:** Alphabet letters to which children are more frequently exposed individually (such as their name) and generally (signs, frequently read children's books) are learned more easily. The more often a child is exposed to specific letters, the more easily they are learned. Edward Fry (2004), recognized for developing word lists, lists the following consonants and vowels from most to least frequent.
    - Consonant letters from most to least frequent: *r, t, n, s, l, c, d, p, m, b, f, v, g, h, k, w, x, z, j, q, y*
    - Vowel letters from most to least frequent: *i, a, e, o, u*
- **Letter-name pronunciation advantage:** Students learn letter names that sound like the associated sounds as in /*p*/ for *p* and /*m*/ for the letter *m.* Letters with no connection to the sound are the most difficult to learn such as the letters *y, h,* and *w.*
- **Consonant phoneme acquisition order advantage:** Consonant letters are learned in roughly the order that children acquire them in oral language (Justice et al., 2006). For example, children developmentally acquire the following phonemes from birth to four years old—*n, m, p, h, t, k, y, f, ng, b, d, g, w, s.* The consonant letters associated with these consonant phonemes would likely be learned earlier than the remaining consonants.

Teachers in kindergarten and first grade spend a lot of time teaching and engaging students through song and chants practicing alphabet recognition with both upper- and lowercase letters.

Four Phases of Word Learning

When teaching phonics, it is important to keep in mind that children go through phases as they build their understanding of the alphabet and how it works, as demonstrated in the example in figure 3.1.

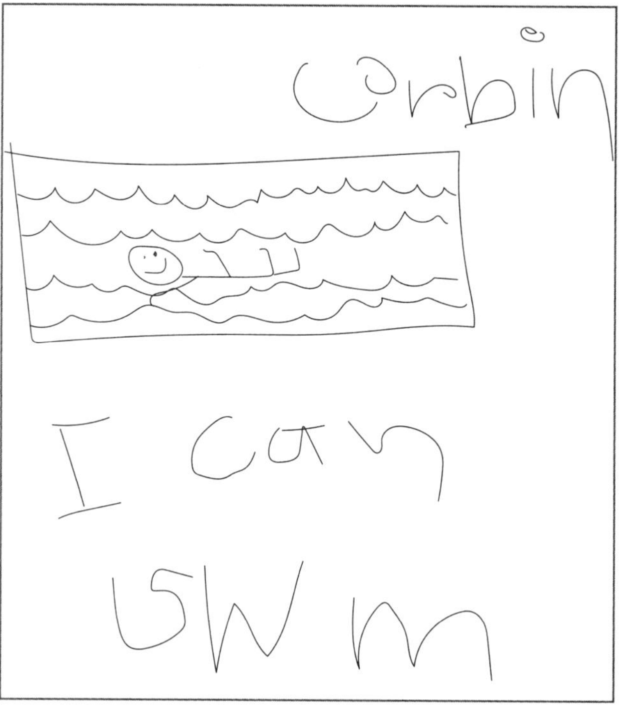

Figure 3.1: Student's early writing at the partial alphabetic phase.

Linnea C. Ehri (1998, 2005), a prominent researcher who focuses on how children learn to read, identifies four phases of word learning. These phases are shown in table 3.1 along with the characteristics of each phase and the suggested text type to support readers in each phase of word learning.

Table 3.1: Four Phases of Word Learning

Phases of Word Learning	Reader Characteristics	Text Type
Phase 1: Pre-alphabetic	• Limited alphabet knowledge • Children recognize words in their environment that have a distinctive shape but don't pay attention to their individual features. • Example: Children may recognize words from a cereal box by visual clues but do not have letter-sound correspondence.	• Predictable texts • High-quality, authentic children's literature
Phase 2: Partial alphabetic	• Children have emerging skills and know a few letters and sounds and use them to predict words. • Example: Typically, students use invented spelling with only consonants as in "wrk" for the word *work*.	• Decodable texts
Phase 3: Full alphabetic	• Children combine major letter-sound correspondences with spelling, pronunciation, and meaning. • Typically occurring in kindergarten and first grade, children are also able to commit words to memory and exhibit increasing automatic word recognition.	• Decodable texts • Less-controlled texts • High-quality, authentic children's literature
Phase 4: Consolidated alphabetic	• Children use their knowledge of letter-sound correspondence to blend whole words and parts of words into chunks in order to read them. • For example, in the word *sandbox*, the student would notice *sand* and *box* to read the word, rather than trying to read it letter by letter. • Readers can generalize and read many words by sight.	• Less-controlled texts • High-quality, authentic children's literature

PHONICS

Instructional Implications

Teaching the alphabet to automaticity is the goal in kindergarten and first-grade classrooms. While there is no best sequence for systematically teaching letters and sounds (Shanahan, 2023), there are instructional implications, such as the following, that emerge from the research to guide your decisions as you teach the alphabet.

- Teach high-frequency letters first, which are previously listed.
- Separate teaching visually and auditorily similar letters (for example, *b* and *d, p* and *q, h* and *u*).
- Introduce single letter sounds first, and then progress to more complex sounds, including digraphs (for example, *ch, sh*) and then trigraphs (for example, *dge, igh*).
- Begin with a limited set of letters that can be combined to make a number of simple VC (for example, *at, in, up*) and CVC words (for example, *pan, bet, hop*) in order to help students learn how to blend and segment.

- Employ brief, daily lessons that provide plenty of exposure to and practice with letters including lots of repetition rather than a letter-of-the-week instructional format. Jones and Reutzel (2012) propose grouping the letters into chunks and teaching a letter-of-the-day format with time for practice and review between letter groupings. In other words, don't teach twenty-six letters in twenty-six days; rather, allow time for practice and rehearsal.
- Spend more instructional time teaching and practicing letters that are more difficult to learn, such as those whose name does not match the sound, as in *w* (Jones & Reutzel, 2012).

Systematic Approaches

The NRP reviewed thirty-eight studies focused on phonics and examined both the value of phonics instruction and the effectiveness of varied instructional approaches (NICHD, 2000a). These findings support a systematic approach to teaching phonics, or one that builds from simple to more complex, with a cycle of review and repetition. Systematic phonics instruction is better than a non-systematic approach or no phonics instruction. Students in grades K–2, along with older students needing remediation, benefit from phonics instruction. Additionally, the panel finds that phonics instruction that begins in kindergarten provides students with an early advantage, and skills continue to develop with additional instruction in grades 1 and 2.

Systematic approaches teach the entire array of letter-sound correspondence. This includes consonant sounds, short and long vowels, consonant digraphs (for example, *sh, th, ck*), diphthongs (for example, *ai, ea, ou*), blends (for example, *sp, bl, tr*) and final stems (for example, *–ack, –up, –ot*). In short, phonics instruction has a positive effect on students' word recognition skills, spelling, and comprehension.

In contrast, non-systematic approaches typically include an emphasis on teaching high-frequency words such as those found in E. W. Dolch's (1936) list. This list, developed in 1936, includes 220 high-frequency words such as *ten*, *pretty*, and *small* found in children's literature at that time. In this approach, students are encouraged to recognize these words instantly without needing to sound them out. Many educators seem to think the words on the Dolch list should be memorized because they do not follow phonetic principles. However, while some words such as *laugh* and *once* do not follow phonetic principles, most do. When teaching phonics, instruction typically falls into two instructional approaches, synthetic phonics and analytic phonics.

- *Synthetic phonics* is when students are taught to convert letters into sounds and to blend those sounds to form a word. Sometimes we think of this approach as whole-to-part-to-whole. For example, when students see the word *pet* (whole), they decode the word by saying the sounds corresponding to the letters and blend them—*/p/ /ĕ/ /t/* (part)—to read the word *pet* (whole). As students become automatic readers, they'll see the word *pet* as a whole and no longer need to blend the letters. Automaticity, a characteristic of fluency, leads to better comprehension.

- *Analytic phonics*, on the other hand, emphasizes larger sound units when decoding. This approach uses word families or known words as analogies to figure out unknown words. For example, when students see the word *pet*, they might reason: "Well, I know the word *pat* and *bet* . . . the word begins with */p/* like in *pig* and ends in */et/* like in bet, so it must be *pet*."

While both synthetic and analytic approaches can be effective for teaching phonics, the NRP found no difference between using the two approaches (NICHD, 2000a). Later studies, however, find advantages for the synthetic approach (de Graaff, Bosman, Hasselman, & Verhoeven, 2009) specific to phonemic awareness, spelling, and reading at the end of kindergarten (Johnston & Watson, 2004), with positive effects for word reading and comprehension seven years later (Johnston, McGeown, & Watson, 2012).

These findings do not mean that a phonics approach based on analytics does not have merit. Since both methods have value, using formal and informal assessments provides information about which method may best support individual learner needs. Some students may benefit most from a word family-analogy approach, particularly as they become more proficient at decoding using basic letter-sound correspondence. The analytic approach is also useful for proficient readers to use when decoding unfamiliar words. Adept readers quickly (and often unconsciously) compare the word to other known words to make a best guess at pronouncing the word.

Resources to Support Phonics Instruction

- *A Fresh Look at Phonics, Grades K-2: Common Causes of Failure and 7 Ingredients for Success* by Wiley Blevins (2017)
- *Differentiating Phonics Instruction for Maximum Impact: How to Scaffold Whole-Group Instruction so All Students Can Access Grade-Level Content* by Wiley Blevins (2024)
- *Letter Lessons and First Words: Phonics Foundations That Work, PreK-2* by Heidi Anne Mesmer (2019)
- *Phonics Poetry: Teaching Word Families, K-3* by Timothy V. Rasinski & Belinda S. Zimmerman (2001)

Decoding Practice

Phonics instruction must include decoding practice, both in isolation and within connected text. Decoding includes a broader array of skills, including phonological awareness, phonemic awareness, alphabet knowledge, sight vocabulary, phonics, and spelling. Reading and writing activities should frequently be integrated with phonics instruction, as they provide a context that is helpful to the reader. Practicing with predictable and decodable text, particularly, can provide support. When practicing decoding in isolation, without textual clues, readers must rely solely on phonics skills (Rayner & Pollatsek, 1989). Most reading curriculum includes both kinds of practice: practice through stories and practice outside of context.

Let's consider text selection for a moment. Picture, if you will, three stacks or piles of books. Each is a different text type that supports readers as they practice and extend their literacy skills. Each of the three stacks are made up of predictable texts, decodable texts, and authentic children's literature. The first two types of texts—predictable text and decodable text—are specifically for early readers and provide a great deal of support for decoding practice. The third stack, children's literature, rounds out the selections from which students should be listening and reading independently. We'll take a look at predictable and decodable texts first and then at how children's literature can round out the stacks of books to support a healthy diet for reading (Pennell et al., 2024).

Predictable Text

As you may recall from the key vocabulary chart at the beginning of the chapter (page 92), *predictable text* is a type of controlled text that includes repeated phrases or sentences on each page with one new word that changes in the refrain. Consider the following example in figure 3.2.

Figure 3.2: Example of predictable text.

Students in grades K–1 will have varied literacy skill levels, likely ranging from those who have little or no alphabet knowledge and print awareness to students who are reading connected text. You'll need to meet the needs of each of these readers through a variety of text types during instruction and during both supported and independent reading.

Predictable text, such as that in the preceding list or in the beloved picture book *Brown Bear, Brown Bear, What Do You See?* (Martin, 2012), provides the scaffolding students who have little alphabet knowledge and print concepts need. Though very simple, such text is supportive. Using predictable text, students practice skills such as matching speech-to-text, developing understanding of print concepts, and gaining confidence in reading at the level at which they conceive reading, which is empowering.

Decodable Text

Once again, as you may recall from the key vocabulary chart at the beginning of the chapter (page 92), *decodable text* is text written using letter-sound correspondence that students have learned, and it provides practice for early readers to apply their growing phonics skills. Consider the following text in figure 3.3, which supports practice with the short */ă/* sound.

Figure 3.3: Example of decodable text.

Students in grades K–3 need daily opportunities to read connected text in order to build fluency, accuracy, and comprehension (Institute of Education Sciences, 2016). A comprehensive approach to phonics includes providing students with ample time to engage with and listen to high-quality texts. Students need to read a variety of text types, including decodable texts, which are designed to support decoding (Pennell et al., 2024). Decodable texts, written using letter-sound correspondence that students have learned, provide practice for early readers to apply their growing phonics skills.

While many students who have limited decoding ability are able to read predictable text, the skills for reading decodable text emerge from scaffolded support and direct phonics instruction.

While practicing skills through decodable text is crucial, it's important to note that not all decodable texts are created equally. In decodable picture books, the words and pictures often support each other, although at times the images extend the text by adding more information. When evaluating decodable texts, keep in mind such features as the degree of decodability, quality of illustrations (and how these illustrations support and extend the text), cultural context, and how motivating the text appears to be.

It's important to match readers with a decodable text that allows them to practice the skills they've learned within context. In order for students to benefit most, they should have previously been exposed to the word patterns in the text. When reading decodable texts, students are more likely to apply their phonics skills and read more accurately with less assistance (Mesmer, 2005). Decodable texts, in summary, are intentionally selected to support beginning readers as they practice and firm up their decoding skills. However, as you incorporate them into your phonics instruction and practice, you'll want to intentionally select other authentic trade books and high-quality children's literature to build vocabulary, fluency, and comprehension.

Authentic Children's Literature

In primary classrooms, authentic high-quality children's literature is often integrated through picture books, read alouds by teachers, and trade books. Children's literature is important to include in a well-rounded reading diet since the true-to-real-life writing and narrative is often engaging for readers. In addition, since it's not tied to specific word length or sentence length (readability features), students are exposed to vocabulary and high-quality illustrations not found within their predictable and decodable texts. The vocabulary, illustrations, and narrative provide lots of opportunities for extended, enriched conversation, which builds background knowledge and word learning.

In a literacy-rich classroom, the classroom library should include a well-rounded selection of books from which children can choose. In chapter 1, there are lots of ideas for building a classroom library that supports your students as readers and writers. In primary classrooms, the selection will likely include less-controlled predictable books, more-controlled decodable books, and authentic trade books. Trade books and picture books—read aloud daily—help students build their vocabulary, background knowledge, reading stamina, and comprehension skills (Pennell et al., 2024).

Orthographic Mapping

Orthographic mapping is when students learn words in a way that maps the sounds and spelling in the brain leading to automatic retrieval and word recognition. In other words, students read words by sight (Ehri, 2005, 2014, 2020). We often think of irregular or high-frequency words as sight words, but all words that we read automatically can be considered sight words because they are orthographically mapped, which supports instant retrieval. Students need proficiency in three areas—(1) phonemic awareness, (2) phonics, and (3) the alphabetic principle—in order to orthographically map words in long-term memory, which allows them to retrieve words instantly and automatically.

Decoding, while critically important, is not the entire picture of word recognition. When we teach phonics, we must also reinforce word meanings. When students understand word meanings, the brain automatically connects the printed word to pronunciation and meaning through orthographic mapping (Ehri, 2022). While students must learn how to blend individual sounds in order to decode words, orthographic mapping is the process by which students become automatic readers. When words are mapped, such as in figure 3.4, students almost instantly recognize them, and they connect them to pronunciation and meaning. Fluent readers, discussed at length in the next chapter, are automatic readers, which allows them to focus on comprehension, rather than decoding.

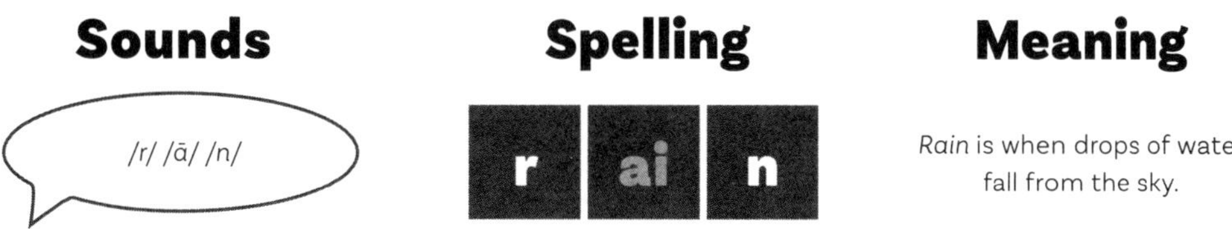

Figure 3.4: The process of orthographic mapping.

To better understand orthographic mapping, let's look at the word *rain* as shown in figure 3.4. The reading brain maps the three phonemes /r/ /ā/ /n/ to three graphemes—*r*, *ai*, and *n*—made up of four letters—*r*, *a*, *i*, and *n*. In the example using *rain*, students must understand grapheme-phoneme relationships and how to segment the word in order for the brain to map this word.

Orthographic mapping is the process by which the brain permanently connects sounds to their spelling (Ehri, 1984, 1987, 2014). It speeds up retrieval and enables students to become automatic, or fluent, readers. Orthographic mapping is a reminder that the skills we teach do not exist in a vacuum. Phonemic awareness, the alphabet, phonics, and vocabulary (meaning) are intertwined, each dependent on the other when reading. Each links to the other to create fluent, automatic readers who comprehend proficiently as shown in figure 3.5 (page 106).

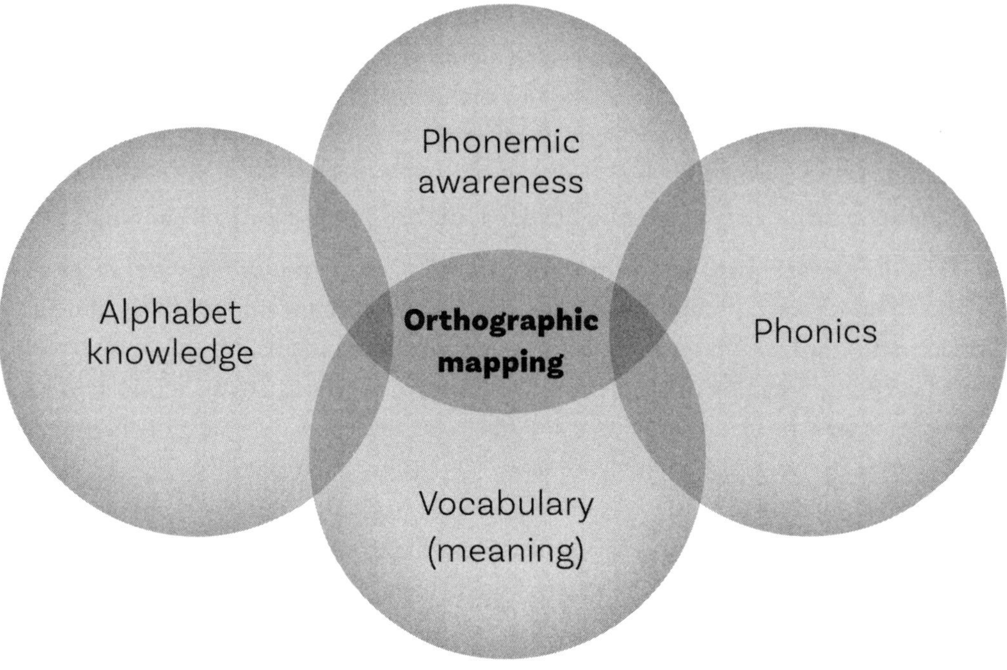

Figure 3.5: The interconnectedness of orthographic mapping.

What Works in the Classroom?

Educators who teach phonics must have a toolbox that includes explicit instructional routines and strategies. The good news is that there are plenty of research-based strategies that support early readers as they learn how to apply phonics skills.

The content and strategies in this resource are curriculum-agnostic and therefore not dependent on a specific curriculum used in your school or district. Regardless of your curriculum, the following generalizations for phonics instruction are clear.

- Teach both *decoding* and *encoding*. In other words, directly teach students how to both read and write (spell) words. Teaching decoding and encoding concurrently supports students as they make the connection between sounds and letters. Students need practice, over time, recognizing words automatically in order to become fluent readers.
- Embed phonemic awareness into phonics instruction, helping students firm up sound-symbol correspondence.
- *Recognition* and *retrieval* are both important elements of phonics instruction. For example, students can more easily recognize letter patterns and familiar words than instantly retrieve words from memory since retrieval is a more complex process than recognition. Retrieval requires repeated practice and exposure in order to orthographically map words for instant recognition.
- Integrate and practice reading and writing connected text (Serravallo, 2023a).

Research teaches us a great deal about effective instructional practices when teaching children how to read. In this section, we'll explore characteristics of effective phonics instruction along with strategies to implement with your students.

Characteristics of Effective Phonics Instruction

There are numerous characteristics common among strategies that support effective phonics instruction. In the following table 3.2, you'll find a summary of each characteristic. I suggest keeping these characteristics in the forefront of your mind as you plan systematic and explicit phonics instruction.

Table 3.2: Characteristics of Effective Phonics Instruction

Begin Instruction at the Right Grade Level	Phonics instruction that begins in kindergarten provides students with an early advantage, and skills continue to develop with additional instruction in grades 1 and 2 (NICHD, 2000a). Instruction using a synthetic approach that continues to grade 2, regardless of students' word reading skills, helps them become better readers (Connor et al., 2007).
Group Appropriately for Instruction	Phonics instruction can take place in whole groups, small groups, and individually. You'll recall that when teaching phonemic awareness, small-group instruction is the most effective, whereas phonics instruction is effective with varied group sizes. For students who are struggling, small-group instruction and tutoring continue to be beneficial.
Use Systematic and Explicit Instruction	Instruction that is systematic and explicit is beneficial for all students and particularly for those who may have difficulty learning to read or may be at risk for future reading problems (Armbruster et al., 2009; Ehri et al., 2001; Mesmer & Griffith, 2005; National Early Literacy Panel, 2008; NICHD, 2000b). *Systematic instruction* refers to a scope and sequence. Scope includes the content of phonics instruction, and sequence refers to the order for teaching letter-sound relationships. Systematic instruction is recognized as an instructional sequence that organizes skills, in this case phonics, into a logical sequence that makes clear letter-sound relationships, larger units of sound/letter combinations (onsets and rimes), and spelling patterns (*ea, ie, oa, ou*). *Explicit instruction* refers to how one teaches, or the instructional delivery. For example, teachers are clear, and their language is direct, such as, "The letters *c-h* make the */ch/* sound, as in *chase*." Some phonemic awareness and phonics strategies are very direct or explicit, such as this example and the sequential protocols for Elkonin boxes (see chapter 1 and later in this chapter). In addition to systematic and explicit instruction, authentic reading and writing activities should frequently be integrated with phonics instruction. Students should practice reading and writing letters and reading words, sentences, and stories both aloud and silently. Phonics instruction that incorporates writing instruction strengthens phonics acquisition (Ray, Dally, Colyvas, & Lane, 2021; Xue & Meisels, 2004). Rather than focusing solely on phonics skills, students should be reading and writing every day, along with building vocabulary, fluency, and language comprehension through read alouds.

continued ▶

Incorporate Word Study	Word study is an approach to spelling instruction that moves away from focusing on memorization and shifts to paying attention to the meaningful study of words. The goal of word study, or *word work,* is to provide students with lots of opportunities to explore and study the alphabet and the relationships between letters and sounds. As their knowledge grows, they can apply their word understanding to contextual reading and writing (Bear, Invernizzi, Templeton, & Johnston, 2016; Bear & Templeton, 1998). Students need explicit instruction along with contextual practice (Allington, 2009). Word study helps students focus on and analyze word features such as short and long vowels, digraphs, diphthongs, and more. The goal is for students to gradually deepen their "understanding of how spelling works to represent sound and meaning" (Bear et al., 2016, p. 5). While instruction can occur in a whole-group setting, in *Words Their Way* (Bear et al., 2016), the authors suggest beginning with a spelling inventory (in the book) to determine individual learners' strengths and gaps in order to differentiate instruction. For instructional routines, Bear and colleagues (2016) suggest a "circle-seat-center" routine, which includes targeted small-group instruction, literacy centers, and independent word work activities at their desks.
Include Spelling	Reading and spelling are reciprocal (Ehri, 1989; Shanahan, 1984) in nature. Spelling is important to reading, and vice versa. There is strong and consistent support for teaching spelling as revealed in a meta-analysis of fifty-three studies with over 6,000 K–12 students (Graham & Santangelo, 2014). Spelling instruction not only improves spelling, but it also improves phonological awareness (0.53), reading (0.44), and writing (0.94). Students who are learning to read and write go through developmental stages. They'll often use invented spelling, in which they write words based on sounds, which has been found beneficial for children to learn phonics (Shanahan, 2003). Although invented spelling isn't accurate spelling, it doesn't mean we don't care about spelling. By the end of kindergarten and in first grade, students should be able to spell words correctly that follow consistent CVC patterns, as in *hat* and *sit,* that have previously been taught.
Support English Learners	We are still discovering how to best support English learners in acquiring reading skills. Generally speaking, what we know about teaching literacy for non-ELs is also the foundation for teaching reading for English learners (Goldenberg, 2020). Additionally, ELs who experience difficulty learning to read can benefit from the same type of interventions as non-EL students, with more of it (Gersten et al., 2007).
Support Struggling Readers	Students who struggle with phonics skills often benefit from more systematic, explicit, and multisensory instruction. To begin, I suggest assessing phonemic awareness skills to determine whether students could benefit from additional time with isolating, segmenting, and blending sounds. To reinforce the letter-sound connection, I recommend following the protocol later in this chapter for Elkonin boxes using letter tiles (page 124). The protocol can be found in the What Works in the Classroom section of this chapter. I also frequently relied on the Orton-Gillingham approach (Gillingham & Stillman, 1960) for struggling readers who needed a very explicit and sequential approach to learn phonemic awareness and phonics.

As you integrate the characteristics described previously into your phonics instructional routines, students will be supported as they acquire their phonics skills. In the next section, you'll find strategies for implementing phonics strategies in your classroom to secure students' early reading development.

Strategies to Develop Phonics Skills

Building phonics skills takes up a large chunk of the literacy block in kindergarten through second grade. In this section, you'll find strategies to blend and strengthen your phonics instruction. As I mentioned previously, teach phonic skills both in isolation and immersed within reading and writing. Additionally, don't tip the scales too far in one direction so that you're focusing solely on phonics and phonemic awareness. You'll also want to intentionally support fluency, vocabulary, and comprehension growth—all necessary for students to become proficient readers.

The Language Experience Approach

The language experience approach is an instructional strategy that integrates concepts of print, phonics, and word study as an authentic reading and writing activity. It has been around as an instructional approach since the 1960s and perhaps much longer. I appreciate using this approach to support early literacy acquisition because it so nicely connects speaking and listening with reading and writing. It exemplifies the full circle of literacy, namely, *what we say can be written*, and *what we write can be read.* Another way of expressing this is that language experience helps students connect *speech to print* and *print to speech.*

The conceptual knowledge behind speech to print can be summarized with the following key ideas.

- Letters are symbols that represent sounds.
- Sounds can be represented by one, two, three, or four letters as in m*a*p (one letter), t*ea*m (two letters), h*igh* (three letters), and *eigh*t (four letters).
- One sound, /ā/, can be represented by many spellings as in *late, pain, sway,* and *great.*
- One spelling can have many sounds, as in *weak* /ē/, *break* /ā/, and *bread* /ĕ/.

In the strategy in figure 3.6 (page 110), you'll find simple directions for how you can use the language experience approach to reinforce concepts of print and support students as they connect sounds and symbols.

Early and emerging readers need to see the connection between listening, speaking, writing, and reading. The language experience approach through conversation, writing, and reading makes these connections apparent for our earliest learners.

Strategy: Language Experience Approach

Pillar: Phonics

Grade Level:

- ☑ K
- ☑ 1
- ☑ 2
- ☑ 3
- ☐ 4
- ☐ 5
- ☐ 6

Instructional Grouping:

- ☑ Whole Group
- ☑ Small Group
- ☑ Individual

Materials:

- Large chart paper and wide-tip markers

Consider This:

- The language experience approach (LEA) can be easily implemented as a whole-group strategy and just as easily with small groups of students.
- If used individually to support readers, students draw on an experience in their lives.

What is it? The language experience approach is an instructional model in which the teacher (or tutor) writes, in the student's language, about an experience. It helps make clear the connection between speaking, writing, and reading.

Why is it important? Connecting listening, speaking, writing, and reading is crucial for young learners. The language experience approach is an instructional strategy that makes the connection explicit for students. Additionally, the LEA supports students' understanding of print concepts such as print moving from left to right, letters making up words, space between each word, and how what we say can be written using letters of the alphabet.

What works in the classroom?

Simple Steps

Shared event: The first step when using the LEA as a whole-group activity is a shared event of some sort, such as a hands-on activity like observing the weather, engaging in a science activity, or even cooking. For example, I remember going on a brief walk with my kindergarten students, noticing the changing colors of leaves in fall, and gathering them to bring back to the classroom for an art activity.

Class conversation: Once the experience is complete, gather the students around a chart with a marker in hand. Prompt students to talk about the experience, perhaps begin in groups of two or three. You can also ask students specific questions to prompt their retelling of the event. The idea is that students understand what is experienced can be retold through language and speaking.

Record sentences: Tell students you want to write a story or article about the experience. Ask students if they have something they'd like to share about the experience. If a child responds with a one-word response such as "colorful," going back to the example, you can prompt them with something like, "Were the leaves colorful?" to which the student may say, "The leaves were colorful and crunchy." Then, record their sentences on the chart paper. Stay with this process until you've written several sentences or paragraphs.

Read aloud: When you've written four or five sentences, read the sentences aloud with expression, using your hand to move from left to right under the text.

Fluency practice: Following this, engage in echo reading with students, having them try to follow along and sound just like you.

Follow-Up Teaching Opportunities

Concepts of print: Conduct a brief lesson highlighting print concepts, including letters making up words, words having space between each other, periods being placed at the end of sentences, and words being read from left to right and top to bottom.

Echo and choral reading: Revisit the article or sentences and have students read it aloud several times using echo reading and choral reading strategies. You could divide students into A and B groups. Have group A read one sentence and group B read the next, for example, and alternate until complete.

Paired reading: Print copies of the sentences. Using the paired readers protocol (see chapter 4, page 151), intentionally form pairs, and have students reread the sentences with or to one another.

Word study: Choose several words and conduct word studies with them. Write words separately and then compare them to each other, pointing out common endings, beginnings, digraphs, or diphthongs. Students can extend their learning by adding words to individual printed or digital word journals.

Figure 3.6: Strategy—Language experience approach.

Visit ***go.SolutionTree.com/literacy/FSK6*** *and enter the unique access code found on the book's inside front cover to access a reproducible version of this figure.*

Word Building

We've established that explicit and systematic phonics instruction works and is endorsed by literacy experts (NICHD, 2000a). Additionally, connecting phonemic awareness with letters is impactful once students have mastered the alphabetic principle. When students have had explicit instruction in sounds and letters, students should then have ample time to practice those skills both within connected text and outside of text.

Word building strategies that help students construct words by manipulating letters and letter combinations provide a context, separate from text, in which students play with and manipulate letters and sounds to explore how words work. Word study often takes place with manipulatives such as letter tiles, magnetic letter tiles, or whiteboards and markers so that students can easily change a letter or letters or identify patterns within word families. Including these strategies during small-group instruction allows for lots of opportunities to differentiate skills (beginning, middle, and ending sounds) and complexity (one-syllable versus multisyllabic words) depending on the needs of individual students.

In the next four strategy figures, you'll find simple directions for word building strategies—blending (figure 3.7, page 112), word awareness (figure 3.8, page 114), word sorts (figure 3.9, page 116), and word ladders (figure 3.10, page 117).

Strategy—Word Building: Blending Sounds and Letters

Pillar: Phonics

Grade Level:

- ☑ K
- ☑ 1
- ☑ 2
- ☑ 3
- ☐ 4
- ☐ 5
- ☐ 6

Instructional Grouping:

- ☑ Whole Group
- ☑ Small Group
- ☑ Individual

Materials:

- Letter cards (cardstock with letters printed on them), letter tiles, magnetic word building boards, or foam word building blocks
- If you're using cardstock letters, have a bag for each student with all letters. At the beginning of the week, list the letters students will need for the week and have them place them in a "letters for the week" bag. It will make the word building activities go much more smoothly.

Consider This:

- Routinely provide a simple definition of target words to support ELs and students with vocabulary gaps.

What is it? Word building is a phonics strategy in which students practice and apply their knowledge of letters and sounds outside of connected text by building and manipulating letters to form words.

Why is it important? Students must become skilled and automatic at using their understanding of letters and sounds to manipulate letters (deleting, adding, and substituting) in words to form new words.

What works in the classroom?

Learning goal: In this format, students change one letter, which you specify, to form a new word. The goal is for students to blend the new sound with the ending and read the new word.

Show Me: Provide several examples with a CVC word using an explanation similar to the following.

T: "Today we are going to make words and change one letter to make a new word. The word is *pet*, *p-e-t*, *pet*. Read *pet* with me." (*Run your finger from left to right under the letters, stretching the sounds.*)

S and T: "Pet."

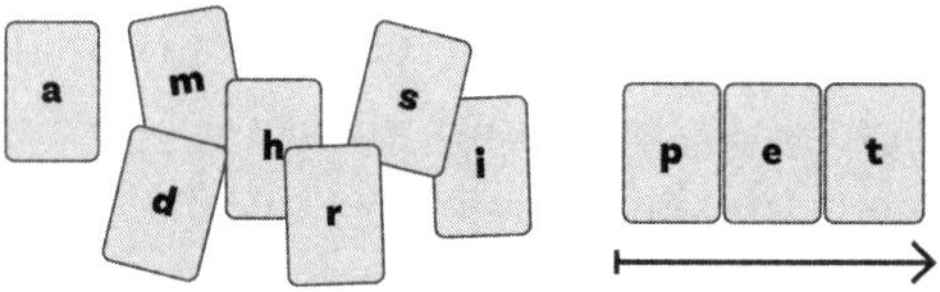

T: "I'm going to change one letter in *pet* to make a new word. Let's change the *p* to an *m*. The new word is *met*, *m-e-t, met*." (*You could also ask students what the new word is.*) "Let's blend the sounds together. Read *met* with me." (*Stretch the sounds.*)

S and T: "Met." (*Run your finger or hand from left to right under the letters.*)

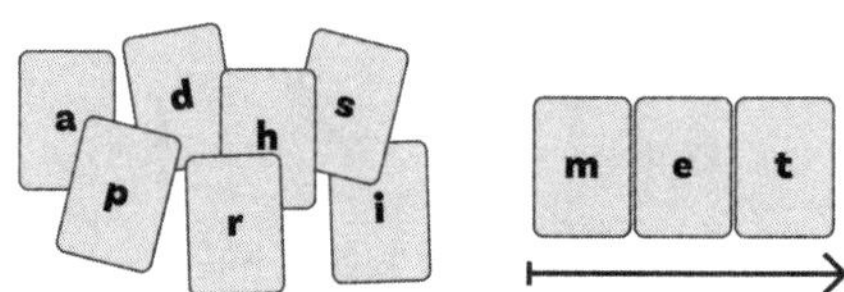

Help Me: Have students mimic your example at their desk or table.

T: 1. "Make the word *met* with your letter cards."

2. "Now let's change the *m* to an *s*."

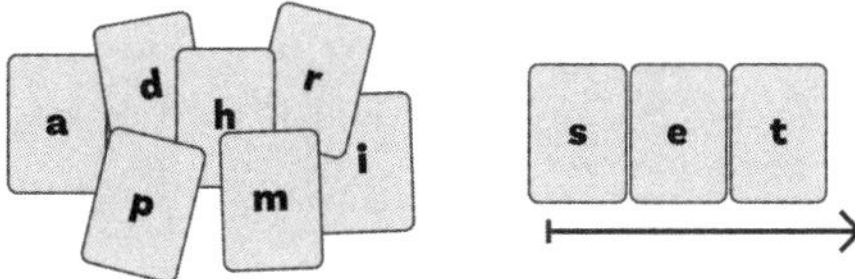

3. "What is the new word? Let's blend the sounds together and read the new word."

Let Me: Go on to provide several more examples, changing the initial letter, and have students do them independently (or with a partner if needed).

T: 1. "Make the word *hat* with your letter cards."

2. "Now change the *h* to an *s*."

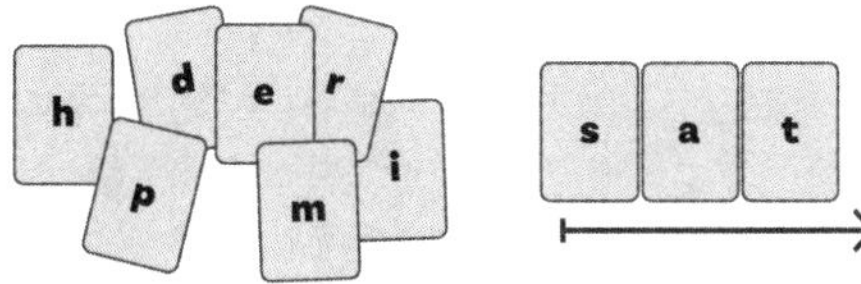

3. "What is the new word? Let's blend the sounds together and read the new word."

S and T: "*Sat.*"

Extensions and Follow-Up

- **Ending sounds/letters and middle sounds/letters:** As students grow in their proficiency, have students change ending sounds and middle sounds to form new words (middle is the most challenging).
- **Independent practice:** During small-group instruction, students can work independently or in pairs and change letters to make new words using a list of words with a self-checker. Focus on one sound—beginning, middle, or end.
- **Connect to writing:** Have students dictate a few sentences using the target words while you write them. Read them orally with students. As students progress, have students write a few sentences independently using the target words.
- **Onset and rimes, blends, and digraphs:** Word building blocks are one of my favorite manipulatives to use with early learners. They are colorful foam blocks on which are printed consonants, vowels, onsets, rimes, blends, and digraphs. Each side of the block has a different consonant, vowel, or cluster on it. And, they're organized by color. They were originally produced by Lakeshore Learning, and although they were discontinued, they are regularly available on eBay (www.ebay.com). I love them because they're just the right size for little hands to manipulate.
- **Word building blocks:** Use word building blocks to support individual and small-group instruction. For example, place about ten to twelve blocks on the table and while students get settled for small group, they make words using the blocks. Before instruction, each student reads the word/s they made. It's a quick but purposeful activity that reinforces how to build words.

m ate

- **Phonemic awareness tie-ins:** Separate the blocks and delete the onset or rime and ask students what sound remains.

Figure 3.7: Strategy—Word building: Blending sounds and letters.

*Visit **go.SolutionTree.com/literacy/FSK6** and enter the unique access code found on the book's inside front cover to access a reproducible version of this figure.*

Strategy—Word Building: Word Awareness

Pillar: Phonics

Grade Level:

- ☑ K
- ☑ 1
- ☑ 2
- ☑ 3
- ☐ 4
- ☐ 5
- ☐ 6

Instructional Grouping:

- ☑ Whole Group
- ☑ Small Group
- ☑ Individual

Materials:

- Letter cards (cardstock with letters printed on them), letter tiles, or magnetic word-building boards

Consider This:

- If you're using cardstock letters, have a bag for each student with all letters. At the beginning of the week, list the letters students will need for the week and have them place them in a "letters for the week" bag. It will make the word building activities go much more smoothly.
- Always provide a simple definition of target words to support ELs and students with vocabulary gaps.

What is it? Word awareness is a word-building strategy in which students practice and apply their knowledge of letters and sounds, outside of connected text, by building and manipulating letters to make new words.

Why is it important? Students must be able to use their understanding of letters and sounds to manipulate letters (deleting, adding, and substituting) in words to independently form new words.

What works in the classroom?

Show Me: Provide several examples making a CVC word with letters using an explanation similar to the following.

T: "Today we are going to make words and change letters to make new words."

T: "The word is *mad, m-a-d, mad*. Read *mad* with me." (*Run your finger or hand from left to right under the letters.*)

S and T: "Mad."

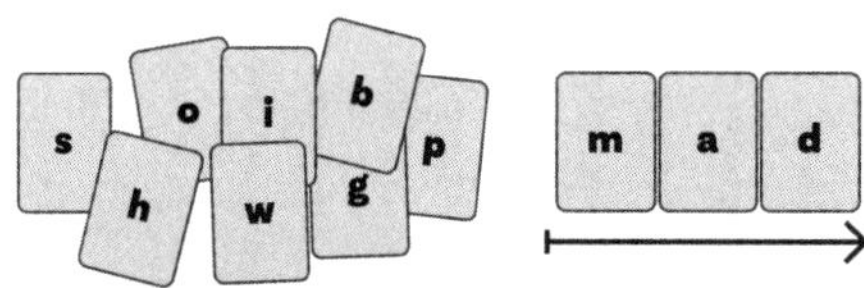

T: "Watch me as I change *mad* to *dad*." (*Think aloud as you say letter names and sounds of tiles until you select the* d *for* dad.)

T: "The new word is *dad, d-a-d, dad*. Read the new word with me."

S and T: "Dad." (*Run your finger or hand from left to right under the letters.*)

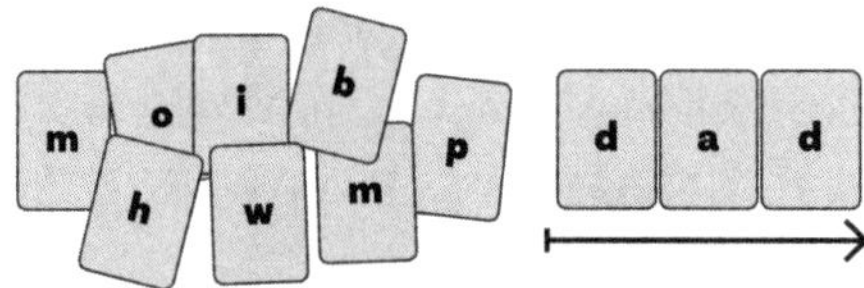

Help Me: Have students mimic your example at their desk or table.

T: "Make the word *mop* with your letter cards."

S and T: "Let's read it together, *mop*." (*Run your finger or hand from left to right under the letters.*)

T: "Now change *mop* to *hop*." (*Students work independently or with a partner as you support.*)

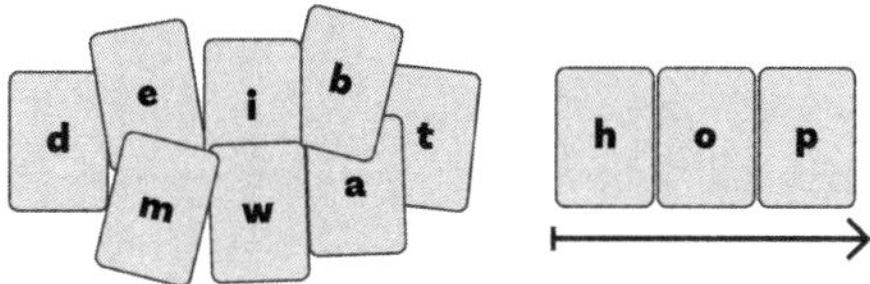

T: "What letter did you change to go from *mop* to *hop*?"

T: "Let's read the new word together."

S and T: "Hop, *h-o-p*, hop."

Let Me: Go on to provide several more examples, having students make new words independently or with a partner.

T: "Make the word *bin* with your letter cards."

T: "Change the word *bin* to *win*."

T: "Let's read the new word together."

S and T: "Win, *w-i-n*, win."

Follow-Up Teaching Opportunities

- **Ending sounds/letters and middle sounds/letters:** As students develop in their proficiency, provide new target words and change the word by having students replace ending sounds/letters and middle sounds/letters.
- **Multisyllabic words:** Increase the complexity by targeting words with two syllables.
- **Connect to writing:** Have students dictate a few sentences using the target words while you write them. Read them chorally with students. Students can also write a few sentences independently using the target words.
- **Independent practice:** During a small group instructional cycle, students can work independently or in pairs and change letters to make new words using a list of words, with a self-checker, that you've provided.

PHONICS

Figure 3.8: Strategy—Word building: Word awareness.

Visit ***go.SolutionTree.com/literacy/FSK6*** *and enter the unique access code found on the book's inside front cover to access a reproducible version of this figure.*

Strategy—Word Building: Word Sorts

Pillar: Phonics

Grade Level:

- ☑ K
- ☑ 1
- ☑ 2
- ☑ 3
- ☐ 4
- ☐ 5
- ☐ 6

Instructional Grouping:

- ☐ Whole Group
- ☑ Small Group
- ☑ Individual

Materials:

- Students need word cards with the pattern/s you are teaching and reinforcing. Each student should have a bag of word cards that will be used during the week.

Consider This:

- Word sorts are a perfect way to differentiate instruction based on students' assessed phonics skills.

What is it? Word sorts support word study, spelling, and observing patterns in words, which include vowel patterns, prefixes and suffixes, and stems and roots.

Why is it important? Word sorts help students make sense of words, which includes categorizing, pronouncing, spelling, and word knowledge.

What works in the classroom?

Teacher preparation: Determine the focus for the week for each group of students. Place word cards in bags that students will use during the week.

Sound sort example: *-ee -ea* sounds

- **Read and define words:** To begin, read the *-ee* and *-ea* word cards with students to be certain students can read each word.
- **Choose instructional sequence:** Two examples are provided.

Direct Instruction, Example 1

- After reading, discuss the sounds that students hear in the words. After determining that all the words have the long /ē/ sound, place the *-ee* and *-ea* headers at the top of the pocket chart.
- Discuss that *-ee* and *-ea* are spelled differently but both make the same long /ā/ sound.
- One by one, read and discuss each word and have students determine under which heading it belongs. If a student makes an error, allow them time to self-correct.

Direct Instruction, Example 2

- Place one word card with the *-ee* and *-ea* spelling at the top of the pocket chart, say *weed* and *team.*
- Discuss that *-ee* and *-ea* make the same long /ē/ sound.
- Have students select another card, let's say it's *sweet.* Read aloud together.
  - **T:** "Look at the word *sweet.* Where would you place it on the chart?"
  - Let students discuss and add it under *weed.* (*If they place it under* team, *allow it to be there, and eventually they'll likely self-correct.*)
- Continue until all the words are placed under *weed* and *team.*
- Discuss where the headers *-ee* and *-ea* should be and add to the top of each column of words.

Extension

- **Students write words:** Have students write all the *-ee* words and another day write all the *-ea* words while reading each word after writing. Students can also write them on the whiteboard underneath the chart, as shown in the earlier figure.
- **Dictating:** Have students dictate several sentences using these words while you write them.
- **Students write sentences:** Have students write a sentence each day using one of the words from either column.

Figure 3.9: Strategy—Word building: Word sorts.

Visit ***go.SolutionTree.com/literacy/FSK6*** *and enter the unique access code found on the book's inside front cover to access a reproducible version of this figure.*

Strategy—Word Building: Word Ladders

Pillar: Phonics

Grade Level:	Instructional Grouping:	Consider This:
☑ K ☑ 1 ☑ 2 ☑ 3 ☑ 4 ☑ 5 ☑ 6	☑ Whole Group ☑ Small Group ☑ Individual	• Model how to work through a word ladder with students. • When beginning word ladders with early learners, I suggest beginning with a five-rung ladder and moving to a ten-rung ladder when they get the gist. • Word ladders can be done in any configuration, including as a quick whole-class activity, as pairs, or individually.

What is it? Word ladders is a strategy that helps students think about and play with words in order to form new words. It also draws students' attention to word spelling.

Why is it important? Playing with words is another way to expand and reinforce students' vocabulary. Word games engage students in a different manner than through direct instruction and cause students to think metacognitively about words.

What works in the classroom?

Prep

- Download the eight- and ten-rung word ladder template (www.timrasinski.com/resources.html) or create your own.
- The words you select for the word ladder can come from recent vocabulary in a content unit of study, a read aloud, or words your class has been collecting.
- For a prep-free experience, print themed word ladders from Tim Rasinski's resources, one for grades 2–3 and another for grades 4–5.

Figure 3.10: Strategy—Word building: Word ladders.

continued ▶

Steps

- The first and last words are always related. The first word is provided.
- Students read the directions and work through each rung of the ladder, adding or deleting letters, until they arrive at the final word.
- Example: Beginning Word—read
    - *read* (change a letter; this is a small, rounded piece of glass often used in jewelry)
    - *bead* (subtract a letter; this is the opposite of good)
    - *bad* (add a letter; this means having no hair)
    - *bald* (change a letter; this is a round toy)
    - *ball* (change a letter; this is the opposite of short)
    - *tall* (change a letter; you pay this when you drive)
    - *toll* (change a letter; a screwdriver or hammer is one of these)
    - *tool* (change a letter; Yesterday we ___ a test.)
    - *took* (change a letter; this is what you read)
    - *book* (Final Word)
- In the example, *read* is provided for students as they begin the ladder. *Read* and *book*, the first and final words, are related.

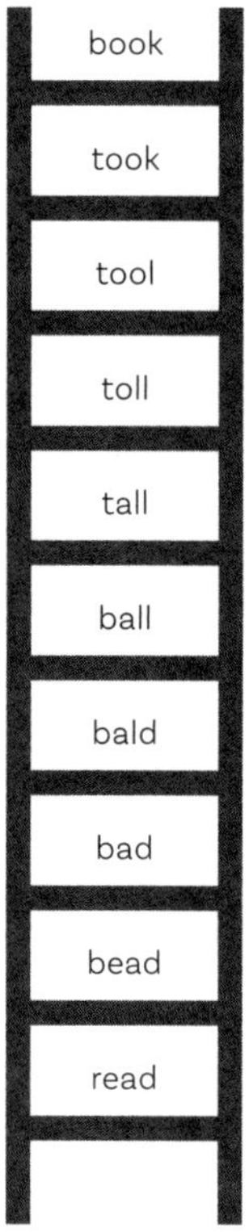

book

took

tool

toll

tall

ball

bald

bad

bead

read

Visit ***go.SolutionTree.com/literacy/FSK6*** *and enter the unique access code found on the book's inside front cover to access a reproducible version of this figure.*

Word awareness may seem like a repeat of word blending, but it's actually a more advanced skill that requires the student to make decisions about letters or sounds and placement (beginning, middle, end) during the word building sequence. Other decisions include how the target word varies from the new word, which letter needs to be removed to make the new word, and which letter must be selected to form the new word. You'll see these decisions play out as you follow the sequence described in the word awareness strategy table (figure 3.8, page 114).

In word sorts, students learn more about words by observing likenesses and differences. This can be done in a variety of ways and with all types of words. Word sorts provide a useful combination of direct instruction along with students constructing their knowledge about words. Word sorts can also be used for varied literacy skills, such as another example you'll see in chapter 5 (page 210). I've provided a few examples in the strategy box in figure 3.9 (page 116), along with generalizations about how to make word sorts meaningful for students.

Word ladders (Rasinski, 1995; Rasinski & Padak, 2001) is a strategy that helps students think about and play with words in order to form new words. Students move from one word to the next, adding, subtracting, or changing one letter at a time. The last word in the ladder is connected to the first word in some way. Word ladders can serve as a great review on Friday after students have had the opportunity to have multiple exposures to vocabulary words during the week. Word ladders are a great individual or paired activity, and students love them (so do I!). Please see figure 3.10 (page 117) for an example of how to structure this kind of exercise.

If you follow Tim Rasinski on Blue Sky, (https://bsky.app/profile/timrasinski.bsky.social) you'll see he features Word Ladder Wednesday and posts a new word ladder for download each week. He also developed two resources brimming with word ladders that you can print and use with students or send home as a parent-child activity (Rasinski, 2005a, 2005b).

Root Words

The study of word parts—affixes, prefixes, and Greek and Latin root words—occurs most significantly between fourth grade and high school (Nagy et al., 1993). The sequence for teaching roots (Bear et al., 2008) is to generally begin with Greek number prefixes and then move to Greek roots and then to frequently occurring Latin roots. Finally, students would explore additional Latin and Greek prefixes and common Greek suffixes.

The root of the day strategy (figure 3.11) is an interactive and fun way to build knowledge of roots, prefixes, and suffixes among intermediate students (Bloodgood & Pacifici, 2004).

Strategy—Word Building: Root of the Day

Pillar: Phonics

Grade Level:	**Instructional Grouping:**	**Materials:**
☐ K ☐ 1 ☐ 2 ☑ 3 ☑ 4 ☑ 5 ☑ 6	☑ Whole Group ☑ Small Group ☐ Individual	• Use the whiteboard or online tool such as Padlet (www.padlet.com) for this strategy. The advantage of using the whiteboard is that students easily add words during the day and other students can see the web of words. Using Padlet provides a more permanent collection of words developed over time. • Resources for Roots: *The Reading Teacher's Book of Lists* (Kress & Fry, 2016); *Words Their Way* (Bear et al., 2016) **Consider This:** • To support English learners, provide a simple definition of each word that is added to the root web.

What is it? Root of the day is a simple, incidental word study strategy to strengthen and advance root word knowledge along with prefixes and suffixes.

Figure 3.11: Strategy—Root of the day.

continued ▶

Why is it important? Knowledge and use of root words expands students' word building and vocabulary knowledge. Students discover word meanings from known roots.

What works in the classroom?

1. **Write the root word** on the whiteboard as shown for the example *photo-*.
2. **Students add words** throughout the day that have *photo-* as the root.
3. **Lead a conversation** about the root and the words that students added with *photo-* as the root. Have a student rearrange the words listed to show connections like the following.

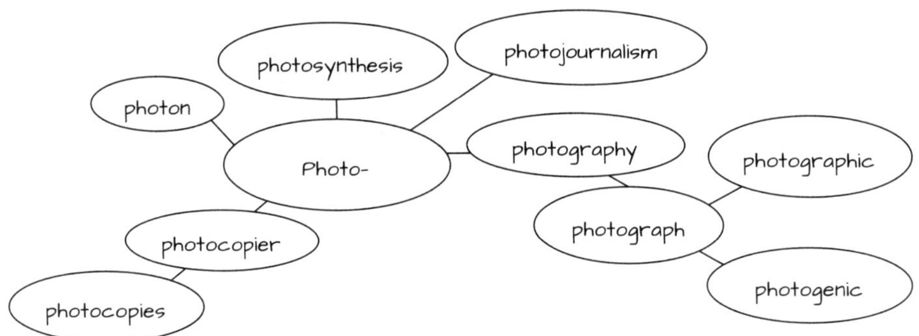

4. **Students guess what the root *photo-* means** based on the words listed and their common features or meanings. Add the meaning of *photo-* (light).
5. **Have several students look up the definitions of the words** each day during the class discussion. Additionally, common prefixes and suffixes and their meanings can be discussed as well as their connections to parts of speech.

Visit ***go.SolutionTree.com/literacy/FSK6*** *and enter the unique access code found on the book's inside front cover to access a reproducible version of this figure.*

Multisensory Approaches

Multisensory strategies use more than one sense, or modality, as students learn reading skills. Visual, auditory, kinesthetic, and tactile strategies incorporate seeing, hearing, kinesthetic or body movement, and touching. In working with students in a reading clinic setting, I provided explicit instruction along with incorporating visual, auditory, kinesthetic, and tactile strategies to support struggling readers. Several of these types of strategies aim to support spelling and attention to letters and syllables, summarized in the following.

- **Writing in the air:** Using kinesthetic (movement) pathways, students can write letters in the air to reinforce spelling and vocabulary. It is an easy way for students to visualize letters, spell the word, and write it from left to right, thus internalizing the connection between letters and spelling. As students write each letter, they say the letter aloud. The Orton-Gillingham approach (Peavler & Rooney, 2019) suggests that students use their predominant arm and use large muscle movement when writing letters. I suggest having students write letters and words in the air frequently to reinforce spelling and to cement new vocabulary words that you teach following a read aloud.

- **Writing in sand or on sandpaper:** Fill a shallow tray with sand. As you name (call out) letters, students write them in the sand and say the letter aloud as they write it. You can also use sandpaper and have students form the letter using their index finger. While you can't see the letter in sandpaper like you can in sand, it adds the tactile experience to writing letters, and it's a lot less messy.
- **Arm tapping:** Students use arm tapping to tap out syllables, sounds, or letters of a word when spelling. As the teacher presents a target word such as *big,* students use their dominant hand to tap the phonemes */b/ /i/ /g/* beginning at their shoulder or forearm and tap, tap, tap while saying the letters aloud and moving toward the hand. Finally, students read the target word, *big,* aloud while making a sweeping motion down their arm.
- **Mirrors:** Mirrors can be a helpful addition when teaching phonics skills. For example, you may model pronouncing the short */ă/* and long */ā/* sound and show students how your mouth moves. Students listen and watch your mouth closely. Then, using small, handheld mirrors, students practice making the short and long */ā/* sounds while watching their mouth formation and articulation. You can extend this by asking what students notice about their mouth, tongue, and jaw when they make the sounds and then match it to an image on the sound wall.
- **Auditory activities:** Auditory activities connect listening and identifying sounds and then matching those sounds to letters. For example, show students a tray with a number of objects on it. First, identify the items on the tray. Then, ask students to group the objects that begin with the */b/* sound. Students select items such as a ball, beans, and a box. Students orally identify the beginning sound */b/* and then write the letter *b* on their whiteboard. Another simple auditory activity is to show cards with images on them. For example, show cards with images of a cat, bat, and pot. Identify the pictures and say their names aloud. Have students say them with you. Then, ask students to identify the sound they hear that is the same in the pictures. In this case, it is */t/.* Students write the letter *t* on their whiteboard.
  You'll notice that the first task I described is simpler than the second task. In the first task, the teacher identifies the common sound, */b/,* and prompts students to find objects that begin with that sound. In the second task with picture cards, students must pronounce each image and identify the matching sound with no prompt, which is a more complex skill. With your grade-level team, you can think of additional auditory or listening activities to support phonics.

The following visual, auditory, kinesthetic, and tactile strategy—read it, build it, write it, connect it (figure 3.12)—focuses on irregular spelling by drawing students' attention to the spelling using several steps and connections to the word. The simple steps are easy to follow (Orton-Gillingham.com, n.d.).

Strategy—Read It, Build It, Write It, Connect It

Pillar: Phonics

Grade Level:	**Instructional Grouping:**	**Materials:**
☑ K ☑ 1 ☑ 2 ☑ 3 ☐ 4 ☐ 5 ☐ 6	☐ Whole Group ☑ Small Group ☑ Individual	• Pencil, crayon, letter cards, or letter tiles • If providing letter cards or tiles, I would provide a sampling of letters rather than all 26 letters. **Consider This:** • To support English learners, provide a simple definition of the target words.

What is it? Read it, build it, write it, connect it is a strategy that works well to practice and cement the spelling of irregular words.

Why is it important? Irregular words that don't follow a common spelling pattern are more difficult to learn to read and spell correctly, particularly for struggling readers. Following a simple instructional format provides a routine to practice irregular words.

What works in the classroom?

Simple Steps

Provide a box with three spaces labeled with "Read It," "Build It," and "Write It.".

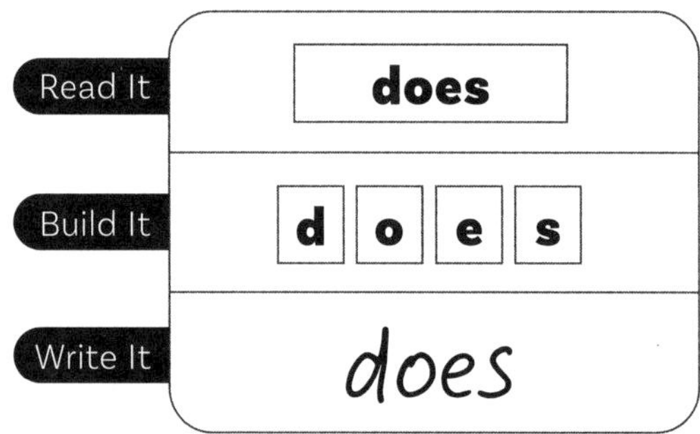

T: "Today, we're going to look closely at words that don't follow a spelling pattern we would expect. We'll read, build, and write them. I'm going to show you a few examples before we begin." *(Model several examples as shown in the figure.)*

Read It

T: "The word is *does*. Let's read the word in the 'Read It' box together."

T and S: "Does."

T: "What makes the spelling of this word different from how we expect it to be spelled?"

S: (*Students may respond in various ways, which may include, "oe sounds like /uh/. Usually that's spelled with a u." Another may say, "The s sounds kind of like a z."*)

T: "Let's name the letters and read it again."

T and S: "*D-o-e-s, does.*"

Build It

T: "Use your letter cards (tiles) to build the word *does* next to 'Build It.'"

S: (*Students use their letter cards and build the word.*)

T: "Let's name the letters and read it aloud together."

T and S: "*D-o-e-s, does.*"

Write It

T: "Use your pencil to write *does* next to 'Write It.' Say the letters quietly as you write each letter to spell *does*."

S: (*Students write the word in the space.*)

T: "Let's name the letters and read it aloud together."

T and S: "*D-o-e-s, does.*"

Connect It (to Writing)

T: "Let's write the word *does* in a sentence. Can someone use *does* in a sentence?"

S: (*Students respond with a sentence.*)

T: "Great! I'm going to write, 'He *does* not like carrots.' (*Write the sentence on a whiteboard.*) "Let's read it together."

T and S: "He *does* not like carrots." (*Have students write the sentence on their whiteboard.*)

Extension

- **Tracing letters:** Students can spell, or trace, the word in their hand as they say each letter aloud.
- **Air writing:** Students can also air write the letters to reinforce the spelling of the target word while saying it aloud.

PHONICS

Figure 3.12: Strategy—Read it, build it, write it, connect it.

*Visit **go.SolutionTree.com/literacy/FSK6** and enter the unique access code found on the book's inside front cover to access a reproducible version of this figure.*

Strategies for Struggling Readers

Struggling readers will likely need instruction that is even more explicit, systematic, and multisensory than the average reader of the same age or grade level. With students who are not progressing as anticipated, we must work harder to make the invisible visible in order to address their gaps in knowledge and understanding.

A good scope and sequence, along with gathering understanding through assessment data, will help you know where those gaps exist in order to address them. For example, some students may need a solid review of short vowel sounds applied to CVC words. Others may need additional support with vowel teams such as *ai*, *ay*, *ea*, and *ee* and see those applied within words, both in connected text and independent of text.

Many students in grades 3–6 with reading difficulties are missing key skills, which often result in halted, disjointed reading and poor reading comprehension. It is easy to assume that these students missed key phonics skills and proceed directly to addressing the sequence of skills.

However, research reveals that struggling readers have primary issues that trace back to poor phonemic awareness (Ashby et al., 2023; Fletcher, Lyon, Fuchs, & Barnes, 2019; Kilpatrick, 2015), which contributes to a lack of phonological processing. If students struggle with phonics, they likely need additional practice developing how they process speech sounds within words. In other words, when students have poor phonics skills, it likely stems from poor phonemic awareness.

As teachers of reading, it is relatively easy to identify poor phonemic awareness and to provide explicit and systematic instruction to gird up these skills. Struggling readers in grades two or beyond will likely know letter-sound correspondence. However, when activities are focused on phonemic awareness, use blank tokens to represent sounds rather than letter tiles (Ashby et al., 2023). This keeps the focus and memory-building on sounds and sound sequences rather than letter-sound connections. Letter-sound mapping and spelling can take place during other English or language arts instruction.

Elkonin Boxes

Elkonin boxes (Elkonin, 1963), or sound boxes, which I mentioned previously (page 84) as a method for providing additional support in phonemic awareness for students who need it, serve as a concrete way for students to identify and manipulate phonemes to make the sound-symbol match. For example, students move a blank token (for phonemic awareness) or letters (for phonics) into small square boxes representing each sound or sounds they hear.

In my clinical work and when supporting primary teachers, I have found Elkonin boxes also support students as they begin segmenting sounds and attaching letters to those sounds. Struggling readers typically need additional practice with segmenting sounds. Keep the following guidelines in mind as you plan instruction and practice the following strategy (figure 3.13).

- When addressing phonemic awareness, stick with blank tokens in order to keep the focus on segmenting sounds.
- Use one-syllable words.
- Select words that are familiar to the student.

- Include digraphs (for example, *sh, ch*) and diphthongs (for example, *ai, oa*) to reinforce the concept that two letters can make one sound.
- Include words with the silent *e*.
- As the student progresses, have the student make decisions about how many boxes they need in order to complete the task.

Strategy: Elkonin Boxes for Phonics

Pillar: Phonics

Grade Level:

☑ K
☑ 1
☑ 2

Struggling Readers:

☑ 3
☑ 4
☑ 5
☑ 6

Instructional Grouping:

☐ Whole Group
☑ Small Group
☑ Individual

Materials:

- See the reproducible template online for making your own Elkonin boxes. I make mine using cardstock and laminate them.
- Letter tiles or letter cards

Consider This:

- This strategy is fairly intense; about ten minutes is adequate with kindergarten and first-grade students. For second grade and beyond, I'd work no longer than fifteen minutes.

What is it? Elkonin boxes help students form the foundational skill of isolating, identifying, segmenting, and manipulating letters/sounds in words. Elkonin boxes are small square boxes into which students move a letter or letters representing each sound they hear in a word.

Why is it important? Isolating, segmenting, and blending sounds to say words are three critically important skills as students learn to read. Elkonin boxes can help the invisible become visible for struggling readers in particular. They assist students in isolating, identifying, and segmenting initial, medial, and final sounds in words.

What works in the classroom?

The sequence I use may be slightly different from others you have seen. Coming from a clinical setting, the sequence I use may be more rigid than some. In my professional opinion, the sequence should be routinized and followed, especially with struggling readers.

Modeling the Strategy

Depending on the skill level of students, always begin with a simple word with two (VC) or three sounds (CVC) so that the student experiences success.

Words With Two Sounds (VC):

Place the two-box sound box and about eight letters on the table, most of which the student will use during the session along with a few extra letters (distractors).

Connect to Meaning:

Before beginning the protocol, define the target word and use it in a sentence to support students with word gaps and English learners.

Figure 3.13: Strategy—Elkonin boxes for phonics.

continued ▶

Instructional Protocol

1. **Segment the word into phonemes.**

   T: "I'm going to say a word. Then, you'll repeat the word after me. As you say the word, think about the sounds you hear. As you stretch the sounds, tell me how many sounds you hear. Touch each sound box as you say the sounds. The word is *it*. Say the word *it*." (*Touch the sound box to match each sound.*)

   S: "It." (*The student says the word* it *slowly and touches each sound box for each sound.*)

   T: "How many sounds do you hear in *it*?"

   S: "Two."

2. **Match the sounds to letters.**

   T: "Now you'll move a letter into the sound box for each sound you hear." (*Model several times using a two-sound sound box and a word such as* it. *Following this, do several more two-sound words with the student.*)

   Note: You can also have students begin by moving colored tokens into the boxes to represent sounds and then replace them with letters. I typically just use letters.

   T: "What is the first sound you hear in *it*?"

   S: "/ĭ/."

   T: "What letter makes the /ĭ/ sound? Name the letter and move it to show me where the /ĭ/ sound is in *it*."

3. **Move letters into boxes.**

   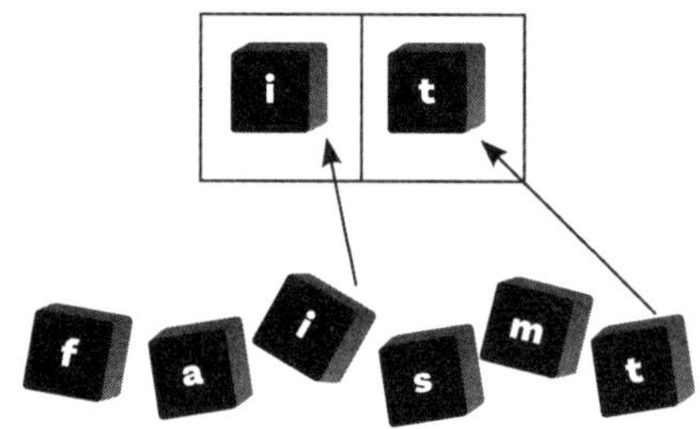

   S: (*The student moves the letter* i *into the first box.*)

   T: "What is the next sound you hear in *it*?"

   S: "/t/."

   T: "Name the letter and move it to show me where the /t/ sound is in *it*."

   S: (*The student moves the letter* t *into the second box.*)

   T: "The word is *it*. Say the word *it* with me." (*Slide your finger beneath the boxes from left to right as you say* it.)

   T and S: "It." (*Slide fingers beneath the discs from left to right.*)

4. **Write the word.**

   T: "Now write the word *it*."

   (*Present four to five additional target words following the sequence. Keep the same vowel pattern. See the following CVC example*).

5. **Read all the words.**

   T: "Now let's read all the words with the short /ă/ sound."

   T and S: (*Read the list of words orally.*)

Words With Three Sounds (CVC)

The target word is *hop*. Place the three-box sound box with the assortment of letters on the table in front of the student. Follow the same protocol used for a CVC word.

Digraphs and choosing sound boxes

Begin the session by placing a two-sound, three-sound, and four-sound set of boxes on the table. Letter tiles, along with a few distractors, should also be on the table.

Choosing boxes. As the student progresses, I place two or three sets of sound boxes in front of the student, one with two boxes, three boxes, and four boxes. The student listens to the target word and then makes a decision regarding which set of boxes to choose that matches the number of sounds. If the student does not choose correctly, I do not correct them. Usually, as the student moves through the task with the target word, they note their error and self-correct, which is an important metacognitive behavior.

Connect to Meaning: Define the target word *fish* and use it in a sentence.

Instructional Protocol

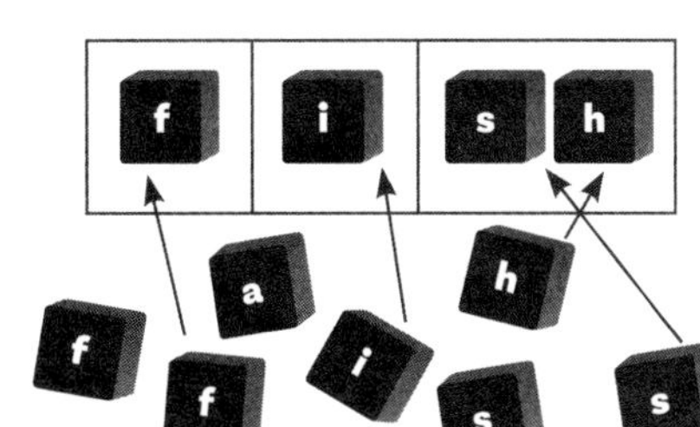

1. **Segment the word into phonemes.**

   T: "The word is *fish*. Say the word *fish*."

   S: "Fish." (*The student says the word* fish *slowly.*)

   T: (*Touch the sound box to match each sound.*) "How many sounds do you hear?"

   S: (*The student says the word* fish *slowly and touches each sound box.*) "Three sounds. /f/ /i/ /sh/."

   T: "Choose the boxes that you will need." (*Wait until the student selects the three set of boxes and moves the others aside.*)

2. **Match the sounds to letters.**

   T: "Now say *fish* slowly, listening for the sounds."

   S: "Fish. /f/ /ĭ/ /sh/."

   T: "What is the first sound you hear in *fish*?"

   S: "/f/."

3. **Move letters into boxes.**

   T: "Move the letter that matches the /f/ sound into the box that shows where you hear the sound." (*Proceed with the second and third sounds or letters until the word is complete. Have a discussion about how /sh/ makes one sound.*)

   T and S: "*Fish.*" (*Have the student slide their hand under the word while reading aloud.*)

4. **Write the word.**

   T: "Now write the word *fish*."

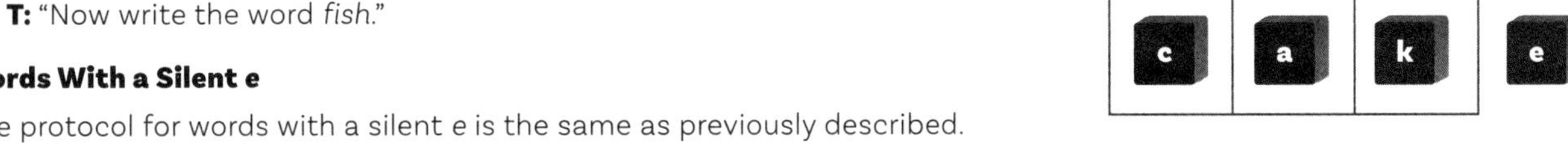

Words With a Silent e

The protocol for words with a silent *e* is the same as previously described.

Use words which have previously been introduced.

If the target word is *cake*, the number of boxes needed is three because the *e* is silent. I have the student place the *e* outside of the third box so that we remember the *e* is part of the spelling but silent.

Visit ***go.SolutionTree.com/literacy/FSK6*** *and enter the unique access code found on the book's inside front cover to access a reproducible version of this figure.*

When using Elkonin boxes, you'll follow an instructional routine. The protocol is intentional in order to be clear about the task and to break down the decisions students make. These include how many sounds they hear, how many boxes they will need, the letters that make the sounds, which combination of letters make one sound, and so forth. Become familiar with the sequence outlined in the Elkonin boxes strategy table.

Elkonin boxes are an important choice among a collection of strategies that support emerging and early readers. They can be used in a variety of ways to support students who do not yet understand the alphabetic principle as well as for those who have made the sound-symbol match. Use them regularly, in small doses of time, to support students as they increase their proficiency in hearing, segmenting, blending, and manipulating sounds.

Wrapping It Up

There are a lot of considerations in order to implement effective phonics instruction, the third pillar. Systematic and explicit instruction is critical in order for students to make the sound-symbol match. Understanding your students' strengths and skill deficits will help you target instruction and intervention decisions for individual students. School leaders can use the Leader's Lens (figure 3.14) to support teachers moving forward with effective literacy practices. As you consider the Five Key Takeaways (page 130), think about what resonated most with you and perhaps where you may make adjustments after becoming familiar with the what, why, and how as related to phonics instruction. Think about intentionality as it relates to your instruction and literacy environment as you consider the Five Key Next Steps (page 130).

Leader's Lens

Phonics

Consider the following supervision supports and classroom connections as you lead and guide teachers as they implement effective phonics instruction.

Supervision Supports	
Practical Research	• Have you shared current understandings about the importance of phonics that are aligned to the science of reading research? • Have you shared the direct link between phonemic awareness and phonics or phonics' role as a building block for fluency?
Professional Development	• What do you consider essential professional development for phonics? Where would you begin? • How would you support collaborative teams as teachers implement phonemic awareness practices within the literacy block? • Have you shared materials and resources that support best practices in phonics instruction that is intentional and aligned to the science of reading?
Feedback and Expectations	• Does my feedback support phonics instruction that is systematic and explicit? • Have you provided specific expectations regarding what phonics instruction should look like in the classroom?
Financial Focus	• Is there money budgeted to provide materials that could be used for phonics instruction?
Classroom Connections (Look-Fors)	
Literacy-Rich Environment	• Does the classroom environment intentionally support letters, clusters, and phonics instruction? • Does the classroom library include predictable text, decodable text, and authentic children's literature?
Direct Instruction	Notice the following instructional practices, which include: • Systematic and explicit instruction • Lessons that are differentiated based on student needs • Phonics instruction that is integrated with phonemic awareness, fluency, read alouds, word learning, and comprehension • Use of multisensory approaches for struggling readers and English learners • The use of manipulatives for students who could benefit from additional supports

Figure 3.14: Chapter 3 leader's lens.

Visit ***go.SolutionTree.com/literacy/FSK6*** *for a free reproducible version of this figure.*

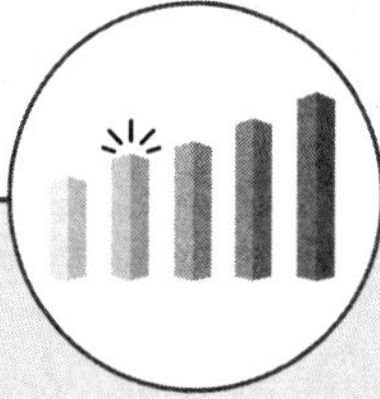

Five Key Takeaways

Consider the following key ideas gleaned from the chapter individually or discuss them with your collaborative grade-level team.

1. **Alphabet considerations:** This chapter includes several advantages related to teaching the alphabet along with the four phases of word learning, which details the phases students pass through as they build their understanding of the alphabet and how it works.
2. **Text types:** As readers build their skills, several types of text support their growth. These include predictable text, decodable text, and authentic children's literature. Use a healthy dose of variety for students as they build their decoding skills.
3. **Orthographic mapping:** Orthographic mapping is when the brain permanently connects sounds, spelling, and meaning, which provides quick retrieval of words and reading automaticity, important for comprehension.
4. **Systematic and explicit instruction:** Systematic and explicit instruction are not synonymous terms. The term *systematic* typically refers to a scope and sequence while the term *explicit* refers to how one teaches, or the instructional delivery.
5. **Phonics strategies:** There are seven strategies in the chapter that support word study, writing, multisensory approaches, and strategies for struggling readers. Phonics instruction should be integrated with read alouds, reading connected text, writing, word learning, and comprehension.

Five Key Next Steps

Consider the following questions and discussion prompts individually or have a conversation with your collaborative grade-level team.

1. **Alphabet recognition advantages:** What did you think about the alphabet recognition advantages and instructional implications for teaching the alphabet? Did these resonate with you? Why or why not?
2. **Explicit and systematic phonics instruction:** Consider your current phonics instruction. Is it explicit and systematic? Do you follow a scope and sequence? What about a synthetic or analytic approach? There is a lot to consider. Engage in discussion with your collaborative team.
3. **Effective phonics instruction:** Review the characteristics of effective phonics instruction. Did any of these surprise or resonate with you? What are your next steps for integrating?
4. **Text selection:** Consider text selection with early readers. Review the "phases of word learning" table for suggested texts for students as they progress through the phases of word learning. Do you use a variety of texts to support your students? Discuss with your collaborative team.
5. **Phonic strategies:** Think about the strategies included for phonics skill development. Are there any specific ones you want to try? Share with your grade-level team. Consider trying several and discussing them with your grade-level team.

Key Vocabulary

Fluency

Accuracy	The ability to read or decode words accurately and without pronunciation errors
Automaticity	The ability to read with little cognitive effort and with adequate speed
Choral Reading	An oral reading strategy in which students read a text, poem, or song aloud in unison with expression; a teacher or model reader may serve as the lead reader.
Dyad Reading	A form of paired reading in which a lead reader (more-skilled reader) and an assisted reader (less-skilled reader) read chorally side by side
Echo Reading	An oral reading strategy in which a teacher, adult, or peer reads a poem, text, or song lyrics aloud and then a student or group of students repeat, or echo, the reading with the aim of sounding just like the model
Effect Size	Measures how meaningful the relationship between variables is in a research outcome; effect sizes, reported frequently in research, are useful because we can compare the results of varied studies on the same topic (for example, phonemic awareness, vocabulary, or comprehension). We interpret effect sizes as follows: below 0.20 is negligible, between 0.20 and 0.39 is small, between 0.40 and 0.79 is moderate, and over 0.80 is large.
Fluency	The ability to read with accuracy, appropriate speed, and meaningful expression
Neurological Impress Method	An oral reading fluency intervention strategy designed to support struggling and striving readers through repeated reading; the model reader (usually the teacher) reads aloud by the student's ear slightly louder and faster than the student until the student is confident to read the text independently.
Prosody	Refers to being able to read with expression and proper phrasing, often indicating the reader understands what they are reading
Read Alouds	A "shared literacy experience engaging children and adults in conversation and engagement around a high-quality text" (Ness, 2023, p. 3)
Reader's Theater	An engaging instructional approach in which students expressively read a script aloud for performance purposes; built on the premise of repeated reading, students practice scripts repeatedly and perform for their classmates or special guests by reading orally directly from the script.
Reading Rate	Reading rate, as related to fluency, is measured in number of words read per minute.
Repeated Reading	The primary instructional strategy that supports fluency development; repeating reading strategies helps students improve fluency and comprehension.

CHAPTER 4

Fluency
Growing Fluent Readers

Good oral reading instruction involves reading to children, reading with children, and listening to children read.

—Tim Rasinski

FLUENCY

Reading fluency, the third of the five essential pillars of reading success, has waxed and waned in terms of attention within the field of literacy. I'm in agreement with literacy researchers (NICHD, 2000a) who concur that fluency is often neglected and does not get the attention it deserves. In this chapter, I share why I believe reading fluency has earned its place among the five pillars and should receive more attention both in research and during reading instruction. While the characteristics of effective fluency instruction and the associated strategies are the heart of this chapter, I encourage you to spend some time in the sections What Is Reading Fluency? and Why Is Fluency Important? (page 135), where I share the basics of reading fluency and practical research that affirms its importance in the literacy continuum.

In my work, I've found that when teachers understand the importance fluency plays in developing proficient readers, they want to explore strategies and methods that help students become fluent readers. I trust this chapter will support your efforts as you develop classroom routines and strategies that grow fluent readers.

What Is Reading Fluency?

What do you think of when you hear "oral reading fluency?" Reflect for a moment. Is fluency something you recognize when you hear a student decoding accurately and without hesitation while also reading with expression? Do you think about the reader who reads quickly but sounds like a robot? Or do you think about the student who labors over every single word, sounding it out letter by letter? Some of your students are proficient readers or "good" readers. They also tend to be fluent readers. You also have students who are struggling readers, sometimes referred to as "poor" readers in the literature. These dysfluent students labor when reading and typically read word by word, which impairs comprehension.

Oral reading fluency, or fluency for short, includes three dimensions, as shown in the following list.

- **Accuracy in word decoding:** *Accuracy* is the students' ability to read or decode words accurately and without pronunciation errors.
- **Automatic text processing:** *Automaticity* refers to the readers' ability to read with little cognitive effort and with adequate speed (measured as words correct per minute). Automaticity is a critically important aspect of fluency because it frees up the reader to shift their cognitive energy to comprehension.
- **Prosodic reading:** *Prosody* refers to being able to read with expression and proper phrasing, often indicating the reader understands what they are reading.

The three dimensions of fluency are interdependent as students develop into proficient readers. Readers who are proficient understand how to make reading sound like speech, as if talking to a friend. They raise or lower their voice, emphasize specific words, slow down, speed up, and perhaps pause for dramatic effect. I'll blend these three dimensions together to form a definition.

Oral reading fluency is the ability to read with accuracy, speed, and meaningful expression. I'll add one more qualifier to the definition. Oral reading fluency is the ability to read with accuracy, *appropriate* speed, and meaningful expression. I'll share much more about why appropriate speed is important as we think about fluency.

Oral reading fluency is measured by calculating automaticity, which is words correct per minute. You've probably experienced students reading as quickly as they can during a timed oral fluency measure. They read so quickly they often lose all expression and sound more like a speed reading machine. This happens because many readers equate speed with fluency. In some circles, we've prioritized speed over all else, and many students seem to know this.

Noted researchers Jan Hasbrouck and Gerald Tindal (1992, 2006, 2017) co-developed the oral reading fluency measure in the early 1990s, which still serves as a reliable and valid measure of fluency. Hasbrouck addressed the issue of speed readers in a podcast of *Melissa & Lori Love Literacy*, episode 153 (Loftus & Sappington, 2023).

She recommends that when a student begins an oral reading fluency measure by speed reading, the teacher should acknowledge the student's speed and then redirect them to begin again with the direction to "read well or like you're talking." Otherwise, the norm-referenced measurement will not be accurate.

Adding the descriptor *appropriate* before speed reminds us we must always keep in mind that speed is relative. When students read independently, they may read with greater speed when they know the topic well. On the other hand, when reading challenging text, a student's appropriate speed should be much slower, with more attention going toward unusual vocabulary and comprehension. Reading rate, or speed, does not equal comprehension.

Unpacking the definition a little further, accuracy means being an automatic reader. When students achieve automaticity, they don't have to think about the process of decoding every word. They accurately decode most words and can turn their attention toward reading at an appropriate speed with meaningful expression.

We can also assess fluency by evaluating prosody. The third dimension of fluency includes the elements of reading associated with expression. Reading with meaning may include slowing down and speeding up for effect, reading with good phrasing, varying the tone of the voice to display emotion, and reading at an appropriate pace. In addition to the oral reading fluency measure, Jerry Zutell and Timothy V. Rasinski (1991) developed the *multidimensional fluency rubric* to evaluate prosody. The four-point rubric includes expression and volume, phrasing, smoothness, and pace, providing a broader view of fluency.

In the following section, we'll take a closer look at the importance of reading fluency in relation to comprehension.

Why Is Reading Fluency Important?

Although fluency is in the spotlight as the third of the five pillars of reading, it is not a new aspect of reading that emerged with the science of reading. Oral reading was a common practice in the colonial period and early 1900s in the United States, when students frequently read orally from the Bible and other texts in one-room schoolhouses. Specific to literacy research, its roots trace as early as the 1900s (Huey, 1908/1968). Two highly regarded researchers, David LaBerge and S. Jay Samuels (1974) conducted seminal research in reading, which brought fluency into the spotlight. It was also identified as one of the "big five" by the renowned team of experts who made up the National Reading Panel in 2000 (NICHD, 2000a). The panel concluded that empirical research provides evidence that fluency instruction improves decoding, word reading, fluency, and reading comprehension in grades 1–4. Additionally, fluency instruction supports struggling reader improvement in grades 1–12.

For the past few decades, interest and attention surrounding fluency and fluency instruction has been uneven. Timothy Rasinski, professor emeritus of literacy education at Kent State University, has probably done more than any literacy educator or researcher to keep pushing forward the importance of fluency in developing proficient readers. He has written countless articles, conducted research, and authored or coauthored many resources that aid teachers in implementing fluency strategies in their classrooms.

The science of reading has brought fluency to the forefront again, and it has re-emerged as important within schools and states that have adopted the science of reading as the framework for their core literacy instruction.

Fluency as a Bridge to Comprehension

At the heart of fluency is comprehension, the ability to decode *and* comprehend at the same time. It is not enough for students to be accurate decoders; they must also read at an appropriate speed and with expression to become fluent readers. And, if they're not fluent, it becomes a hurdle to comprehension (Stanovich, 1991; Torgesen et al., 2001; Torgesen et al., 2003).

Fluency has been studied as a predictor of comprehension and *embodies* reading for meaning. Think of fluency as a bridge. On one side of the bridge is decoding, and on the other is comprehension. Fluency bridges the gap between decoding and comprehension (Duke & Cartwright, 2021; Duke et al., 2021; Pikulski & Chard, 2005), as shown in figure 4.1. Let's explore this analogy in more depth.

Figure 4.1: Fluency as a bridge to comprehension.

Though attention is often on reading rate or automaticity when measuring fluency, meaningful expression (prosody) is also a contributor to comprehension. Rate is only part of the bridge; it must be coupled with prosody. For example, when speaking with our friends or family, expression and phrasing is a natural part of how we communicate meaning. We slow down and speed up, talk loudly and softly, and create meaning through our expressiveness. Encouraging readers to use similar expressiveness when they read orally often takes practice through repeated reading, and it pays off.

In a 2015 study, researchers found that fourth-grade students who demonstrated natural intonation when reading aloud had better comprehension than those who simply demonstrated adequate reading rate (Veenendaal, Groen, & Verhoeven, 2015). In another study, second-grade students who participated in oral reading fluency strategies for a semester performed better on comprehension measures than their counterparts who participated in round robin reading (Reutzel & Hollingsworth, 1993). Fifth-grade students, who similarly took part in reader's theater, paired reading, and reading with audiobooks outperformed the control group on speed, prosody, and comprehension measures (Kanik Uysal & Duman, 2020).

These and other studies show that students who read orally with meaningful expression tend to have better comprehension when reading silently than students who have less expressive oral reading skills. Prosody plays an important role in both fluency and overall reading proficiency. As teachers who desire students to comprehend well, it is vitally important to include oral reading strategies in the literacy block to help students improve their rate, prosody, and comprehension.

Fluency is more than its simple definition comprising accuracy, appropriate speed, and meaningful expression. It also has to do with cognitive capacity and attention. Researchers David LaBerge and S. Jay Samuels (1974) argue that we can only really focus on one thing at a time. Fluent readers spend the majority of their cognitive energy on making sense or comprehending text, with only a fraction of their attention going toward decoding, as shown in figure 4.2 (page 138). They are automatic readers who flip back and forth easily between slowing down to decode an unusual word and comprehending. As proficient readers, they also likely have a more rich and nuanced vocabulary.

In contrast, struggling readers have great difficulty shifting between decoding and comprehension. They employ the majority of their cognitive energy on decoding, often reading word by word. Because they spend so much attention on decoding, they have little capacity remaining for comprehending (Kuhn & Stahl, 2003), which is illustrated in figure 4.3 (page 138).

Not only does a lack of fluency impact a young reader's ability to gain information and enjoyment from a single given text, but it may also continue to have a negative impact on their lifetime experience with reading. In his landmark research, which coined the term *Mathew effect*, Keith E. Stanovich (1986) argued that students who read fluently also engage in reading more frequently. The term is taken from the biblical passage that describes "the rich get richer, and the poor get poorer" phenomenon (*Literal Word*, n.d.). Similarly, Stanovich uses it to describe the relationship between voluminous reading and comprehension (Pfost, Hattie, Dörfler, & Artelt, 2014; Stanovich, 1986). Thus, avid readers continue to gain fluency in all aspects of proficient reading while, at the same time, struggling and striving readers who read less continue to fall further behind.

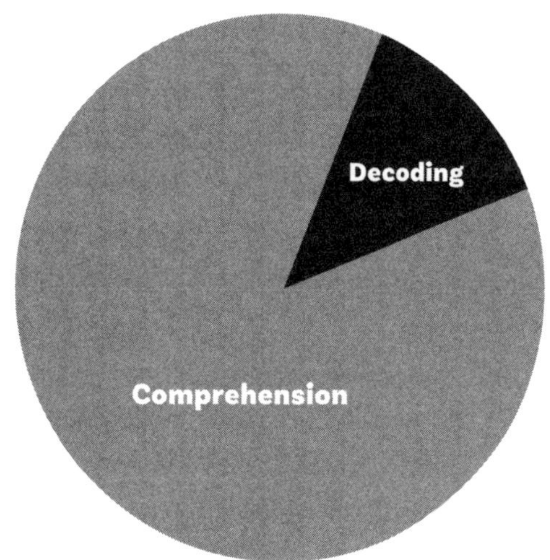

Figure 4.2: Fluent readers' cognitive attention is focused on comprehension.

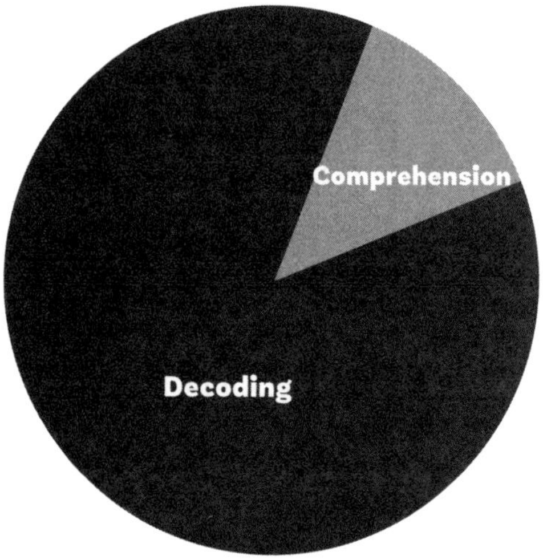

Figure 4.3: Struggling readers spend most of their cognitive capacity on decoding.

Fluency is more than the sum of its parts. Fluency bridges the gap between word recognition and comprehension. Fluent readers also comprehend more ably. While spending time supporting students as they become fluent readers is time well spent, doing so is not without challenges. In the next section, I'll discuss some specific challenges to teaching fluency as well as preview ways to address these challenges.

Challenges of Fluency Instruction

Fluency issues increasingly impact comprehension as students read more challenging texts laden with academic vocabulary. Instruction can be challenging, and I've summarized a few of the underlying reasons why.

- **Lack of phonics skills:** Students who lack phonics skills and are word-by-word readers pour their cognitive energy into decoding, rather than comprehension. These students likely need additional instruction in phonemic awareness skills such as isolating, blending, and segmenting sounds.
- **Difficulty with independent reading:** Students who lack fluency skills are often reluctant or striving readers who may not engage in frequent independent reading. Finding books that interest students is one important step toward motivating them to read more (Tompkins, 2006). For fluency development, reader's theater can provide just the type of ongoing practice from which these students can benefit. Additionally, intentionally pairing students can also provide oral reading practice within authentic text. Audiobooks, another viable option, are discussed in chapter 6 (page 226).

- **Few models of fluent reading:** Students who are dysfluent may lack models of fluent readers. Daily read alouds undoubtedly provide one such important model. Additional models for primary and intermediate students are necessary in order to provide ongoing support for fluency. For intermediate students, following or reading along with an audiobook provides a model of strong prosody and pacing and a meaningful support for decoding. And, it may just provide the motivation for these students to read more frequently.

In summary, the benefits of addressing fluency far outweigh the challenges since fluency directly impacts comprehension. Challenges that impact instruction include students who have deficient phonics skills, students who do not engage frequently in reading independently, and students who lack models of fluent reading. In the following sections, I articulate a foundation for how to build fluency along with specific strategies that support your students as they become fluent readers.

Fluency Can Be Taught

Fluency instruction and ongoing practice must be intentional and consistent and use authentic texts as much as possible as students develop their fluency skills. The following sections explore intentional, consistent methods.

Classroom Structures to Support Fluency Practice

Classroom routines, structures, and the literacy environment are building blocks that support effective fluency instruction. Consider making space in the literacy block, if you haven't already, for frequent time devoted to one (or more) of the many evidence-based strategies described in this chapter.

For example, the whole-class Fluency Development Lesson (page 162) is a lively method for modeling fluency, having students orally practice their fluency skills, and engage in reading text to others. Additionally, struggling readers can benefit greatly from assisted reading and paired reading strategies. Struggling readers benefit from strategies such as the Neurological Impress Method (page 156). All students should be participating in paired reading and repeated reading strategies such as reader's theater. Ideally, students should routinely be rehearsing a script or text selection for fluency practice in preparation for performing for classmates.

Too often, fluency practice is either ignored or treated as a once-and-done activity. In order to become proficient in accuracy, rate, *and* prosody, students need to hear fluent models and engage in repeated reading. Let's consider round robin reading, a common fluency practice, but one that is actually not particularly effective.

Round robin reading, sometimes called popcorn reading, is when the teacher randomly selects students to read aloud a portion of a text. At its core, it is simply unrehearsed oral reading. At face value, it may seem to have merit since the teacher has the opportunity to hear and assess students' oral reading skills. However, there are glaring issues with round robin reading summarized next. First, round robin reading often results in choppy, dysfluent reading filled with many oral reading errors because students haven't had the opportunity to practice reading silently first. Next, students who read at a faster pace than the student reading often subvocalize or read under their breath while the student is reading. Instead of supporting fluency, subvocalizing slows down more-able readers and impairs comprehension. Finally, the emphasis in round robin reading is on decoding accurately. Word calling, or accurate decoding, does not equal comprehension. Comprehension is multifaceted and includes activating prior knowledge, understanding vocabulary, and reading fluently. In the What Works in the Classroom section, we'll explore instructional strategies that support the benefits of oral reading without causing undue anxiety for students.

Practice Builds Fluent Readers

Becoming more proficient at any skill, strategy, or task requires practice. Fluency instruction is similar and effective (Kuhn & Stahl, 2003). Becoming automatic so that you can perform a skill without thinking requires repeated practice over time. As adults, we master many tasks and perform them automatically. For some of you, it may be playing an instrument; for others, it may be knitting or playing a sport like pickleball or tennis. We did not become proficient at these tasks all at once.

While writing this book, I decided to add Ai Chi (Tai Chi but in a heated pool) to my exercise routine and was reminded how much practice it takes before becoming fluent at a skill. The first few times, I stood near the instructor and watched her like a hawk as she performed the movements. I'd also refer frequently to the large poster featuring visuals of each move. When I wasn't making the movements correctly, the instructor would gently correct me or model the move. Each week, I recalled a few more of the movements and slowly learned the routine. Many months later, I enjoy the class while also receiving the stretching and mental centeredness benefits of Ai Chi. Why? Because ongoing practice and rehearsal gradually shifted my skills to automaticity. My cognitive energy is no longer maxed out thinking about each move and how to do it. I'm on autopilot, and my body and mind receive the full benefit of Ai Chi (which I highly recommend).

With reading, it's a similar process. Students become automatic through lots and lots of practice. Reading becomes more accurate by practicing along with reading often and widely across many types of text. As students become automatic readers, they can turn their attention to prosody, or expressive reading. They begin to naturally notice punctuation and attend to phrasing, thus influencing comprehension. Practice and rehearsal is vital for growing proficient readers and should include repeated reading, especially for struggling readers. Repeated reading becomes the vehicle for improving fluency and increased comprehension; read on to become familiar with the strategies that are built on repeated reading.

What Works in the Classroom?

In reading instruction, depending on grade level, teachers spend time each day teaching phonemic awareness and phonics along with comprehension. Fluency and vocabulary development often get the short end of the stick in terms of time and attention, although both have an influence on comprehension—the goal of reading.

Fluency is identified by research as a set of tools and evidence-based strategies that are effective in developing fluent readers. Strategies include modeled reading, assisted reading, and repeated reading. The thread across these strategies is support for struggling and striving readers, fluency development, and increased comprehension.

Resources to Support Fluency Instruction

- *Build Reading Fluency: Practice and Performance With Reader's Theater and More* by Timothy Rasinski and Chase Young (2024)
- *Developing Fluent Readers: Teaching Fluency as a Foundational Skill* by Melanie R. Kuhn and Lorell Levy (2015)
- *The Fluent Reader: Oral and Silent Reading Strategies for Building Fluency, Word Recognition and Comprehension (2nd edition)* by Timothy Rasinski (2010)
- *The Megabook of Fluency: Strategies and Texts to Engage All Readers* by Timothy V. Rasinski and Melissa Cheesman Smith (2018)

Characteristics of Effective Fluency Instruction

Fluency strategies that include practice and repeated reading make a positive impact on fluency development. The key is ongoing practice rather than a once-and-done fluency activity. Consistency is key. The characteristics in table 4.1 (page 142), based on research evidence, are suggested to inform effective fluency instruction.

Table 4.1: Characteristics of Effective Fluency Instruction

Engage in Repeated Reading	Engaging students in fluency activities that encourage repeated reading (sometimes for an audience) supports fluency growth (NICHD, 2000a). Repeated reading, according to Rasinski and Smith (2018, p. 12), "is just another name for rehearsal. Rehearsal is not about reading quickly, but about communicating with meaning for the enjoyment of a listening audience." Choral reading, echo reading, and reader's theater are among the most common repeated reading strategies.
Use Authentic Text	High-quality picture and trade books, poems, scripts, speeches, and songs are meant to be performed orally. Jump-rope chants, jokes for kids, and tongue twisters add lots of variety to reading, and they lend themselves well to fluency practice. English language arts curriculum typically includes diverse text selections; however, there are many resources available online and through educational publishing companies that support classroom fluency practice. Taking the time to collect and gather texts that are meant to be read orally and with expression will pay off to support students' fluency goals.
Practice Wide Reading	Repeated practice leads to fluency in many skills such as playing an instrument, driving, and riding a bike. Reading frequently and widely leads to reading growth (Kuhn et al., 2006). Students need to be independently reading large amounts of text daily.
Support English Learners	ELs benefit from social interaction and develop confidence and motivation from interacting and receiving support from their peers (Genishi & Dyson, 2009). Fluency strategies that include choral reading and repeated reading strategies using poems and texts that are relevant to their home cultures are an opportunity for ELs to build their vocabulary, pronunciation, and fluency. ELs greatly benefit from partner reading to support fluency and comprehension, particularly in mathematics, science, and social studies (Calderón, 2011). Strategic pairing, discussed later in this chapter, is an important step to support your ELs. Buddy by my side, a paired reading strategy for fiction and informational text (see chapter 6), includes questioning protocols that support ELs and native speakers.
Support Struggling Readers	Read alouds, intentional paired reading, choral reading, and reader's theater support struggling readers by providing opportunities to build fluency by rereading text. Additional strategies found in the next section that support these readers also include paired reading (page 151), Neurological Impress Method (page 156), and dyad reading (page 153).

Integrating the characteristics of effective fluency instruction summarized in the table will support your students as they become fluent readers. In the next section, you'll find specific strategies for building fluency through regular, meaningful practice.

Strategies to Grow Fluent Readers

Helping students grow in their fluency—automaticity, appropriate speed, and meaningful expression—can be a vital and energetic element of reading instruction. In the next section, as you learn more about fluency strategies, think intentionally about the gradual release framework described previously (page 27) as *show me*, *help me*, and *let me*.

First, model each strategy; be clear about the why or objective for each strategy and share the objective clearly with students. Additionally, consider implementing a collaborative model as recommended by Fisher and Frey (2008). For example, fluency strategies are often implemented best in models that include paired readers or small groups of students. Next, provide feedback to your students as they engage in these strategies. Fluency practice should be student-centered and responsive. Finally, fluency is not a once-and-done activity written into lesson plans on occasion. Practice should be ongoing with a good deal of monitoring and support, perhaps done during small-group or individual instruction.

The fluency strategies presented here are divided into three strands: (1) assisted reading or modeled reading strategies, (2) synchronous paired oral reading techniques (SPORT), and (3) repeated reading strategies. Read on to explore strategies to enhance and improve your students' fluency skills.

Assisted Reading and Modeled Reading Strategies

Striving readers who are working to achieve fluency can benefit from hearing a model reader who reads orally or through audio text. Assisted reading or modeled reading strategies are those in which a proficient reader provides the exemplar of a fluent reader who reads accurately, effortlessly, and with expression. Several strategies are included here that provide models for students as they grow their fluency skills.

Assisted Reading Through Technology

As I've noted, students benefit from hearing adults model fluent reading aloud from high-quality books when they are learning to read. I do not get excited about many computer-assisted reading programs in which students stare at a screen with little or no human interaction.

On the other hand, when we use the power of technology coupled with a supportive adult, we have something worth talking about. One More Story (www.onemorestory.com), an online library filled with about one hundred award-winning picture books read by masterful and fluent readers, is my personal favorite technology-assisted read aloud. One More Story includes Caldecott winning titles such as *The Snowy Day* by Ezra Jack Keats, *Crow Boy* by Taro Yashima, *Stellaluna* by Jannell Cannon, and *Pete's Pizza* by William Steig. It is a subscription-based model that can be purchased individually by families or schools. One More Story can be a useful resource for early readers, and, coupled with the routine suggested in this section, it supports fluency practice and comprehension.

One More Story includes several features such as "read-along" mode and "I can read it" mode, which are explained in figure 4.4. I've also included a few steps to use alongside the features to support growing readers as they build fluency and comprehension.

Strategy: One More Story

Pillar: Fluency

Grade Level:	**Instructional Grouping:**	**Consider This:**
☑ K ☑ 1 ☑ 2 ☐ 3 ☐ 4 ☐ 5 ☐ 6	☐ Whole Group ☐ Small Group ☑ Individual	• Consider incorporating One More Story as a routine students can add to their independent reading to support listening and fluency practice. • You can view a brief clip of an early reader engaging with the "I can read it" mode on my YouTube channel (www.youtube.com/watch?v=ZNw8Y8tUbWI).

What is it? One More Story (www.onemorestory.com) is an online library filled with award-winning picture books read aloud by fluent, masterful readers in which students can listen, read independently, and practice individualized word learning.

Why is it important? Early readers need many opportunities for practice as they build their fluency skills. One More Story provides a means in which students can listen to model reading and practice reading aloud until they experience fluency. With the help of a teacher or another adult, they can retell the book and merge fluency with comprehension.

What works in the classroom?

Before Reading: Time with teacher, aide, or caregiver

- The student selects a book from one of the bookshelves shown on the screen.
- Side by side with the adult, they talk about the cover of the book and flip through the book to predict what the book may be about and think about the characters and setting.

During Reading: Independent reading

- The student listens to the book using the "read-along" mode. They listen several times until they feel confident to move to the "I can read it" mode. The student reads the book aloud, clicking on words as they need support with pronunciation.
- The student practices the words in their "my word" list with the goal of moving them to the "learned words" list.

After Reading: Time with teacher, aide, or caregiver

- When the student is ready, they join the adult to read the book aloud.
- The teacher, aide, or caregiver offers support and encouragement specifically in regard to the aspects of fluency.
- Following reading, the teacher, aide, or caregiver asks the student to retell the story and asks several comprehension questions.
- The adult and student discuss which book the student may choose next.

Figure 4.4: Strategy—One more story.

Visit ***go.SolutionTree.com/literacy/FSK6*** *and enter the unique access code found on the book's inside front cover to access a reproducible version of this figure.*

Freddy Fluency

Prosody, or reading with expression and proper phrasing, is a skill that we need to consistently bring to readers' attention. Modeling expression and appropriate phrasing through read alouds reminds students that these aspects help us understand, enjoy, and make meaning of text.

Students also learn about fluency by non-examples or contrasting experiences. Every once in a while, consider reading in a staccato, flat, or robot voice to show students the stark difference between expressive and non-expressive, boring reading. When I read this way, my students always got a kick out of "robot reading" and would give me tips for reading better. We can agree that it's much more enjoyable to listen to a person who reads with great expression and phrasing.

One day, when I was working with teachers on fluency development, a primary teacher shared with us the stoplight puppet figure that she created and pulled out whenever students were working on fluency, particularly prosody (figure 4.5).

Freddy Fluency helped students visualize and talk about the third aspect of fluency—expression and phrasing. I thought it was a

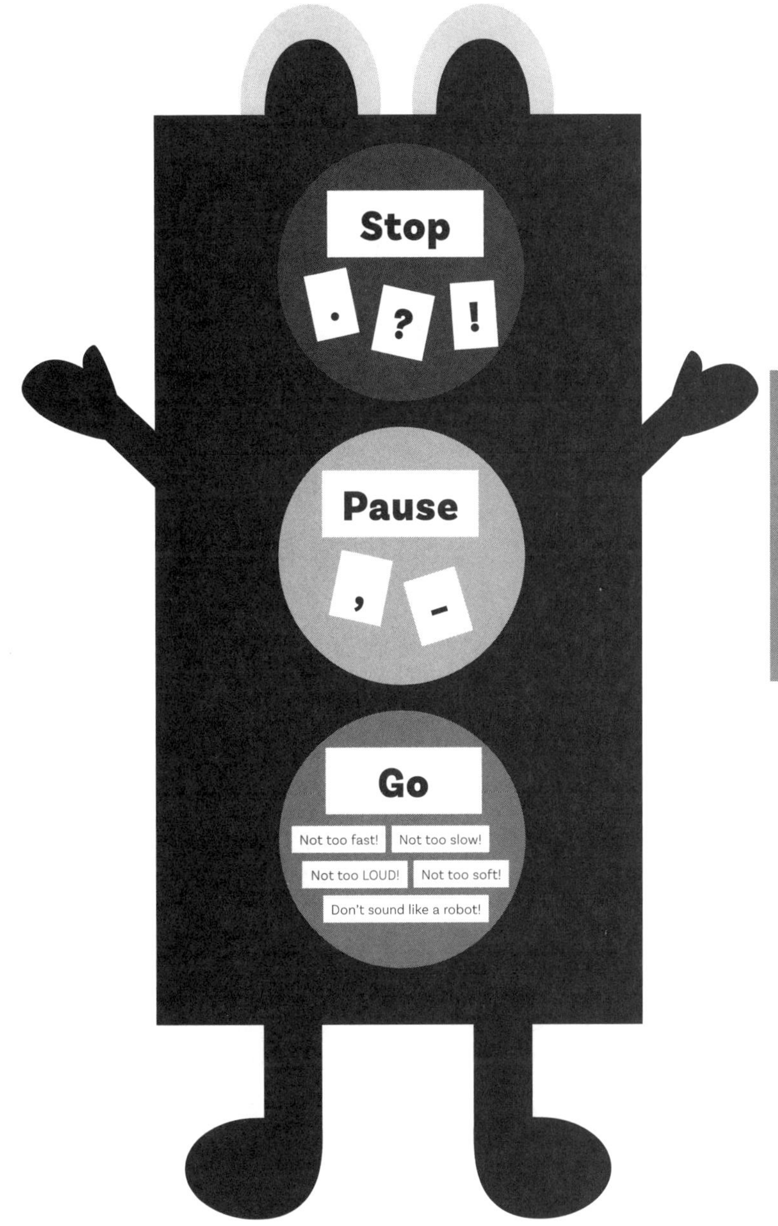

Figure 4.5: Freddy Fluency supports readers as they develop fluency.

clever visual application for primary students. See figure 4.6 for a simple explanation of how to use Freddy Fluency, and perhaps create your own Freddy Fluency to use during fluency practice.

Strategy: Freddy Fluency

Pillar: Fluency

Grade Level:	Instructional Grouping:	Consider This:
☑ K ☑ 1 ☑ 2 ☐ 3 ☐ 4 ☐ 5 ☐ 6	☑ Whole Group ☑ Small Group ☐ Individual	• Have a conversation with students about punctuation—periods, commas, question marks, and exclamation points—along with expression and phrasing and how they affect reading for meaning.

What is it? Freddy Fluency is a visual stoplight model used to remind students of specific aspects of prosody to create meaning when reading.

Why is it important? As students make gains in word recognition and automaticity, their reading should also become more expressive. Reading expressively with proper phrasing and intonation lends itself to better understand and make meaning from the text.

What works in the classroom?

- You can use Freddy Fluency in a variety of ways to support the aspects of fluency—accuracy, automatic reading, and expression. In addition, Freddy can help early readers notice punctuation and adjust their reading.
- As you introduce Freddy, discuss the three aspects of fluency in a way that makes sense to your students.
- Freddy's red, yellow, and green lights mean the following:
    - **Red light:** Stop! Stop at periods, question marks, and exclamation points.
    - **Yellow light:** Caution! Pause when you see commas or dashes.
    - **Green light:** Go! Don't read too fast or too slow. No robot reading. Try not to read too loudly or too quietly. Read with expression and phrasing.
- Each time you bring out Freddy before reading orally or having students read chorally, have students briefly engage in a discussion about fluency, reminding one another about what the red, yellow, and green lights mean as we read.

Figure 4.6: Strategy—Freddy Fluency.

*Visit **go.SolutionTree.com/literacy/FSK6** and enter the unique access code found on the book's inside front cover to access a reproducible version of this figure.*

Fast Start

With regard to helping students become fluent readers, nurturing the school-home connection can help, particularly for students in early grades. Including parents in reading with children and listening to them read can have great results. A meta-analysis of sixteen studies reveals that parental involvement, overall, has a positive effect on children's reading acquisition (Sénéchal & Young, 2008). Further, when parents engaged in specific literacy activities with their children, this involvement produced a larger effect than when just listening to their children read books.

Fast Start (Padak & Rasinski, 2005; Rasinski, 1995) is a reading-at-home strategy that has had considerable success. It is recommended as a daily activity in which parents or caregivers spend around ten to fifteen minutes reading with and listening to their child read along with engaging in additional word study. Research support is considerable (Padak & Rasinski, 2004); parents who used Fast Start saw their students make the greatest gains in reading in first grade (Rasinski, 1995). In a three-year longitudinal study, parental involvement made a substantial impact on children's reading fluency over children whose parents participated in a limited way or not at all (Crosby et al., 2015). Moreover, parents of both kindergarten and first-grade students perceived value in the lessons they provided their children. In addition, struggling readers made the most gains using the Fast Start protocol (Rasinski & Stevenson, 2005; Stevenson, 2001).

The Fast Start strategy (figure 4.7) includes easy-to-implement steps and a suggested resource. If you've been desiring to increase the read-at-home connection with parents as a means to increase fluency, consider the evidence-based Fast Start protocol.

Strategy: Fast Start

Pillar: Fluency

Grade Level:	**Instructional Grouping:**	**Consider This:**
☑ K ☑ 1 ☑ 2 ☐ 3 ☐ 4 ☐ 5 ☐ 6	☐ Whole Group ☐ Small Group ☑ Individual	• Select texts with a lot of variety, including poems, songs, nursery rhymes, and very brief text. • Provide simple directions for parents and model the activity via a video to which you can direct parents. Perhaps post the video on your classroom website. • Time commitment for parents is 10-15 minutes per night. • Scholastic produces a resource for this activity, *Fast Start for Early Readers*, by Nancy Padak and Tim Rasinski (2005). It includes sixty reproducibles (poems and text) with activities for parents to do with their children and will save you lots of preparation time.

What is it? Fast Start is a home-reading program in which parents or caregivers read brief selections each day with their child, listen to their child read, and engage in additional word study activities.

Figure 4.7: Strategy—Fast Start.

continued ▶

Why is it important? Supporting early readers by reading at home and engaging in brief, purposeful reading and word study activities can have positive results on fluency and literacy acquisition.

What works in the classroom?

Planning and Preparation

Provide texts for parents. Provide texts along with word study activities for parents or caregivers to do with children. It is recommended to primarily use poems, songs, or rhymes for reading.

Steps for Parents

- **The parent/caregiver reads the poem aloud:** The parent/caregiver reads the poem expressively several times (two to four times), sitting side by side with the child, and they point to the words as they read aloud.
- **Talk about meaning:** The parent/caregiver and child stop to talk about the poem and its meaning.
- **The child reads the poem aloud:** After a few times, the parent/caregiver invites the child to orally read the poem (two to four times) while pointing to each word. The adult can provide support and read in a quiet voice if needed (similar to the Neurological Impress Method strategy described later in this chapter). The parent/caregiver provides lots of feedback and praise.
- **Additional literacy connections:** After reading, the parent or caregiver engages in some type of phonemic awareness, phonics, or word study activity to extend the reading connections. Examples include:
    - *Phonics*—Find and circle words that begin with the same letter.
    - *Phonemic awareness*—Find words that begin with the same sound and read them aloud.
    - *Phonemic awareness*—Notice rhyming words and word families (for example, *-op*, *-ant*, -ess). The parent writes the words on the sheet and the parent and child read them aloud together.
    - *Word study*—Select a few words, talk about their meaning, and write them on a whiteboard, index cards, an iPad, or on the sheet where the poem is written. If the words are written on cards, they can be used for word sorts at a later time.

Extension

- **School connection:** Every so often, the teacher prints the poem, projects the poem, or records it on chart paper. The class reads the poem chorally, through echo reading, or in pairs. Students can also engage in word study.

Visit ***go.SolutionTree.com/literacy/FSK6*** *and enter the unique access code found on the book's inside front cover to access a reproducible version of this figure.*

Choral Reading

Choral reading is an oral reading strategy that supports students who are less fluent as well as English learners. Students read a text, poem, or song in unison with expression. A teacher or model reader may serve as the lead reader. Some students may be familiar with choral reading as a common practice in their worship setting. Others may not be, but it's very easy to implement and provides perfect support for struggling readers and English learners.

Choral reading, though frequently done in unison, can also include many variations that keep it interesting and motivating for students. For starters, selecting appropriate text is important. Look for texts, poems, and songs that have good rhythm and distinct parts for the following variations.

For primary students, the *You Read to Me, I'll Read to You* series of books by Mary Ann Hoberman are excellent choices. Two parts are clearly differentiated for groups *a* and *b*, and there is a choral refrain that all students can read together! You can view a brief video (https://youtu.be/ABgAr-igg80) featuring two first-grade students orally reading a poem titled "I Like" while taking the *a* and *b* parts displayed in the book. The remaining students join in and chorally read the refrain together.

For intermediate students, you can use poetry or texts that have historical value and align with your state standards. Historical selections such as the Gettysburg Address may be a good choice, since this type of reading includes unfamiliar language and thus promotes language development. You can view a brief video of students engaging in a choral reading of an excerpt from "Paul Revere's Ride" (https://youtu.be/NJLT7axMwz0). After rehearsing, one student takes the lead while the remaining students chorally read the refrain.

Resources for Choral Reading

- *You Read To Me, I'll Read to You Series* by Mary Ann Hoberman
  - *Very Short Stories to Read Together* (2006)
  - *Very Short Scary Tales to Read Together* (2009)
  - *Very Short Fairy Tales to Read Together* (2012)
  - *Very Short Mother Goose Tales to Read Together* (2012)
  - *Very Short Fables to Read Together* (2013)
  - *Very Short Tall Tales to Read Together* (2019)
- *Texts for Fluency Practice* by Timothy Rasinski and Lorraine Griffith (2005)
  - *Level A* (grade 1)
  - *Level B* (grades 2-3)
  - *Level C* (grades 4-8)

Try to routinely revisit previously selected texts or poems so that less-fluent readers can practice and build their confidence while chorally reading. If you're trying a variation, and students will be reading alone or with pairs, provide a copy of the text in advance and have students practice during small-group instruction and independently. You'll find a summary of choral reading in figure 4.8, along with several variations (Rasinski & Smith, 2018).

Strategy: Choral Reading

Pillar: Fluency

Grade Level:	Instructional Grouping:	Consider This:
☑K ☑1 ☑2 ☑3 ☑4 ☑5 ☑6	☑ Whole Group ☑ Small Group ☐ Individual	• Provide a brief introduction to the piece the group will be reading. • The activity will take about five to ten minutes depending on the length of text. • Consider sending some of the poems home so students can read them for fluency practice to a listener at home.

What is it? Choral reading is an oral reading strategy in which the teacher or lead reader leads a class or group of students in reading a text, poem, or song aloud in unison.

Why is it important? A well-rounded fluency program supports all readers, particularly those who need fluency practice. Choral reading provides a social and community setting that provides support while building students' fluency and self-confidence as readers. Through choral reading, all students can achieve fluency.

What works in the classroom?

Preparation

- Select a poem, brief text, or historical piece that would be appropriate for choral reading. If projecting, use a large font so students can easily see and read the text.
- For variations summarized in the next section, students should have a copy of the text/poem/script.

Choral Reading Variations

- **Unison:** Choral reading typically takes place with students reading a selected piece of text, poem, or song in unison with the teacher as the lead.
- **Line-a-child:** The group begins by reading the first few lines together. Then each student reads a line or two of text individually with the group reading the closing lines together. (You'll need to mark the text/poem carefully so students can follow along. You can vary the readers over time so all can participate as solo readers.)
- **Dialogue with narrator:** Similar to reader's theater, use a brief reader's theater script. A student or the teacher can be the narrator, and the class reads the dialogue portions together. Or, assign a few students to each character and have them read the character's lines together. (You'll need to mark the poem/script carefully so students can follow along.)
- **Solo line:** Poems work particularly well for solo line choral reading. Select a nursery rhyme or poem. The solo reader reads the first line of each stanza (boldface the line), and the class reads the remaining lines of the stanza. Students practice their solo line before the group choral reading so they are able to read expressively.

Figure 4.8: Strategy—Choral reading.

*Visit **go.SolutionTree.com/literacy/FSK6** and enter the unique access code found on the book's inside front cover to access a reproducible version of this figure.*

Paired Oral Reading Strategies

Oral reading practice is particularly important for improving reading fluency. Shanahan (2005), who served on the National Reading Panel, points out that of the fifty-one studies of oral reading fluency instruction that the NRP examined, there was a substantial pattern of evidence that teaching oral fluency improves reading achievement. He goes on to say that "research has consistently supported the positive impact of oral reading practice, while silent reading has had less consistent positive results" (Shanahan, 2005, p. 19). Put simply, we need to have struggling and striving readers engage in oral reading more often with varied texts and text levels, particularly with a more-skilled reader.

Educational researchers provide a historical review of oral reading practices pairing more-skilled and less-skilled readers (Downs, Mohr, & Young, 2023). Several methods that consistently show great promise with dysfluent readers include those shared in the following sections. These methods rely on a proficient reader, often the teacher or another adult, who provides a model of fluent reading for the student. All of these strategies share a fundamental trait—paired synchronous oral reading between a more-skilled reader and a less-skilled reader.

Paired Readers Protocol

Partner reading, also known as dyad reading, can be an effective literacy practice with a bit of consideration when creating pairs. Intentionally pairing students for maximum effectiveness is important and grounded in Vygotsky's (1978) Zone Of Proximal Development research because pairing provides a level of scaffolding for students (see the Gradual Release of Responsibility section, page 27). There is a preferred way to pair students for practice, and it is not randomly throwing students together and hoping for the best. It's also not pairing the very best readers with the most struggling readers, although that may seem like a good idea.

To begin, collect beginning-of-year (BOY) oral reading data and list each student's scores in order from least proficient to most proficient. In table 4.2, students' BOY grade-level reading scores range from 3.2 (third grade, month 2) to 4.8 (fourth grade, month 8) for a theoretical fourth-grade class. Note that readers with scores that indicate some struggle are paired with readers with higher scores.

Table 4.2: Intentional Paired Readers BOY Grade Level Reading Data

Fourth-Grade Students	
BOY Scores	**BOY Scores**
Jasmine 4.8	Brandon 3.8
Corbin 4.6	Jaclyn 3.7
Max 4.5	Victor 3.6
Elizabeth 4.4	Charleen 3.5
Taylor 4.3	Gregory 3.5
Phoenix 4.3	Ben 3.4
Colton 4.2	Tyson 3.4
Morgan 4.2	Beau 3.2
Heather 4.0	Charlotte 3.2
Molly 4.0	Andrew 3.1

I've used the paired readers' protocol for years with great success. I suggest using the following protocol (Fuchs, Fuchs, & Burish, 2000) for pairing readers in your own classroom (figure 4.9, page 152).

By following the simple steps in figure 4.10 (page 153), you'll have more purposeful pairs for fluency development and other paired literacy activities.

Strategy: Paired Readers Protocol

Pillar: Fluency

Grade Level:	Instructional Grouping:	Consider This:
☐ K ☑ 1 ☑ 2 ☑ 3 ☑ 4 ☑ 5 ☑ 6	☐ Whole Group ☐ Small Group ☑ Pairs of Readers ☐ Individual	• Follow the following steps to pair readers. However, keep an eye on students as they read together and remain fluid in regrouping students to create pairs that benefit both students.

What is it? The paired readers protocol is a method for pairing readers to support maximum effectiveness for both students.

Why is it important?

- When pairing students for literacy practice, we desire a good fit between the two students so that each benefits from the paired instructional activity.
- Some teachers may be inclined to pair the most able, expressive readers with struggling, word-by-word readers who need a lot of support. However, pairing good readers with poor readers usually results in a frustrating experience for both students. If you pair these two readers for oral reading, the proficient reader gets frustrated and typically takes over. The more-able reader often simply reads the text rather than taking turns in order to support the less-able reader.
- The suggested protocol creates student pairs that provides the most benefit to each reader.

What works in the classroom?

Steps for Pairing Students

1. **Students as readers:** Think about your students as readers, specifically their fluency skills.
2. **Data:** List appropriate data for each student.
3. **List students from the most able to struggling readers:** Using the tool for pairing readers (figure 4.10), begin the first column by listing the most able reader at the top, and keep listing students from the most able readers to least . Mid-level readers will be toward the bottom third of the first column and the top third or so of the second column until that column ends with the most struggling readers.
4. **Pair students:** Now pair students across the columns from one another. Using this format, the most able readers will be paired with mid-level readers who have some fluency skills but could still benefit from reading with highly skilled, fluent readers. And mid-level readers will be paired with more struggling readers. The mid-level reader will likely not be frustrated by students who read with less proficiency. Using this protocol, all students experience challenge without the frustration that sometimes accompanies pairing (Alexander, 2024).
5. **Model expectations:** Pairing students using this method will set up both students for a successful experience. Along with modeling expectations, students will be better suited so that both benefit from the paired reading experience.

Figure 4.9: Strategy—Paired readers protocol.

Visit ***go.SolutionTree.com/literacy/FSK6*** *and enter the unique access code found on the book's inside front cover to access a reproducible version of this figure.*

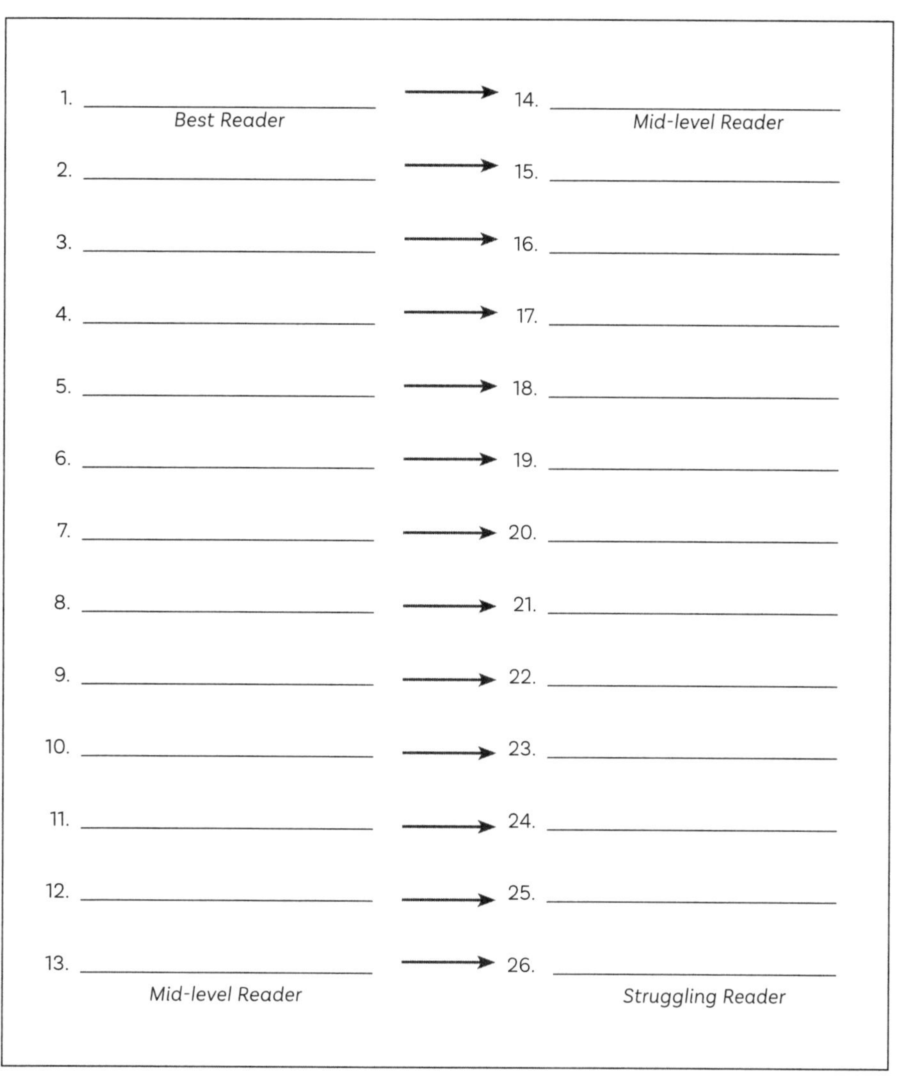

Figure 4.10: Tool for pairing readers.

Visit ***go.SolutionTree.com/literacy/FSK6*** *for a free reproducible version of this figure.*

Dyad Reading Strategy

Dyad reading is a form of paired reading in which a lead reader (more-skilled reader) and an assisted reader (less-skilled reader) read chorally side by side. It is an effective means for building fluency skills for the less-skilled reader. It follows a stricter protocol than some paired reading models, including how to pair readers, which aligns with the paired reading protocol described in the previous section. Dyad reading can take many different forms, including the following.

- Teacher and student
- Aide and student

- Parent, caregiver, or volunteer and student
- Students from different grade levels (such as a fourth-grade student and a second-grade student)
- Students of different reading proficiency levels

Figure 4.11: Dyad reading intentionally pairs a more-skilled reader and a less-skilled reader.

Dyad reading, as shown in figure 4.11, is a paired reading strategy that provides a protocol for practicing oral reading skills and provides support for students who need to develop their fluency skills. Dyad reading is not nearly as intensive as the Neurological Impress Method, described later in the section, which is directed by the teacher or interventionist.

Researchers J. Lloyd Eldredge and D. William Quinn (1988) show dyad reading to be an effective reading strategy by closely monitoring the reading growth of second-grade students. After nine months of dyad reading, second graders who were poor readers achieved nearly one more year's growth in reading achievement on the Gates-MacGinitie Reading Tests when compared with sixty-one poor readers who did not participate in dyad reading. And, twenty-seven of the thirty-two students in the experimental group who participated in regular dyad reading scored on or above grade level when compared with only six of the thirty-two control group students. They even found that less-skilled readers could make quicker progress by reading materials with the skilled reader that were two grade levels above their instructional level.

In another qualitative dissertation study with second-grade students learning English, Michelle Lynn Klvacek (2015) finds that a quality paired reader match is important. She also finds that teachers need a good amount of books to maintain student interest. Students expressed an increase in confidence in their reading skills and reported liking the nonfiction selections more than fiction (students read equal amounts of fiction and nonfiction). Klvacek (2015) also reports that, with second graders, dyad reading or "follow the reader" required more repeated modeling than she had anticipated. I suggest providing ongoing modeling with fiction and nonfiction text in order for students to gain benefit from paired reading.

Finally, it is understandable that we look carefully at the impact of strategy instruction on striving readers' reading improvement. However, it is important to also look at skilled reader development. In a study of dyad reading with third-grade students, researchers (Brown et al., 2018) find skilled and less-skilled readers make reading gains when compared to a control group. Additionally, they find that less-skilled readers make the most gains when reading text two grade levels above their instructional levels.

Please see figure 4.12 for simple steps in dyad reading.

Strategy: Dyad Reading

Pillar: Fluency

Grade Level:	Instructional Grouping:	Consider This:
☐K ☐1 ☑2 ☑3 ☑4 ☑5 ☑6	☐ Whole Group ☐ Small Group ☑ Pairs of Readers ☐ Individual	• Model dyad reading with a reader for students to observe and follow. Consider making an anchor chart with simple steps to follow. • To pair students, use the paired reader protocol shown earlier in this chapter. • Reading material should include both expository and narrative text selections. Preferably, text should be at the instructional level (90–95 percent accuracy in word recognition) of the more-proficient reader. This means the less-skilled reader will be reading more challenging material than typical.

What is it? Dyad reading, sometimes called "duolog reading," is a form of reading where two readers, one more proficient and one less, read together chorally.

Why is it important? The less-proficient reader experiences side-by-side choral reading with a supportive and more-skilled reader who can model appropriate speed, accuracy, and meaningful expression. It also provides a means of reading more challenging text.

What works in the classroom?

Teacher/Aide and Student

- **Provide a selection of books:** Provide several options of books from which the striving reader may choose. It may be at the student's frustration level. It's also helpful if the books are of interest to the reader.
- **Introduce the book:** Provide a brief introduction to the book and have a conversation with the students while previewing the book.
- **Read together:** For a brief segment, read together for about five to ten minutes. Read at a moderate pace, neither too fast or too slow.
- **Guide below the text:** Use your hand or finger as a guide as you read orally. Make sure your hand or finger is below or touching each word as you read so the striving reader can match the spoken word with the written word. The purpose is for striving readers to match text/print with pronunciation.
- **Read slightly louder than the student:** While reading, don't hesitate to read slightly louder than the student.
- **Comprehension conversation:** Always complete the choral reading session by talking about the text to support comprehension.

Student (More-Able Reader) and Student (Less-Able Reader)

- **Reading options:** With students, provide some options for them to read that are at the instructional level of the lead reader.
- **Talk about the book:** Have students begin by talking about the book, what they notice, and why they selected it.
- **Read together:** Students read together for a brief segment, no longer than about ten minutes in total. The skilled reader should not read too fast or too slow.
- **Guide below the text:** The skilled reader should use their hand or finger as a guide as students read orally. Their hand or finger should touch or be below the word they are reading so the less-able reader can match the spoken word with the written word.
- **Comprehension conversation:** Students complete the choral reading session by talking about the text. If students need support, you can develop or co-develop a brief protocol that students can follow to respond to text following reading.

Figure 4.12: Strategy—Dyad reading.

*Visit **go.SolutionTree.com/literacy/FSK6** and enter the unique access code found on the book's inside front cover to access a reproducible version of this figure.*

Neurological Impress Method

The Neurological Impress Method (NIM; Heckelman, 1969) is an essential intervention strategy designed to support struggling and striving readers. R. G. Heckelman, a psychologist, developed NIM with the purpose of helping struggling and striving readers become fluent readers through repeated reading with a model reader. In her research, Heckelman (1969) finds NIM to have positive effects on students' overall reading ability. In fact, one student made gains of nearly six grade levels in six weeks with numerous fifteen-minute sessions a week. Numerous literacy researchers have also had positive results using NIM with elementary and secondary students (Eldredge, 1990; Eldredge & Quinn, 1988; Henk, 1981; Topping, 1987; Young, Durham, & Rosenbaum-Martinez, 2018).

NIM is a powerful strategy in which the model reader (typically a teacher or paraprofessional) reads aloud by the student's ear slightly louder and faster than the student until the student is confident to read the text independently. I've implemented NIM with great success in my work with struggling readers in several clinical settings, reading clinics, and in my private practice, and it's been a privilege to watch students' skills grow along with their confidence. Probably my favorite star student was my son, who struggled with fluency. To this day, *Mañana, Iguana* by Ann Paul holds a special place in our hearts because it was the primary picture book that we used over and over again using NIM. My son's confidence and fluency skills grew, as did our love for the beautifully illustrated and lively picture book.

If you'd like to see NIM in action, view the brief video of me reading with a first-grade struggling reader using the NIM strategy (https://youtu.be/3dG8z8N06Y0). After introducing the book and briefly previewing, you'll see us reading together (1:00 in the clip) as I run my finger beneath the text and read slightly louder and faster than the student, both NIM protocols. Specific steps and tips are included in the NIM strategy (figure 4.13).

Repeated Reading Strategies

Repeated reading is the primary instructional strategy that supports fluency development. It was first articulated by S. Jay Samuels (1979) who notes that students greatly improve their fluency when they read a short passage of fifty to two hundred words several times, both silently and aloud, until they obtain sufficient rate and accuracy. Later, students should also receive feedback from an adult and use skills like goal setting and self-monitoring.

Research clearly shows the power of repeated reading to improve fluency and comprehension. Betty Ann Levy, Andrea Nicholls, & Dafna Kohen (1993) report that students in grades 3–5 reading on grade level and below grade level increased their error detection and comprehension through repeated reading. Several researchers conducted a meta-analysis in which they reviewed many research studies that looked at the effect of repeated reading on fluency.

Strategy: Neurological Impress Method

Pillar: Fluency

Grade Level:	Instructional Grouping:	Consider This:
☑K ☑1 ☑2 ☑3 ☑4 ☑5 ☑6	☐ Whole Group ☐ Small Group ☐ Pairs of Readers ☑ Individual	• Select a text at the student's instructional level. Ideally, choose a text that is interesting to the student. • As the student progresses, consider a slightly more challenging text, which is possible because you are side-by-side supporting the student. • This strategy is fairly intense and should be used for about ten minutes with primary students and slightly longer for intermediate students.

What is it? NIM is a multisensory oral reading fluency intervention for striving readers that involves paired choral reading.

Why is it important? Striving readers need proficient fluency models and side-by-side support as they practice and improve their fluency skills.

What works in the classroom?

Before Reading

- **Preview the text:** Prior to reading, preview the text, picture book, or trade book selection. To begin, the book or text selection should be at the student's instructional level. As the student progresses, have the student choose from several more challenging text selections or books.

During Reading

- **Sit side by side with the student:** Sit next to the student so that you and the student can share a text. The student should be able to see and hear the words you are reading as your finger or hand follows below the text.
- **Read aloud with the student:** Here is where the magic happens.
  - **Read the text aloud:** Use your finger or hand to indicate where you are reading.
  - **Read slightly louder and slightly faster than the student as you read together:** Make a conscious effort to read into the student's left ear, "imprinting" the sound-symbol correspondence for the student. (The student will typically read more slowly and try to keep up with your pace. Adjust your speed based on the student's rate, slowing down and speeding up appropriately.)
  - **As the student's fluency and confidence improves, gradually switch roles:** Slowly lower your voice so that the student's voice is more prominent while you follow the student's lead until the student is reading independently. If the student isn't quite ready, shift back into the role of model reader.

After Reading

- **Comprehension conversation:** Always talk about the text or book following reading to connect the dots for the student. Reading IS meaning.

Figure 4.13: Strategy—Neurological Impress Method.

*Visit **go.SolutionTree.com/literacy/FSK6** and enter the unique access code found on the book's inside front cover to access a reproducible version of this figure.*

While repeated reading can take various instructional forms, the goal is always to increase reading rate, accuracy, and prosody. For example, repeated reading is a foundational aspect of reader's theater. Some criticize reader's theater because they think that it only has a positive fluency impact on the text in front of students, but that's not the case. Two meta-analyses by William J. Therrien (2004) and Jiyeon Lee and So Yoon Yoon (2017) find strong transfer benefits for repeated reading to new, unrehearsed text. Additionally, repeated reading is also fundamental to echo reading, in which a student or group of students echoes the teacher or another proficient reader. In this chapter, you'll find several additional strategies that are built on repeated reading. These include read-listen-reflect along with radio reading, reader's theater, and the fluency development lesson.

While repeated reading is an effective instructional strategy to improve fluency, Rasinski (2006) cautions us that repeated reading for the sole purpose of improving accuracy and rate misses the mark. At the heart of fluency is comprehension, meaning that fluency practice should be coupled with a focus on comprehension. When guiding readers, we should always return to the meaning of the text, rather than focusing on rate, accuracy, and prosody alone. The following strategies are enjoyable for students while at the same time include a large dose of repeated reading and support for readers as they grow in their fluency.

Read, Listen, Reflect Strategy

While the proliferation of repeated reading research and observations are accomplished without tapping into technology, Ness (2017) merged the power of technology with repeated reading. Read-listen-reflect, the first strategy in this section, is the result of incorporating iPad tablets into the repeated reading process through the power of video self-modeling, which is the simple act of students recording themselves for the purpose of reflecting in order to improve their performance.

Using the iPad, Ness (2017) focuses on video self-modeling to improve fluency through self-reflection with third-grade students. She notes that, even though she implemented this strategy with third-grade students, students in even lower grades were able to record themselves using the iPad. She finds that the iPads and self-reflection motivate students as they self-selected text to improve their fluency through practice.

Find steps for read-listen-reflect (adapted from Ness, 2017) in the strategy detailed in figure 4.14.

While read-listen-reflect is a fluency development strategy that uses technology to support repeated reading, it can also be connected to the before-, during-, and after-reading processes described in chapter 6. I would suggest also connecting the reading processes to student's self-reflection, which is also included in the reflection form.

Strategy: Read-Listen-Reflect

Pillar: Fluency

Grade Level:	Instructional Grouping:	Consider This:
☐ K ☐ 1 ☑ 2 ☑ 3 ☑ 4 ☑ 5 ☑ 6	☐ Whole Group ☐ Small Group ☐ Pairs of Readers ☑ Individual	• Initially, help students choose appropriate text or provide text for students at their instructional or independent reading level.

What is it? Read-listen-reflect uses technology, such as an iPad, as students engage in repeated reading with text. Through video self-modeling, students are able to self-reflect on their performance and improve fluency.

Why is it important? As mentioned previously, repeated reading is an evidence-based strategy to improve students' fluency. Tapping into technology while implementing repeated reading is also effective. Additionally, building metacognitive skills applies not only to fluency but also to all aspects of learning.

What works in the classroom?

Model this strategy before students record themselves. Specifically, model how to mark errors in reading.

Record

- **Read:** Students read a brief text passage at their independent or instructional reading level. They should need minimal assistance.
- **Record:** Students record themselves while reading.

Listen

- **Listen:** Readers view and listen to their recording as they note their accuracy, automaticity, and prosody. Encourage students to listen to their recording more than once.
- **Mark errors:** Students mark their errors and pay attention to prosody and intonation, as well as punctuation. Errors students mark include—
    - Omitting a word
    - Substituting a word
    - Inverting the order of words
    - Inserting a word not in the text

Reflect

- **Evaluation:** Students complete a brief evaluation and set goals for the next rereading. The Reading Checklist, shown beside, provides fluency aspects for students to think about during self-reflection.
- **Feedback:** The teacher, peers, and a proficient reader can also provide feedback to the student.

Name: ______________________ **Date:** ____________

Title of the Text: ______________________

Watch your video. Think about your own reading. Ask yourself these questions.

	Well Done	Needs Improvement
Did I take my time and read at the appropriate pace?		
Did I pay attention to punctuation and what it means?		
Did I sound expressive?		
Did I pause at the correct places?		
Did I read clearly?		
Did I say each word correctly?		
Did I self-correct if I made a mistake?		

I made ______ mistakes (fill in the number). Next time, I'm aiming for ______ mistakes (fill in the number).

It took me ______ seconds (fill in the number). Next time, I'm aiming for ______ seconds (fill in the number).

Here's where I ran into trouble:

Here's my plan for next time to address that trouble:

Other comments I want to make about my video:

Extension

- **Re-record:** Students re-record text until they select a "showcase" video.
- **Showcase videos:** The showcase video is uploaded to a private YouTube channel where parents or caregivers can view the videos and write encouraging comments under videos.

Figure 4.14: Strategy—Read-listen-reflect.

*Visit **go.SolutionTree.com/literacy/FSK6** and enter the unique access code found on the book's inside front cover to access a reproducible version of this figure.*

Radio Reading Strategy

Radio reading (Opitz & Rasinski, 1998; Rasinski, 2010) is another instructional approach that has repeated reading at its core. Today, it might be more appropriately named news anchor reading or YouTube reading because I doubt many students have experience listening to readers on the radio. Radio reading differentiates itself from some other strategies because readers practice and rehearse in order to read like a radio (or news) announcer, emphasizing aspects of prosody, including tone and phrasing, to create interest and engagement in the news story.

Figure 4.15 includes my suggestions for implementing radio reading with students. You can also view two students engaging in an animated radio reading on my YouTube channel (https://youtu.be/z0IHoPDqwYc). The students featured in the video selected a sports reporting script from a snippet included in *National Geographic Kids* magazine. The steps to implement radio reading are simple, and I think you'll find that students enjoy performing while improving their tone, phrasing, and reading with meaning.

Radio reading is a fun, personalized, and energetic experience for students. It allows students to select reading material that interests them, provides an audience, and creates the venue for students to practice and reread with purpose.

Reader's Theater Strategy

Reader's theater, one of my favorites, is an instructional approach in which students expressively read a script aloud for performance purposes. It is a fun and entertaining way to engage students in repeated reading to increase fluency. After practicing a script repeatedly, students read and perform for their classmates or special guests by reading orally directly from the script. Reader's theater should be one strategy, along with other fluency strategies, to support students. In an interview with Jen Serravallo (2023b), Tim Rasinski notes that reader's theater not only improves automaticity, prosody, and expression, but readers' comprehension, word recognition, and accuracy also improve.

Curriculum series frequently include reader's theater scripts here and there; in my professional judgment, however, it's not frequent enough to move the dial to improve fluency. For improvement to occur, reader's theater should be implemented in a regular and ongoing fashion along with other fluency strategies. Ongoing use of reader's theater, as described in this section, is better in terms of achieving changes in fluency.

Not only do gains in fluency transfer to unfamiliar, unrehearsed text (Lee & Yoon, 2017; Therrien, 2004), but overall reading comprehension and reading achievement also improve (NICHD, 2000a; Rasinski, Reutzel, Chard, & Linan-Thompson, 2011; Rasinski & Hoffman, 2003; Therrien, 2004), especially with students with learning disabilities (Stevens et al., 2017). I'm intentionally repeating this important finding. *Not only does repeated reading improve fluency and comprehension on the selected text the*

Strategy: Radio Reading

Pillar: Fluency

Grade Level:	Instructional Grouping:	Consider This:
☐ K ☐ 1 ☑ 2 ☑ 3 ☑ 4 ☑ 5 ☑ 6	☐ Whole Group ☑ Small Group ☑ Pairs of Readers ☑ Individual	• Radio reading can be done individually, with a pair of readers, or in small groups of three to five students. • Allowing students to choose the text is highly motivating (Tompkins, 2006). Radio reading lends itself to students' selecting texts that interest them and that their classmates would want to listen to! Scripts can be from trade books you have in the classroom library or school library as well as magazines and newspapers. • Although props aren't necessary, students enjoy using a large, handheld microphone (pretend or a non-functioning microphone) as they're reading their part.

What is it? Radio reading is a fluency strategy that includes repeated reading and expressive reading to create meaning and engage an audience.

Why is it important? Repeated reading is fundamental for increasing fluency, and strategies that help students improve their tone, expression, and pacing are important. Providing an audience encourages rehearsal and practice!

What works in the classroom?

Preplanning Steps

- **Model:** Model radio reading as a read aloud for students. Select a high-interest piece that lends itself well to expression, tone, and phrasing.
- **Distribute scripts:** Distribute scripts during small-group instruction or allow students to select a script or piece of text. Highlight each student's part or assign parts as you deem appropriate according to reading proficiency.
- **Read the text:** Have students read the text silently. Read the text aloud to or with the students.
- **Practice:** Students should have a few days to practice the text independently or with a partner. Encourage them to take the text home to practice it there as well, reading to a family member (or pet). Students can adopt the voice or tone of a newscaster or just read expressively.

Performance Day

- **Sign-up:** I prefer sign-up sheets so that when students think they're ready to perform, they sign up, indicating they have practiced and are ready to read their script aloud.
- **Perform:** Students—pairs or small groups—perform their script for the class using their best expression and tone! (If students encounter any pronunciation issues, support them as discreetly as possible.)
- **Notice and note:** Have classmates pair up and share what they noticed about the performance, then have a discussion focused on primarily positive feedback.
- **Assess comprehension:** You can choose to have students develop a few comprehension questions prior to the performance or just lead a discussion about the text.

Post-Performance

- **Discussion:** If you've organized this around small instructional groups, the next time you meet, offer encouragement, debrief, and talk about the performance.

Figure 4.15: Strategy—Radio reading.

Visit ***go.SolutionTree.com/literacy/FSK6*** *and enter the unique access code found on the book's inside front cover to access a reproducible version of this figure.*

student is practicing, but fluency and comprehension also improve when reading new, unrehearsed text selections. Repeated reading has a positive impact!

To see reader's theater in action, you can check out a fun, multi-grade reader's theater of "The Three Wishes," a folktale play, on my YouTube channel (https://youtu.be/SHi7OKuxadc). In this performance, there were six parts, including three narrators. Notice a few things as you watch. First, you'll see that students are wearing name tags with their part written on the nametag. You'll also notice each student steps forward and states their role before the presentation begins.

Organizing reader's theater and the scripts you select will be dependent on the grade and reading levels of your students. One of my favorite resources for intermediate students is the *Stand Up and Speak Out* series by National Geographic Learning, which features historical fiction reader's theater. The series is made up of content-based chapter books designed with parts and narrator roles for reader's theater. Since they are chapter books, you could assign different students roles from each chapter to continue the story.

Titles include *The War of the Roses,* about obtaining women's right to vote, and *A Road to Freedom,* which chronicles the events of a family who helped slaves find freedom through the Underground Railroad. You can view a brief reader's theater with several students performing *Divided Loyalties,* which tells the story of the turmoil a colonial family faces as they decide whether they should support the Patriot cause or the Loyalist cause. You'll notice in this reader's theater that there are no props and that students are seated for the performance (https://youtu.be/MRAFRKIrZR8). There are many great resources available online and through publishers (see examples on page 165). Many scripts are free and available to download.

In the reader's theater strategy (figure 4.16), you'll find a suggested implementation plan that I've used with teachers. While there is no perfect plan, you'll want to make certain that reader's theater is part of an integrated plan to improve fluency through regular and ongoing practice.

Reader's theater is a lively repeated reading strategy that engages readers who range from emerging skills through proficiency. Its structure and audience provide the opportunity to practice with purpose.

The Fluency Development Lesson Strategy

The Fluency Development Lesson (FDL) strategy, as developed by Rasinski (2010), is a single whole-group lesson that includes a short passage (predictable poems, story segments, or other 50–200 word selections) that is read aloud expressively by the teacher. Then, students read and reread the text or poem with group support using a specific protocol. This strategy is based on the well-documented premise that repeated reading improves fluency, and it is one of my personal favorite whole-group strategies because it provides energetic fluency practice for primary students. FDL is fast-paced

Strategy: Reader's Theater

Pillar: Fluency

Grade Level:	**Instructional Grouping:**	**Materials:**
☐ K ☑ 1 ☑ 2 ☑ 3 ☑ 4 ☑ 5 ☑ 6	☐ Whole Group ☑ Small Group ☐ Pairs of Readers ☐ Individual	• I save my name badges from conferences and collect them from others. Then, I print the name of characters and narrators and slide them into the badge holders. Students wear these on performance day and always seem to enjoy it. You can see students wearing these in the YouTube videos. • Folders for scripts • Simple props (optional) **Consider This:** • Before the performance begins, students step forward and introduce themselves and their role in the script.

What is it? Reader's theater is a lively, entertaining performance activity that provides opportunities for students to engage in repeated reading, which helps build oral reading fluency.

Why is it important? Students need many opportunities to engage in repeated reading, a strategy known to improve fluency. Reader's theater is a strategy that provides the motivation for students to reread for a purpose and another opportunity for them to engage in fluency practice.

What works in the classroom?

A Quick Guide to Organizing Reader's Theater

Scripts

- **Resources:** There are many online resources to find scripts, many of which are free. Picture books can also be reformatted into scripts fairly easily for classroom use.
- **Folders for scripts:** I suggest printing scripts and stapling them inside simple colored folders. Highlight each student's part in the script. Label the front of the folder with the title of the script. With this simple prep, you'll be able to use the scripts repeatedly. It also lends to the performance aspect and provides something for students to hang onto so they don't drop scripts during the performance. You can see students holding folders with scripts inside in the multi-age reader's theater "The Three Wishes" video.
- **Assigning scripts:** Don't be too concerned about the reading level for each character or narrator. As a whole group or during small-group instruction, you'll introduce the script and read through it with students. With lots of practice and motivation, many students can perform scripts that exceed their independent reading level.

Props

- You can choose whether to include props. They are not necessary; however, some teachers keep a basket of items that can be easily incorporated into performances.

FLUENCY

Figure 4.16: Strategy—Reader's theater.

continued ▶

Weekly Cycle

The suggested organization allows for all students to engage in reader's theater every week with a Monday to Friday cycle.

- **Preplanning:** Have a script printed for each student with parts highlighted. All students will perform from the same script. Divide students into groups, the amount depending on the number of parts and narrators in the script.
- **Monday:** Introduce the reader's theater script for the week. Provide any background information necessary to build context. Read the script aloud to students while they follow along. Distribute scripts to students with their individual parts highlighted.
- **Tuesday–Thursday:** Students practice with partners, perhaps during small-group instruction, and receive feedback. If students are practicing around the room, it's the perfect opportunity to circulate and provide specific, immediate feedback and encouragement to students. Additionally, students also take scripts home and practice there.
- **Friday:** Each Friday is performance day. Typically groups meet together for about fifteen to twenty minutes to practice the script together before the performance, then each group has an opportunity to perform the script for the class and any other visitors. It's a perfect time to invite parents and caregivers, another class, the principal, instructional coaches, or the librarian. With technology, you could also record students and upload onto a private blog that parents could view.

Feedback

- Self-reflection, a metacognitive behavior, can easily be included following a reader's theater performance. In the image shown, you'll see a rubric well suited for early readers to provide feedback.
- You may want to create a more in-depth evaluation to use with students in grades 3-6.

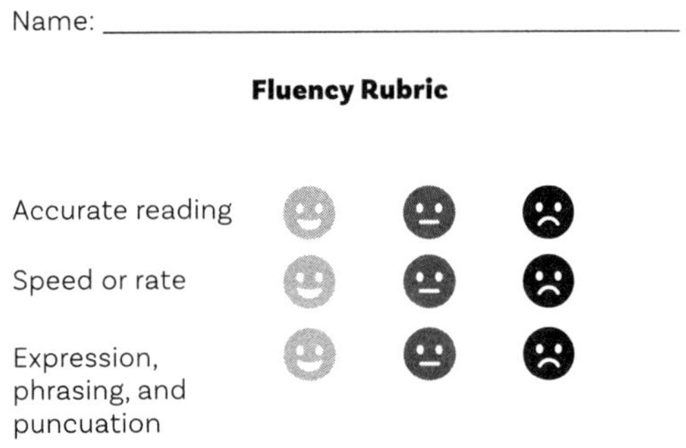

Name: ______________________

Fluency Rubric

Accurate reading	🙂	😐	☹
Speed or rate	🙂	😐	☹
Expression, phrasing, and puncuation	🙂	😐	☹

Variation

- **Paired poetry performance:** You can vary reader's theater in many ways. For example, students can read poetry as a paired performance. They practice independently, together, and then perform on Friday or even at the end of the literacy block since the performance is brief. View a paired performance with two second-grade students on my YouTube channel (https://youtu.be/JVJR0aCAUEc). You'll notice the poetry pieces were stapled in a folder for ease and re-use.

*Visit **go.SolutionTree.com/literacy/FSK6** and enter the unique access code found on the book's inside front cover to access a reproducible version of this figure.*

and takes about fifteen to twenty minutes, in which students hear a model reader and then read the text or poem several times chorally and with a partner. However, the learning from this strategy doesn't end after in-class practice. Students are encouraged to take a copy of the selection home and read to a family member, the dog, or whoever will listen.

Resources for Reader's Theater

- Building Fluency Through Reader's Theater [Grades 1-2, 3-4, 5-6] themed sets, such as *Folk and Fairy Tales* by Teacher Created Materials
- Reader's theater themed sets by Benchmark Education (www.benchmarkeducation.com)
- *Just Right Plays: 25 Emergent Reader Plays Around the Year* by Carol Pugliano-Martin (1999)
- *Fluency Practice Read-Aloud Plays: Grades 1-2* by Kathleen M. Hollenbeck (2006)
- Reader's theater scripts from www.thebestclass.org/rtscripts.html
- Reader's theater scripts from www.aaronshep.com/rt/index.html
- Reader's theater scripts from www.teachingheart.net/readerstheater.htm
- Reader's theater scripts from www.mrsjudyaraujo.com/free-readers-theater-scripts

Selecting text is an important consideration, especially when using it to support choral or echo reading. When choosing texts for echo, choral, or another repeated reading strategy, I suggest selecting passages or poems that are interesting and can be read expressively. "Good Conduct," by Douglas Florian (2000), has been one of my favorite poems to use with students and to model FDL for teachers. The poem is brief—only ten lines—but lively. It includes juicy vocabulary such as *conduct*, *aloof*, *amuse*, and *jolt*, and I wrote the poem in large print on chart paper so that students could follow along as I modeled and expressively read the poem aloud using various voices.

Specific steps for FDL are detailed in figure 4.17 (page 166). Have fun with it!

In short, the Fluency Development Lesson is a lively whole-group activity that employs the teacher or a proficient reader who models fluency—appropriate speed, accuracy, and expressive reading—for students. It incudes repeated reading in a variety of forms, including choral reading, and supports readers who need fluency practice most.

Resources for Poetry

- *Big Talk: Poems for Four Voices* by Paul Fleischman (2008)
- *Everything is a Poem: The Best of J. Patrick Lewis* by J. Patrick Lewis (2014)
- *How to Write a Poem* by Kwame Alexander and Deanna Nikaido (2023)
- *Lemonade Sun: And Other Summer Poems* by Rebecca Kai Dotlich (1998)
- *National Geographic Book of Animal Poetry: 200 Poems with Photographs that Squeak, Soar, and Roar!* by J. Patrick Lewis (2012)
- *Meet Danitra Brown* by Nikki Grimes (1997)
- *My America: A Poetry Atlas of the United States* by Lee Bennett Hopkins (2000)
- *Say My Name* by Joanna Ho (2023)
- *Welcome to the Wonder House* by Rebecca Kai Dotlich and Georgia Heard (2023)
- *Where the Sidewalk Ends: The Poems and Drawings of Shel Silverstein* by Shel Silverstein (1974)

Strategy: Fluency Development Lesson

Pillar: Fluency

Grade Level:	**Instructional Grouping:**	**Consider This:**
☐ K ☑ 1 ☑ 2 ☑ 3 ☑ 4 ☑ 5 ☑ 6	☑ Whole Group ☑ Small Group ☐ Pairs of Readers ☐ Individual	• Carefully select a predictable poem or brief text selection. For example, the poem could simply be for enjoyment, or a text selection could be tied into a content unit of study and be broken into several segments and practiced over several days. • For primary students, I suggest writing the poem on chart paper. Students can return to the anchor charts and reread them independently or with a partner.

What is it? FDL is a whole-group lesson that takes place several times a week and includes modeling, repeated reading, and practice to build fluency. It includes brief passages (poems, story segments, or other 50–200 word selections) that students read and reread aloud using a specific protocol summarized as follows. FDL only takes fifteen to twenty minutes and includes modeling, choral reading, and repeated reading.

Why is it important? There are many ways to develop fluency; one of the primary strategies is repeated reading to build automaticity and fluency. FDL builds fluency using repeated reading both chorally and individually using high-quality texts, including poetry.

What works in the classroom?

Preplanning Steps

1. **Select poems:** Choose poems of all sorts—predictable, humorous, more sophisticated, and so on. Alternatively, select a brief text of 100–200 words, perhaps tied to a content unit of study. You can also select a longer text segment and divide it across several days.
2. **Record the text or poem:** I prefer printing the poem or text in large text on a chart paper, but you can also project it on a whiteboard.
3. **Make copies for students:** Make two copies of the text or poem, one for students to use in paired reading and one for students to take home.

Simple Steps

4. **Model:** Read a poem or text aloud several times using different voices or tones while students follow along. Have students talk about the meaning and what they noticed in terms of expression.
5. **Read and reread:** Invite students to read with you several times using variations of choral reading. For example, divide by boys and girls, front of the room and back of the room, students wearing blue and students in other colors. Don't think too hard and mix up the groups frequently!
6. **Pair up students to reread:** Immediately following the choral reading, have students read the selection to one another for five or ten minutes, taking turns in groups of two or three. Each student should read the text aloud three times, with the listener offering coaching comments and feedback. Circulate around the room and provide feedback and encouragement to students.

Extended Practice

7. **Students read to anyone who will listen:** Students take an extra copy of the poem home and read it to a family member, a bus driver, an aunt through FaceTime, or a willing dog—anyone who will listen. That person (or paw) signs the back of the poem and students return to school. When individual students acquire a specific number of signatures, they join the Lucky Listener Club. I've seen some teachers make a fluency bulletin board and post snapshots of students holding one of the poems.
8. **Discuss meaning and vocabulary:** Return to the text and discuss meaning along with vocabulary. In "Good Conduct," I highlighted the words *conduct*, *aloof*, *amuse*, and *jolt*. Students can also choose these words along with two or three additional words to add to their personal vocabulary journal or digital word bank. Additionally, play with words through a word sort or word ladder (see chapter 3, page 116).
9. **Students reread the previous day's poem or text:** The following day, students chorally reread the previous day's poem or passage.

Figure 4.17: Strategy—Fluency Development Lesson.

Visit ***go.SolutionTree.com/literacy/FSK6*** *and enter the unique access code found on the book's inside front cover to access a reproducible version of this figure.*

Wrapping It Up

Reading fluency is an important pillar and literacy skill serving to bridge the gap between word recognition and comprehension. In this chapter, I encouraged you to make fluency a dynamic part of your literacy block. Many fluency strategies are built on repeated reading, which a great deal of evidence suggests increases fluency and comprehension. Use the Leader's Lens (figure 4.18) to deepen your thought process and support teachers as you move forward. As you review the Five Key Takeaways (page 170), consider how you will integrate fluency strategies into daily instruction to support readers as you move forward to vocabulary, the next integral pillar tied to comprehension. Think about intentionality as it relates to your instruction and literacy environment as you consider the Five Key Next Steps (page 170).

Leader's Lens

Fluency

Consider the following supervision supports and classroom connections as you lead and guide teachers as they implement effective fluency instruction.

Supervision Supports	
Practical Research	• Have you shared practical fluency research with teachers? What do you consider essential to know? • Have teachers discussed the bridge analogy? How can you help teachers explore how fluency bridges the gap between decoding and comprehension?
Professional Development	• What do you consider essential professional development for fluency? • How would you support collaborative teams as teachers implement fluency practices within the literacy block? • How would you provide professional development for important assisted reader strategies for struggling readers? • Consider conducting teacher and interventionist training in the strategies, such as Neurological Impress Method and dyad reading, that support struggling readers.
Feedback and Expectations	• What expectations do you have for integrating fluency practice into the literacy block? • How would you provide feedback as teachers implement fluency strategies?
Financial Focus	• Is there money budgeted to provide materials that would be beneficial for fluency practice? • Is there money budgeted to provide classroom materials that could be used for fluency support?
Classroom Connections (Look-Fors)	
Literacy-Rich Environment	• Notice if there are fluency resources and materials to support fluency practice. • Are there paired reading books (fiction and nonfiction) to support paired reading?
Assisted Reading and Modeled Reading	• Notice teacher read alouds. Are the three dimensions of fluency explicitly mentioned—reading at an appropriate speed, phrasing, and expression? • Do students participate in choral reading and echo reading? • Notice if technology-assisted reading strategies are used purposefully
Paired Oral Reading Strategies	• Notice if teachers integrate Neurological Impress Method and dyad reading with struggling readers. • Notice if teachers are pairing students strategically according to the paired reading protocol.
Repeated Reading Strategies	• Notice if fluency instruction incorporates repeated reading strategies. • Do students participate in reader's theater? Consider providing resources for teachers to support reader's theater.

Figure 4.18: Chapter 4 leader's lens.

Visit ***go.SolutionTree.com/literacy/FSK6*** *for a free reproducible version of this figure.*

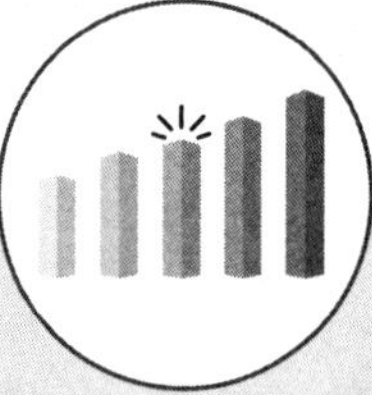

Five Key Takeaways

The following takeaways summarize the key elements in the chapter. Consider them individually or discuss them with your collaborative grade-level team.

1. **Oral reading fluency:** Oral reading fluency refers to the ability to read with accuracy, appropriate speed, and meaningful expression. Fluency is an important literacy pillar to regularly include as we develop proficient readers who comprehend well.
2. **Bridging the gap:** Fluency bridges the gap between word recognition and comprehension. Word-by-word, or dysfluent, readers spend most of their cognitive capacity sounding out each word with little energy left for comprehension. Fluent readers, in contrast, read automatically and with meaningful expression and phrasing. In doing so, they can focus their attention on comprehension—the heart of reading.
3. **Fluent readers:** Becoming a fluent reader is not only related to greater prosody, but it also includes comprehension and reading stamina. Increased comprehension and stamina typically motivate students to increase the time they spend reading, which, in turn, strengthens their reading and comprehension skills (Shanahan, Fisher, & Frey, 2012).
4. **Repeated reading:** Repeated reading is the primary manner in which we develop fluency. Instructional strategies in the chapter included assisted reading strategies, synchronous paired oral reading techniques, and repeated reading strategies.
5. **Fluency strategies:** Fluency strategies include choral reading, echo reading, paired reading, reader's theater, repeated reading strategies, FDL, radio reading, and others.

Five Key Next Steps

Consider the following questions individually or discuss them with your collaborative grade-level team.

1. **Read alouds:** Consider your read alouds in connection to fluency. Do you vary the type of text you read and intentionally slow down or speed up? Do you sometimes sound like different characters or vary your tone for emphasis?
2. **Paired reading:** Pairing readers for fluency practice is an effective strategy. Have you considered pairing students using the pairing protocol included in this chapter? Why or why not?
3. **Fluency development lesson:** Have you tried FDL? If so, what type of reading selections have you chosen to use? What has been your experience with the strategy?
4. **Reader's theater:** If you've implemented reader's theater, share with colleagues what you've learned and how students are progressing. Do you have a favorite source for scripts? Share with your collaborative team.
5. **Struggling reader strategies:** Consider implementing NIM and dyad reading with struggling readers and share your experience with your collaborative team members.

Key Vocabulary

Vocabulary

Direct Vocabulary Instruction	Instruction that includes identifying target vocabulary and explicitly teaching word meaning through examples, visuals, context, analogies, and more.
Expressive Vocabulary	Refers to those words we use when speaking and writing
Indirect Vocabulary Instruction	Indirect word learning includes lots of opportunities for students to experience and learn words indirectly. Examples include a print-rich environment that features books, word walls, posters, anchor charts, word games, digital tools, and language.
Linguistic Strategies	Refers to word-based vocabulary strategies
Nonlinguistic Strategies	Refers to vocabulary strategies that include images, symbols, mental pictures, skits, and pantomimes
Receptive Vocabulary	Those words we understand when we listen and read
Tiered Vocabulary	An organizational framework for categorizing words; the tiered framework includes three levels, with tier one being made up of everyday words and tiers two and three made up of academic words.
Vocabulary	Refers to the words we use to communicate effectively when we listen, speak, read, and write
Word Clusters	Refers to semantically related words
Word Gap	Refers to the vocabulary gap that exists when students enter school; this occurs because of differences in socioeconomic backgrounds.

CHAPTER 5

Vocabulary
Word Learning Matters

In settings where literacy achievement is going well, teachers flood the classroom with vocabulary and vocabulary instruction.

—Michael Pressley

The importance of a rich and broad vocabulary cannot be understated. It is well known that vocabulary knowledge is related to becoming a proficient reader (Ricketts, Nation, & Bishop, 2007; Wright & Cervetti, 2017) and general academic achievement (Graves, 2016). Building vocabulary begins in the home, and there is a wide divide among students' word knowledge as they enter school (MacDonald & Figueredo, 2010). Students with limited word knowledge are at a disadvantage to those students who have a broader, more diverse vocabulary.

Conservative approaches to vocabulary—such as teaching a limited number of words, typically prescribed by the curriculum—aren't sufficient to address the word gap many students experience. Edna Brabham, Connie Buskist, Shannon Coman Henderson, Timon Paleologos, and Nikki Baugh (2012) observe that "in settings where literacy achievement is going well, teachers flood the classroom with vocabulary and vocabulary instruction" (p. 523).

In this chapter, you'll find a wealth of information about vocabulary and its primary importance as a pillar of effective reading instruction. We begin by exploring the relationship between vocabulary and comprehension, what it means to know a word, and how to select and organize vocabulary for direct instruction. Next, we'll look at the characteristics of effective vocabulary instruction and easy-to-implement strategies for building vocabulary both directly and indirectly with your students. Finally, you'll be equipped with specific strategies for helping students acquire and deepen their understanding of new words. In the conclusion, you'll find the chapter's Five Key Takeaways and Five Key Next Steps along with the Leader's Lens reproducible tool. I hope you and your students will have fun with words and your classroom becomes flooded with resplendent word growth.

What Is Vocabulary?

Vocabulary can be defined in a myriad of ways. For the purposes of this discussion, let's keep it simple. *Vocabulary* "refers to the words we use to communicate effectively when we listen, speak, read, and write" (Tyson & Peery, 2017). However, taking an understanding of vocabulary a step further, it can be useful to think of words as existing in two discrete buckets—receptive vocabulary and expressive vocabulary. *Receptive vocabulary* includes those words we understand when we listen or read, while *expressive vocabulary* is made up of words that we use when we speak and write. We have many, many more words in our receptive vocabulary than in our expressive vocabulary. When intentionally developing vocabulary, our goal is to deliberately engage students in practice and review in order to shift words from receptive to expressive vocabulary. By doing so, our students will engage in higher-level conversation, increase comprehension, and improve their writing.

By the nature of this definition, we must provide ongoing opportunities for students to listen to both everyday language and specific, descriptive, and academic vocabulary coupled with opportunities to use their newly acquired words. Students need to hear vocabulary in oral conversation as well as engage with words within narrative and informational text. As students hear words repeatedly within varied contexts, they gain familiarity and the ability to begin using the words when they speak and write.

While each of the five pillars calls for specific instructional strategies to support students as they develop discrete skills, vocabulary is foundational to literacy learning. Emerging readers benefit greatly from vast amounts of oral language to build general everyday vocabulary and learn how language works. Vocabulary knowledge not only supports students as they make sound-letter connections but likewise also connects letters to words that carry meaning. As students progress through the grades, there is greater need for acquring specific content and academic vocabulary that supports recognizing words easily while reading and positively influences fluency. Additionally, word knowledge is critical to supporting comprehension as students connect what they know with what they are learning.

Why Is Vocabulary Important?

It can be argued that vocabulary is fundamental to the other four pillars. Understanding words, both general and academic, is critically important to listening and speaking. Word knowledge plays a pivotal role in comprehension as students read an increasing number of nonfiction texts as they progress through the grades. Since it is estimated that about 85 percent of comprehension relies on understanding vocabulary in content area texts, it stands to reason that if a student doesn't know the majority of the words in the text, the text is difficult to comprehend (Ibrahim, Sarudin, & Muhamad, 2016).

In the following sections, we examine the relationship of vocabulary to comprehension, the challenges common to vocabulary instruction, and the reasons why we know vocabulary can be taught.

Vocabulary's Relationship to Comprehension

Vocabulary has been the focus of decades of research that consistently show vocabulary knowledge is strongly correlated to reading comprehension. Vocabulary and comprehension are interconnected, so much so that the National Reading Panel reported that separating them "is difficult, if not impossible" (NICHD, 2000b, p. 239).

Developing vocabulary begins long before formal schooling through oral language and conversations. Oral language begins in the home and plays an important role in how children become familiar with language and how words work. We know there is a wide divide between the oral vocabulary of students from low-income families and those from middle-income and professional homes as evidenced in groundbreaking research by Betty Hart and Todd R. Risley (2003). Hart and Risley (2003) spent two and a half years observing forty-two diverse families, nearly equally divided among socioeconomic groups. They spent time with each family monthly, observing what went on as children were learning to talk. The amount of words children heard per hour was starkly different among the three groups. Children in professional families heard 382 different words per hour, compared to 251 words per hour in working-class families and 167 different words in the families with the lowest incomes. By age 3, children's vocabularies mirrored their parents. Children in the families of the lowest incomes used about half the words per hour (149 different words) than their counterparts (297 different words) living in homes of professional families.

Students who lack word knowledge are at a distinct disadvantage for many reasons, one of which is that early word knowledge is predictive of later reading comprehension. For example, kindergarten students' word knowledge predicts their reading comprehension in second grade (Catts, Fey, Zhang, & Tomblin, 1999; Roth, Speece, & Cooper, 2002) and fourth grade (Wagner, Muse, & Tannenbaum, 2007). Even more stunning,

Anne E. Cunningham and Keith E. Stanovich (1997) find first-grade students' word knowledge is a strong predictor of their reading comprehension in eleventh grade.

Based on Hart and Risley's (2003) research, an extrapolation from the averages of words children are exposed to results in the commonly used phrase *30 million word gap by age 3*. An average child in a professional family would have been exposed to 45 million words, a child in a middle-class family would have experience with 26 million words, and the average child in a welfare family may have experience with 13 million words, thus accounting for the 30 million word gap.

Clearly, the numbers are telling and substantially significant, and they provide a perfect formula for an ongoing game of catch-up from day one as students enter preschool or kindergarten. However, without intentional effort on the part of educators, these students will never make up their vocabulary deficits. Research surrounding the word gap shows the positive effects of reading to children from storybooks (Logan et al., 2019). Books include many more specific and diverse words than we use orally and can provide students with enriched vocabulary. Further, the results of reading with children can be extrapolated to five years before entering kindergarten. Parents who read one picture book with their child every day provide an estimated 78,000 words per year. Over the course of five years, that is a cumulative 1.4 million more words from reading than children who were never read to (Logan et al., 2019). Because of this finding, many public libraries have bags filled with books ready to be loaned to caregivers and parents.

Including *dialogic conversations*—thoughtful and structured processes to support students as they engage and respond to text—can be useful to teachers in helping students expand their understanding and use of oral language.

While spending time with phonemic awareness, phonics, fluency, and comprehension is important, these must be intentionally coupled with a heavy dose of purposeful vocabulary development. In the What Works in the Classroom? section (page 188), you'll find vocabulary and word learning strategies for both primary and intermediate students.

Helping students develop a broad and rich vocabulary is an intentional practice and one that needs a plan. Researchers (Ibrahim et al., 2016) recommend that teachers help students develop their knowledge of both low-frequency and high-frequency words. It is recommended that students continue to develop their knowledge of high-frequency words at a rate of 5,000 and 10,000 words each year and, at the same time, expand their knowledge of low-frequency words.

Finally, teachers need to play a more active role in creating awareness of the importance of vocabulary-related activities in building students' vocabulary size. By the end of this chapter, you should be well equipped to define a plan for yourself or with your collaborative team that creates in students a love (or at least enjoyment) of words and the ability to reap all the benefits of a rich vocabulary!

Challenges of Vocabulary Instruction

A limited vocabulary impacts comprehension particularly as students read more challenging text, but helping students make gains in their vocabulary is not always easy. Here we'll look briefly at a few of the challenges related to vocabulary instruction.

- **Oral language:** The size of children's vocabulary plays out specifically when they are learning to read. When following children from age three to third grade, researchers (NICHD, 2005) find that oral language plays both a direct and indirect role in word recognition. It will not surprise teachers of young children that students with limited oral language exposure often have poor phonological awareness, which impacts their ability to learn to read (Snyder & Downey, 1997). Many also have little understanding of how print and books function. Fill your classroom with print and elevated language; additionally, talk about words both casually and intentionally.
- **Vocabulary gap:** For students who have gaps in word knowledge, exposure to rich oral language is crucial for building vocabulary and reading skills since students who have large oral vocabularies learn to read more easily. Primary teachers play a significant role in helping make up the word gap some students have as they enter school. It's an important role and a doable one. For example, morning meetings are an ideal setting for sharing conversation and building word consciousness along with social skills. Conversations about daily activities, the calendar, the weather, and seasons are all ways to increase word knowledge within everyday context. Additionally, reading aloud from picture books supports word learning by introducing students to specific, unique vocabulary within narrative or informational text.

  Intermediate teachers have a responsibility to create a classroom that inspires word awareness as well. It is well substantiated that students with broad vocabularies tend to read more (Stanovich, 1986). Consequently, students who read more continue to grow their word knowledge through frequent exposure to new words. As students read more and become richer in word knowledge, the gap between good and poor readers widens over time and is often referred to as the Matthew effect (Stanovich, 1986), which I previously discussed in chapter 4 (page 137). Combat this trend by reading aloud to students, providing paired reading opportunities and audiobooks along with print books and materials students want to read.

- **Selecting vocabulary:** There are so many words to learn it can feel overwhelming to decide where to begin. In *Blended Vocabulary for K–12 Classrooms* (Tyson & Peery, 2017), Angela B. Peery and I go into depth regarding how to classify and select vocabulary. Our suggestions include general knowledge words (referred to as tier one vocabulary), words that appear in state standards, districtwide core vocabulary lists, words from literature and read alouds, and Spanish words in classrooms with English learners. Develop word lists, such as the one depicted in figure 5.1 with your collaborative team, taking into consideration your grade level, students, and content areas.
- **Lack of an instructional plan:** While planning effective vocabulary instruction takes time and effort, leaving vocabulary and word learning up to chance is not a plan, and the lack of a plan is one that ultimately harms students. While the curriculum is a guide for vocabulary, it's not enough to create a classroom flooded with words (Pressley, 2002), which is what many students need. I suggest a balanced approach to word learning that helps students expand and deepen their understanding of words and includes these three areas.

Figure 5.1: Posting Spanish and English words supports students.

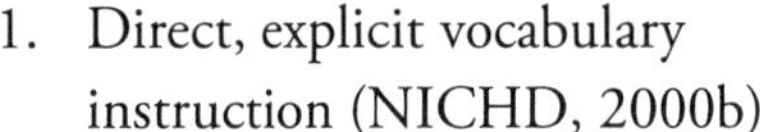

1. Direct, explicit vocabulary instruction (NICHD, 2000b)
2. A literacy-rich environment that includes lots of print and supports incidental word learning (NICHD, 2000b)
3. Modeling excellent word use and using digital tools to provide opportunities for practice and review (Tyson & Peery, 2017)

Vocabulary Can Be Taught

Vocabulary is one of the building blocks of language and impacts fluency, comprehension, and student achievement. Vocabulary instruction and ongoing practice must be intentional and consistent, using direct and indirect methods to help students build robust vocabularies. As educators, we must feel an urgency to teach and expose students to words. Direct instruction, oral language, and wide reading all contribute to vocabulary growth. We'll look at several models of word learning and viable places to begin your efforts, but first we'll examine what it means to truly *know* a word.

What It Means to Know a Word

As you target words for direct instruction, it can be helpful to know your students' familiarity with specific words. Gauging their understanding doesn't have to be complicated. However, it isn't as simple as having students think about words dichotomously as contained in two buckets of words, one labeled "know" and the other "don't know."

Rather, students should think of learning words as a gradual process. It is more accurate to think about knowing words (for students and adults) as falling on a continuum of understanding. The stages of word learning were developed by Edgar Dale (1965), an American researcher, and stand the test of time. Students at all grade levels can use these stages to think about their word knowledge, and the following activity can help you gauge students' knowledge of specific words prior to instruction. Even better, this continuum can be used with young learners as well as students in more advanced grades.

The four stages of word learning as described by Dale (1965) are shown in figure 5.2 and phrased with *I can* statements (read them beginning at the bottom with number 1).

Figure 5.2: Four stages of word learning.

You could describe the four stages using the analogy of raising the brightness on a smartphone or digital device such as an iPad. Similar to how raising the bar causes the screen to become brighter, multiple exposures to words helps deepen understanding over time. For example, the word *effusive* can move from stage 2 (having heard the word but not being able to provide the meaning) to stage 4 (being able to use it in conversation and writing) only after the person hears and reads the word in varied contexts, which helps form a rich and nuanced understanding of the word.

Let's look at an example specific to mathematics instruction for third-grade students. The target word is *trapezoid,* which the teacher writes on a whiteboard and pronounces. Students proceed to think about the term and determine at which stage of understanding they are. Each student could simply lift one to four fingers to represent their level of understanding as a quick formative assessment. If the teacher will be introducing numerous terms, students could use a chart (shown in the strategy table, figure 5.3) to record the words at the appropriate level.

Strategy: Four Stages of Word Learning

Pillar: Vocabulary

Grade Level:	**Instructional Grouping:**	**Consider This:**
☐ K ☑ 1 ☑ 2 ☑ 3 ☑ 4 ☑ 5 ☑ 6	☑ Whole Group ☑ Small Group ☐ Individual	• Prior to teaching this strategy, create a list of several target words related to a unit of study to use for modeling. • Create an anchor chart for reference. • Primary students: Draw or post a picture of a hand with four fingers held up. As you describe each stage of understanding words, write a brief explanation by each of the four fingers. • Intermediate students: Create a simple chart or a template (see the following) that students can access in print or on a laptop or digital tablet.

What is it? The four stages of word learning is a way of thinking about how well we know and can use specific words. Students can use this strategy to help them think about or gauge their understanding of words. The four stages can also help teachers get a sense of students' overall understanding of specific terms prior to reading or studying a content unit.

Why is it important? It is helpful for students to understand that, when learning new words, their understanding will gradually deepen over time. As they hear and read words repeatedly across contexts over time, they'll deepen their understanding and be able to use the word themselves.

What works in the classroom?

- **Talk about the four stages:** Have a discussion about the four stages of word learning and provide examples for each stage. Consider using the screen brightness analogy to demonstrate how we understand words better as we continue to hear them used and read them repeatedly.
- **Create an anchor chart:** With students, develop an anchor chart listing each stage and what it means.

Early Learners

- **Raise fingers to represent stages:** To provide practice with early learners, have students display their understanding of each target word by raising one to four fingers.

One finger
I don't know the word; I've never heard the word.

Two fingers
I think I've heard the word, but I don't really know what it means.

Three fingers
I think I might be able to put the word in a category.

Four fingers
I know this word! I can use it when I'm talking and writing.

- **Read aloud tie-in:** As you read informational picture books aloud and target specific vocabulary, consider having students think about and display their understanding using fingers on their hand.

Intermediate Students

- **Discuss the four stages:** Have a discussion about the four stages of word learning and provide examples for each stage. Record your knowledge of the words on the chart the students will use. Consider using the screen brightness analogy discussed previously.
- **Record understanding using a chart:** For intermediate students, I suggest that they use a simple chart, which follows, to think and record their understanding of specific words.

Title or Content: ______________________________

Directions: Read the words at the bottom of the page or on the whiteboard. After you read each one, write the word in the column that best describes how much you know about each one.

Stage 1	Stage 2	Stage 3	Stage 4
I don't know the word at all.	I have seen or heard the word; I don't know the meaning.	I think I know the meaning (I might know the meaning in context).	I know the meaning.

- **Select academic words and provide practice:** Provide practice for students using academic words from a chapter or unit of study.
- **Provide definitions:** As you display and orally read each word, provide a brief definition or synonym.
- **Students record words:** Students record the word in the category on the template that best describes their knowledge of each word.
- **Note students' record of familiarity with vocabulary:** Circulate the room to get a sense of which categories represent your students' understanding. You'll get a good idea of students' familiarity with the content words prior to teaching the unit of study.
- **Revisit the stages periodically:** Consider having students use this template at the beginning of some content units of study to familiarize themselves with the vocabulary prior to classroom discussions and reading.

Figure 5.3: Strategy—Four stages of word learning.

Visit ***go.SolutionTree.com/literacy/FSK6*** *and enter the unique access code found on the book's inside front cover to access a reproducible version of this figure.*

The stages aren't just nice to know. Students should clearly understand them and be able to use the stages metacognitively as they tackle new vocabulary, particularly content area terms. Hearing words pronounced and spelled aid students as they read, just as thinking about word knowledge prior to the unit of study provides students with a quick check to reflect on how familiar they are with the content.

Models of Word Learning

Vocabulary building should begin with intentionality. It is vitally important to have a systematic and explicit plan to address the vocabulary deficits many students have. Researchers have described comprehensive vocabulary programs (Beck, McKeown, & Kucan, 2013; Graves, Schneider, & Ringstaff, 2018; Marzano, 2004; Tyson & Peery, 2017; Zucker, Cabell, & Pico, 2021) based on evidence of what works to acquire new words. Next, I'll summarize several models of word learning, one for early learners, another for intermediate students, and a blended model that integrates digital tools into word learning.

Word Learning Model for Grades PreK–1

The approach described in the following section is specifically for students in preK through first grade who do not yet read widely and are not able to use reference materials such as dictionaries. This comprehensive vocabulary approach for young children includes three components.

1. **Word consciousness:** Elicit word play, explain the power of words, and motivate students to use new words while modeling academic language.
2. **Vocabulary learning:** Provide shared book reading, turn-and-talk conversations, and opportunities to learn words through content area instruction.
3. **Vocabulary instruction:** Teach individual words in texts and units of study and encourage students to ask adults what words mean as a word learning strategy (Zucker et al., 2021).

Word Learning Model for Grades 2–6

Students in grades 2–6 have more advanced skills that facilitate learning new words in a variety of ways. A comprehensive approach for older students differs slightly from one for younger learners and includes a four-part model (Graves et al., 2018) based on Michael F. Graves' (2000) original word learning model. Its components are described as the following.

- **Foster word consciousness:** Encourage students to become aware of language all around them, both orally and in print.
- **Encourage wide reading:** Promote wide reading in a variety of genres and text types.
- **Teach individual words:** Directly introduce and teach individual words, particularly academic vocabulary.
- **Teach word learning strategies:** Teach students a variety of independent word learning strategies.

In grades 2–6, you'll notice that encouraging students to read widely along with how to independently use word learning strategies is different from the approach for younger students. These two elements are important to add with age-appropriateness because we know that wide reading introduces students to many specific words they won't hear in everyday conversations, and acquiring word learning strategies helps students independently learn new words, a skill that supports comprehension and lifelong learning.

Blended Vocabulary Word Learning Model

In our book, Peery and I introduced a new model for word learning that takes into consideration elements of previously existing models along with harnessing the power of digital tools to increase engagement and support differentiated practice, as illustrated in figure 5.4.

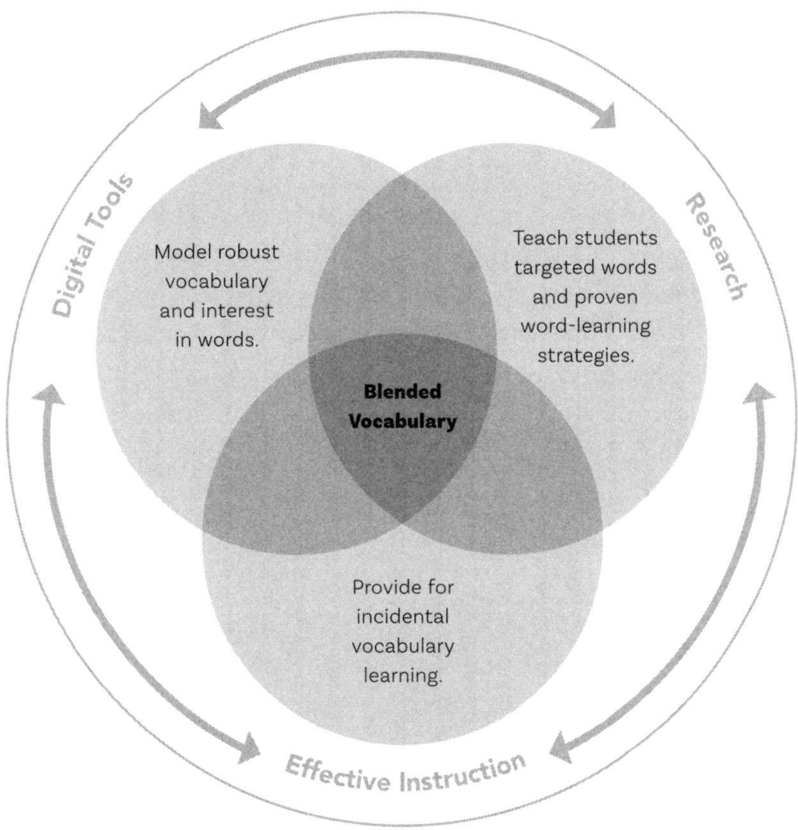

Source: Tyson & Peery, 2017, p. 21.

Figure 5.4: Blended vocabulary model for word learning.

The blended vocabulary model includes three elements as summarized.

1. **Modeling:** Model robust vocabulary and interest in words. All adults with whom students interact during the school day should model using vocabulary relevant to what they do (such as a lunchroom worker or gym teacher).
2. **Explicit instruction:** Teach students targeted words and proven word learning strategies so they can tackle learning words on their own. Use digital tools as part of instruction, review, and practice.
3. **Incidental learning:** Provide for in-school incidental vocabulary learning experiences, including creating literacy-rich classroom environments, read alouds, dialogic conversations, word walls, and independent reading. You'll find many ideas for community-wide experiences that support incidental word learning in *Leading a Culture of Reading* (Radice, 2024). Radice includes diverse opportunities such as launching a community-wide reading campaign, dramatic performances, reading parades, family literacy nights, and poetry slams, to name just a few. These rich experiences provide the backdrop and support for rich, incidental word learning.

Direct vocabulary instruction is an important part of all teaching models and selecting that vocabulary for instruction can be an in-depth and, at times, confounding task. It's natural to wonder, "Which words do I teach?" Tiered vocabulary is an organizational structure I've used frequently with much success. *Tiered vocabulary*, developed by Isabel L. Beck, Margaret G. McKeown, and Linda Kucan (2002, 2013) at the University of Pittsburgh, is an organizational framework for categorizing words. The tiered framework includes three levels, with the first tier being made up of everyday words and the second and third tiers made up of academic words. Since the framework is recognized as an excellent method for selecting and sorting vocabulary for direct instruction, it works well for sorting words to teach early learners as well as high school students and any grade level in between.

You may be familiar with tiered vocabulary through the Common Core State Standards Initiative (National Governors Association [NGA] Center for Best Practices & Council of Chief State School Officers [CCSSO], 2010), which included the tiered framework as a focus for vocabulary instruction. Following, I briefly highlight how the framework can be used for sorting and selecting words along with direct implications for instruction and student use. The three tiers, along with words categorized in each tier, are shown in figure 5.5.

As you may note from figure 5.5, tier one includes words used in everyday language. These words are part of most native speakers' vocabulary and are learned over time through conversation with family, friends, and interactions at places such as school, the grocery store, and church. Examples include *house*, *fruit*, *vegetables*, *table*, *desk*, *restroom*, *teachers*, *cafeteria*, *pew*, *aisles*, *groceries*, *scanners*, *preacher*, and *priest*. Before writing off

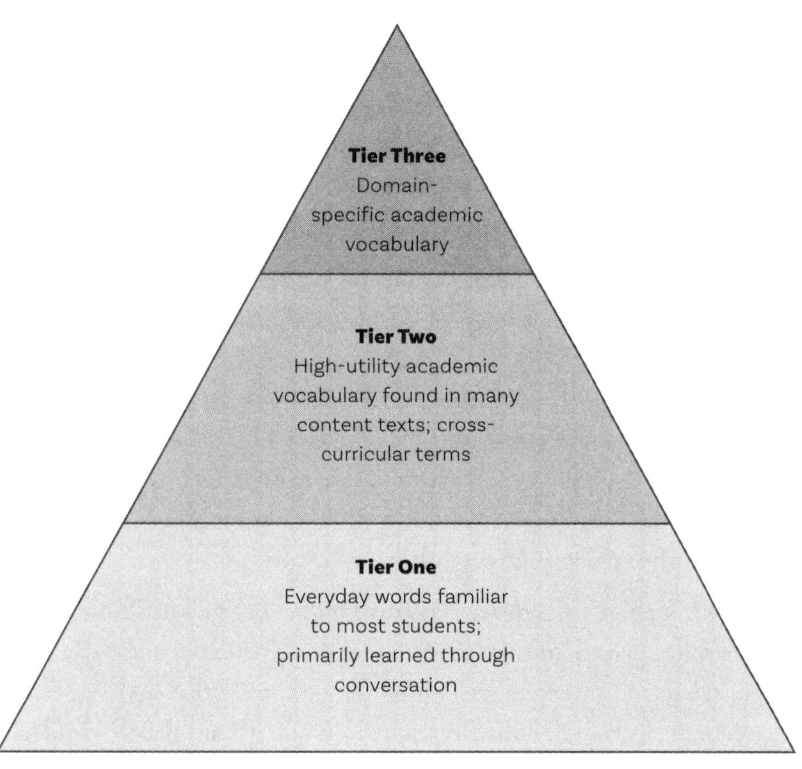

Source: Tyson & Peery, 2017, p. 310.

Figure 5.5: Tiered vocabulary.

tier one words as ho-hum and unimportant, however, I'll provide a word of caution. Tier one terms are important in that they enable us to communicate and navigate our everyday lives. As schools become increasingly diverse, we have more English learners in our classrooms who lack experiences with everyday vocabulary acquired through conversations. If this describes your setting, directly teach tier one words and label the environment, as illustrated in figure 5.6, to support English learners as they acquire language. Another excellent way to build tier one vocabulary is through oral language and dialogic conversations. In other words—talk, talk, and more talk.

Figure 5.6: Simple labels in the classroom support English learners.

Tier two words include general academic terms that frequently occur across content areas. This category is made up of high-utility, cross-curricular words. Students primarily learn these words through reading and explicit instruction, rather than through oral language, as they would with tier onee words. Tier two words are far more likely to appear in texts and newspapers than in general conversation. They are a powerhouse in that they have high utility across a wide range of contexts and topics, and allow students to access informational, technical, and literary texts (Ferlazzo, 2017). Examples include *observe*, *compare*, *contrast*, *justify*, *summarize*, *reason*, and *accumulate.* Tier two words also allow us more specificity when we speak and write. For example, using the word *saunter* rather than *walk* or *loquacious* instead of *talkative.*

It is suggested that tier two words should be the bulk of instructional focus since they serve as a bridge between more general, everday vocabulary and specialized terms (Beck, McKeown, & Kucan, 2008). Why? One reason is that tier two words are generalizable to many settings and appear frequently in both fiction and nonfiction as well as oral language. Since students learn these words primarily through reading and instruction, you'll want to spend most of your time focusing on tier two words through explicit, direct instruction and review. In short, students get more "bang for their buck" when they master these words.

Words in the tier three category are also academic words, but these terms are low-frequency, specialized, academic terms. They are described as *domain-specific*, meaning the terms are related to a specific discipline (Beck et al., 2008, 2013). For example, fifth-grade students learning about electricity and magnetism need to understand key vocabulary such as *conductor*, *circuit*, *insulator*, *static electricity*, and *magnetic field.* These terms are critically important to reading, writing, and speaking about electricity; however, they're not generalizable like tier two words. Students can typically find these terms in the glossary or as bold-faced terms in the text.

There are several important implications for instruction. First, it is recommended to display tier three words, pronounce them, and succinctly preteach them. Sometimes this is referred to as *front-loading*, which can be done through oral discussion and using a Padlet or Smartboard to display the words in order for students to reference as needed. Or, simply, teach tier-three words in context as the need arises (Beck et al., 2013).

Spending some time identifying vocabulary for a unit of study and then sorting them into tiers is time well spent. Very quickly, you'll be able to easily identify the difference between tier-two and tier-three words in order to create your focus for instruction. To help with that, use the reproducible activity "Sorting Vocabulary Into Tiers" (figure 5.7) to help you and your collaborative team practice sorting tier one, tier two, and tier three words (Tyson & Peery, 2017).

Tiered vocabulary can also be used as a guide to create content vocabulary lists. Creating must-know (tier two) and nice-to-know (tier three) words by grade level and content area supports vertical and horizontal alignment. This benefits teachers as they prepare units of study and students as they build their repertoire of vocabulary.

Sorting Vocabulary Words Into Tiers

Try your hand at sorting vocabulary words into three tiers. Read the following terms from a sixth-grade social studies unit about volcanoes, then sort them according to the three tiers. Write the terms in the boxes provided following the terms. Then compare your results with colleagues. Keep in mind that there is some subjectivity around placement of specific words into the three tiers, but if a term can be used only in one discipline and only in one specific way, it's definitely a tier three word.

soda bottle	tectonic plates	solid	magma	erupt
expand	geologist	pressure	lava	fall
prediction	smoke	mantle	avalanche	

Tier One: Common Words
Tier Two: Cross-Curricular Words
Tier Three: Technical and Academic Vocabulary

Source: Tyson & Peery, 2017, pp. 36–37.

Figure 5.7: Sorting vocabulary into tiers.

Visit ***go.SolutionTree.com/literacy/FSK6*** *for a free reproducible version of this figure.*

When we select words to teach directly, it makes sense to think about how to organize them. While tiered vocabulary is one way, there are others, some of which may complement tiered vocabulary. Related terms are referred to as language gestalts, semantically related words, or, more simply, *word clusters* (Marzano, 1984; Marzano & Marzano, 1988; Marzano, 2020). Robert J. Marzano (1984), a vocabulary expert, recommends teaching all vocabulary in word clusters.

For example, a word cluster of tier one words related to school may include *classroom, hallway, restroom, lesson, coatrack, cafeteria, gym,* and *playground.* For a fourth-grade unit on weather, a tier three word cluster could include *air pressure, drought, climate, atmosphere, heat wave, heat index, ozone, forecast,* and *humidity.* The word cluster approach makes the terms easier to hang together as students become familiar with these words.

For extensive word cluster lists, there may be no better source than *Teaching Basic, Advanced, and Academic Vocabulary* (Marzano, 2020) for grades K–5. It includes 420 word clusters specific to tier one and tier two words that include parts of speech, words that denote emotion, nouns, verbs, mammals, occupations, the fine arts, and many more topics.

Text sets, which should be a part of classroom libraries, provide another means for students to acquire clustered vocabulary. By hearing thematically clustered words through read alouds and then reading additional words in the cluster during independent reading, students more easily build their vocabulary. Texts should be carefully selected to build a themed set on a single topic such as *desert animals, electricity,* or *transportation.* Resources can also include articles, videos, websites, and infographics. I suggest including books of varied levels of complexity that offer more general and accessible vocabulary to build background knowledge. You can also extend the learning by creating a digital word wall where students who read these books can record the new vocabulary they learn. Word learning that includes direct and indirect methods along with digital tools creates an integrated and holistic approach to word learning.

Students cannot learn all the words they need to know incidentally through conversation. It is important to carefully plan which words to explicitly teach using the tiered or clustered approach. Teachers must help students develop their knowledge of low-frequency and high-frequency words (Ibrahim et al., 2016). Once you've got a plan for how to select and organize the words you'll target, you can move to strategies that will help students move words up the stages of word learning.

In the following sections, word learning strategies are divided into two categories—direct and indirect strategies for increasing word learning. You'll find both *linguistic* and *nonlinguistic* strategies, both important ways we store information. Linguistic strategies are focused on words, and nonlinguistic strategies include images, symbols, mental pictures, and skits or pantomimes (Marzano, 2009; Marzano, 2020; Marzano & Simms, 2013). Images and mental pictures have a powerful impact on learning, and adding them when learning new words helps students deepen their understanding of terms (Marzano & Simms, 2013).

What Works in the Classroom?

A culture of word learning is one in which students are immersed with language and words across the school day (Tyson & Peery, 2017). Building a culture of word learning with your colleagues and school staff benefits students. The school environment offers immersive supports for word learning—in classrooms and hallways as well as the lunchroom and gymnasium. For example, bulletin boards in the hallway featuring "Top Books for Dinosaur Lovers" or "Grab this Mystery!" are simple ways of promoting reading and building specific, novel vocabulary.

A favorite hallway bulletin board in an elementary school featured nonlinguistic vocabulary words along with images of students acting them out (Marzano, 2009; Marzano & Simms, 2013). Students would routinely stop and stare at the vocabulary and images that rotated regularly. Another way to create a schoolwide environment that values and immerses students in language is to label objects in the cafeteria, for example, *dish racks* or *lunch menus*. Labeling can be continued throughout the school in places such as the gymnasium, school library, and front office.

Resources to Support Vocabulary Instruction

- *Blended Vocabulary for K–12 Classrooms: Harnessing the Power of Digital Tools and Direct Instruction* by Kimberly Tyson and Angela Peery (2017)
- *Bringing Words to Life: Robust Vocabulary Instruction (2nd edition)* by Isabel L. Beck, Margaret G. McKeown, and Linda Kucan (2013)
- *Inside Words: Tools for Teaching Vocabulary, Grades 4–12* by Janet Allen (2007)
- *Reading Aloud Across the Curriculum: How to Build Bridges in Language Arts, Math, Science, and Social Studies* by Lester L. Laminack and Reba M. Wadsworth (2006)
- *Teaching Basic, Advanced, and Academic Vocabulary: A Comprehensive Framework for Elementary Instruction* by Robert J. Marzano (2020)
- *The Vocabulary-Enriched Classroom: Practices for Improving the Reading Performance of All Students in Grades 3 and Up* by Cathy Collins Block and John N. Mangieri (2006)
- *Vocabulary in a SNAP: 100+ Lessons for Elementary Instruction* by Angela B. Peery (2017)
- *Vocabulary in a SNAP: 100+ Lessons for Secondary Instruction* by Angela B. Peery (2017)
- *Words, Words, Words: Teaching Vocabulary in Grades 4–12* by Janet Allen (1999)

Characteristics of Effective Vocabulary Instruction

There are numerous characteristics common among strategies that support effective word learning. As you plan purposeful vocabulary instruction, please note the important characteristics of effective vocabulary instruction I've summarized within table 5.1.

When directly or indirectly teaching vocabulary, the characteristics described in the table will go a long way to support word learning among your students. In the following section, I'll outline both direct and indirect strategies that will strengthen your vocabulary instruction and student word learning.

Strategies to Increase Vocabulary and Word Learning

As educators, we need a plan for teaching and increasing word learning in and out of the classroom. A comprehensive vocabulary program is often more effective than simply selecting words and direct instruction. I always suggest a balanced approach to word learning that includes direct and indirect word learning opportunities. This approach includes three areas of emphasis: (1) explicit, direct instruction focused on selected vocabulary, (2) creating literacy-rich classrooms that support and promote incidental word learning, and (3) modeling vocabulary orally and providing practice and review through games and digital tools (Tyson & Peery, 2017).

In the following sections, we'll look at numerous strategies that, when used in a balanced approach, help students become independent word learners.

Direct Word Learning Strategies

Direct word learning strategies focus on intentional word learning with specific, targeted words. Providing direct instruction about specific words you have targeted is an important element of a comprehensive word learning program. First, you need to determine which words you will explicitly teach. Though you'll likely prioritize words from the curriculum, you'll also want to include other words depending on your student population. For example, you may select words from read alouds, current events, or seasonal words.

Some teachers begin with tier two academic words that have wide generalizability. And, depending on the number of English learners, they also focus on tier one words during small-group instruction. Open your eyes to the possibilities of words that should be taught directly. The following strategies can be incorporated into direct instruction. Some are more linguistic based and focus on words while others are more nonlinguistic and include images, visual representations, and movement.

Table 5.1: Characteristics of Effective Vocabulary Instruction

Provide Multiple Exposures to Words	One of the key characteristics of effective vocabulary instruction is that meaning is shaped through multiple exposures to words. "Once and done" doesn't work. Students need many opportunities to hear words used in various contexts in order to know a word well enough to shift it from receptive to expressive vocabulary. Marzano and Pickering (2005) suggest at least six exposures to new words, and additional research (Ricocomini et al., 2015) suggests students need at least sixteen exposures to new words in order to own words. In other words, to move an unknown word up the stages of word learning so that students can use it when they speak and write requires hearing and reading the word in many and varied contexts.
Front-Load Vocabulary	Teaching targeted vocabulary can occur both within the context of the lesson or as a preteaching opportunity. Specifically when teaching content, preteaching select words aids students in comprehending text (Alamri & Rogers, 2018; Elleman, Lindo, Morphy, & Compton, 2009). Preteaching challenging words in particular aids students with reading difficulties and limited language. Keep in mind that front-loading, as described, doesn't have to take a lot of time nor should it. It can be as brief as projecting several academic or highly technical words and pronouncing them. Students can add what they know, and you can provide a brief, easy-to-understand meaning.
Teach Independent Word Learning Strategies	Because you can't possibly teach all the words students need to learn, they need to acquire a few independent word learning strategies. Three basic strategies include (1) use of context, (2) use of word parts, and (3) use of reference materials (Graves et al., 2016). Using context is more reliable in nonfiction or informational text than in fiction. As students become familiar with how texts are structured to define vocabulary, they'll be able to use context more effectively. Word parts—affixes, prefixes, and Greek and Latin root words—should be included in a comprehensive vocabulary effort. In addition, digital texts provide the opportunity for students to click on a word, which provides a definition or synonym in a manner more expedient (and less distracting) than referring to a dictionary or glossary.
Actively Engage Students in Learning	Students need to practice, review, listen, read, and play as they deepen their understanding of specific words. Word learning *can* and *should* be fun! Use games such as Boggle and Scrabble to review and revisit words along with digital tools. Flashcard Stash is a great tool for reviewing words and Free Rice (www.freerice.com) is a fun online game that differentiates word learning for each student.
Support English Learners	English learners, in general, benefit greatly from everyday teacher talk and conversation because it provides opportunities for word learning and practicing new vocabulary, deepening understanding of new ideas, and building rapport (Calderón, 2011). As you select vocabulary, keep the following tips in mind. While ELs also benefit from many of the same strategies as native language speakers, they also need direct instruction in both high-frequency words, everyday words (tier one vocabulary) as well as low-frequency, academic vocabulary (tier two and tier three vocabulary; Ibrahim et al., 2016). Calderón (2011), an English learner researcher, also suggests selecting vocabulary that aligns to standards and tests, supports comprehending a specific text selection, is used in formal writing, and supports academic success.

Motor Imaging Strategy

As we all know, students love to move! Motor imaging is the perfect nonlinguistic strategy to combine word learning with movement or gestures. In motor imaging, as students learn meanings of words, they link a bodily movement with the word meaning, which engages both the mind and the body (Casale, 1985). It's a simple but effective strategy that integrates word learning with physical movement. It appears that motor imaging (Manzo et al., 2006) is a form of *dual coding* (Paivio, 1986), which is when new learning is provided in two different formats—verbal and nonverbal—at the same time. In motor imaging, dual coding combines learning new vocabulary with movement, which, in turn, helps the learner understand and recall the information more effectively from long-term memory.

Motor imaging is easy to naturally integrate into classroom routines and instruction. For example, if you're reading aloud with first-grade students and the author uses the term *abode,* you'd briefly explain that the word *abode* means a home. Then you'd ask students to use their body to show you how they'll remember the *abode.* Next, scan the room and choose the common image, which might be hands formed in the shape of a triangle like the roof of a home. Finally, you'd show that gesture to students, and they would mirror the image while repeating the word *abode* using the gesture. Finally, you'd remind them that each time you read the word *abode*, they'll make the image with their hands.

The simple steps for motor imaging are included in the following strategy (figure 5.8; Casale, 1985). I encourage you to incorporate it with read alouds and with general and specific vocabulary found in informational text.

List-Group-Label Strategy

List-group-label (Massey et al., 2008; Taba, 1967; Tierney & Readence, 2000) is a powerful prereading and vocabulary-building strategy that provides context for word learning. It is an ideal strategy to elicit students' prior knowledge and build background knowledge for those who may know little about the topic. Additionally, list-group-label is a before-, during-, and after-reading strategy that engages students to think about specific terms at each stage of reading. The process encourages students to find connections between words and uses *semantic mapping* (or graphic organizers) to represent relationships among words. This typically takes the form of a web of words that shows the relationship between a word or phrase and related words or concepts. Students actively engage with the content terms through discussion with peers as they categorize and group words. It provides an ideal forum for seeing and discussing meaningful relationships between and among words.

Consider the following example for fifth-grade students studying volcanoes. Following each of the steps listed, the class reconvenes to discuss and record. Begin this strategy with a good deal of teacher support, direction, and discussion following each step.

1. **Introduce:** The teacher introduces the volcano unit, and students pair up or get in small groups and begin brainstorming words related to volcanoes.

Strategy: Motor Imaging

Pillar: Vocabulary

Grade Level:	**Instructional Grouping:**	**Consider This:**
☑K ☑1 ☑2 ☑3 ☑4 ☑5 ☑6	☑ Whole Group ☑ Small Group ☐ Individual	• Motor imaging doesn't have to be reserved for young learners. Connecting bodily representations for words can help cement vocabulary for students of any grade level. • The strategy doesn't work with every word. Try it with words that are easily represented by gestures or bodily movement. • When selecting words from a read aloud, select one or two words that are integral to understanding the story. Focusing on too many words may result in kids focusing on gestures and acting out rather than the words themselves.

What is it? Motor imaging is a word learning strategy that combines learning words with bodily movements and gestures that represent words.

Why is it important? Nonlinguistic representations of words help anchor the word's meaning (figure 5.10, page 195) when students are learning new words (Marzano, 2009; 2020).

What works in the classroom?

Five Simple Steps

1. Introduce the target word and provide the definition (linguistic).
2. Each student chooses and demonstrates their own simple pantomime or gesture (nonlinguistic).
3. Scan the students' gestures. Then, select a common gesture and demonstrate for all students to see.
4. Have students repeat the word while doing the common gesture or movement.
5. The class engages with text that uses the target word in context. Each time the word is repeated, students do the bodily movement.

Figure 5.8: Strategy—Motor imaging.

Visit ***go.SolutionTree.com/literacy/FSK6*** *and enter the unique access code found on the book's inside front cover to access a reproducible version of this figure.*

2. **List:** On the SMART Board, record the following words that students provide: *lava*, *fire*, *explosion*, *dust*, *destruction*, *mountain*, *death*, *Mount Saint Helens*, *Hawaii*, *cinders*, *ash*, *smoke*, *earthquakes*, *rocks*, and *heat*. Add a few other words to the list including: *molten*, *eruption*, and *magma*. Make certain to read each word aloud so that students connect each word with the spelling and pronunciation.
3. **Group:** In pairs or small groups, students review the words and create groups of words that have something in common. Notice that terms may be in more than one group. It could look something like the three groups shown here.

VOCABULARY

- lava, ash, rocks, dust, smoke
- lava, fire, cinders, molten, magma
- explosion, destruction, death, earthquakes

4. **Label:** Groups of students read over the words and look for common characteristics. Then, they determine labels for the groups of words, which might be as follows.
    - Things That Come Out of a Volcano—Lava, ash, rocks, dust, smoke
    - Hot Parts—Lava, fire, cinders, molten, magma
    - Results of an Eruption—Explosion, destruction, death, earthquakes
5. **Read and revise:** The teacher directs students to the text to read (or the teacher reads aloud a brief section of the chapter) about volcanoes with a focus on looking for terms they may have missed. The class reconvenes and revises any of the groups of words or the labels.

A completed list-group-label template is shown in figure 5.9 to give you an idea of how students complete the template. Use the reproducible version provided online at **go.SolutionTree.com/literacy/FSK6** as you implement list-group-label. The strategy table in figure 5.10 summarizes the easy-to-follow steps.

List-Group-Label

- **List** all the words or terms you can think of and record them in the large box.
- After reading or class discussion, **group** the words or terms according to what they have in common.
- **Label** each group of terms.

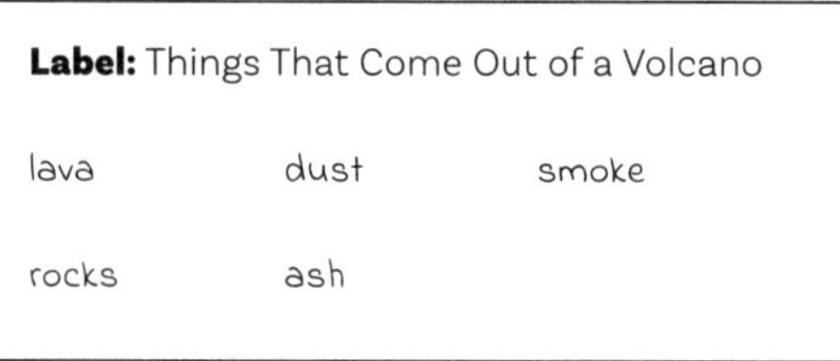

Label: Hot Parts

lava cinders magma

molten fire

Label: Results of an Eruption

explosion death

destruction earthquake

Label:

Figure 5.9: List-group-label volcano example.

*Visit **go.SolutionTree.com/literacy/FSK6** to access this free reproducible.*

Strategy: List-Group-Label

Pillar: Vocabulary

Grade Level:	**Instructional Grouping:**	**Consider This:**
☑K ☑1 ☑2 ☑3 ☑4 ☑5 ☑6	☑ Whole Group ☑ Small Group ☐ Individual	• This strategy is suitable for grades K–6, with the teacher providing writing and structure for younger students. • Consider introducing this strategy as a whole-group activity. Model the steps and record students' thinking and terms so they understand the process. • Later, have students work in pairs or small groups as they discuss terms and provide labels for the groups of words. • The list of words that students brainstorm, which will be grouped and labeled, should be manageable. Depending on grade level, about fifteen to thirty words work well.

What is it? List-group-label is an interactive strategy, built on semantic mapping, that helps students think deeply about content terms as they see relationships among them in order to group and label those terms. It also draws on students' background knowledge as they build relationships between existing vocabulary and new words.

Why is it important? As students draw on their background knowledge and see relationships among academic words, they'll expand their word knowledge more quickly.

What works in the classroom?

Simple Steps

- **List:** Select a topic or concept from a reading selection or content area text. Before reading, have students brainstorm all the words they know related to this topic, thus activating their prior knowledge. *List* those words on the SMART Board in no particular order. Don't edit their words, and add a few of your own.
- **Group:** In small groups, students review the words and look for commonality and shared features among the words. Then they *group* the words according to their shared features or relationships. Students need to be able to support the reasoning behind each group of words.
- **Label:** Students *label* each group of words.
- **Read and Revise:** Have students *read* the text and then *revise* their list. After reading, they may delete irrelevant terms, add new terms, create a new group of words, or change a label for a group of related words.

Figure 5.10: Strategy—List-group-label.

Visit ***go.SolutionTree.com/literacy/FSK6*** *and enter the unique access code found on the book's inside front cover to access a reproducible version of this figure.*

Alphaboxes Strategy

Alphaboxes (Hoyt, 2009) is one of those rare strategies that can be used before, during, and after reading. If you're looking for a strategy that supports word learning in informational and nonfiction text, alphaboxes is a perfect choice. The simple process, outlined in the alphaboxes strategy table, activates students' prior knowledge and creates the opportunity for students to make connections to vocabulary and concepts before reading, which aids comprehension. Then, following reading, students revise the words listed in the alphaboxes chart. The power of alphaboxes lies in the discussion about vocabulary that occurs among students.

For example, if you were teaching a geography unit of study in fifth grade, students could enter a few terms they know before reading, such as *equator* and *hemisphere,* in their alphabox. During reading, students can add additional terms they notice to their template, such as *landforms* and *latitude*. Following reading, listening, or watching a video, students reconvene in small groups or as a whole group and share terms they learned from reading or listening. For example, students may add *longitude* and *map scale,* which were part of the reading.

The alphaboxes template, found in figure 5.11, can be reproduced and used with students in your setting. In the alphaboxes strategy (figure 5.12), you'll find tips and simple steps to easily integrate it into your content area and vocabulary instruction.

Indirect Word Learning Strategies

Effective vocabulary instruction includes both direct and indirect opportunities to support word learning. While direct instruction is imperative, we must also create many indirect occasions for students to listen, speak, read, and write in order to extend their vocabulary. While some strategies such as read alouds may be found within other chapters, they are included here because of their impact on vocabulary and word learning. Some strategies are summarized, and others are described more fully within a strategy table. The strategies in this section help enrich your students' vocabulary incidentally.

a	b	c	d	e	f	g	h
i	j	k	l	m	n	o	p
q	r	s	t	u	v	w	x, y, z

Figure 5.11: Alphaboxes template.

Visit ***go.SolutionTree.com/literacy/FSK6*** *for a free reproducible version of this figure.*

Strategy: Alphaboxes

Pillar: Vocabulary

Grade Level:	Instructional Grouping:	Consider This:
☑K ☑1 ☑2 ☑3 ☑4 ☑5 ☑6	☑ Whole Group ☑ Small Group ☑ Individual	• Alphaboxes can be used with students of any grade level. Teachers provide more direct instruction, recording words in kindergarten and first grade. • Consider making a large, laminated alphabox to use and display during the content unit, recording terms as the unit progresses.

What is it? Alphaboxes is a strategy that activates students' prior knowledge and serves as a tool to build, record, and see relationships among academic vocabulary, thus increasing comprehension.

Why is it important? The more attention we bring to vocabulary, the better. The steps in alphaboxes, along with the graphic organizer, provides a vehicle for students to think about and reflect on vocabulary before, during, and after reading.

What works in the classroom?

Simple Steps

- **Select text:** Select informational text or a nonfiction selection from a content area text.
- **Announce topic:** Prior to reading and discussion, announce the topic or concept. Ask students to brainstorm terms that are connected to the topic, thus drawing on background knowledge.
- **Record words:** As students share words, record them alphabetically on the alphaboxes grid in the appropriate square.
- **Discuss each word:** Discuss each word briefly as it is added to the chart. Ask students how they think it is related to the topic to add to the discussion.
- **Add a few additional terms:** Before reading, you may add a few terms to the chart that you think are critical to understanding the content.

Early Learners

- **Teacher-directed instruction:** For early learners, this strategy will be more teacher directed; however, students can suggest words while the teacher records them on the alphabox organizer.
- **Read aloud:** The teacher reads aloud the informational text selection, projecting it if possible.
- **Edit words after reading:** Following reading, return to the chart and add or edit words in each appropriate lettered square.

Intermediate Students

- **Students record words:** For intermediate students, each student should have a copy of the alphabox chart. Using this tool, students record new terms as they read, listen to a discussion, or watch videos related to the content. Each student's chart will be different and reflects their word learning needs.
- **Students discuss words in small groups:** In small groups, have students review and justify word selections in their alphabox chart. Students can edit their charts based on the discussion, adding and deleting words.
- **Use the alphabox for review:** The alphabox chart can also serve as a tool for review, individually or in small groups, prior to an assessment.

Figure 5.12: Strategy—Alphaboxes.

Visit ***go.SolutionTree.com/literacy/FSK6*** *and enter the unique access code found on the book's inside front cover to access a reproducible version of this figure.*

Literacy-Rich Environment

Students need to be exposed to oral language and print throughout the day. An environment brimming with print and language—at all grade levels—provides students with opportunities to refine their language and vocabulary through reading labels, signs, anchor charts, graphs, books, and other materials from the classroom library. For example, when frontloading vocabulary, you could create an anchor chart featuring prefixes, as shown in figure 5.13. Students could suggest words prior to reading a text selection. Over time, add more prefixes and students can add corresponding words acquired through reading, listening, and conversation.

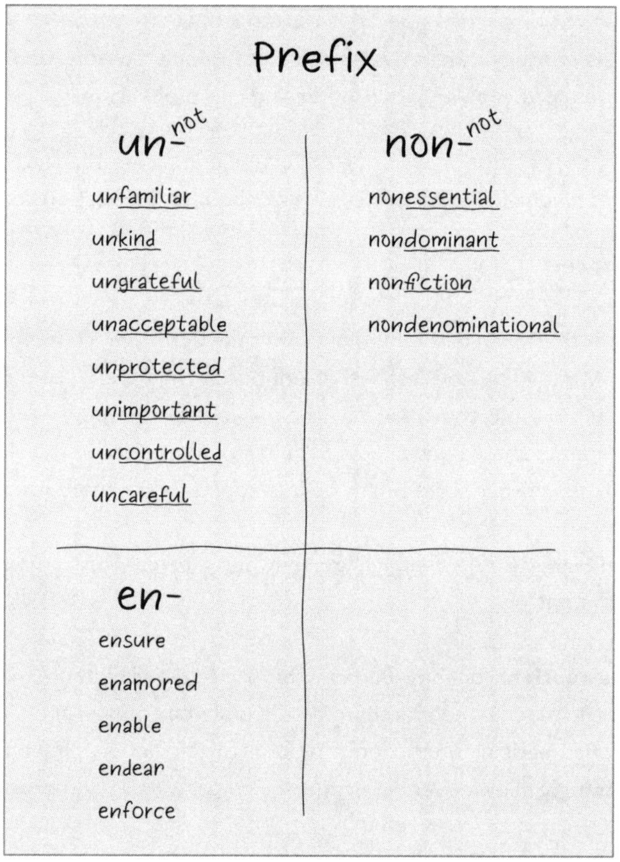

Prefix

un- (not)
unfamiliar
unkind
ungrateful
unacceptable
unprotected
unimportant
uncontrolled
uncareful

non- (not)
nonessential
nondominant
nonfiction
nondenominational

en-
ensure
enamored
enable
endear
enforce

Figure 5.13: An anchor chart highlights how prefixes change word meanings.

A graffiti wall is another fun and interactive way to encourage students to use vocabulary and respond to timely questions. A graffiti wall, as shown in figure 5.14, lines the main hallway of an elementary school. Every few weeks, students respond to new questions posted in the hallway, which is a novel way to support word learning.

As stated previously, students have many words to learn, including everyday, commonplace words as well as academic vocabulary. Immerse students in words and word learning opportunities. A simple way of extending vocabulary is to mix up the words

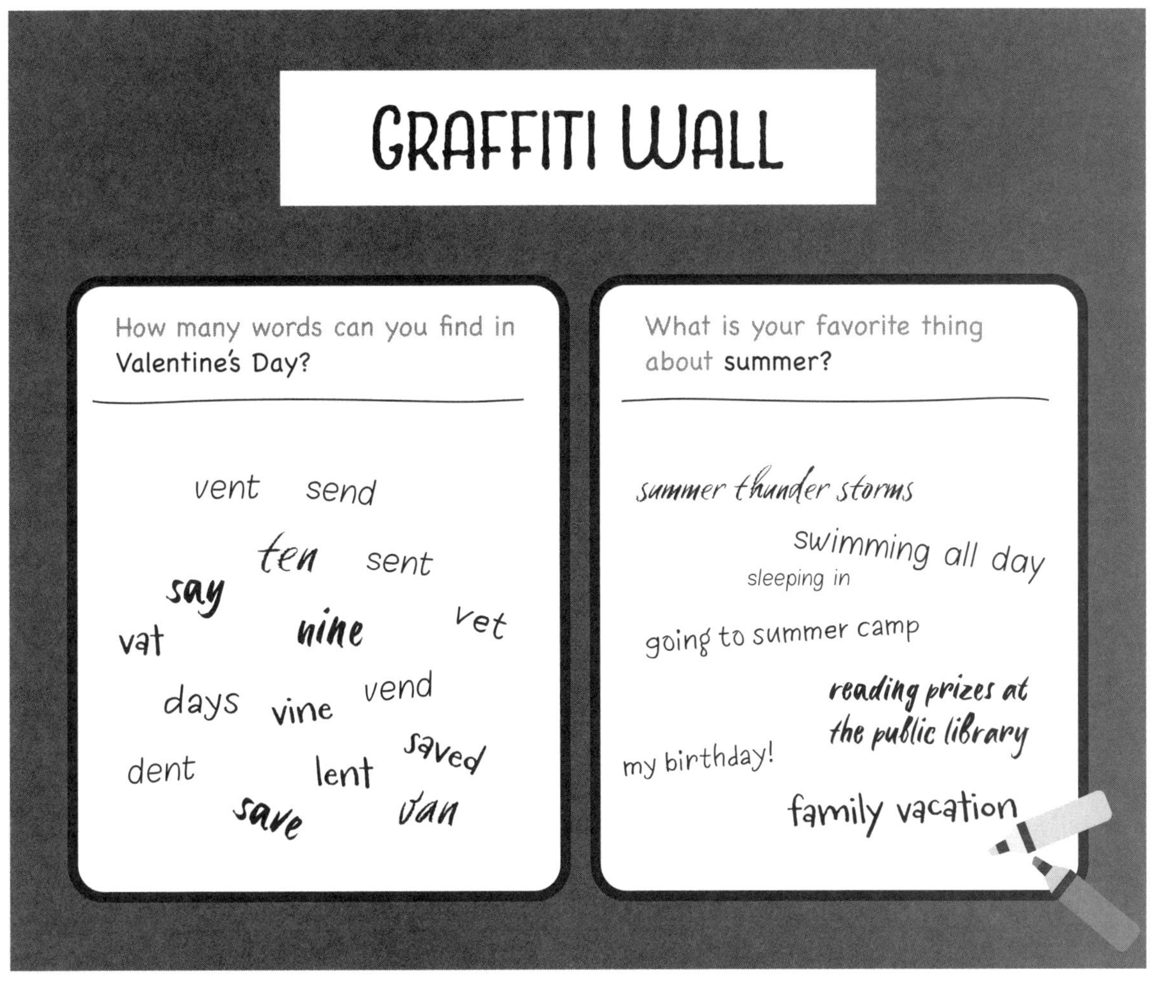

Figure 5.14: Graffiti walls help students explore lansuage and vocabulary.

you use commonly everyday. Instead of using the same words every day to describe something, change it up. Think of synonyms you can use in place of words used frequently, such as "Let's line up *quickly*" instead of "Let's line up *fast.*" Or use *alarmed* in place of *scared* or *ecstatic* instead of *happy*. You can also easily use transition times to review words that have been taught. When lining up for an activity, read aloud words from the word wall. When a student provides the meaning, they join the line of students. Don't belabor this, but a few words at a time is great reinforcement.

Wide Reading

There are so many words to learn and so little time! We all use a limited number of words when we speak and thus hear many of the same words over and over. One of the most expedient ways to increase exposure to more words is through independent, wide reading. Encouraging wide reading can take a variety of forms, some of which may include competition and incentives. I prefer to support wide reading through a less competitive, well-rounded approach that includes read alouds, book talks, guest readers, book clubs, and reading challenges.

The Forty Book Challenge is one of my preferred challenges and was originated by Donalyn Miller (2009), who is a classroom teacher and author and recognized across the United States as an expert in reading. In her best-selling book, *The Book Whisperer* (Miller, 2009), she describes the challenge as a way to support her students individually and collectively to expand their reading lives by expanding their book selections. It's a personal challenge for each student, rather than a competition. Overall, we desire for students to become engaged readers. Some avid readers may read far beyond forty books across the school year while others read twenty; in doing so, they may discover a favorite author, series, or genre by reading outside of their typical selections.

In short, reading widely exposes students to new and specific vocabulary in a variety of contexts. Students need access to text along with time to read those texts. Drawing from your classroom library and school library, encourage reading by establishing routines and opportunities to read self-selected materials across the school day as an integral way to strengthen reading and vocabulary-building skills. I encourage you to strategize with your grade-level collaborative team about how to support vocabulary growth through well-rounded wide reading activities.

Read Alouds to Build Vocabulary

Read alouds expose students to print awareness, text structure, language, and vocabulary, and they are commonplace in elementary classrooms (Smith et al., 2022). An interactive read aloud provides many benefits for students as they hear the teacher model ways of thinking and comprehending while building meaning with their classmates (Acosta-Tello, 2019; Wiseman, 2011).

In addition to comprehension benefits, reading one picture book each day provides young children exposure to 78,000 words per year (Logan et al., 2019). Early learners can learn advanced vocabulary through read alouds before they can read independently (Wright, 2019). Selecting several words each time you read, briefly discussing them within context, and circling back to them at other times increases specific word learning through exposure and context.

Read alouds not only provide many benefits specific to vocabulary development for primary students but also for intermediate students. They serve as a scaffold for struggling readers since students can focus on comprehension rather than decoding (Hurst & Griffity, 2015). Additionally, tier two words (Beck et al., 2013), or academic words, are commonly found in books and other reading materials. Teachers can identify several tier two words and explicitly teach them in the context of the read aloud (Barnes et al., 2019). While teachers commonly read aloud from fiction, be intentional about incorporating nonfiction and informational text that supports your grade-level standards.

Read alouds can include speeches, letters, newspaper and magazine articles, and poetry. Nonfiction is particularly rich in word learning opportunities that include specific academic vocabulary.

Anchored Word Learning Strategy

Anchored word learning (Beck et al., 2013) is a read aloud strategy that capitalizes on the elevated vocabulary found in read alouds. Picture books are an ideal choice for teaching vocabulary since they typically include a higher level of vocabulary and more unusual words than those to which young students are exposed when reading independently. Anchored word learning provides a simple but effective plan for selecting words from read alouds that will intentionally expand your students' vocabulary. It is an excellent example of a simple routine for purposefully exposing students to words through read alouds. For example, if you read aloud once a day and introduce three words during a read aloud, that's an additional 540 words per year. And, at the rate of twice a day, you can easily expose students to more than 1,000 words a year in addition to curriculum selections. These types of intentional word learning choices begin to put the dent in the word gap that exists between groups of students.

It's important to intentionally select words, such as tier two words, as outlined in the anchored word learning strategy table (figure 5.15). By selecting these words, you'll benefit students by providing them with a good number of words that they will understand orally and recognize as they read increasingly challenging text. In appendix B of *Blended Vocabulary for K–12 Classrooms* (Tyson & Peery, 2017, p. 121), we listed tier two words from read alouds for primary and intermediate students. You can also access this online as a reproducible, titled "Suggested Books Containing Tier-Two

Strategy: Anchored Word Learning

Pillar: Vocabulary

Grade Level:	**Instructional Grouping:**	**Consider This:**
☑ K ☑ 1 ☑ 2 ☑ 3 ☑ 4 ☑ 5 ☑ 6	☑ Whole Group ☑ Small Group ☐ Individual	• Select three tier two words that are important to the selected read aloud and provide vocabulary growth. • Periodically revisit words since multiple exposures are key to helping students deepen their understanding of words.

Figure 5.15: Strategy—Anchored word learning.

continued ▶

What is it? Anchored word learning is a strategy for intentionally integrating word learning opportunities with daily read alouds.

Why is it important? Students need both direct and indirect word learning opportunities across the school day. Since most elementary teachers engage in read alouds daily, it is efficient to do double-duty and combine targeted, advanced word learning with your read alouds.

What works in the classroom?

Pre-Steps

- **Select a read aloud:** Choose books by your favorite authors, books recommended by others, favorite books, and picture and trade books.
- **Identify three words for instruction:** Preview the book prior to the read aloud and select three tier two words that both expand students' vocabularies and will likely appear in other texts.
- **Mark the three words with a sticky note the first time each appears in text:** Place a sticky note on each page where a targeted word appears. Additionally, write the three words on a sticky note and place it on the inside cover of the book to remind yourself of the targeted words as you reread the book in future years. Two examples are as follows:
  - *Toy Boat* (de Sève, 2014) selected words: *gliding, afloat, bellowed*
  - *I Got an Elephant* (Ginkel, 2006) selected words: *confused, absurd, sturdy*

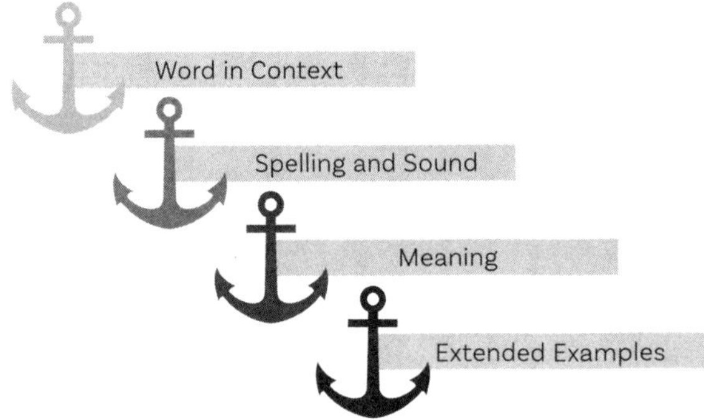

- **Read the targeted word in context:** Read each word aloud in context and briefly bring attention to it. Don't engage in a lengthy discussion as you read the word aloud in context. Students should initially hear the word in a complete, fluent reading selection.
- **Teach spelling and sound:** Read the word aloud and have students repeat it. Then, write the word on a sentence strip, saying the letters aloud as you write the word. Have students notice the spelling and voice anything they notice that is unusual about the spelling, such as double letters, a silent *e*, and so forth. Have early learners air write the word while saying each letter aloud. Older students can spell the word with their hand by forming each letter on the palm of the opposite hand or tracing letters on their desks.
- **Provide the meaning:** Reread the words in context and provide the meaning of each with a student-friendly definition.
- **Give extended examples:** Provide examples for each word beyond the context of the story. Encourage students to provide examples of their own so they personalize the word, relating it to their own context.

Extension

- **Create a community read aloud word wall or poster:** Create a community word wall or poster featuring words specifically found in read alouds. The power of word learning is in multiple exposures and review! The community wall provides a simple, accessible way to return to words and review their meanings during read aloud time, thus providing multiple oral exposures and increased familiarity with the words.

Visit ***go.SolutionTree.com/literacy/FSK6*** *and enter the unique access code found on the book's inside front cover to access a reproducible version of this figure.*

Vocabulary Words for Primary and Intermediate Grades" (visit **go.SolutionTree.com/literacy**).

Selecting read alouds that specifically encourage students to notice and collect words is a perfect way to create a word-rich classroom. Read alouds can help to create an energy and enthusiasm about vocabulary and word choice while also including dynamic and colorful illustrations.

Resources for Read Alouds

- *A Walk in the Words* by Hudson Talbott (2021)
- *Big Words for Little People* by Jamie Lee Curtis (2008)
- *Colossal Words for Kids: 75 Tremendous Words—Neatly Defined to Stick in the Mind* by Colette Hiller (2024)
- *Donovan's Word Jar* by Monalisa DeGross (1994)
- *Max's Words* by Kate Banks (2006)
- *Miss Alaineus: A Vocabulary Disaster* by Debra Frasier (2000)
- *The Boy Who Cried Fabulous* by Lesléa Newman (2004)
- *The Boy Who Loved Words* by Roni Schotter (2006)
- *The Weighty Word Book* by Paul M. Levitt, Douglas A. Burger, and Elissa S. Guralnick (2009)
- *The Word Collector* by Sonja Wimmer (2012)
- *Words are CATegorical book series* by Brian P. Cleary and Brian Gable (1999–2012)

Word Walls

Create word walls *with* students and *for* students. Word walls and intentionality go hand in hand. They can be a vital element of a literacy-rich environment. *Intentionality* is key. In my estimation there are two key elements that have potential to make word walls serve as vocabulary enrichment for students: (1) *co-construction* and (2) *review*. See figure 5.16 (page 204) for an example of a social studies word wall created with students and displayed on chart paper.

Word walls are not meant to be static, never-changing elements in the classroom. They don't have to be fancy, either. For example, simple paper displayed on a cabinet suffices to record key vocabulary from a social studies unit. During lessons, the teacher and students determined specific words to record. As students co-constructed and added words relative to the content unit, they engaged with tier two and three vocabulary (Shanahan, 2021). When created and used purposefully, word walls provide another opportunity for repeated exposures to words—students can see, hear, and discuss words in another context as you co-develop word walls. Word walls need to be regularly tied to instruction, practice, and review.

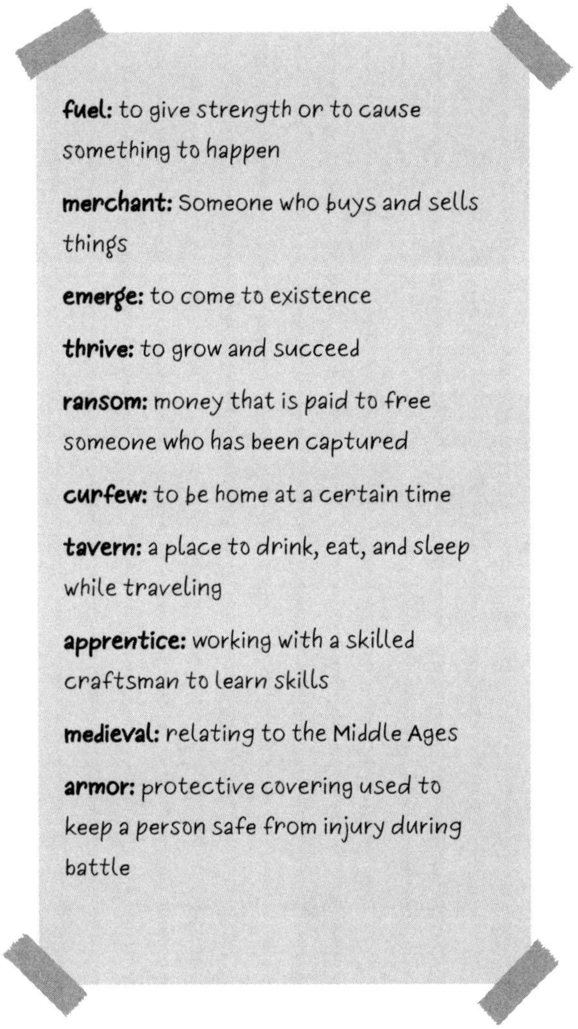

fuel: to give strength or to cause something to happen

merchant: Someone who buys and sells things

emerge: to come to existence

thrive: to grow and succeed

ransom: money that is paid to free someone who has been captured

curfew: to be home at a certain time

tavern: a place to drink, eat, and sleep while traveling

apprentice: working with a skilled craftsman to learn skills

medieval: relating to the Middle Ages

armor: protective covering used to keep a person safe from injury during battle

Figure 5.16: Key vocabulary recorded with students for a social studies unit of study.

In addition to how you use word walls, development begins with selecting words to display. There are endless possibilities for which words to include on word walls. If you're a primary teacher, you may want to develop a high-frequency word wall so that students see these commonly used words and have a reference for spelling. Emerging writers can also create their own "portable" word wall using a file folder. Alongside each alphabet letter, students print words they are learning or wish to use when writing, as shown in figure 5.17.

Words specific to the season or a unit, for example, can be written on a poster board to aid students as they read and write. Perhaps your school has many students who are English learners. Consider co-creating a word wall that features common Spanish words alongside equivalent English words, as shown earlier in this chapter.

A middle school in Indiana created a "word splash" hallway bulletin board featuring tier two and tier three vocabulary for their fifth- and sixth-grade students (see similar example in figure 5.18). Teachers agreed to focus on these words during instruction and conversation, and students watched the colorful display of words grow over time.

Finally, displaying words doesn't have to be limited to traditional bulletin boards. Use poster boards, the back of bookshelves, and sticky notes. Digital word walls using tools such as Padlet work well, too. The choices you make will depend on your students, how you will incorporate them into instruction and review, and available technology.

In the word walls strategy (figure 5.19, page 206), I've provided a simple, five-step process that I developed to ensure your word walls support continuous vocabulary development for your students.

Games and Gamelike Activities to Support Word Learning

Since an important aspect of word learning is hearing and experiencing words in varied contexts, games provide the perfect opportunity to have fun with words and use them orally with classmates. They're so effective that Robert J. Marzano (2009, 2020) included games as the sixth step in his six-step

Figure 5.17: A student's portable word wall using a file folder.

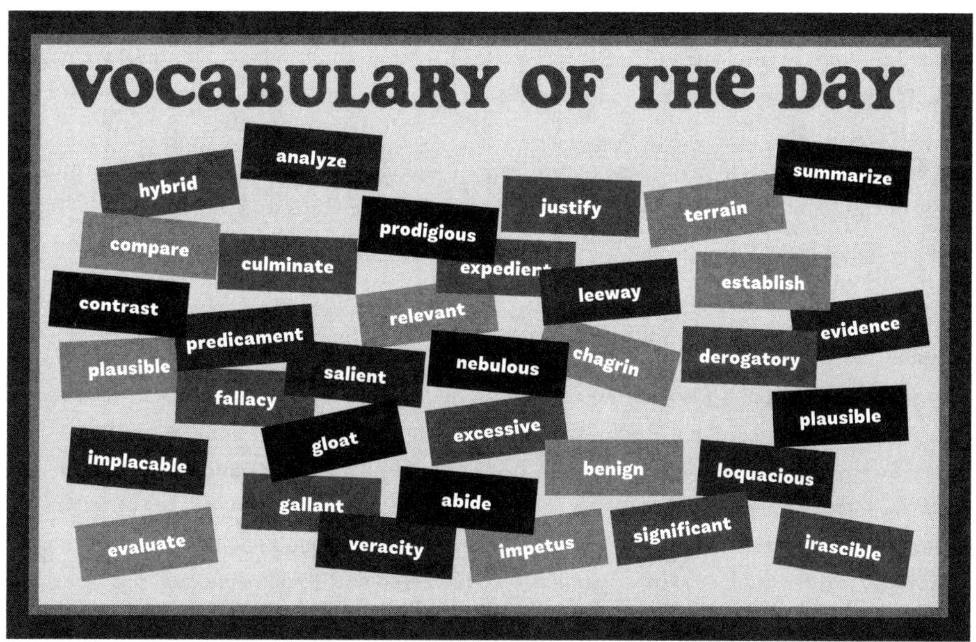

Figure 5.18: Word splash hallway word wall of tier two and tier three vocabulary.

Strategy: Word Walls

Pillar: Vocabulary

Grade Level:

- ☑ K
- ☑ 1
- ☑ 2
- ☑ 3
- ☑ 4
- ☑ 5
- ☑ 6

Instructional Grouping:

- ☑ Whole Group
- ☑ Small Group
- ☐ Individual

Consider This:

- Create words walls that will be integrated into instruction, practice, and review.
- Change words frequently using the following suggestions.
- Develop word walls *with* your students.

What is it? Word walls are a visual display of words that serve as a reference to students when they speak, write, and read.

Why is it important? Word walls help immerse students in a print-rich environment and provide additional opportunities for students to engage with words. The key is actively engaging students in developing, selecting, and using the words in speaking and writing. Using word walls as part of instruction and review provides additional instances in which students hear words used in varied contexts, thus refining their understanding of specific vocabulary.

What works in the classroom?

Five Simple Steps to Make Word Walls Support Learning

1. **Create word walls with your students:** Create word walls alongside your students as part of an ongoing direct instruction and review cycle. Consider organizing words using the word cluster approach as previously discussed and change them frequently. Have students develop them collaboratively using an app such as Padlet while they are engaged in a unit of study, book study, or independent research.
2. **Display them your way:** There are so many ways to display words other than the typical bulletin board. Assess your room and get creative. Think about using the backs of bookshelves, poster boards, the side of a cupboard or filing cabinet, or a pocket chart.
3. **Change up your word walls:** As an intentional strategy, word walls should be dynamic and changed frequently. As stated previously, there are so many words to learn! Create a read aloud word wall or poster. Make a fun "trash" word wall that includes words students agree not to use frequently when they write. Trash words may include *nice*, *said*, *good*, and so on. And for lots of cluster word groups and ideas, check out Marzano's (2020) *Teaching Basic, Advanced, and Academic Vocabulary: A Comprehensive Framework for Elementary Instruction.*
4. **Add images to accompany words:** Most word walls that we typically see display words alphabetically. How about including images, symbols, or pictographs with words—referred to as nonlinguistic representations (Marzano, 2009, 2020)? Think about word walls featuring each word alongside nonlinguistic representations like pictures of students acting out the words. Images, symbols, and examples are powerful reminders and hooks to learn and recall vocabulary. (See figures 5.20 and 5.21 for examples.)
5. **Review and play games:** Playing games with words helps students experience vocabulary in a new and different context. Save the last word for me is a fun and interactive game described in the following pages. Games don't have to be complex. For example, play a simple game of flashlight vocabulary. Provide a flashlight to each group of three or four students. Begin by providing brief definitions of words displayed in the classroom. When the group identifies the word, they shine their flashlight on it. Along with traditional games such as Boggle, you'll find fun and engaging games online. Marzano (2020) and Marzano, Katie Rogers, and Julia A. Simms (2015) include a number of games and directions in their vocabulary books.

Figure 5.19: Strategy—Word walls.

Visit ***go.SolutionTree.com/literacy/FSK6*** *and enter the unique access code found on the book's inside front cover to access a reproducible version of this figure.*

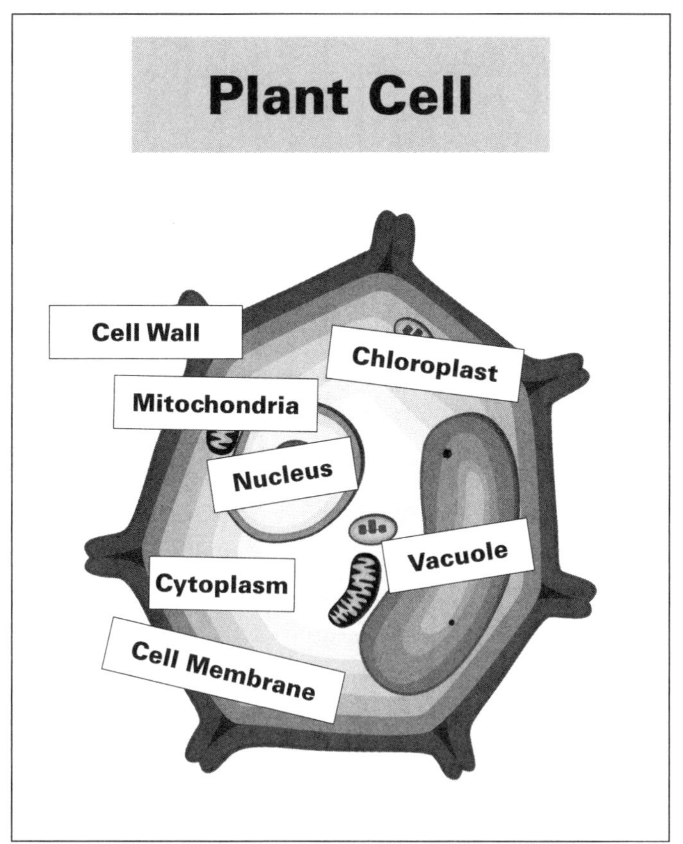

Figure 5.20: Learning about plant cells with movable tier three vocabulary.

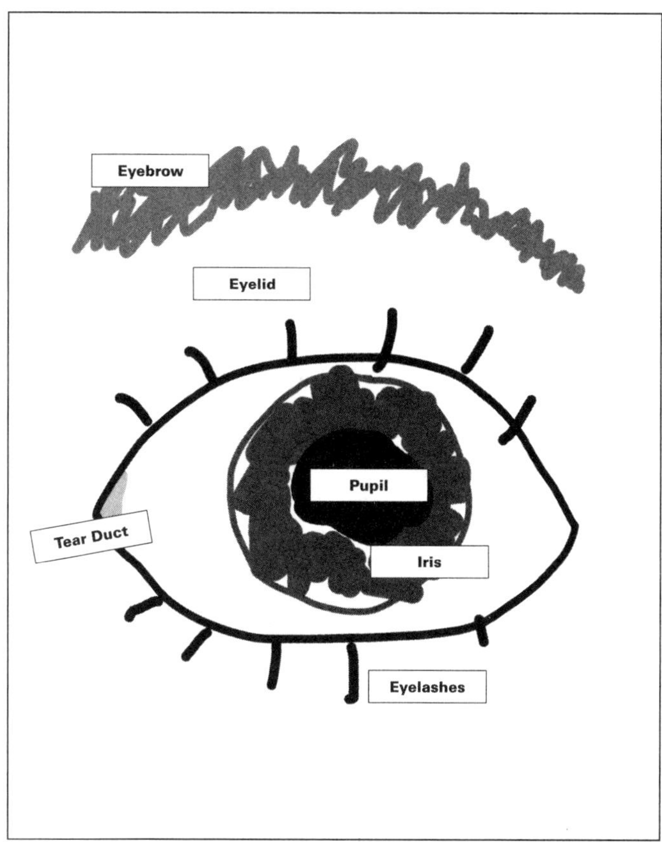

Figure 5.21: Primary students label an eye they created, which supports word learning.

word learning process. They're a great way to engage students in review in a relaxed, playful environment.

Classroom games like Pictionary, Boggle, and Scrabble are easy items to include on a shelf in the classroom library. Additionally, previously described strategies such as word walls and save the last word for me are ways to infiltrate the class day with word learning activities that are fun and interactive. Digital tools can fill this niche as well. Kahoot! (www.kahoot.com), Flashcard Stash, and Free Rice (www.freerice.com) all provide ways to review words. Finally, if you're looking for varied vocabulary games, check out *Vocabulary Games for the Classroom* (Carleton & Marzano, 2010), a resource that fills the need for adding word games of all sorts to your classroom. The following sections offer two additional strategies you can utilize in your classroom.

Save the Last Word for Me

Vocabulary strategies can take a gamelike form as you provide students review opportunities. Save the last word for me is a gamelike activity that works best with students in the intermediate grades (Beers, 2003). The clearly defined process provides a structure for students to review words and deepen their content understanding through discussion.

Since students are active participants as both speakers and listeners, the game encourages deeper understanding, which, in turn, moves words up the stages of word learning. The strategy can be used as students are acquiring vocabulary related to a unit of study or prior to an assessment to help students practice and review vocabulary.

In the save the last word for me strategy, you'll find how to develop the vocabulary game and implement it with your students. I've used this strategy with students and teachers; the ensuing discussion never disappoints. I've also developed student-friendly directions, captured in a reproducible, which you can use with your students (see figure 5.22).

Save the Last Word for Me Directions

- One student selects a card from the deck of terms and shares the term with the other members in the group.
- On a piece of paper, each student jots down what he or she knows about the term. (This can also be in one's head, with each student thinking about what he or she knows about the meaning of the term.)
- When they are finished, each student takes a turn sharing his or her reflections and responses. As each participant shares his or her thoughts, other students can share their own thoughts and responses.
- The student who drew the card gets the last word by sharing his or her reflections and reactions or by stating a fresh view if the responses of others have altered his or her original thinking about the term. If students are unsure, they can refer to the text or handouts for clarification.
- Next, another student draws a new card, and the process repeats.

Source: Tyson & Peery, 2017, p. 70.

Figure 5.22: Student-friendly directions for save the last word for me.

*Visit **go.SolutionTree.com/literacy/FSK6** for a free reproducible version of this figure.*

The strategy is further detailed in figure 5.23.

Strategy: Save the Last Word for Me

Pillar: Vocabulary

Grade Level:	**Instructional Grouping:**	**Materials:**
☐K ☐1 ☑2 ☑3 ☑4 ☑5 ☑6	☐ Whole Group ☑ Small Group ☐ Individual	• Pre-made sets of vocabulary terms placed in bags for each group • If the unit of study has a lot of terms, consider printing a master set of vocabulary terms and place about six terms in each bag. After a few minutes, signal the groups to trade the bags of terms so each group has a new set of terms. **Consider This:** • Divide students into groups of three to five students. Small groups are better for interactive discussion. • Second-grade students may not be ready for this strategy, but students in third grade should be able to benefit from the targeted discussion of content area words.

What is it? Save the last word for me is a gamelike strategy that provides the vehicle for students to deepen their understanding of academic vocabulary. Even though it's low tech, save the last word for me serves as an interactive, engaging way to review and extend word learning and is well suited to academic vocabulary found within content texts.

Why is it important? Students need multiple exposures to words in order to learn them deeply. The goal is for students to review and refine understanding of concepts and specific terms. When they hear words in varied contexts, they'll deepen and extend their understanding.

What works in the classroom?

Preplanning

- **Make one set of vocabulary terms for each group of students:** The word and definition can be printed on opposite sides or the same. The terms should come from a content area chapter or unit of study. (If the unit of study has a lot of terms, consider printing a master set of vocabulary terms while only putting about six terms in each bag. After a few minutes, signal the groups to trade the bags of terms so each group has a new set of terms.)
- **Print the directions for each group** Place the printed directions and terms in a plastic bag or clear sleeve for each group of students.
- **Divide students into groups of three to five:** It's important that groups are small so students have the opportunity to participate and discuss word meanings.

Steps for the Game

1. One student draws a card from the deck and reads it aloud.
2. Remaining students write (or think about) a brief definition for the word.
3. Moving around the circle, the first student provides a definition, and then other students add to the definition, refining and adding examples along the way.
4. The person who drew the card gets the last word and can add to the definition or revise it before students agree on a definition. If students don't know a specific term or concept, they can agree to use the text, a glossary, or an online dictionary to gain clarity.
5. Students take turns drawing cards and repeat the process previously described.

Figure 5.23: Strategy—Save the last word for me.

*Visit **go.SolutionTree.com/literacy/FSK6** and enter the unique access code found on the book's inside front cover to access a reproducible version of this figure.*

Word Sorts Strategy

Word sorts are a word study activity in which students group or sort words according to their common features. Sorting can be done in a variety of ways including shared features such as meaning, beginning or ending sounds, letters, spelling patterns, and parts of speech. Word sorts can be used in a variety of ways. One way is to use word sorts as a semantic mapping activity that helps students see relationships among words and concepts. Students need many opportunities to see these relationships and talk about how words are related. Word sorts, for vocabulary development, is a strategy done best in pairs or small groups using vocabulary with which students have familiarity. In the stages of word learning, word sorts fit into level three, when students begin understanding that words fit into categories or word clusters. See the simple steps to implement word sorts with your students (figure 5.24), providing additional supports or scaffolds based on student needs and grade level.

Strategy: Word Sorts

Pillar: Vocabulary

Grade Level:	Instructional Grouping:	Consider This:
☑K ☑1 K-1 teacher supported ☑2 ☑3 ☑4 ☑5 ☑6	☐ Whole Group ☑ Small Group ☐ Individual	• Consider using word sorts related to content area terms your students have been learning. • For K-3, consider modeling the word sorts strategy as a teacher-directed whole-group activity using a document camera to display words, categories, and show movement of words into appropriate categories.

What is it? Words sorts is a semantic mapping strategy that engages students in identifying relationships between words. Students categorize sets of words into groups based on common features.

Why is it important? Students need many opportunities to engage with words, both through direct instruction and through indirect word learning opportunities that allow them to deepen and extend their understanding of words.

What works in the classroom?

Preparation

- Create sets of word cards to support a unit of study such as *volcanoes*, *the colonial era*, or *mammals*.
- Create sets of cards that name the categories into which the words fall. Using the volcano example from list-group-label, the three labels would be: Things that Come Out of a Volcano, Hot Parts, and Results of an Eruption.

Word Sort Activity

Primary Students

- For primary students, you will determine the labels for each group of words and provide students with labels prior to the activity.
- Working in small groups, students place the words in front of them and sort them according to common features. They then place each group of words under the matching label that identifies the feature or characteristic the words have in common.

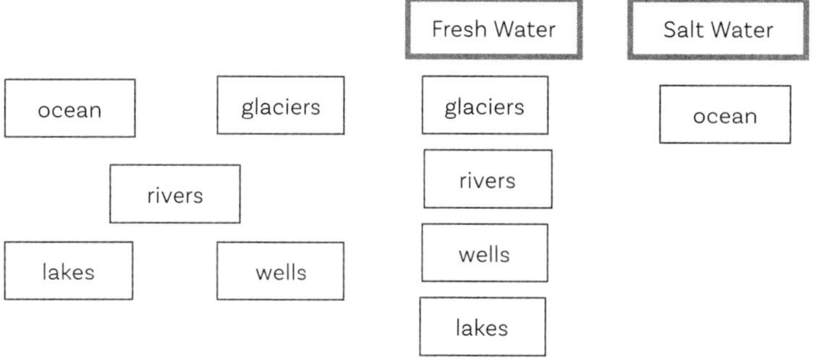

- Consider an example of a word sort from a second-grade unit of study about bodies of water. As a recap of the unit, the teacher provided the headings "salt water" and "fresh water." In small groups, students categorized the cards with the bodies of water listed on them under the appropriate heading.

Intermediate Students

- Working in small groups, students place the words in front of them and sort them according to common features.
- Through group discussion, students decide how to categorize each group.
- Students make a label for each group of words and place the label above each group.
- Students circulate and observe how other groups sorted and labeled each group of words.
- To extend the vocabulary discussion, bring the class together to discuss how each group sorted and labeled the terms.

Figure 5.24: Strategy—Word sorts.

Visit ***go.SolutionTree.com/literacy/FSK6*** *and enter the unique access code found on the book's inside front cover to access a reproducible version of this figure.*

Fly Swatter Vocabulary (Flashlight Vocabulary) Strategy

Looking for a quick, energetic game to engage students while reviewing vocabulary? Fly swatter vocabulary serves that purpose. Word learning can be fun, and this fast-paced game provides that. Students love it, and you can use it as a quick five-minute review before lunch or at the close of the day. Please see figure 5.25 (page 212) for a detailed outline of the strategy.

Digital Tools to Support Word Learning Strategies

Word learning takes many forms, and digital tools provide another avenue to explore a broader array of information about words than traditional tools alone. And, as I established, students need a wide range of tools and opportunities to enrich their vocabulary while experiencing words in many different contexts.

One advantage of digital tools is the ability they offer to customize word lists to support content goals so that students can easily practice and review. While digital tools vary, many allow students to do the following.

Strategy: Fly Swatter Vocabulary

Pillar: Vocabulary

Grade Level:	Instructional Grouping:	Consider This:
☑ K ☑ 1 ☑ 2 ☑ 3 ☑ 4 ☑ 5 ☑ 6	☑ Whole Group ☐ Small Group ☐ Individual	• You can choose to keep points in this game or just play for review. • This game is perfect for reviewing vocabulary from a content unit of study or words collected during read alouds. • You can also turn this into flashlight vocabulary and use a flashlight in place of the fly swatters.

What is it? Fly swatter vocabulary is a simple and fun game to review vocabulary—content area terms work quite well.

Why is it important? Students need many exposures to words when they are acquiring vocabulary to be able to use them as part of their expressive vocabulary—words they can use when they speak and write.

What works in the classroom?

- **Project words:** Write, post, or project each vocabulary term on the board.
- **Teams:** Divide the class into two teams.
- **Provide definition:** Read the definition of one term at a time.
- **Students find the word:** One student from each team scans the board with the goal of swatting the correct word first.
- **Context:** Then, read aloud a sentence using the target word in context to provide additional opportunity for students to hear the word used correctly within context.
- **Play on:** Continue this routine until all students have an opportunity to participate.

Figure 5.25: Strategy—Fly swatter vocabulary.

*Visit **go.SolutionTree.com/literacy/FSK6** and enter the unique access code found on the book's inside front cover to access a reproducible version of this figure.*

- Hear pronunciations
- Read words in a variety of authentic examples
- View photos and images related to words (especially important for English learners)
- Reinforce word learning through interactive games
- Play with and manipulate language
- Discover rhyming words
- Collaborate with classmates to create virtual word walls
- Develop personalized word banks

There are many ways that digital tools can be integrated into word learning and vocabulary instruction. Carefully select the tools that support your instructional practice and review goals. Some tools are particularly useful in supporting English learners and others are well suited for primary or intermediate students.

In *Blended Vocabulary for K–12 Classrooms* (Tyson & Peery, 2017), we explored the many ways digital tools can be integrated into word learning and vocabulary instruction. This exploration of digital tools is not an in-depth review nor exhaustive of all the digital tools that support word learning. We've also developed guidelines to help you think more deeply about which tools to select. Go to **go.SolutionTree.com/literacy** and select the page for *Blended Vocabulary for K–12 Classrooms* to access the free reproducible "Using Digital Tools: Questions for Consideration." In the following list, you'll also find categories of tools (along with ideas of where to find them) that encourage differentiated word learning, review, and playing with language.

- **Reference tools:** There are a wide variety of online tools that are easy to use, even for primary students. Many include a visual display of words, words used with context and grouped by theme. Some of my favorite tools include Lexipedia (www.lexipedia.com), Lingro (www.lingro.com), and a Maths Dictionary for Kids (www.amathsdictionaryforkids.com). More visual dictionaries include Shahi (http://blachan.com/shahi) and Snappy Words (www.snappywords.com). Share several dictionaries with students and have them choose which ones they prefer. A few additional online dictionaries are Wordnik (www.wordnik.com), which includes a word-of-the-day feature, and Your Dictionary (www.yourdictionary.com), which boasts a clutter-free display, provides words within context, and saves custom word lists.
- **Word clouds:** *Word clouds* are a visual display of words within a specific context—such as words that have to do with weather, words that express joy, words connected to a specific content unit, and so on. While they don't build vocabulary, they do create interest and build word consciousness. Tagxedo (www.tagxedo.com), a free word cloud tool, creates word clouds in specific shapes! Wordle (www.wordle.net) generates word clouds based on text entered and can be used to generate a cloud based on words that students enter related to a content unit, for example. In short, the more frequently students enter each specific word, the larger and more prominent the words appear in the cloud. WordSift (http://wordsift.com) is another tool similar to Wordle. Beneath the cloud, it groups words semantically, which is a big plus for students making connections between words.
- **Games and review:** Games and gamelike activities can be especially motivating and increase engagement for some students. For English learners in particular, English Vocabulary Word Lists (www.manythings.org/vocabulary) includes numerous handy word lists accompanied by games, quizzes, and puzzles. Flashcard Stash (http://flashcardstash.com) helps

students build instant recognition and fluency with words, taking one step toward moving up the progression of understanding the meaning of words. Teachers can also create flash cards to support units of study. Free Rice (www.freerice.com) has been one of my favorite online gamelike activities. Students match words to the correct definition, which, in turn, donates rice at the same time. For each correct answer, the United Nations World Food Program donates ten grains of rice to a country in need. How's that for combining word learning with social consciousness? In addition, students see a visual display of rice added to a bowl each time they make a correct response. With sixty levels and many subject areas, it's differentiated for each student. It's a winner!

- **Concept maps:** *Concept maps* help students see the logical or causal relationships among topics, events, or issues. The defining or overarching topic typically appears in a large circle or box with subtopics in smaller circles or boxes surrounding the topic. Lines connect the shapes, which help visually define relationships. Concept maps are a great way to tap into higher-level thinking when students develop the maps themselves. When working with a partner or in small groups, students have the opportunity to build and expand their vocabulary and word knowledge. Popplet (https://popplet.com) is a free, web-based digital tool and app that allows students to create their own concept map. Bubbl.us (https://bubbl.us) and Mind Map (https://lucidspark.com) are similar digital tools with which to familiarize yourself.
- **Word walls:** As I mentioned previously in this chapter, word walls are a teaching, discussion, and review tool. Additionally, student-generated word banks or word journals are a good way to have students take control of their own word learning. ThingLink (www.thinglink.com) can be used to help build background knowledge before a unit of study. You begin by uploading an image, which ThingLink makes dynamic. From there, you identify hotspots on specific parts of the image and add text or web links. ThingLink is available in both free and paid versions. Padlet (https://padlet.com) is another favorite digital tool that is used to create a collaborative, digital word wall. It's interactive in that students can create sticky notes that include text, images, links, or videos. You can also embed the digital word wall on a class website, which provides easy access for students. For primary students, teachers will probably want to create the wall ahead of time with words and links for students. Intermediate students could add text and images to the word wall during class discussion. Padlet has both free and paid versions with varied capabilities. Learn more about how to integrate Padlet into

your classroom by viewing Teacher's Tech's (2022) YouTube video "How to Use Padlet."

- **Assessment:** Want to engage in formative assessment to assess general or specific word knowledge? Kahoot! (https://getkahoot.com) is a site that allows you to create multiple-choice items and turn them into games in which students use their devices to select answers before time runs out. Data on the results are instantly displayed. Check out lots of Kahoot! games that teachers have shared. Plickers (www.plickers.com), another quick-check tool, are cards containing QR codes that teachers create and print. Students hold up the cards in response to questions posed to the whole class. The way students turn their cards reflects each student's response (usually A, B, C, or D for multiple-choice items). You simply snap a photo of the entire class holding up their individual cards, using a phone or tablet. Then the Plickers app reads all the cards and shows the teacher real-time data based on students' responses. No devices are required for students to participate; they need only to hold up their pre-printed cards with the QR code displayed.

Encouraging word learning through direct and indirect strategies supports students as they expand their word knowledge. Digital tools can be used in a variety of ways to bolster word learning and sometimes provide more information about words than more traditional tools. Additionally, digital tools are typically engaging for learners and support independent word learning with groups of students as they review and expand their understanding of general and academic vocabulary. In summary, digital tools and apps show great promise in rounding out a classroom filled with word learning opportunities.

Wrapping It Up

Vocabulary is a foundational pillar that is integral to the four remaining pillars. Word knowledge has an impact on how easily students acquire phonemic awareness and phonics, influences reading fluency, and impacts comprehension. In this chapter, we looked at how to select and teach words, how to develop a comprehensive vocabulary program, and how to use direct and indirect strategies to increase word learning for your students. Use the Leader's Lens (figure 5.26, page 216) to deepen your thought process as you move forward. Consider the Five Key Takeaways (page 217) as you implement these strategies. Think about intentionality as it relates to your instruction and literacy environment as you consider the Five Key Next Steps (page 217).

Leader's Lens

Vocabulary and Word Learning in the Classroom

Consider the following supervision supports and classroom connections as you lead teachers to create a classroom brimming with word learning opportunities.

Supervision Supports	
Practical Research	Have you shared research and key understandings such as: • Current research on classroom environments that support literacy and word learning • *The why* behind vocabulary development and word learning • The research behind the word gap and how to address it • The four stages of word learning
Professional Development	• What do you consider essential professional development for vocabulary? Where would you begin? • How would you support collaborative teams as teachers implement effective vocabulary practices within the literacy block? • Are there professional vocabulary resources to support teachers as they learn more about the importance of intentional vocabulary instruction?
Feedback and Expectations	• Have you provided expectations specific to effective instruction and the literacy environment that support vocabulary instruction aligned to the science of reading?
Financial Focus	• Is there money budgeted to provide books for read alouds and materials that can support rich vocabulary instruction?
Classroom Connections (Look-Fors)	
Oral Language	• Notice the level of vocabulary used during direct and indirect instruction. • Notice the intentional use of read alouds to support word learning.
Literacy-Rich Environment	• Notice the evidence of vocabulary instruction within the classroom. • Notice the purposeful use of wall space or anchor charts to support vocabulary acquisition. • Notice if the environment is labeled to support English learners.
Direct Instruction for Word Learning	Notice the following direct instructional practices, which include: • Explicit vocabulary instruction of tiered vocabulary • Direct instruction of vocabulary tied to standards and content units • Varied linguistic and nonlinguistic strategies for word learning
Indirect Word Learning Opportunities	Notice indirect instructional vocabulary practices, which include: • The classroom atmosphere and the utilization of tools—print and digital—that can enhance vocabulary acquisition • The evidence of vocabulary development through the use of read alouds • Tier one and tier two vocabulary used throughout the day • The amount and frequency of oral language and dialogic conversation across the school day

Figure 5.26: Chapter 5 leader's lens.

*Visit **go.SolutionTree.com/literacy/FSK6** for a free reproducible version of this figure.*

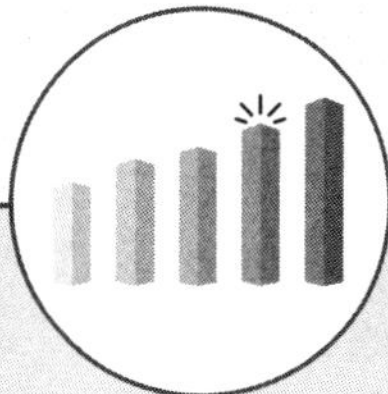

Five Key Takeaways

Consider the following takeaways individually or discuss them with your collaborative grade-level team.

1. **Vocabulary impacts comprehension and achievement:** Vocabulary, the fourth pillar of the big five, "refers to the words we use to communicate effectively when we listen, speak, read, and write" (Tyson & Peery, 2017, p. 1). At its core, vocabulary has a direct impact on comprehension and general academic achievement.
2. **Address word gaps:** Some students enter school with a large repertoire of words, while others have very limited vocabularies, which creates a substantial word gap between the two groups. To address this deficit, provide both direct and indirect word learning opportunities to support students as they acquire and deepen their understanding of words.
3. **Implement a balanced approach to word learning:** A balanced approach to word learning includes (1) explicit, direct instruction focused on selected vocabulary, (2) creating literacy-rich classrooms that support and promote incidental word learning, and (3) modeling vocabulary orally and providing practice and review through games and digital tools (Tyson & Peery, 2017).
4. **Use organizational structures to select vocabulary for direct instruction:** Tiered vocabulary (Beck et al., 2002, 2013) and cluster vocabulary (Marzano, 1984; Marzano & Marzano, 1988; Marzano, 2020) are two organizational structures which provide a framework for selecting and organizing words for direct instruction
5. **Provide multiple exposures to words:** Students need multiple exposures to words in order to learn them. Direct instruction, independent reading, and engaging students in games with words allow them to play with and explore words in a relaxed setting and provide for additional exposure to words in order to understand them well.

Five Key Next Steps

Consider the following questions individually or discuss them with your collaborative grade-level team.

1. **Word gap:** Have you considered whether your students have experienced a word gap as they entered school? If so, what are ways you can address the gap to support their learning?
2. **Tiered vocabulary:** How does tiered vocabulary and the cluster approach impact your vocabulary instruction? Have you considered the ways your classroom supports direct and indirect word learning opportunities?
3. **Direct instructional strategies:** How do the direct instructional strategies in this chapter compare with vocabulary strategies you currently use? How are they similar or different?
4. **Direct and indirect strategies:** Select a direct and indirect strategy to implement with your students and share with your collaborative team. With your team, discuss why you selected a specific strategy, how you implemented it, and what you have learned.
5. **Digital tools:** Do you use digital tools and apps to support and extend word learning? If so, discuss with your team which you prefer and why. If not, is there one shared here that you may explore with your students?

Key Vocabulary

Comprehension

Before-, During-, and After-Reading Strategies	A common framework used to describe the cognitive behaviors of proficient readers during each phase of reading.
Comprehension	Refers to the process of constructing meaning through the dynamic interaction among (1) the reader's existing knowledge, (2) the information suggested by the text being read, and (3) the context of the reading situation
Comprehension Monitoring	The process in which readers actively determine whether they understand what they are reading and what to do if comprehension breaks down.
Expository Text	Text that presents information or ideas
Fiction Text	Fiction writing is a piece of writing, or other narrative work, created in the author's imagination and typically includes characters, dialogue, plot, events, places, and setting.
Fix-up Strategies	Refers to the techniques or strategies readers use during reading to improve comprehension.
Front-Loading Vocabulary	Refers to an instructional strategy that provides scaffolding for students prior to reading; front-loading can be as simple as drawing students' attention to bold-faced vocabulary in informational text or briefly defining academic terms.
Informational Text	A subset of nonfiction writing, informational text is designed to inform or educate the reader about a specific topic. They typically include text features such as glossaries, bullet points, headings, subheadings, and images to aid the reader.
Narrative Text	Text that tells a story or describes a sequence of events
Nonfiction Text	Text that includes verifiable information, real-life events, or real people, divided into two main categories: biographies and informational books (Young et al., 2020)
Prior Knowledge	Also called background knowledge, it refers to the knowledge someone already possesses prior to reading a text (ILA, 2023b)
Schema Theory	An explanation or theory about how readers use their background knowledge of a text topic and their skills as a reader to interact with and make sense of or comprehend the information in the text (ILA, 2023b)
Story Grammar	An organization of consistent features that represent the basic structure of a narrative text.
Text Structure	The way information is organized within a text
Think-Alouds	When the teacher models their invisible behaviors by thinking aloud or talking about and demonstrating their thinking, and they read narrative and expository text.

CHAPTER 6

Comprehension
The Heart of Reading

Today a reader, tomorrow a leader.

—Margaret Fuller

We have arrived at the final essential pillar of reading—comprehension. Comprehension is arguably the most important pillar of the five. The previous four pillars—phonemic awareness, phonics, fluency and vocabulary—all point toward comprehension, the bull's-eye of the literacy target. Comprehension, at its simplest, is the heart of reading.

As you've read, digested, and implemented each pillar, you've undoubtedly noticed that the five pillars are interconnected. Each pillar has a specific purpose, but woven together, they have the power to develop strong, capable readers. For example, phonemic awareness and phonics are reciprocal processes that support emergent readers. As students' proficiency in phonemic awareness deepens, their proficiency in phonics deepens as well. Automatic decoding is dependent on decoding *and* word knowledge in order to map words proficiently. As students orthographically map words (all words they can read automatically), their fluency becomes more automatic. And automaticity is the bridge between decoding and comprehension.

In this chapter, we'll briefly look at several theories of comprehension that serve to frame both how we think about comprehension and how to best support students as they listen and read. Additionally, I've summarized the challenges of comprehension instruction, text structure, and the characteristics of effective comprehension instruction.

Finally, you'll be equipped with strategies for supporting students before, during, and after reading. Strategies include specific actions for activating prior knowledge, monitoring comprehension during reading, and deepening processing after reading. We'll conclude with Five Key Takeaways and Five Key Next Steps along with the Leader's Lens. I encourage you to reflect on your instruction as you strive to strengthen your students' most important skill—comprehension.

What Is Comprehension?

Comprehension isn't just a goal for readers, it is *the* goal. Even though comprehension is the heart of reading, it doesn't mean that comprehending is simple. Rather, comprehension is a complex process.

Several years ago, when I was working with a group of K–12 teacher leaders, we delved deeply into vocabulary and comprehension. At one point, I encouraged each small group to develop their own definition of comprehension. Read through them in the following list. They'll cause you to think about the varied ways we consider the factors that make up comprehension.

- Comprehension is a process in which information from the text and the knowledge possessed by the reader act together to construct meaning.
- Comprehension is the ability to decode printed text and recognize and understand words. Word recognition is the foundation for reading.
- Comprehension is transacting with text in order to create meaning from it.
- Comprehension is the process of constructing meaning through the dynamic interaction among (1) the reader's existing knowledge, (2) the information suggested by the text being read, and (3) the context of the reading situation.
- Comprehension is the thinking done before, during, and after reading.
- Comprehension is intentional thinking during which meaning is constructed through interactions between the text and the reader.

How we think about comprehension impacts our instruction. In my professional opinion, all of these definitions are accurate on some level. While one definition places more emphasis on the decoding and word recognition aspect of comprehension, most of these definitions lean toward a constructivist and transactional view of reading, which draws heavily from schema theory (Anderson & Pearson, 1984) and prior knowledge.

Schema theory, in brief, draws from cognitive science and seeks to explain how we organize and interpret information based on our personal mental frameworks. Schema, or an individual's mental organization of a topic, is based on the person's experiences and prior knowledge, thus differing from person to person. Some people find it helpful to think of schema as file folders, which are useful for both organizing and retrieving information while also changing and evolving over time. A person uses their background knowledge as they read text or other reading material to interact with and make sense of the information as they comprehend the text (ILA, 2023b).

For example, let's think about two people—one with a great deal of baking experience and the other a novice baker—who are attempting to make chocolate croissants. The skilled baker uses her background knowledge and well-honed experience to easily make sense of a complicated recipe for making chocolate croissants and also produce a perfectly crispy, delicious croissant. Her well-developed schema is based on years of prior baking experience, which helps her read, interpret, and easily understand the steps in the recipe. In contrast, a new baker with less-developed schema for baking would likely have difficulty following the recipe. Their lack of background knowledge and experience limits their understanding of the importance, for example, of chilling butter and cutting it in or the process of laminating as it relates to making croissants. In time, the new baker's schema would expand and refine as they gained skills, vocabulary, and experience.

Similarly, your students bring varied experiences and background knowledge to the classroom, which impacts both learning to read *and* reading to learn. Related to instruction, it's why I suggest routinely taking a few moments to preteach vocabulary and have students briefly talk about the topic. Having a brief discussion helps students activate their prior knowledge and begins building schema before reading, which, in turn, improves comprehension.

Understanding this lends importance to spending a few moments preteaching vocabulary prior to reading and filling in obvious content knowledge gaps. With this further explanation of schema and background knowledge, I encourage you to return to the definitions of schema and reread them. The interaction between the text and the reader implied directly and indirectly in many of these definitions points to the importance of schema theory. Selecting from these definitions, my preferred view of comprehension is the process of constructing meaning through the dynamic interaction among:

1. The reader's existing knowledge
2. The information suggested by the text being read
3. The context of the reading situation

Why Is Comprehension Important?

Each of the five pillars are key to building competent readers. Comprehension, however, is the primary outcome of the essential pillars and is also integral to student achievement and lifelong success.

The NRP reviewed 205 studies about reading comprehension. In their summary, they note three primary themes relative to developing comprehension.

1. The role of vocabulary as it relates to comprehension is integral.

2. Explicit comprehension strategy instruction positively impacts understanding.
3. Teachers should be better equipped through professional development to effectively teach comprehension strategies (NICHD, 2000a).

Let's look at each theme a bit further. First, vocabulary is intimately related to and directly impacts comprehension. Vocabulary and word learning must be an integral part of comprehension instruction. In chapter 5, there are many direct and indirect strategies that can strengthen vocabulary instruction and teach students how to independently learn vocabulary, which benefits their comprehension as they read narrative and informational text.

Next, direct instruction in comprehension strategies makes a difference in students' understanding of text (NICHD, 2000a). Students can learn to be active, engaged, and metacognitive as they read in order to construct meaning from text. In the What Works in the Classroom? section of this chapter (page 228), you'll find nine strategies to implement before, during, and after reading to support your students.

Third, teachers need practice and support through professional development to learn how to best teach comprehension strategies. Ideally, this would take place through ongoing professional learning opportunities and coaching. However, in the absence of this support, I suggest you support each other through your grade-level or collaborative team. Better yet, form a cross-grade-level group or schoolwide book study where you delve deeply into these evidence-based strategies and others (there are many more). Learn, discuss, and implement. Reflect and come back together to discuss what worked well along with specific challenges you faced. Learn from one another. We still have a lot to learn about comprehension strategies and their effectiveness at different grade levels and with different student populations.

Theories of Comprehension

Going back to the 20th century, we have learned a lot about comprehension through research and practice. Several models of comprehension have emerged that help us think about how readers make meaning from text. The three models that inform how we think about comprehension are schema theory, the transactional theory, and the constructivist theory of comprehension. I summarize each theory briefly in table 6.1.

If you briefly recall the previously listed definitions developed by teachers, you can see these theories reflected within the teachers' definitions. I'll offer one final definition of comprehension from the International Literacy Association (2023b), which is the following:

> Making meaning of what is viewed, read, or heard. Comprehension includes understanding what is expressed outright or implied as well as interpreting

Table 6.1: Theories of Comprehension

Comprehension Theories	Description
Schema Theory (Anderson & Pearson, 1984)	• Readers use prior knowledge to create meaning from text. • Readers must have adequate background knowledge and activate their prior knowledge (Langer, 1984) in order to understand what they read.
Transactional Theory (Rosenblatt, 1938, 1978)	• Readers bring different experiences to reading, which impacts what they take away from a given reading experience. • Reading is a transactional process between the reader and the text.
Constructivist Theory (Dixon-Krauss, 1996)	• Readers construct meaning based on their own knowledge by making connections to the text and their prior knowledge. • As readers actively construct meaning by creating representations and interpreting the text, comprehension improves.

> what is viewed, read, or heard by drawing on one's knowledge and experiences. Comprehension may also involve application and critical examination of the message in terms of intent, rhetorical choices, and credibility.

Once again, the ILA (2023b) definition is influenced by the three theories from table 6.1. In short, whichever definition you prefer should include threads from these theories of comprehension that guide your instruction and the strategies you select to support your students. However, even with awareness of the theories of comprehension and a knowledge of instructional strategies to support engagement before, during, and after reading, you will undoubtedly face challenges. In the following section, I examine some of these challenges.

Challenges of Comprehension Instruction

Comprehension involves developing skills and background knowledge, for which full proficiency occurs over time. Students who have poor comprehension may lack a variety of skills on which comprehension is built. We'll look at each of these briefly.

- **Lack of background knowledge:** Students may have limited background knowledge and poorly developed schema for specific topics, which, in turn, negatively impacts comprehension. Several strategies in this chapter and in previous chapters address how to help increase students' background knowledge.
- **Lack of fluency:** If students lack fluency and automaticity, a great deal of their cognitive energy is focused on decoding, with little remaining for comprehension. As described in chapter 4 (page 156), repeated reading is one of the most effective strategies for increasing fluency. In addition to the

strategies I provide in chapter 4, keep in mind that providing audiobooks can also be beneficial for these students and allow them to focus their attention on comprehending text rather than decoding.

- **Fluency is strong, but comprehension is poor:** Students may be fluent readers but still have poor reading comprehension. Focus on specific comprehension strategies, such as reciprocal teaching (Brown & Palincsar, 1987; Palincsar & Brown, 1984), so that students who are proficient at decoding also become proficient at understanding what they read (Lee & Tsai, 2017).
- **Limited vocabulary:** The majority of reading beyond the early grades is nonfiction and informational text, which include a great deal of academic vocabulary. When students have limited word knowledge, their comprehension is severely impacted as they move into upper elementary and middle school. Additionally, English learners may lack understanding of basic, everyday words known as tier one vocabulary (Beck et al., 2013), which makes comprehension challenging in both narrative and expository text.
- **Lack of familiarity with text types:** Students may have little familiarity with how texts are structured. Understanding how texts are structured impacts how students read and supports comprehension.
- **Learning disabilities and dyslexia:** Language learning disabilities such as dyslexia may impact understanding oral and written language and listening comprehension. Additionally, students with disabilities may have difficulty efficiently decoding, which, in turn, impacts comprehension.

Comprehension Can Be Taught

Students who are skilled readers use a variety of strategies when reading and comprehending text (Stanovich, 2000; Sweet & Snow, 2003). These include predicting, activating prior knowledge, generating questions, monitoring comprehension, drawing inferences, identifying text structures, and creating summaries (NICHD, 2000a).

However, many students don't acquire these skills naturally. This instruction actually begins early through explicit and systematic phonemic awareness and phonics instruction (pillars one and two) and lots of fluency practice (pillar three). Vocabulary (pillar four) and building background knowledge through oral conversation and read alouds is also integral to comprehension. Finally, we need to explicitly teach and model comprehension skills and strategies (Block & Pressley, 2002; Pressley, 2002, 2006), which results in "substantial improvements in student understanding of text" (Pressley, 2002, p. 12).

In education, there is a commonly repeated statement that goes, "In the primary grades, students *learn to read,* and then they *read to learn.*" This statement, which reflects a mindset, is troublesome. While it's true that educators focus on teaching the building blocks of reading in K–2, the mental and attitudinal framing this statement creates is dangerous. Along with teaching fundamental phonemic awareness and phonics skills, we must support comprehension at the same time. *All* reading should focus on meaning, including reading for emerging readers.

Students, even early primary students, can learn how to comprehend through direct strategy instruction. They can learn intentional actions—predicting, questioning, summarizing, and mapping—to monitor their comprehension as they read independently or listen to narrative and expository text.

Language (Listening) Comprehension

Language comprehension refers, in a broad sense, to one's acquired language related to cultural and content knowledge. That knowledge and related vocabulary may have been obtained through conversation and from text. While reading comprehension receives a great deal of attention in books and journals, listening comprehension garners much less focus, which minimizes its importance. In actuality, language skills develop from birth, long before children can speak. In the classroom, we need to begin early to intentionally continue developing oral language and listening comprehension. Through read alouds, everyday conversation, and intentional conversation specific to content, we can lay the groundwork needed for independent reading comprehension (Duke & Cartwright, 2021).

It's important to note that the skills required for listening comprehension are virtually the same as those required for reading comprehension (Clinton, 2019). While predictable and decodable texts are often limited in meaning, we can build listening comprehension through read alouds with authentic texts, such as high-quality picture books, trade books, and informational texts. Further, since many students enter our classrooms with enormous gaps in vocabulary and background knowledge, we must address both gaps through oral language and intentional instruction.

Before students are independent readers, reading aloud is an ideal way to build topical knowledge and vocabulary, both of which are necessary for comprehension. For example, while research shows that teachers predominantly read aloud from fiction (Giles & Morrison, 2023; Smith et al., 2022), you should intentionally select nonfiction and more complex texts than students can read independently. Since you provide the model of a fluent reader and provide the scaffolding for students, their cognitive energy can go toward comprehending the text through listening.

To make the experience beneficial, be intentional about learning outcomes and use a sequence that resembles the following. First, always preread the text and think about the questions you'll ask, connections you'll highlight, and vocabulary you will teach through the read aloud (Watts & Gandy, 2024). Allow students time to make connections and respond orally to the text, which is important for developing language, vocabulary, and comprehension (Bruner, 2021; Kaefer, 2020). Ideally, in order to build knowledge, students should read several texts or excerpts on a single topic or thematic unit being studied. Reading several types of text on a single topic helps students build richer connections and knowledge about specific topics such as transportation, volcanoes, or machines. And, by highlighting a few related books in the classroom library, students can read more on the topic and will likely read at a higher level than typical because of their increased background knowledge and broader vocabulary.

Not only do read alouds build language comprehension skills for primary students, but intermediate students can also benefit from intentional text conversations along with vocabulary and knowledge building based on the text. *Reading Aloud Across the Curriculum* (Laminack & Wadsworth, 2006) is an excellent resource for diverse, content-based read alouds to support building background knowledge and comprehension. In addition, intermediate students who have limited decoding skills may also benefit from listening to audiobooks. Listening to audiobooks is not a "less than" form of reading. When listening, students listen to a fluent reader who provides access to topics, grade-level information, and authors these students may not be able to read independently. Additionally, the social-emotional benefit for students reading below grade level who now have access to on- and above-grade-level topics and materials, and the ability to select "hot topic" books and interesting authors, may build personal autonomy and much-needed confidence.

Reading Comprehension

Comprehension typically refers to an independent meaning-getting process that occurs as a transactional process between the reader, the text, and the context. It is affected by what the reader is reading and why they are reading it. So much so that in a 2010 review, researchers Nell K. Duke and Kathryn L. Roberts "identified at least 18 differences between narrative and informational reading processes" (Duke, Ward, & Pearson, 2021, p. 666). For example, text structure differs between narrative and informational text and impacts how the reader approaches reading the text. Additionally, the reader's purpose for reading narrative differs greatly from reading an informational text, which is typically based on a specific topic. Vocabulary load for each text type also varies greatly and impacts how a reader approaches and comprehends text.

Teaching strategies that support comprehension from narrative and informational text help students build their repertoire of independent text strategies. Strategies that include developing a purpose, building vocabulary and background knowledge, understanding text structure, and summarizing information all support deeper text comprehension. Research supports the effectiveness of direct instruction in comprehension strategies for both younger students (Mahdavi & Tensfeldt, 2013) and students in grades 3–12 (Okkinga et al., 2018).

Direct instruction in comprehension, as with the other pillars, requires systematic and explicit instruction. Teaching students comprehension strategies with the purpose of making comprehension processes visible is vital to comprehensive literacy instruction. Gerald G. Duffy (1993), a well-respected literacy researcher, argues that strategy instruction should not consist of skill and drill—rather, they should be taught as a way for readers to construct meaning from text. Focus should be not on teaching comprehension strategies in a lock-step manner but rather on helping students understand that strategies are flexible and good readers frequently alter and adjust them to make meaning from text. Our aim is to support students as they become strategic readers. Ellin Oliver Keene and Susan Zimmermann (2013), the best-selling authors of a book about comprehension strategy instruction, also remind their readers that strategies are not the end goal; instead, we teach strategies to help students become active readers who monitor their comprehension.

Even with our earliest readers, we must allocate time for frequent conversations and direct instruction about how we make meaning from text. Unfortunately, observational research paints a rather bleak picture of explicit strategy instruction. Dolores Durkin (1978), a well-known literacy researcher, conducted a landmark study in which she observed primary classrooms during reading and social studies. She found very little comprehension instruction occurring during observations. Rather, teachers spent most of their time teaching phonics and giving and checking assignments. None used social studies as an opportunity to teach comprehension.

Unfortunately, additional studies report similar findings. For example, Barbara M. Taylor and her research colleagues (2000) report that comprehension instruction in grades 1–3 is minimal and focuses primarily on asking literal questions during small-group instruction. In grades 3–6, researchers (Pressley et al., 1998) are "struck by the almost complete absence of direct instruction about comprehension strategies" (p. 172). Ness (2011) finds that teachers in grades 1–5 devote about 25 percent of instructional time to comprehension, and a 2021 meta-analysis (Duke, Ward, & Pearson, 2021) reports a mean of 8.4 sessions devoted to comprehension instruction over the course of thirty-five school days. In short, our earliest learners need teachers who consistently prioritize comprehension instruction alongside the other pillars, including phonics.

While it appears that explicit comprehension instruction is not routine in many classrooms, it can and should be. Going back to the initial premises I laid out, intentionality makes a difference. Through think-alouds, where we reflect on our thinking and comprehension processes, we can begin to make the invisible processes visible for students. In the next section, you'll find numerous comprehension strategies that will help you make the processes in which readers engage visible and apparent for students, including the earliest readers.

What Works in the Classroom?

Educators can rely on decades of research for evidence-based recommendations specific to how to best support language and reading comprehension. In the following sections, we'll review characteristics of effective comprehension instruction along with specific instructional strategies to support students' thinking about and making meaning from text.

Characteristics of Effective Comprehension Instruction

Positively influencing comprehension begins long before strategy instruction since comprehension is dependent on phonological and phonemic awareness, phonics, fluency, oral language, and vocabulary. Based on a growing body of research, we better understand the characteristics of effective comprehension instruction. Once again, there is plenty of evidence that supports viewing the five pillars as interconnected and interdependent. Instructional approaches that acknowledge and support this interdependence are most effective. The following sections explore the components that support comprehension instruction, beginning with the characteristics of effective comprehension instruction found in table 6.2.

Table 6.2: Characteristics of Effective Comprehension Instruction

Develop Foundational Skills	Foundational skills such as concepts of print, phonemic awareness, and phonics skills are essential and have a positive impact on reading comprehension (Suggate, 2016). Students must be able to automatically read or decode most of the words in text in order to comprehend.
Consider Morphological Awareness	Developing *morphological awareness* means teaching the smallest, meaningful parts of words, including roots, affixes, and compound words, is beneficial as students develop foundational skills (Duke & Cartwright, 2021). Based on a meta-analysis of thirty studies, morphological awareness has been shown to positively impact reading comprehension (Goodwin & Ahn, 2013). In fact, teaching morphology not only benefits young children but also older students, sometimes benefiting reading comprehension years after the instruction (Lyster et al., 2016).
Address All Grade Levels	Teaching comprehension practices and metacognitive strategies should begin early *and* often. Remind students to activate their prior knowledge, think about their overall purpose for reading, preview reading material, and notice text structure before reading. Talk with students about narrative elements—characters, setting, theme, and plot—to support their schema when reading narrative. Show *and* tell students about nonfiction text structure and how it helps us when we read.

Ensure Thoughtful Grouping for Instruction	While whole-group instruction has positive results for comprehension strategy instruction (Okkinga et al., 2018), small-group instruction is particularly effective (Palinscar & Brown, 1984). As you assess your students formally and informally to understand their strengths and challenges specific to comprehension, you'll likely want to support students in smaller groups. In that setting, you'll be able to scaffold and differentiate instruction based on specific reader needs, selecting text types to best support comprehension growth.
Build Background Knowledge	Students create meaning based on their background knowledge about general and specific topical knowledge. When exploring topics that are likely unfamiliar to students, create and add to existing general knowledge through read alouds, preteaching vocabulary, and viewing images and videos to build students' understanding. Creating text sets—books of varied readability levels and types—around the topic is another way to support students as they independently read to deepen and build their schemata, or background knowledge, about specific topics.
Engage in Vocabulary Building	Vocabulary knowledge, based on both quantitative and qualitative research, is strongly correlated to comprehension (Dong et al., 2020). In fact, vocabulary and comprehension are so interconnected that the National Reading Panel reported that separating them "is difficult, if not impossible" (NICHD, 2000a, p. 239). Building students' vocabulary breadth and depth through direct and indirect instruction, read alouds, discussion, and through independent reading supports comprehension.
Engage in Comprehension Instruction in Content Areas	In elementary schools, we routinely partition English language arts as instruction separate from science and social studies, both of which often get pushed to the side (Schwartz, 2024a). Integrating comprehension instruction into science and social studies makes sense since students need ongoing practice in connecting ideas, learning academic vocabulary, and analyzing texts. With the push toward knowledge building as highlighted within the science of reading, we should intentionally integrate literacy instruction within science and social studies. Direct instruction, along with think-alouds using informational text, support students as they navigate learning how to read more challenging expository text.
Teach Responsive Writing	Engaging students in writing as a response to reading capitalizes on the reciprocal relationship between reading and writing and improves reading comprehension (Graham et al., 2018). Students need lots of opportunities to engage in language as they translate their thoughts and responses from speech to print for both narrative and informational text.

continued ▶

Teach Responsive Discussion	Emerging readers and those with more well-developed skills benefit from talking about reading, or dialogic conversations about text (Whitehurst et al., 1988). In brief, dialogic conversations are a thoughtful and structured process to help students engage and respond to text. Dialogic conversations can occur with a teacher or parent, a small group of students, or as a class. Behavioral and conversation tools can provide scaffolds as students discuss texts. For example, simple behavioral reminders such as, "Look at other students as you respond," "Be respectful," and "Take turns responding," set students up for success. And conversation starters such as, "One part I really enjoyed was ____________________" or "I didn't understand why ____________________ did ____________________" can be printed for students to use as reference. These simple tools are beneficial to provide support as students engage in dialogic conversation in small groups. You can also develop more text response prompts suited to varied text types. In order for all students to participate and benefit from text conversations, consider intentionally pairing students to support struggling readers and English learners (see chapter 4). Additionally, consider beginning dialogic conversations with two-person structured turn and talks. Then shift to a structured three-person conversation before moving to a group of four or five students.
Encourage Independent Reading	Independent reading plays a direct and impactful role in building fluent readers (Castles, Rastle, & Nation, 2018; Stanovich & West, 1989), and fluent readers comprehend better than those who are less fluent (NICHD, 2000a). Research affirms that students who read more are also better readers (Anderson et al., 1985; Cunningham & Stanovich, 1998; Guthrie et al., 1999). Comfortable seating in a classroom can encourage students to pursue reading more diligently. Reading volume, both in and out of school, makes a difference and is associated with higher reading achievement (Allington, 2002; Campbell et al., 1998). Children who are proficient readers tend to enjoy reading and engage in reading more frequently (Anderson et al., 1988). They also take on more challenging reading tasks whereas poor, or struggling, readers typically enjoy reading less and engage in reading less frequently. A 2020 study pinpointed what types of students benefit from leisure reading. Researchers (Torppa et al., 2020) found that students who were reading at the third grade level and above improved their fluency and comprehension through independent reading. Those reading lower than the third grade threshold needed more scaffolding and support in order to make fluency and comprehension gains. These students benefit more from read alouds, intentional paired reading, supported practice, and audio texts (see chapter 4).
Support English Learners	English learners benefit from instruction related to the five pillars, as do native speakers (Shanahan & Beck, 2006). They also benefit from oral discussion following read alouds, preteaching vocabulary to support comprehension, and prereading activities to build relevant background knowledge (Manyak & Bauer, 2008). When explicitly teaching comprehension strategies with ELs, Calderón (2011) suggests using a text slightly above students' reading level, both to model fluency and the types of reading strategies students can use. Two strategies, buddy by my side and questioning the author (Beck & McKeown, 2006), are described later in this chapter and provide support for ELs to discuss text, clarify confusions, and apply comprehension strategies.

Support Struggling Readers	There are many students in our classrooms who do not fall under the avid reader description. Some haven't acquired all the skills of their more proficient counterparts and are striving to build those skills. Struggling readers frequently lack foundational skills, background knowledge, or language proficiency. Providing word recognition scaffolds such as front-loading vocabulary support students, particularly those in grades 3 and above, who struggle with decoding (Mesmer, 2024). Students with less proficient skills will still be exposed to on-grade-level texts and content to build comprehension and vocabulary skills, but with additional scaffolds through teacher read alouds and listening to text. Additionally, these students will need more support and scaffolding in order to benefit from time spent reading. For these students, independent reading includes intentional paired reading (see chapter 4) with strategies such as buddy by my side, described in the What Works in the Classroom section of this chapter. When paired with a more proficient peer, students can typically comprehend text up to two grades above their assigned levels (Brown et al., 2018; Morgan et al., 2000). Expanded reading opportunities can also include close reading with teacher support and repeated reading activities such as reading scripts in preparation for reader's theater (see chapter 4, page 160).

Comprehension instruction is challenging and multifaceted. Whether you teach students in primary or intermediate grades, your students can benefit from direct instruction to develop their language and reading comprehension.

Strategies to Develop Reading Comprehension

Students who comprehend proficiently engage in a variety of metacognitive behaviors and activities that support understanding text (Pressley & Afflerbach, 1995). While some students seem to develop these skills naturally, many students will not and would benefit from direct instruction in before-, during-, and after-reading strategies.

Comprehension can be taught, and there are several considerations to keep in mind as you develop a structured plan.

1. **Text structure is important and impacts how we read and comprehend fiction and nonfiction text:** Teaching text structure is rather straightforward and can be revisited frequently as students encounter new books and resources.
2. **The before-, during-, and after-reading framework is commonly used for organizing comprehension strategies and is built around the actions readers engage in during each stage of reading:** I've used this framework as an organizational structure for the strategies in this chapter. In my experiences, this framework makes sense to our earliest readers and intermediate students as well.

3. **Model, model, and model again:** Use the show me, help me, let me scaffolded instructional sequence (gradual release of responsibility). Make invisible comprehension processes visible by thinking aloud. In *Comprehension Connections*, a favorite resource of mine, Tanny McGregor (2007) helps bridge the abstract with concrete examples, along with visuals and strategies to support comprehension. Also, keep in mind that when students learn new strategies, there is sometimes a slight dip in comprehension because their attention has shifted to paying attention to the strategy, which can negatively affect comprehension. Over time, strategies shift to more natural behaviors without garnering attention away from comprehension. Revisit strategies regularly with students so they have plenty of opportunities to become automatic.

The strategies found in the following sections are organized first around those for teaching students about text structure and then around before-, during-, and after-reading strategies.

Text Structure Strategies

Text structure was first described by Bonnie J. F. Meyer (1975), a researcher. Text structure simply refers to the way that information is organized within a text. It is not unusual for students to be unaware of text structure. Today, the term is commonplace, but teaching text structure is relatively recent within comprehension instruction.

Teachers play an important role in helping students learn how to identify and use text structures as they read, and text structures should be a part of explicit and systematic comprehension instruction (Dymock & Nicholson, 1999; Pearson & Duke, 2002; Sweet & Snow, 2003). Students who understand how to use expository text structures comprehend better (Dymock & Nicholson, 1999); as such, they need to learn specific strategies and features for different text types (Beach & Appleman, 1984).

In this section's set of strategies, you'll find student-friendly descriptions of text structures to share, information on how to introduce text structures outside of text, and information on how signal words can help students navigate text.

Expository Text Features

Expository texts are informational in nature and are the primary source of reading material students encounter related to academic content. They present information, facts and concepts, and explanations for how things work. Social studies and science texts are a type of expository text. Expository texts are often dense with academic and technical vocabulary, lots of facts, and unfamiliar content. As such, they present more difficulty for students to comprehend than narrative text (McCormick & Zutell, 2015).

There are five text structures that appear commonly in informational text: (1) description, (2) compare and contrast, (3) sequence, (4) cause and effect, and (5) problem and solution. Awareness of text structures serves as a schema or mental framework for students as they read and comprehend informational text. The student-friendly descriptions and examples in table 6.3 help text structure make sense to students.

Table 6.3: Student-Friendly Descriptions and Examples of Five Text Structures

Text Structure	Description	Examples
Description	The author tells us about something. They may describe it, tell us the characteristics, and provide facts.	• Transportation systems • Weather patterns • Land masses
Compare and Contrast	The author shows us how two things are similar and different.	• Cities and towns • Boats and airplanes • Lakes and oceans
Sequence	The author tells us things in order. It may include steps, a timeline, or a cycle.	• Life cycle of a butterfly • Steps to the scientific method • Timeline of the Industrial Revolution
Cause and Effect	The author tells us how an event leads to an outcome. The relationship between the cause (the event) and the outcome (the result).	• Garbage and overflowing landfills • Automobiles and the development of better roadways • Lightning strikes a tree, and the tree burns
Problem and Solution	The author tells about a problem and how to solve it.	• Overflowing landfills and making recycling easy • Too much time on devices and setting a daily time limit for phones and iPads

When teaching text structure, consider beginning *outside of text*, with simple classroom discussions using the text structures (Roehling et al., 2017). I've provided a few examples of conversation topics that will likely be familiar to children and are also examples of text structures. Following each classroom discussion, label the example with the type of text structure.

- **Description:** Describe our classroom morning routine to someone—a friend, parent, or caregiver—who has never been in our classroom.
- **Compare and contrast:** Let's talk about how apples and oranges are similar and different (Alvermann, 1981).
- **Sequence:** Explain how to make a peanut butter and jelly sandwich.
- **Cause and effect:** What happens if you forget your lunch at home? What happens if we have a tornado or emergency warning during the school day?

- **Problem and solution:** What is a problem we have in our classroom sometimes, and how do we solve it? (Students are talking loudly, not sharing, or being unkind.)

On another day, layer or scaffold instruction using examples of informational text. Have a discussion about how authors write about information. For example, they describe how specific rocks are similar and different (compare and contrast). In texts, authors may describe types of clouds (description) or tell us what happens to the environment if we ignore our landfills (cause and effect). Then, display the text and point out how the text is organized as well as specific vocabulary or sentence structures the author used. Finally, label each text structure. You'll find an example in figure 6.1.

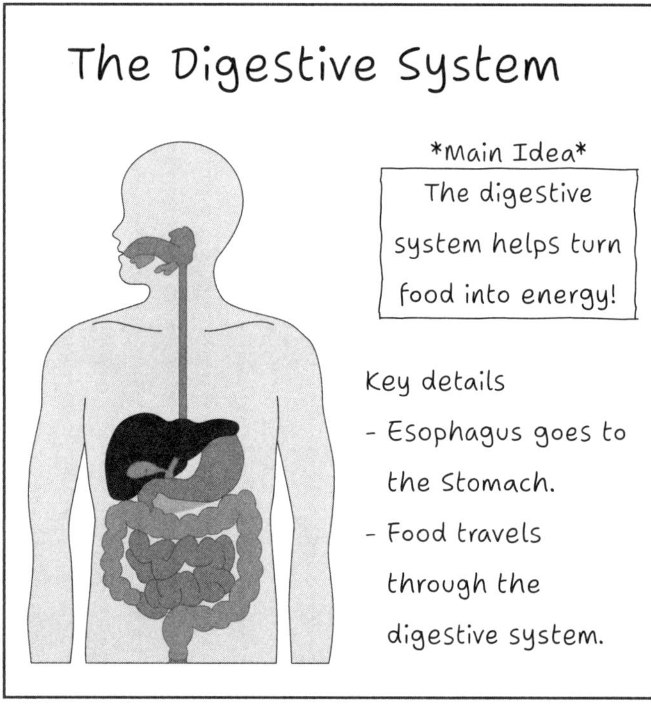

Figure 6.1: An anchor chart summarizing the digestive system using a sequence text structure.

Another text feature found routinely in expository text is the use of *signal words*, which are specific words found in informational text that signal the text structure to the reader. You may refer to signal words by other names, such as *text clues* or *clue words*. Teach signal words in context, always emphasizing text structure. When modeling, perhaps note signal words using highlighting tape. Students, working in pairs, could do this as well. If reading text on a device, students can mark up or highlight directly on the device.

Be aware that spending too much time teaching signal words could result in students over-focusing on finding signal words without realizing they simply help us navigate and identify text structure, which, in turn, creates a mindset to help us comprehend. It's another case of, they are a *means* to an end, *not* the end. Become familiar with the signal words listed for each text structure shown in table 6.4.

Narrative Text Features

Narrative text is a type of text that tells a story or describes a sequence of events. Generally, narrative text is found in literature selections and tells what happened, to whom, and why. When narrative text is written and organized following story grammar, it is easier to comprehend (Thorndyke, 1977).

Story grammar represents the basic structure of a narrative text. It is a hierarchy or organization of sorts for consistent features found in narrative text. The concept of story grammar was introduced by David E. Rumelhart (1975), a researcher, and has been applied to narrative since then. The story grammar framework serves as a schema

Table 6.4: Text Structures and Common Signal Words

Text Structure	Signal Words
Description	To begin, an example of, for example, looks like, sounds like, acts like
Compare and contrast	**Compare:** same as, similar, alike, both, in common **Contrast:** in contrast to, on the other hand, different from, not alike, in comparison
Sequence	First, next, last, finally, before, after, then, now
Cause and effect	As a result, because, since, may be due to, if . . . then, consequently
Problem and solution	The problem/issue/dilemma/difficulty is . . . , one answer is, the solution is, one reason for the problem is . . .

or mental framework for students as they read and comprehend a story (see figure 6.2).

Common story grammar includes a setting, theme, characters, plot, and resolution. Many students, as they enter school, understand that stories have a beginning, middle, and end. Story grammar helps provide more definition and detail to a story rather than just referring to the sequence of events. Understanding story grammar benefits students' comprehension. For example, students in grade 1 who were taught story grammar outperformed students who did not have that instruction (Baumann & Bergeron, 1993). The comprehension of third- and fourth-grade students, including struggling readers, improved with an understanding of story grammar instruction (Idol, 1987), and sixth-grade students improved their listening comprehension through story grammar (Chuang & Wang, 2015). Further, there was a positive correlation between listening comprehension and reading achievement. Finally, a meta-analysis (Pico et al., 2021) confirms that instruction in story grammar improves students' comprehension.

Figure 6.2: Story grammar, or elements, captured in an anchor chart.

The focus of instruction in story grammar should include the following elements, adapted from Susan Dymock (2007).

- **Setting:** The setting establishes where and when the story takes place.

- **Characters:** The characters in a story carry the plot or sequence of events. Students should understand that there are major characters and minor, less important, characters.
- **Plot:** The plot is the sequence of events within a story. The plot describes what happens and why it happens. The plot can be divided into four parts, which include the problem, response, action, and outcome. Each answers a question. "**Problem**. *What is the problem in the story?* **Response**. *How do characters respond to the problem?* **Action**. *What do characters do about the problem?* **Outcome**. *What is the outcome?"* (Dymock, 2007, p. 163).
- **Episodes:** The plot can usually be divided into episodes, each with a problem that results in an action, outcome, or solution. Sometimes it is helpful to create a simple diagram that lists each episode and the resulting action, outcome, or solution.
- **Theme:** The theme represents the underlying message of the story. It is often interpreted by the reader, similar to the theme of a movie. Have students turn and talk to gather ideas about the theme. For some students, identifying a theme is challenging. It is, of course, much less direct since it requires reader interpretation. Discuss the theme with students and ask for text evidence to support their ideas. Themes may include *kindness*, *good versus evil*, *love*, *life's challenges*, *friendship*, *loneliness*, and *justice*, to name just a few.

Before-, During-, and After-Reading Strategies

Thinking about comprehension in terms of the cognitive activities that take place before, during, and after reading is a common framework used to describe the behaviors of proficient readers during each phase of reading. These behaviors, of course, look different depending on the reader, the text, and the reader's purpose for reading—be that pleasure reading or reading for a specific task.

When teaching strategies, we must be explicit and provide examples with many types of text so that students have a clear understanding of what the strategy looks like within text. The NRP (NICHD, 2000a) and other literacy experts (Keene & Zimmermann, 2007) suggest teaching comprehension strategies one at a time.

All students benefit from explicit instruction, struggling readers in particular, as they work toward using independent, strategic reading behaviors. As we teach comprehension strategies, education researchers suggest five critical elements direct instruction and modeling should include, summarized in the following list (Winograd & Hare, 1988).

1. Strategies are **explained carefully** so that they are meaningful and make sense to students. (*show me*)

2. Strategies include a **step-by-step approach** using language such as *first, next,* and *finally*. Steps make it clear how each strategy works. (*show me*)
3. Students **understand the benefit of strategies** and **why they should learn them**. (*help me*)
4. Students learn **when to use each strategy** and **why a strategy is effective**. (*let me*)
5. Students **reflect** on whether or not each strategy works for them and why. (*let me*)

You'll notice that these steps fit into the show me, help me, let me structure previously discussed, which begins with the teacher modeling the strategy and shifting, through repeated practice, to student ownership of the strategy.

Before-reading activities are generally warm-up activities to get one thinking about a specific text. For example, if a student is selecting a book to read for pleasure, they may read the back of the book, flip through a few pages, and talk to friends to see if any have read the book. However, for informational text, the activities are different. Students may preview a chapter to activate prior knowledge, notice bold-faced terms, and think about why they are reading the text or the purpose for reading.

During-reading activities keep the reader engaged and following the text. For example, when reading for pleasure, the reader may form connections to the narrative, absorb the setting and time period, track character development (consciously or unconsciously), and carefully follow the plot.

However, when reading informational text, they engage differently. Since the content may be challenging or new, readers must often engage more actively in order to comprehend. Reading behaviors could include making connections as they read text, monitoring their understanding by underlining or highlighting text, checking vocabulary by using an online dictionary, generating questions, and slowing down and rereading a portion of text if they're confused. All of these behaviors help readers stay attuned, engaged, and support comprehension.

After-reading activities differ as well. For enjoyment or casual reading, they may talk to a friend, family member, or book club about the text. Some readers may quickly go check out another book by the author or read more about the location described in the narrative. Others might look up book reviews, read other readers' responses to the book, or learn more about the author. A few readers may go further and write a blog or an online review about a recently completed book, whether it be fabulous or less interesting than anticipated. Including a few of these on a classroom website is a welcome school-home connection and further supports creating a community of readers.

After reading informational text—often for an assignment—activities range from simple to involved. For example, students could simply think about the information and how it connects to the topic. However, if students need to learn the content more deeply, they may summarize it or write down a few key ideas, look up vocabulary to clear up any confusion, discuss the content with classmates or respond to the text in some fashion.

The bank of comprehension strategies described in this chapter are aimed at supporting readers as they develop these behaviors and will be organized using the before-, during-, and after-reading framework.

Before-Reading Strategies

The primary goal when implementing before-reading strategies is to engage students in thinking about the text by previewing the organization and activating their schema, or prior knowledge.

Activating prior knowledge before reading as a means to develop a purpose for reading is an important activity to ensure comprehension (Marzano, 2004). Prior knowledge, when activated, helps students make predictions when they are reading and supports comprehension. I think about activating prior knowledge as similar to seeing a movie preview. When we see a movie preview and then watch the movie at a later time, the clips from the movie preview often jump out at us. Why? Because we've previously seen and engaged with the content on a cognitive, experiential level, and that simple schema helps us understand the movie better.

By engaging students with text before students read, we activate their prior knowledge and engage them cognitively before reading. Knowing *why* they're reading a text, which is about determining a purpose for reading, is essential. The *why* creates a mindset and focus as students read.

We can engage students through a variety of strategies. A few examples include preteaching vocabulary, engaging in a quick discussion about the topic, developing questions, and previewing the text.

Front-Loading Vocabulary

As students engage with challenging text, front-loading vocabulary is an instructional strategy that provides scaffolding for students, especially English learners, prior to reading (Calderón, 2011). Front-loading doesn't have to be complicated. In informational text, it can be as simple as drawing students' attention to bold-faced vocabulary or providing simple definitions of several academic terms. Using a simple routine such as the one described in figure 6.3, students can build their background knowledge and make connections prior to reading the text.

Strategy: Front-Loading Vocabulary

Pillar: Comprehension

Grade Level:	Instructional Grouping:	Consider This:
☑ K ☑ 1 ☑ 2 ☑ 3 ☑ 4 ☑ 5 ☑ 6	☑ Whole Group ☑ Small Group ☐ Individual	• Keep front-loading brief, just two to four minutes. The strategy is meant to create connections and build background knowledge prior to reading or engaging in a lesson; it is not the lesson. • Choose to front-load when you notice the vocabulary is dense and will likely interfere with comprehension, especially for English learners.

What is it? Front-loading vocabulary is an instructional strategy that provides scaffolding for students prior to reading.

Why is it important? Front-loading has merit. Comprehension increases when students recognize and understand vocabulary from the text they are reading (Pressley et al., 2007).

What works in the classroom?

Choose from these suggestions; you don't have to do each of these every time. However, make it a routine to always write, pronounce, and provide a student-friendly definition of target words.

- **Target words:** Write each target word on the whiteboard and pronounce it so that students connect the spelling to the pronunciation.
- **Student-friendly definition:** Provide a student-friendly definition and use the term in context.
- **Images or videos:** Use an image or video for one or two of the definitions. Use visual dictionaries such as Snappy Words (www.snappywords.com) and Visual Dictionary Online (www.visualdictionaryonline.com) by Merriam-Webster. Visual images help students as they learn new vocabulary (Marzano, 2009) and can be essential for English learners.
- **Latin and Greek roots:** Point out Latin and Greek roots when applicable. Roots such as *anti-* and *tele-* reach far beyond the word in the text and can be briefly discussed. Have students add a few additional words that begin with the root.
- **Graphic organizers:** Have students use a graphic organizer to show relationships among vocabulary or to record definitions as they read. Chapter 5 includes examples of graphic organizers, such as alphaboxes and concept circles. More organizers can be found in *Blended Vocabulary for K–12 Classrooms* (Tyson & Peery, 2017).

Figure 6.3: Strategy—Front-loading vocabulary.

Visit ***go.SolutionTree.com/literacy/FSK6*** *and enter the unique access code found on the book's inside front cover to access a reproducible version of this figure.*

Listen-Read-Discuss Strategy

Listen-read-discuss (LRD) is a strategy which engages students before, during, and after reading (Manzo & Casale, 1985). The LRD strategy provides support for struggling readers and English learners by scaffolding the text along with providing oral discussion. An easy-to-implement strategy, LRD is perfectly suitable for varied disciplines, content area texts, and a range of grade levels. The simple steps are included in the LRD strategy (figure 6.4; Manzo & Casale, 1985).

Strategy: Listen-Read-Discuss

Pillar: Comprehension

Grade Level:	Instructional Grouping:	Consider This:
☑ K ☑ 1 ☑ 2 ☑ 3 ☑ 4 ☑ 5 ☑ 6	☑ Whole Group ☑ Small Group ☐ Individual	• LRD can be adapted to any grade level. Provide more structure, support, and scaffolds (perhaps reading the text aloud) for early readers and less for students who are more-skilled readers. • Students consider varied points of view—the teacher, the author, and other students—as they listen, read, and discuss content.

What is it? Listen-read-discuss is a before-, during-, and after-reading strategy designed to support students' comprehension as they build background knowledge, read, and discuss the content following reading.

Why is it important? As students are introduced to new content or a unit of study, it's important to provide support structures to help them build background knowledge, engage with the text, and discuss new learning.

What works in the classroom?

Listen: Before Reading

- Before reading, students listen to a brief lecture from the teacher that highlights key information about the topic.
- The teacher can use a graphic organizer to show connections between concepts or key information.
- The pre-activities culminate in setting a purpose for reading.

Read: During Reading

- Students then read or listen to a a text selection about the topic and engage in strategies that assist them in making meaning from the text.

Discuss: After Reading

- After reading or listening, students gather in small groups or as a whole group to connect back to the text for discussion. Questions, reflections, connections, and clearing up confusion is encouraged for discussion.
- Depending on the text and the purpose, students may develop a written response, develop a graphic organizer, or respond to questions.

Figure 6.4: Strategy—Listen-read-discuss.

Visit ***go.SolutionTree.com/literacy/FSK6*** *and enter the unique access code found on the book's inside front cover to access a reproducible version of this figure.*

The listen-read-discuss strategy quite simply mimics good, strategic teaching. However, it's sometimes easy to minimize how important it is to connect background knowledge and vocabulary to reading and subsequent discussion. It is especially beneficial for students who struggle with reading and English learners as they connect oral discussion and varied viewpoints with the text selection. Adding a writing component, or quick summary, takes this strategy to another level by connecting listening, reading, and writing.

Anticipation Guide Strategy

Anticipation guides is another novel strategy that begins before reading and extends by engaging readers both during and after reading as well (Bean, Readence, & Baldwin, 2008; Tierney & Readence, 2005). As students engage with the text before reading, they activate their prior knowledge and use it to develop a specific purpose for reading. They use that purpose as they read and discuss the content with peers following reading.

Working with teachers, I refer to anticipation guides as an "Agree or Disagree" activity. I've used this activity frequently before engaging in professional learning, often around the topic of "building vocabulary and word learning." Agree or Disagree is one of my favorite workshop strategies to engage in prior to delivering content because of the conversation it elicits and the ensuing engagement throughout the day. The steps I follow, modified slightly from the original strategy, are summarized here.

First, before the session, I develop about eight to ten statements capturing the most important content elements within the session. Then I record the statements in a Google Doc, followed by printing and cutting them apart so they're movable. After this, I create two larger cards on cardstock, one with *agree* and the other with *disagree* printed on them, and I place the statements and two cards in an envelope.

During the session, I set up the activity by telling teachers they'll read each statement, discuss, and decide whether they agree or disagree with it. I also disclose that I won't immediately provide the "answers." Working in small groups of four to six, teachers place each statement under the "agree" or "disagree" header, forming two columns of statements, as shown in figure 6.5 (page 242). Undoubtedly, there is a great deal of lively discussion. Invariably, some groups place one or two statements in the middle of the two headers, indicating that they can't come to consensus and are unsure whether they "agree" or "disagree." Some even move the statement a little closer to either the "agree" or "disagree" header.

Following this, I typically comment on the statements that are causing the most discussion and then proceed with the session. Keep in mind that the statements were selected and written with intentionality. The content included in each statement is discussed

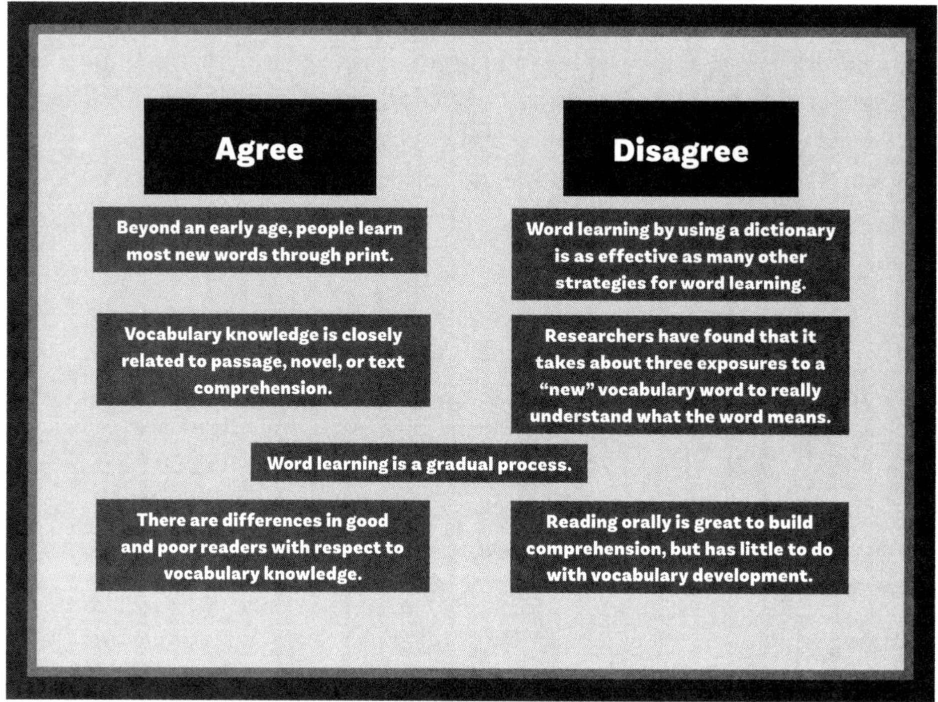

Figure 6.5: Anticipation guide activity.

throughout the vocabulary session. Throughout the day, teachers engage by reading brief selections from *Blended Vocabulary for K–12 Classrooms* (Tyson & Peery, 2017) or a professional article, viewing a video, and interacting with each other and me throughout the day.

Each time the content correlates with one of the statements, everyone notices. And teachers respond with a confirming nod when their response was correct or may seem surprised that they were incorrect in their choice. And, what about the statements stranded in the middle? Teachers usually look at each other, nod their head and smile, and then slide it under the correct header.

Near the close of the session, I intentionally recap the activity by reading each statement and discussing the nugget of content contained in each statement. The statements on which many were indecisive elicit the most discussion, which is good because teachers are imprinting themselves with an important key takeaway about vocabulary and word learning.

I encourage you to implement anticipation guides using the instructions in the strategy table (figure 6.6) or as I do with movable statements (Tierney & Readence, 2005). Either way, they're excellent for building anticipation prior to reading, promoting listening skills, and using text to confirm or deny preconceived beliefs.

Strategy: Anticipation Guide

Pillar: Comprehension

Grade Level:	Instructional Grouping:	Consider This:
☐ K ☐ 1 ☑ 2 ☑ 3 ☑ 4 ☑ 5 ☑ 6	☑ Whole Group ☑ Small Group ☐ Individual	• Developing the guide statements can be challenging. Be certain to develop statements that are experience-based (rather than solely factual) so that students examine their beliefs and opinions about a topic. • Consider developing statements with colleagues who teach the same content.

What is it? This is a before-, during-, and after-reading strategy that engages students as they consider their beliefs and opinions prior to reading and following reading.

Why is it important? Anticipation guides help students engage in activating prior knowledge, developing a purpose for reading, and confirming predictions. All of these are behaviors of readers who comprehend proficiently.

What works in the classroom?

Teacher Preparation

- **Select text:** Select a portion of text on which to base the anticipation guide. Texts that can elicit student opinions or beliefs that can be confirmed or altered by the text work best.
- **Read the text and develop statements:** Read and develop statements that may be opinion or belief based, using the format shown in figure 6.5.

Before Reading

- **Students respond before reading:** Prior to reading the text, students read and respond to each statement individually by circling *A* for agree or *D* for disagree. Responding to the statements helps activate prior knowledge and set a purpose for reading.

During Reading

- **Students read the text:** As students read the text, they can re-examine their beliefs based on the text.
- **Students make notations:** Using the statement or diagram table, students make notations in the third column using notes and page numbers to refer to for later discussion.

After Reading

- **Students reconvene:** Following reading, students reconvene in small groups or as a whole group to revisit the statements as they integrate new information with prior beliefs.
- **Students provide text-based evidence:** During discussion, students should provide text-based evidence to support or alter their original beliefs.

Figure 6.6: Strategy—Anticipation guide.

Visit ***go.SolutionTree.com/literacy/FSK6*** *and enter the unique access code found on the book's inside front cover to access a reproducible version of this figure.*

Generating Questions and Purpose for Reading

Developing a purpose for reading serves as a guide for readers as they comprehend text. Shanahan (2016a) recommends keeping the purpose quite general. The point is that students, at minimum, generate their purpose depending on the text type and generally why they are reading the text.

Framing a purpose and responding to questions about text are common reading behaviors. Some struggling readers have difficulty developing questions in response to reading. ReQuest, a reciprocal questioning strategy, is well suited to support striving readers who often limit questions to literal, "right there" questions (Manzo, 1969). The steps in ReQuest move students beyond the literal into higher-level questions as students respond to text.

Question-answer relationship (QAR) is another strategy that helps students generate questions and responses as they read and navigate text. Question-answer relationship is a strategy that provides a common language for students to think tangibly about the comprehension process as they read expository and narrative text (Raphael & Au, 2005). The QAR structure helps students draw on their prior knowledge when responding to questions and provides support in developing text skills such as skimming, scanning, identifying important information, and making simple and complex inferences. QAR depends on teacher modeling to help students learn the language of generating and answering questions. The simple steps and considerations can be found in the QAR strategy as outlined in figure 6.7 (Raphael & Au, 2005).

Strategy: Question-Answer Relationship

Pillar: Comprehension

Grade Level:	**Instructional Grouping:**	**Consider This:**
☐ K ☑ 1 ☑ 2 ☑ 3 ☑ 4 ☑ 5 ☑ 6	☑ Whole Group ☑ Small Group ☐ Individual	• QAR provides support for all readers. Readers are provided language to discuss all levels of questions rather than being limited to literal questions, which is often the case for striving readers. • Consider creating an anchor chart with examples for students to reference. • Begin simple when teaching QAR. Add more depth, such as described, as students become familiar with the framework. • Don't overdo QAR. Students don't need to label every question and answer they respond to using the QAR framework. Rather, use it as a guide for conversation around text.

What is it? QAR is a strategy that provides a framework for thinking about and verbalizing comprehension processes. It specifically targets the relationships between questions and answers relative to text and background knowledge and experiences.

Why is it important? Students need a common language to discuss on-grade-level text with their peers. QAR helps students connect questions and their responses with text structure and their own background knowledge and experiences.

What works in the classroom?

Pre-Discussion Topics

- **Discuss questions and answers:** Discuss with students that we often ask questions about text and answer them in one of two ways. Talk about where these questions and answers come from, which includes (1) information in the text and (2) our own experiences or prior knowledge.
- **Model the QAR relationships:** Conduct a read aloud with narrative or informational text in order to pose questions that students answer—either from the text or from their prior knowledge. At some point, think about creating an anchor chart using QAR with informational text.

Language of QAR

- **Questions and answers come from two sources:** The two sources are "In the Book" (information in the text) and "In My Head" (background knowledge). In primary grades, you may choose to just introduce these two categories as students think about questions and answers. By second grade, most students can distinguish between the two broad categories (Raphael & McKinney, 1983).
- **Layer learning with QAR framework:** Begin small. Use brief texts including picture books and informational text (several paragraphs) to help students clearly distinguish the two broad categories of "In the Book" and "In My Head" (primary grades).

The Core Question and Answer Relationships

In the Book

- **Right There:** The answer is in one place in the text. Words from the question and words that answer the question are often "right there" in one sentence.
- **Think and Search:** The answer is in the text. Readers may, however, need to "think and search" several sentences or paragraphs or across chapters and maybe even books to answer the question.

In My Head

- **On My Own:** The answer is not in the text. Readers need to use their own ideas and experiences to answer the question.
- **Author and Me:** The answer is not clearly in the text. To answer the question, readers must think about what is in the text and what they already know fit together to answer the question.

Note: Add depth to the QAR framework. As students become proficient in identifying the four categories, add more depth to the framework over time.

- **"In the Book" responses:** "In the Book" responses include *right there* and *think and search*. *Right there* responses are typically straightforward and easy to locate the answer to a question. *Think and search* answers typically require more reading, and the information may be located across paragraphs, a page, a chapter, or more. The text structure may include a simple list, description, explanation, or sequence.

- **"In My Head" responses:** "In my Head" responses, which draw on the text and personal connections, include *author and me* and *on my own* responses. *Author and me* responses include three types of connections to the text. They are (1) text-to-self connections, (2) text-to-theme connections, and (3) text-to-world connections. Provide examples of each and walk through them with students.

Figure 6.7: Strategy—Question-answer relationship.

Visit ***go.SolutionTree.com/literacy/FSK6*** *and enter the unique access code found on the book's inside front cover to access a reproducible version of this figure.*

During-Reading Strategies

Students who read fluently typically connect ideas across phrases, sentences, and chapters within text. They engage in strategic behaviors that keep them active as they read and aid comprehension. For example, proficient readers set a purpose for reading and use their background knowledge to make connections to the narrative while tracking characters, settings, and plot development.

In expository text, fluent readers may quickly preview the text to scan vocabulary and text structure before setting a purpose for reading. Students again connect their background knowledge to new information, and when they find their comprehension breaking down, they may reread the text or look up vocabulary, which is often referred to as "fix-up" behaviors. They try to quickly get back on track and continue reading. In this section, we'll explore a few strategies that support students, including English learners and students with disabilities, as they read and monitor their comprehension.

Monitoring Comprehension With Think-Alouds Strategy

Comprehension processes, as explored previously, are complex and largely invisible. Readers gather information, make connections and inferences, and use their background knowledge as they comprehend. They build mental images as they read, and their comprehension is influenced by many factors including their purpose for reading, prior knowledge, motivation, and culture (Pardo, 2004). Yet, through structured observation and conversation protocols, we know the active behaviors that readers perform while reading and engaging in higher-order thinking skills.

Think-alouds are a viable *and* visible way to tune students into what we do during reading. We sometimes think we provide clear explanations and make our thinking more visible than we do. Beth Davey (1983) first coined the term *think-aloud* to describe the strategy in which teachers model their invisible behaviors by thinking aloud or talking about and demonstrating as a routine part of classroom instruction. A think-aloud can be described as "a teaching strategy in which the proficient reader (in this case, the teacher) verbally reports or models his or her thinking as he or she approaches the text" (Ness & Kenny, 2016, p. 454).

Even though it is a well-seasoned strategy, think-alouds are worth revisiting since they are effective for students ranging from preschool to high school (Dorl, 2007; Lapp, Fisher, & Grant, 2008). A planning and lesson model for effective think-alouds is outlined in the following strategy (figure 6.8; Ness & Kenny, 2016).

Strategy: Think-Alouds

Pillar: Comprehension

Grade Level:	Instructional Grouping:	Consider This:
☑ K ☑ 1 ☑ 2 ☑ 3 ☑ 4 ☑ 5 ☑ 6	☑ Whole Group ☑ Small Group ☑ Individual	• Although think-alouds can be done spontaneously, for the most impact, plan ahead by selecting narrative and informational text that is well suited to think-aloud conversations and comprehension strategies. • A think-aloud is a shared reading experience that prioritizes making apparent the comprehension strategies used within a specific text. • Have sticky notes on hand for preplanning.

What is it? A think-aloud is a strategy in which the teacher explains and demonstrates their reading behaviors and thinking processes while reading text aloud.

Why is it important? Providing a think-aloud model benefits students as they better understand how skilled readers read and comprehend narrative and expository text. Think-alouds done effectively by teachers positively impact student achievement (Caldwell & Leslie, 2010; Coiro & Dobler, 2007; Fisher, Frey, & Lapp, 2011; Loxterman, Beck, & McKeown, 1994; Ortlieb & Norris, 2012). Think-alouds also promote metacognitive thinking as students listen to the teacher describe their reading and comprehension processes and reflect on their own.

What works in the classroom?

Select a text. Think about your purpose for selecting a narrative or informational text. Align the text with your learning targets and the comprehension strategy or strategies you will highlight in the lesson. The following example is with an informational text.

Planning Think-Alouds

- **Preplan with informational text:** Read and mark about eight to fifteen spots as you read the text. Note parts of the text that may provide a challenge to the reader. Examples include academic vocabulary, challenging concepts, and ambiguous connections, to name a few.
- **Reread and evaluate:** Now go back and ask yourself a few questions about each area you marked with a sticky note. Questions may include: What is my intent at each think-aloud spot? Is the stopping point an effective place to make comprehension visible? What will the reader gain from this stopping point?
- **Prepare what you will say:** Think carefully about what you will say during each think-aloud spot. Consider writing down your script so that you don't forget the intent of each spot. Prompts may include: I wonder what . . . I think . . . I predict . . . I don't understand . . . I wonder what this word means . . . This makes me think about . . . I think this might happen next because . . . I'm confused . . . I like this author because . . . I've learned that . . . I picture . . . This signal word means . . . Rereading might help me . . .

  Hopefully, you will soon feel comfortable and not need the script to think clearly about what to say.

  Think about creating a simple chart (Ness & Kenny, 2016) like the following to record your thoughts.

Figure 6.8: Strategy—Think-alouds.

continued ▶

What the Text Says	Teacher Think-Aloud Script	Reading Comprehension Strategy
Jot down the last few words of the sentence you will think-aloud.	Write what you will say during the think-aloud.	Name the comprehension strategy used. (For example, connecting to the text, predicting, confusion, learning vocabulary, visualizing, making inferences . . .)

Variations

Think-alouds are powerful for students. Consider trying one or more of the variations.

- **Differentiate based on student needs:** Doing a brief read aloud in a small-group setting helps provide support and related discussion for specific students.
- **Try doing a think-aloud with challenging text:** Provide experience with how to read and comprehend challenging text.
- **Do read alouds in both narrative and expository text:** Evaluate which is easier for you and why. Which seems to benefit students more and why?
- **Share the load and plan think-alouds with your grade-level team:** Conversations specific to text choice, think-alouds, and comprehension strategies may be effective for think-alouds.

*Visit **go.SolutionTree.com/literacy/FSK6** and enter the unique access code found on the book's inside front cover to access a reproducible version of this figure.*

Buddy by My Side Paired Reading Strategy

Paired reading, or partner reading, is a common practice to build active comprehension and support striving readers. Pairing students with intentionality is key. In chapter 4 (page 151), I include a paired readers protocol and reproducible you can use to maximize the effectiveness of pairs.

Buddy by my side is a paired reading strategy that I've used with early readers, primary students, and intermediate students to support engaging with text and comprehension. It provides just enough support to engage students with narrative or expository text. English learners and struggling readers also benefit from the back-and-forth questioning, conversation, and responding to text. Teacher feedback has consistently been that it's easy to model and implement with students. Figure 6.9 details the buddy by my side strategy.

The *We Both Read* series of books published by Treasure Bay is one of my favorite resources for K–3 students for buddy reading. Their selections include fiction and nonfiction titles in a wide variety of topics. They are a great resource to use with buddy readers because one page includes more text and is intended for the more proficient reader (or parent), and the opposite page features much less text, making it suitable for the less-proficient reader.

Strategy: Buddy by My Side

Pillar: Comprehension

Grade Level:	**Instructional Grouping:**	**Consider This:**
☐ K ☑ 1 ☑ 2 ☑ 3 ☑ 4 ☑ 5 ☑ 6	☐ Whole Group ☑ Small Group ☑ Pairs of Readers ☐ Individual	• Consider modeling this strategy during whole-group instruction and then again during small groups. At that time, students can practice while you monitor. • Resources include (1) a reproducible on which students can write their names as they learn the steps and (2) bookmarks with the steps for narrative and expository text.

What is it? Buddy by my side is a paired reading strategy that provides support for engaging with a buddy reader and promotes active reading within a genuine context. The protocol works well with both narrative and informational text, and there is a protocol for each.

Why is it important? Students need eyes on text and time to practice comprehension strategies. The buddy by my side strategy and protocol provides a supported opportunity for readers to engage with one another while reading, engaging with text, and comprehending.

What works in the classroom?

Preplanning

- **Pair students:** Using the paired reading protocol found in chapter 4 (page 151), determine pairs for reading.
- **Model:** Model the strategy with a student considering who would be a good choice to model the strategy with you. Practice with the student before modeling in front of the class or small group.

Protocols for Narrative and Expository Text

- Students (student A and student B) take turns reading, summarizing, asking and responding to questions, making connections, and predicting using the protocol summarized as follows.
- Students can share a text or each can read from a copy of the text.

Narrative Text: Two Students

- **Student A** orally reads several paragraphs or a page.
- **Student B** summarizes the paragraphs or page.
- **Student A** asks a question or makes a connection to the text.
- **Student B** predicts what will happen next.

(*Have students switch roles.*)

- **Student B** reads several paragraphs or a page.
- **Student A** summarizes the paragraphs or page.
- **Student B** asks a question or makes a connection to the text.
- **Student A** predicts what will happen next.

Figure 6.9: Strategy—Buddy by my side.

continued ▶

Expository Text: Two Students

- **Student A** orally reads several paragraphs or a page.
- **Student B** summarizes the information.
- **Student A** asks a question about the information.
- **Student B** points out key vocabulary, key concepts, or key connections.

(*Have students switch roles.*)

- **Student B** orally reads several paragraphs or a page.
- **Student A** summarizes the information.
- **Student B** asks a question about the information.
- **Student A** points out key vocabulary, key concepts, or key connections.

Visit ***go.SolutionTree.com/literacy/FSK6*** *and enter the unique access code found on the book's inside front cover to access a reproducible version of this figure.*

I've developed two simple guides on which students can print their names, if needed, to guide them as they read with their partner. One guide is for fiction (figure 6.10), and the other for nonfiction and informational texts (figure 6.11).

You may also find that your students prefer the bookmark I've developed with the buddy reading protocols (figure 6.12). You could print and laminate a bookmark for students to place inside the book they are reading with their buddy.

Buddy by My Side

Fiction

Directions:

- Write your names next to the letters (a) and (b).
- Now take turns reading and responding to the story.

Reader a ______________________.

Reader b ______________________.

__________(a) reads several paragraphs or a page.

__________(b) summarizes several paragraphs or a page.

__________(a) asks a question about the selection.

__________(b) predicts what will happen next.

Switch places.

__________(b) reads several paragraphs or a page.

__________(a) summarizes several paragraphs or a page.

__________(b) asks a question about the selection.

__________(a) predicts what will happen next.

Figure 6.10: Buddy by my side—Fiction.

Visit ***go.SolutionTree.com/literacy/FSK6*** *for a free reproducible version of this figure.*

Buddy by My Side

Nonfiction and Informational Text

Directions:

- Write your names next to the letters (a) and (b).
- Now take turns reading and responding to the story.

Reader a ______________________.

Reader b ______________________.

__________(a) reads a paragraph, section, or page.

__________(b) summarizes a paragraph, section, or page.

__________(a) asks a question about what was read.

__________(b) points out key vocabulary or terms.

Switch places.

__________(b) reads a paragraph, section, or page.

__________(a) summarizes a paragraph, section, or page.

__________(b) asks a question about what was read.

__________(a) points out key vocabulary or terms.

Figure 6.11: Buddy by my side—Nonfiction and informational text.

Visit ***go.SolutionTree.com/literacy/FSK6*** *for a free reproducible version of this figure.*

Buddy By My Side

Fiction

____ (a) reads several paragraphs or a page.
____ (b) summarizes several paragraphs or a page.
____ (a) asks a question about the selection.
____ (b) predicts what will happen next.

Switch Places

____ (b) reads several paragraphs or a page.
____ (a) summarizes several paragraphs or a page.
____ (b) asks a question about the selection.
____ (a) predicts what will happen next.

Nonfiction

____ (a) reads a paragraph, section, or page.
____ (b) summarizes a paragraph, section, or page.
____ (a) asks a question about the information.
____ (b) points out key vocabulary, concepts, connections.

Switch Places

____ (b) reads a paragraph, section, or page.
____ (a) summarizes a paragraph, section, or page.
____ (b) asks a question about the information.
____ (a) points out key vocabulary, concepts, connections.

Figure 6.12: Buddy by my side bookmark.

*Visit **go.SolutionTree.com/literacy/FSK6** for a free reproducible version of this figure.*

Pairing students to read and respond to text is a powerful strategy. Use the paired readers protocol protocol (figure 4.9, page 152) to match students purposefully in order for students to gain benefits from both reading and responding to text questions.

Navigating Text Strategies

Navigating text is an important reading skill, one which requires planning and metacognitive behaviors for both narrative and expository text. Increasing the amount students read challenging text is recommended by science of reading advocates and for good reason. The majority of reading beginning in about third grade is expository or informational text. Many students lack the prior knowledge and academic vocabulary to comprehend informational text. Narrative can be challenging as well since it sometimes includes obscure references and themes that may be difficult for students to easily understand.

Proficient readers intentionally use strategies to support comprehension, especially when reading challenging text (Pressley, 2000). The CORE model, which stands for connect, organize, reflect, extend (figure 6.13, page 252; Dymock, 2005), is a useful lesson design to teach students how to identify and navigate the common text model, expository text.

The importance of monitoring comprehension while reading cannot be understated. Helping students learn to read with intention and be aware of their understanding while reading both narrative and informational text is a critical component of comprehension instruction. Using think-alouds with a variety of text types is the perfect way to begin creating awareness for how the reader makes sense of text and what they do when understanding breaks down. Strategies such as buddy by my side and the CORE model also support effective comprehension instruction that highlights reading processes, navigating fiction and nonfiction, and the strategies we use to ensure comprehension. During-reading strategies not only address comprehension but also keep the reader engaged and develop students' metacognitive skills.

Strategy: CORE Model

Pillar: Comprehension

Grade Level:	Instructional Grouping:	Consider This:
☐ K ☑ 1 ☑ 2 ☑ 3 ☑ 4 ☑ 5 ☑ 6	☑ Whole Group ☑ Small Group ☐ Individual	• Students need a good deal of ongoing practice in order to see and identify text structure. • Text structure helps students create a cognitive frame for thinking and learning (Chambliss & Calfee, 1998). • The CORE model can be adapted to grades 1 and 2. Provide more structure, support, and scaffolds (perhaps reading the text aloud) for early readers.

What is it? The CORE model—connect, organize, reflect, extend—is a framework for designing lessons to teach expository text structure (Calfee et al., 1991; Calfee & Patrick, 1995; Chambliss & Calfee, 1998).

Why is it important? Students beyond third grade (and adults) primarily read expository text. In addition, most state assessments include more expository text passages to assess comprehension than narrative selections. Teaching text structure is time well spent so students become increasingly familiar with how expository text is organized, thus aiding comprehension.

What works in the classroom?

CORE Strategy: Lesson Design

- **Connect:** Connect students to the topic and text structure. For example, consider the topic of weather systems. Connect to what students know about the topic (background knowledge) and have a conversation about whatever comes to mind—personal experiences, vocabulary, videos they've seen, stories they've heard, and so on.
- **Organize:**
  - **Expository text organization:** Teach students that information in expository texts is organized in many different structures.
    - In beginning texts, they are often organized in a sequential structure, which include first-to-last and series of events, for example.
    - In more sophisticated texts that intermediate students read, texts are frequently organized in lists, webs, graphic organizers, and compare and contrast. These texts can also include sequence (or string) patterns, which could be a chronological sequence of events in a history text, for example.
  - **How we can organize information:** Model the ways in which we can organize text that help us learn and comprehend the content. The organizational structures include lists, webs, graphic organizers, charts, compare, contrast, and so on.
- **Reflect:** Reflect about text. In an ongoing manner, have students reflect about text. For example, ask questions such as, "What kind of text is this?" "What is an organizational structure that you notice?" "How did you organize information to help you better understand it?"
- **Extend:**
  - **Select new text and topics:** Continually extend learning to new topics and varied texts.
    - For example, during small-group instruction, give each student an informational text and provide time for students to review a chapter or the overall organization of the text.
    - Ask each student to share insights about the topic and how the information is organized in the book. Additionally, have students think about how they could organize the information to better understand it. Ask them to show others by depicting it on a whiteboard.

Figure 6.13: Strategy—CORE model.

*Visit **go.SolutionTree.com/literacy/FSK6** and enter the unique access code found on the book's inside front cover to access a reproducible version of this figure.*

After-Reading Strategies

Thus far, we've looked at strategies that help readers focus on connecting before they read and while they read—both of which increase comprehension. In addition to these activities, readers who engage after reading help cement new learning and make meaning from text. This was the focus of my dissertation study (Tyson, 1993). In that study, college freshmen read expository text and then responded to comprehension questions. In short, students who *did more* comprehended better. Some students underlined text, others wrote key ideas in the margins, and a few summarized the text following reading. Engaging with text increases comprehension.

CORE, the previous strategy, could be considered a before- and after-reading strategy in addition to supporting students as a during-reading strategy. Before reading, students preview the text to discover the text organizational pattern, which supports comprehension. After reading, students return to the text to determine how they could organize the information such as in a web or list, for example, to help them deepen their understanding of the content.

There are a variety of strategies you can teach students and use as part of lesson design to deepen comprehension and extend learning after reading. Remember that the point of after-reading strategies is to deepen understanding. A well-intentioned, post-reading activity that I've observed with frequency is when students create (often elaborate) shoebox dioramas about a novel they read. Can we all agree that this after-reading activity has very little to do with deepening comprehension? They also probably cause parents like me lots of headaches purchasing materials and supporting (or helping) their students the night before it's due.

After-reading strategies that connect active processes to comprehension include the following.

- **Think-pair-share:** Provide a prompt and have students respond to the prompt in pairs or in groups of three.
- **Exit tickets:** Provide a simple reflection such as "Three Key Takeaways" or "I learned" and "I'm confused about _______________."
- **Writing about reading:** Have students write a few sentences about what they learned, a new vocabulary word, or provide an open-ended prompt to which students respond.
- **Graphic organizers:** Students develop a graphic organizer or web individually or with a small group. Students could use Creately (https://creately.com), a digital tool, to develop many types of graphic organizers.
- **Digital word walls:** Create a digital word wall using ThingLink (www.thinglink.com) or Padlet (https://padlet.com). Students can add to the word wall chapter by chapter following reading. Additionally, students could summarize the story using digital tools to create a multimedia summary.

There are additional before-, during-, and after-reading strategies that you may use or learn from colleagues, professional development, or social media. Be careful of cutesy projects that are more arts-and-crafts based than cognitive based. Mike Schmoker (2001), a leading educator and researcher, uses the term *Crayola curriculum* to describe these types of activities (dioramas). In his many classroom observations across the United States, he noted a proliferation of coloring activities in the name of literacy. Let's not contribute to this but rather choose language and thinking-based strategies that extend and deepen text understanding.

The final strategy, High Five!, highlights five before, during, and after reading strategies. Susan Dymock and Tom Nicholson (2010), who developed the strategy, wanted to keep it simple by selecting five strategies that have a lot of research support for their effectiveness. The five strategies are summarized in figure 6.14.

Strategy: High Five!

Pillar: Comprehension

Grade Level:	**Instructional Grouping:**	**Consider This:**
☐K ☐1 ☑2 ☑3 ☑4 ☑5 ☑6	☑ Whole Group ☑ Small Group ☐ Individual	• Teach the High Five! strategies over the course of several weeks using different types of text and create an anchor chart with students that summarizes each strategy. (*show me*) • Consider teaching each strategy during whole-group instruction and following up during small-group instruction with more examples. (*help me*) • Consider making a bookmark for students with each of the strategies along with an icon to represent the strategy for references as they independently use the High Five! strategy. (*let me*)

What is it? The High Five! strategy focuses on five key strategies that support comprehension. These include activating background knowledge, questioning, analyzing text structure, creating mental images, and summarizing.

Why is it important? Good readers use comprehension strategies as they as read (NICHD, 2000b; Pressley, 2006). Learning to use these strategies independently will help students as they read increasingly challenging informational text.

What works in the classroom?

High Five! Strategies

Teach and model each of these strategies with examples from narrative and informational text.

1. **Activating Prior Knowledge:**
   - **Good readers** add to their knowledge by looking up key vocabulary, watching a video, looking up locations on the internet, or viewing a map in the book, for example.
   - **Model** how to review a selection of expository text to determine the topic and teach the importance of activating your prior knowledge before reading.

2. **Questioning:**
   - **Good readers** ask three types of questions: right there (factual), think and search (read and synthesize text to determine a response), and beyond the text (what the text or author is not saying; Dymock & Nicholson, 1999; Raphael, 1982).
   - **Model** how to use text to respond to each of these types of questions.
3. **Creating Mental Images:**
   - **Good readers** create mental images while they read. Mental images can be based on how texts are structured, such as story grammar (narrative) and varied text structures (expository). Mental images can also be created from how the reader connects to text through their schema and background knowledge.
   - **Model** how to create mental images using both narrative and expository text.
4. **Analyzing Text Structure:**
   - **Good readers** preview the text by using text features to navigate and support comprehension. These include print features such as bold print, sidebars, and captions. Graphic aids may be diagrams, maps, charts, and timelines along with photos and other illustrations. Students may also use organizational aids such as the table of contents, chapter headings, the index, and glossary.
   - **Model** how to analyze text structure using several examples, including sequence, cause-effect, description, and problem-solution. Teach each type separately since one type does not transfer to another (Williams, 2009).
   - **Model** how to create different types of graphic organizers—lists, webs, matrix, cause-effect—to organize the information in an expository text.
5. **Summarizing:**
   - **Good readers** can summarize by combining similar ideas, deleting irrelevant details, and determining the main idea.
   - **Model** how to summarize with several different selections from expository texts and short stories.

Figure 6.14: Strategy—High Five!

Visit ***go.SolutionTree.com/literacy/FSK6*** *and enter the unique access code found on the book's inside front cover to access a reproducible version of this figure.*

Wrapping It Up

Comprehension is the heart and soul of reading instruction. This can't be understated. The first four pillars—phonemic awareness, phonics, fluency, vocabulary—are interconnected to support readers as they comprehend text. This chapter included several theories of comprehension, the challenges of teaching comprehension, and characteristics of effective comprehension instruction. The strategies included here and online as bonus content were selected to support your students as they become proficient readers of fiction, nonfiction, and informational texts. Whether you teach primary or intermediate students, literacy instruction leads to one primary goal: comprehension. School leaders can use the Leader's Lens (figure 6.15, page 256) to support teachers moving forward with effective literacy practices. As you consider the Five Key Takeaways (page 257), examine how you can work to bring your students to this primary goal. Think about intentionality as it relates to your instruction and literacy environment as you consider the Five Key Next Steps (page 257).

Leader's Lens

Comprehension

Consider the following supervision supports and classroom connections as you lead and guide teachers in implementing effective comprehension instruction as they develop proficient readers.

Supervision Supports	
Practical Research	• Have I shared current research on the importance of comprehension instruction that is aligned to science of reading research? • Have I shared strategies that enhance understanding of text that leads to high-level comprehension (before, during and after reading)?
Professional Development	• What do you consider essential professional development for comprehension instruction? Where would you begin? • How would you support collaborative teams as teachers implement effective comprehension practices within the literacy block.
Feedback and Expectations	• Are you providing specific and intentional feedback focused on the aspect of comprehension strategies before, during, and after reading? • Are you intentionally addressing comprehension engagement strategies used to enhance understanding of a text?
Financial Focus	• Is there money budgeted to provide materials that could be used to support comprehension instruction? • Are you able to allocate resources for teachers and professional development?
Classroom Connections (Look-Fors)	
Before Reading	• Notice the type of texts used for instruction and read alouds to support comprehension. • Notice strategies used to prepare students for understanding text prior to reading, specifically activating prior knowledge. • Notice whether key vocabulary is highlighted or front-loaded prior to reading.
During Reading	• Notice the strategies used to enhance understanding of text while reading such as the use of text structures and signal words. • Notice how teachers model and support monitoring comprehension. • Notice if students were engaged in paired reading to support comprehension, engagement, and talking about text. What did this look like?
After Reading	• Notice the strategies used to engage in understanding text after reading—what do you see? • How frequently do teachers engage in think-alouds—why?

Figure 6.15: Chapter 6 leader's lens.

*Visit **go.SolutionTree.com/literacy/FSK6** for a free reproducible version of this figure.*

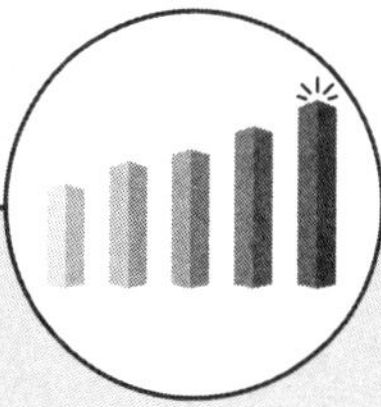

Five Key Takeaways

Consider the following questions individually or discuss them with your collaborative grade-level team.

1. **Defining comprehension:** Refer to the definitions of comprehension developed by teachers and the International Literacy Association. Discuss with your colleagues which you prefer and why.
2. **Theories of comprehension:** Three theories of comprehension include schema theory, transactional theory, and constructivist theory. Each provides a way of thinking about how readers make meaning from text.
3. **Challenges of comprehension instruction:** Teaching comprehension has numerous challenges, which include lack of foundational reading skills, fluency issues, and limited vocabulary, among others.
4. **Text structure:** Teaching text structure positively impacts students' comprehension (Pearson & Duke, 2002). Students need experience and direct instruction in common text structures found within narrative and expository text.
5. **Before-, during-, and after-reading strategies:** Many strategies were included for readers to use before, during, and after reading to engage and deepen comprehension. Eight of these are described in detail within strategy tables.

Five Key Next Steps

Consider the following questions individually or discuss them with your collaborative grade-level team.

1. **Definition of comprehension:** Think about the definition you selected for comprehension. Why did this definition resonate with you? How does this definition impact your instruction?
2. **Challenges of comprehension instruction:** Think about your current challenges relative to comprehension instruction. How do you address these challenges? Discuss with your colleagues and share ideas with one another.
3. **Text structure:** Design a lesson about narrative and expository text structure. The CORE strategy table will help you design a lesson for primary students or intermediate students. How will you intentionally extend student learning beyond the initial lesson?
4. **Before-reading strategies:** Think about the strategies readers engage in before reading. The strategic behaviors include activating prior knowledge, visualizing text, developing a purpose for reading, and generating questions. Select one or two that are new to you and try them with your students. Reconvene with your collaborative team and discuss what went well and what you would do differently next time.
5. **During reading and after reading:** Now reflect on the strategies students can engage in during and after reading. Select one or two that are new to you and implement them with your students. Reconvene with your collaborative team and discuss what went well and what you will do differently next time.

Epilogue

Fifty Strategies to Ensure K–6 Literacy Success: Aligning Instruction to the Five Pillars of Reading wanted and needed to be written. Almost two years after the time I sketched out the table of contents late at night on a plane, it is now complete. Over time, the content has shifted and evolved from the original outline written in my notebook. While the influence of trusted colleagues and classroom teachers have shaped its final form, the purpose has remained the same.

In writing this book, my main objective was to provide a comprehensive and accessible blueprint to assist educators in implementing the five pillars of effective reading instruction—*phonemic awareness*, *phonics*, *fluency*, *vocabulary*, and *comprehension*—which are fundamental to the science of reading. My hope is that the information, research, and strategies provided for each pillar, that is, the *what*, *why*, and *how*, help you become more effective in teaching and supporting your students.

Thank you for joining me in digging deeper into the five essential pillars. I hope, in some way, this book inspires, invigorates, and bolsters you in your professional journey. Our future depends on each of us doing our part to ensure students become strategic and proficient readers, writers, and thinkers.

Appendix

Table A.1 (page 262) serves as a quick reference guide for you to the strategies included in this resource. Each chapter topic is listed across the top of the table and the skill or purpose for each strategy is listed vertically. Glance down the chart to see the names of each strategy, which are connected to the five pillars of reading listed across the top of the table. The bonus online-only free reproducible strategies are indicated with an asterisk and available at **go.SolutionTree.com/literacy/FSK6**.

Table A.1: Five Pillars of Effective Reading Instruction Strategies

	Literacy-Rich Environment	Phonemic Awareness	Phonics	Fluency	Vocabulary	Comprehension
Literacy-Rich Classrooms	Oral Language Labeling the Classroom Learning Targets Anchor Chart Organizing a Classroom Library					
Sounds		Pairing Sounds, Articulation, and Letters* Sound Walls				
Phoneme Isolation		Sound Bingo I Spy Odd Word Out				
Phoneme Blending		Turtle Talk				
Phoneme Substitution		Presto Chango Lucky Roll				
Phoneme Segmentation		Singing and Segmenting Elkonin Boxes				
Word Study			Language Experience Approach			
Word Building			Blending Sounds and Letters Word Awareness Word Sorts Word Ladders Living Words* Root of the Day			
Multisensory Approach Strategies for Struggling Readers			Read It, Build It, Write It, Connect It Elkonin Boxes for Phonics			

Category	Strategies
Assisted Reading and Modeled Reading Strategies	Read Alouds* One More Story Freddy Fluency Fast Start Echo Reading* Choral Reading Phrased Text Lesson*
Paired Oral Reading Strategies	Paired Readers Protocol Dyad Rading Neurological Impress Method Read Two Impress*
Repeated Reading Strategies	Read-Listen-Reflect Radio Reading Reader's Theater Fluency Development Lesson
Direct Word Learning Strategies	Four Stages of Word Learning Motor Imaging Concept Circles* List-Group-Label Alphaboxes
Indirect Word Learning Strategies	Anchored Word Learning Word Walls Word Talks* Word Jars* Save the Last Word for Me Word Sorts Fly Swatter Vocabulary
Before Reading	Front-Loading Vocabulary Listen-Read-Discuss Anticipation Guide Question-Answer Relationship
During Reading	Think-Alouds Buddy by My Side Traffic Light Reading* CORE Model
After Reading	High Five!

References and Resources

Acosta-Tello, E. (2019). Reading aloud: Engaging young children during a read aloud experience. *Research in Higher Education Journal, 37*.

Afflerbach, P., Pearson, P. D., & Paris, S. G. (2008). Clarifying differences between reading skills and reading strategies. *The Reading Teacher, 61*(5), 364–373. https://doi.org/10.1598/RT.61.5.1

Ahlberg, J., & Ahlberg, A. (1978). *Each peach pear plum*. Puffin Books.

Ahmed, Y., Francis, D. J., York, M., Fletcher, J. M., Barnes, M., & Kulesz, P. (2016). Validation of the direct and inferential mediation (DIME) model of reading comprehension in grades 7 through 12. *Contemporary Educational Psychology, 44–45*, 68–82. https://doi.org/10.1016/j.cedpsych.2016.02.002

Alamri, K., & Rogers, V. (2018). The effectiveness of different explicit vocabulary-teaching strategies on learners' retention of technical and academic words. *The Language Learning Journal, 46*(5), 622–633. https://doi.org/10.1080/09571736.2018.1503139

Alexander, K. L. (2024). Using intentional pairing and peer tutoring during structured literacy activities in inclusion classrooms. *The Reading Teacher, 77*(6), 991–996. https://doi.org/10.1002/trtr.2329

Alexander, K., & Nikaido, D. (2023). *How to write a poem*. (M. Sweet, Illus.). HarperCollins.

Allen, J. (1999). *Words, words, words: Teaching vocabulary in grades 4–12*. Stenhouse.

Allen, J. (2007). *Inside words: Tools for teaching vocabulary, grades 4–12*. Stenhouse.

Allington, R. L. (2002). *Big Brother and the national reading curriculum: How ideology trumped evidence*. Heinemann.

Allington, R. L. (2009). If they don't read much . . . 30 years later. In E. H. Hiebert (Ed.), *Reading more, reading better* (pp. 30–54). Guilford Press.

Alvermann, D. E. (1981). The compensatory effect of graphic organizers on descriptive text. *The Journal of Educational Research, 75*(1), 44–48. https://doi.org/10.1080/00220671.1981.10885354

Anderson, R. C. (1995). *Research foundations for wide reading* [Conference presentation]. Center for the Study of Reading, University of Illinois at Urbana-Champaign, special invitational conference.

Anderson, R. C., Hiebert, E. H., Scott, J. A., & Wilkinson, I. A. G. (1985). *Becoming a nation of readers: The report of the Commission on Reading*. The National Academy of Education.

Anderson, R. C., & Nagy, W. E. (1992). The vocabulary conundrum. *American Educator, 16*(4), 14–18, 44–47.

Anderson, R. C., & Pearson, P. D. (1984). A schema-theoretic view of basic processes in reading comprehension. In P. D. Pearson, R. Barr, M. L. Kamil, & P. Mosenthal (Eds.), *Handbook of reading research* (pp. 255–291). Longman.

Anderson, R. C., Wilson, P. T., & Fielding, L. G. (1988). Growth in reading and how children spend their time outside of school. *Reading Research Quarterly, 23*(3), 285–303.

Anthony, J. L., & Francis, D. J. (2005). Development of phonological awareness. *Current Directions in Psychological Science, 14*(5), 255–259. https://doi.org/10.1111/j.0963-7214.2005.00376.x

Anthony, J. L., & Lonigan, C. J. (2004). The nature of phonological awareness: Converging evidence from four studies of preschool and early grade school children. *Journal of Educational Psychology, 96*(1), 43–55. https://doi.org/10.1037/0022-0663.96.1.43

Anthony, J. L., Lonigan, C. J., Driscoll, K., Phillips, B. M., & Burgess, S. R. (2003). Phonological sensitivity: A quasi-parallel progression of word structure units and cognitive operations. *Reading Research Quarterly, 38*(4), 470–487. https://doi.org/10.1598/RRQ.38.4.3

Armbruster, B. B., Lehr, F., & Osborn, J. (2009). *Put reading first: The research building blocks of reading instruction—Kindergarten through grade 3* (3rd ed.). National Institute for Literacy.

Ashby, J., Martin, M., McBride, M., Naftel, S., O'Brien, E., & Paulson, L. H. (2023). *Teaching phonemic awareness in 2024: A guide for educators*. Accessed at https://drive.google.com/file/d/1gjLQmwZ4aLIEOXo5kQqeSdO888KAPclX/view?usp=drive_link on January 24, 2025.

Atwell, N., & Merkel, A. A. (2016). *The reading zone: How to help kids become skilled, passionate, habitual, critical readers* (2nd ed.). Scholastic.

Bailey, A. L. (2007). *The language demands of school: Putting academic English to the test*. Yale University Press.

Baker, L. (2002). Metacognition in comprehension instruction. In C. C. Block & M. Pressley (Eds.), *Comprehension instruction: Research-based best practices* (pp. 77–95). Guilford Press.

Balmuth, M. (2009). *The roots of phonics: A historical introduction* (Rev. ed.). Brookes.

Banks, K. (2006). *Max's words* (B. Kulikov, Illus.). Farrar, Straus and Giroux.

Barger, J. (2006). Building word consciousness. *The Reading Teacher, 60*(3), 279–281. https://doi.org/10.1598/RT.60.3.8

Barnes, E. M., Oliveira, A. W., & Dickinson, D. K. (2019). Teacher accommodation of academic language during head start pre-kindergarten read-alouds. *Journal of Education for Students Placed at Risk, 24*(4), 369–393.

Baron, N. S. (2021). *How we read now: Strategic choices for print, screen, and audio*. Oxford University Press.

Baumann, J. F., & Bergeron, B. S. (1993). Story map instruction using children's literature: Effects on first graders' comprehension of central narrative elements. *Journal of Reading Behavior, 25*(4), 407–437.

Bayer, J. (1984). *A, my name is Alice.* (S. Kellogg, Illus.). Puffin Books.

Beach, R., & Appleman, D. (1984). Reading strategies for expository and literary text types. In A. C. Purves & O. Niles (Eds.), *Becoming readers in a complex society: Eighty-third yearbook of the National Society for the Study of Education* (pp. 115–143). National Society for the Study of Education.

Bean, T. W., Readence, J. E., & Baldwin, R. S. (2008). *Content area literacy: An integrated approach* (9th ed.). Kendall/Hunt.

Bear, D. R., Invernizzi, M., Templeton, S., & Johnston, F. (2008). *Words their way: Word study for phonics, vocabulary, and spelling instruction* (4th ed.). Pearson.

Bear, D. R., Invernizzi, M., Templeton, S., & Johnston, F. (2016). *Words their way: Word study for phonics, vocabulary, and spelling instruction* (6th ed.). Pearson.

Bear, D. R., Invernizzi, M., Templeton, S., & Johnston, F. (2023). *Words their way: Word study for phonics, vocabulary, and spelling instruction* (7th ed.). Pearson.

Bear, D., & Templeton, S. (1998). Explorations in developmental spelling: Foundations for learning and teaching phonics, spelling, and vocabulary. *The Reading Teacher, 52*(3), 222–242.

Beck, I. L., & McKeown, M. G. (2006). *Improving comprehension with questioning the author: A fresh and expanded view of a powerful approach*. Scholastic.

Beck, I. L., & McKeown, M. G. (2007). Increasing young low-income children's oral vocabulary repertoires through rich and focused instruction. *The Elementary School Journal, 107*(3), 251–271.

Beck, I. L., McKeown, M. G., & Kucan, L. (2002). *Bringing words to life: Robust vocabulary instruction*. Guilford Press.

Beck, I. L., McKeown, M. G., & Kucan, L. (2008). *Creating robust vocabulary: Frequently asked questions and extended examples.* Guilford Press.

Beck, I. L., McKeown, M. G., & Kucan, L. (2013). *Bringing words to life: Robust vocabulary instruction* (2nd ed.). Guilford Press.

Beck, I. L., Perfetti, C. A., & McKeown, M. G. (1982). Effects of long-term vocabulary instruction on lexical access and reading comprehension. *Journal of Educational Psychology, 74*(4), 506–521.

Beers, K. (2003). *When kids can't read, what teachers can do: A guide for teachers, 6–12.* Heinemann.

Benning, K. (2014). Independent reading: Shifting reluctant readers to authentic engagement in the middle level. *Journal of Adolescent and Adult Literacy, 57*(8), 632. https://doi.org/10.1002/jaal.298

Berenstain, S., & Berenstain, J. (1985). *The Berenstain Bears forget their manners.* Random House.

Blevins, W. (2017). *A fresh look at phonics, grades K–2: Common causes of failure and 7 ingredients for success.* Corwin Press.

Blevins, W. (2024). *Differentiating phonics instruction for maximum impact: How to scaffold whole-group instruction so all students can access grade-level content.* Corwin Press.

Block, C. C., & Mangieri, J. N. (2006). *The vocabulary-enriched classroom: Practices for improving the reading performance of all students in grades 3 and up.* Scholastic.

Block, C. C., & Pressley, M. (Eds.). (2002). *Comprehension instruction: Research-based best practices.* Guilford Press.

Bloodgood, J. W., & Pacifici, L. C. (2004). Bringing word study to intermediate classrooms. *The Reading Teacher, 58*(3), 250–263. https://doi.org/10.1598/RT.58.3.3

Brabham, E., Buskist, C., Henderson, S. C., Paleologos, T., & Baugh, N. (2012). Flooding vocabulary gaps to accelerate word learning. *The Reading Teacher, 65*(8), 523–533. https://doi.org/10.1002/TRTR.01078

Brady, S. (2020). A 2020 perspective on research findings on alphabetics (phoneme awareness and phonics): Implications for instruction. *The Reading League Journal, 1*(3), 20–28.

Brown, A. L., & Palincsar, A. S. (1987). Reciprocal teaching of comprehension strategies: A natural history of one program for enhancing learning. In J. D. Day & J. G. Borkowski (Eds.), *Intelligence and exceptionality: New directions for theory, assessment, and instructional practices* (pp. 81–132). Ablex.

Brown, K. J., Patrick, K. C., Fields, M. K., & Craig, G. T. (2021). Phonological awareness materials in Utah kindergartens: A case study in the science of reading. *Reading Research Quarterly, 56*(S1), S249–S272. https://doi.org/10.1002/rrq.386

Brown, L. T., Mohr, K. A. J., Wilcox, B. R., & Barrett, T. S. (2018). The effects of dyad reading and text difficulty on third-graders' reading achievement. *The Journal of Educational Research, 111*(5), 541–553. https://doi.org/10.1080/00220671.2017.1310711

Bruner, L. (2021). A well-rounded diet: Fueling children's vocabulary development. *The Reading Teacher, 74*(6), 797–805.

Buckley-Marudas, M. F. (2016). Literacy learning in a digitally rich humanities classroom: Embracing multiple, collaborative, and simultaneous texts. *Journal of Adolescent and Adult Literacy, 59*(5), 551–561. https://doi.org/10.1002/jaal.470

Buffum, A., Mattos, M., & Weber, C. (2009). *Pyramid response to intervention: RTI, professional learning communities, and how to respond when kids don't learn.* Solution Tree Press.

Bus, A. G., & van IJzendoorn, M. H. (1999). Phonological awareness and early reading: A meta-analysis of experimental training studies. *Journal of Educational Psychology, 91*(3), 403–414.

Calderón, M. (2011). *Teaching reading and comprehension to English learners, K–5.* Solution Tree Press.

Caldwell, J., & Leslie, L. (2010). Thinking aloud in expository text: Processes and outcomes. *Journal of Literacy Research, 42*(3), 308–340. https://doi.org/10.1080/1086296X.2010.504419

Calfee, R. C., Chambliss, M. J., & Beretz, M. M. (1991). Organizing for comprehension and composition. In R. Bowler & W. Ellis (Eds.), *All languages and the creation of literacy* (pp. 79–93). Orton Dyslexia Society.

Calfee, R. C., & Patrick, C. L. (1995). *Teach our children well: Bringing K–12 education into the 21st century.* Stanford Alumni Association.

Campbell, J. R., Donahue, P. L., Reese, C. M., & Phillips, G. W. (1996). *NAEP 1994 reading report card for the nation and the states: Findings from the National Assessment of Educational Progress and trial state assessments* (NCES Publication No. 96045). U.S. Department of Education, Office of Educational Research and Improvement, National Center for Education Statistics. Accessed at https://nces.ed.gov/nationsreportcard//pdf/main1994/96045.pdf on January 24, 2025.

Cannon, J. (1993). *Stellaluna.* Clarion Books.

Carleton, L., & Marzano, R. J. (2010). *Vocabulary games for the classroom.* Marzano Resources.

Carnine, D. W., Silbert, J., & Kameenui, E. J. (1997). *Direct instruction reading* (3rd ed.). Merrill/Prentice Hall.

Cartwright, K. B., & Duke, N. K. (2019). The DRIVE model of reading: Making the complexity of reading accessible. *The Reading Teacher, 73*(1), 7–15. https://doi.org/10.1002/trtr.1818

Casale, U. P. (1985). Motor imaging: A reading-vocabulary strategy. *Journal of Reading, 28*(7), 619–621.

Castiglioni-Spalten, M. L., & Ehri, L. C. (2003). Phonemic awareness instruction: Contribution of articulatory segmentation to novice beginners' reading and spelling. *Scientific Studies of Reading, 7*(1), 25–52. https://doi.org/10.1207/S1532799XSSR0701_03

Castles, A., Rastle, K., & Nation, K. (2018). Ending the reading wars: Reading acquisition from novice to expert. *Psychological Science in the Public Interest, 19*(1), 5–51. https://doi.org/10.1177/1529100618772271

Catts, H. W., Fey, M. E., Zhang, X., & Tomblin, J. B. (1999). Language basis of reading and reading disabilities: Evidence from a longitudinal investigation. *Scientific Studies of Reading, 3*(4), 331–361.

Cervetti, G. N., & Hiebert, E. H. (2019). Knowledge at the center of English language arts instruction. *The Reading Teacher, 72*(4), 499–507. https://doi.org/10.1002/trtr.1758

Cervetti, G. N., Wright, T. S., & Hwang, H. (2015, December 3). *The impact of thematic coherence in reading on the quality of student discussions* [Conference symposium]. Literacy Research Association annual meeting, Carlsbad, CA.

Cervetti, G. N., Wright, T. S., & Hwang, H. (2016). Conceptual coherence, comprehension, and vocabulary acquisition: A knowledge effect? *Reading and Writing, 29*(4), 761–779. https://doi.org/10.1007/s11145-016-9628-x

Chall, J. (1967) *Learning to read: The great debate.* McGraw Hill

Chambliss, M. J., & Calfee, R. C. (1998). *Textbooks for learning: Nurturing children's minds.* Blackwell.

Chuang, L., & Wang, C. (2015). Listening enhancement: Converting input into intake. *American Journal of Educational Research, 3*(9), 1091–1097.

Cirino, P. T., Child, A. E., & Macdonald, K. T. (2018). Longitudinal predictors of the overlap between reading and math skills. *Contemporary Educational Psychology, 54*, 99–111. https://doi.org/10.1016/j.cedpsych.2018.06.002

Clayton, F. J., West, G., Sears, C., Hulme, C., & Lervåg, A. (2020). A longitudinal study of early reading development: Letter-sound knowledge, phoneme awareness and RAN, but not letter-sound integration, predict variations in reading development. *Scientific Studies of Reading, 24*(2), 91–107. http://doi.org/10.1080/10888438.2019.1622546

Cleary, B. P., & Gable, B. (1999–2012). *Words are CATegorical* [Book series]. Millbrook Press.

Clemens, N. H., Solari, E., Kearns, D. M., Fien, H., Nelson, N. J., Stelega, M., et al. (2021). *They say you can do phonemic awareness instruction "in the dark," but should you? A critical evaluation of the trend toward advanced phonemic awareness training.* PsyArXiv. https://doi.org/10.31234/osf.io/ajxbv

Clinton, V. (2019). Reading from paper compared to screens: A systematic review and meta-analysis. *Journal of Research in Reading, 42*(2), 288–325. https://doi.org/10.1111/1467-9817.12269

Cohen, A. J. (2020). *Kindergarten from A to Z: Managing your classroom and curriculum with purpose and confidence.* Solution Tree Press.

Coiro, J., & Dobler, E. (2007). Exploring the online reading comprehension strategies used by sixth-grade skilled readers to search for and locate information on the internet. *Reading Research Quarterly, 42*(2), 214–257. https://doi.org/10.1598/RRQ.42.2.2

Connor, C. M., Morrison, F. J., & Underwood, P. S. (2007). A second chance in second grade: The independent and cumulative impact of first- and second-grade reading instruction and students' letter-word reading skill growth. *Scientific Studies of Reading, 11*(3), 199–233. https://doi.org/10.1080/10888430701344314

Conradi Smith, K., Young, C. A., & Yatzeck, J. C. (2022). What are teachers reading and why? An analysis of elementary read aloud titles and the rationales underlying teachers' selections. *Literacy Research and Instruction, 61*(4), 383–401. https://doi.org/10.1080/19388071.2021.2008558

Cowen, C. D. (2016). *What is structured literacy? A primer on effective reading instruction* [Fact sheet]. International Dyslexia Association. Accessed at https://dyslexiaida.org/what-is-structured-literacy on July 1, 2024.

Crosby, S. A., Rasinski, T., Padak, N., & Yildirim, K. (2015). A 3-year study of a school-based parental involvement program in early literacy. *The Journal of Educational Research, 108*(2), 165–172. https://doi.org/10.1080/00220671.2013.867472

Cunningham, A. E., & Stanovich, K. E. (1997). Early reading acquisition and its relation to reading experience and ability 10 years later. *Developmental Psychology, 33*(6), 934–945. https://doi.org/10.1037/0012-1649.33.6.934

Cunningham, A. E., & Stanovich, K. E. (1998). What reading does for the mind. *American Educator, 22*(1–2), 8–15.

Cunningham, A. E., & Zibulsky, J. (2011). Tell me a story: Examining the benefits of shared reading. In S. B. Neuman, & D. K. Dickinson (Eds.), *Handbook of early literacy research* (Vol. 3, pp. 396–411). Guilford Press.

Curtis, J. L. (2008). *Big words for little people* (L. Cornell, Illus.). Joanna Cotler Books.

D'Angiulli, A., Siegel, L. S., & Hertzman, C. (2004). Schooling, socioeconomic context and literacy development. *Educational Psychology, 24*(6), 867–883. https://doi.org/10.1080/0144341042000271746

Dale, E. (1965). Vocabulary measurement: Techniques and major findings. *Elementary English, 42*(8), 895–901.

Daniels, H. (2002). *Literature circles: Voice and choice in book clubs and reading groups* (2nd ed.). Stenhouse.

Davey, B. (1983). Think aloud—Modeling the cognitive processes of reading comprehension. *Journal of Reading, 27*(1), 44–47.

de Graaff, S., Bosman, A. M. T., Hasselman, F., & Verhoeven, L. (2009). Benefits of systematic phonics instruction. *Scientific Studies of Reading, 13*(4), 318–333.

de Sève, R. (2014). *Toy boat* (L. Long, Illus.). Philomel Books.

DeGross, M. (1994). *Donavan's word jar* (C. Hanna, Illus.). Harper Trophy.

Dewdney, A. (2015). *Llama llama red pajama* (A. Dewdney, Illus.). Viking Books.

DiCamillo, K. (2015). *The miraculous journey of Edward Tulane* (B. Ibatoulline, Illus.). Walker Books.

Dimich, N., Erkens, C., Miller, J., Schimmer, T., & White, K. (2022). *Concise answers to frequently asked questions about assessment and grading.* Solution Tree Press.

Diller, D. (2008). *Spaces and places: Designing classrooms for literacy.* Stenhouse.

Dixon-Krauss, L. (1996). *Vygotsky in the classroom: Mediated literacy instruction and assessment.* Longman.

Doberman, M. A. (2009). *Very short scary stories to read together.* Little, Brown Books for Young Readers.

Doberman, M. A. (2012a). *Very short fairy tales to read together.* Little, Brown Books for Young Readers.

Doberman, M. A. (2012b). *Very short Mother Goose tales to read together.* Little, Brown Books for Young Readers.

Doberman, M. A. (2013). *Very short fables to read together.* Little, Brown Books for Young Readers.

Doberman, M. A. (2019). *Very short tall tales to read together.* Little, Brown Books for Young Readers.

Dolch, E. W. (1936). A basic sight vocabulary. *The Elementary School Journal, 36*(6), 456–460. https://doi.org/10.1086/457353

Dong, Y., Tang, Y., Chow, B. W., Wang, W., & Dong, W. (2020). Contribution of vocabulary knowledge to reading comprehension among Chinese students: A meta-analysis. *Frontiers in Psychology, 11*, Article 525369. https://doi.org/10.3389/fpsyg.2020.525369

Dorl, J. (2007). Think aloud! Increase your teaching power. *Young Children, 62*(4), 101–105.

Dotlich, R. K. (1998). *Lemonade sun: And other summer poems.* (J. S. Gilchrist, Illus.). Boyds Mills Press.

Dotlich, R. K., & Heard, G. (2023). *Welcome to the wonder house* (D. Freedman, Illus.). Wordsong.

Downs, J., Mohr, K., & Young, C. (2023). A historical narrative review of paired oral reading practices in elementary classrooms. *Journal of Research in Reading, 46*(1), 42–63. https://doi.org/10.1111/1467-9817.12413

Duffy, G. G. (1993). Rethinking strategy instruction: Four teachers' development and their low achievers' understandings. *The Elementary School Journal, 93*(3), 231–247.

Duke, N. K., & Cartwright, K. B. (2021). The science of reading progresses: Communicating advances beyond the simple view of reading. *Reading Research Quarterly, 56*(S1), S25–S44. https://doi.org/10.1002/rrq.411

Duke, N. K., Ward, A. E., & Pearson, P. D. (2021). The science of reading comprehension instruction. *The Reading Teacher, 74*(6), 663–672. https://doi.org/10.1002/trtr.1993

Durkin, D. (1978). What classroom observations reveal about reading comprehension instruction. *Reading Research Quarterly, 14*(4), 481–533.

Durkin, D. (1981). Reading comprehension instruction in five basal reader series. *Reading Research Quarterly, 16*(4), 515–544. https://doi.org/10.2307/747314

Dymock, S. (2005). Teaching expository text structure awareness. *The Reading Teacher, 59*(2), 177–181. https://doi.org/10.1598/RT.59.2.7

Dymock, S. (2007). Comprehension strategy instruction: Teaching narrative text structure awareness. *The Reading Teacher, 61*(2), 161–167. https://doi.org/10.1598/RT.61.2.6

Dymock, S., & Nicholson, T. (1999). *Reading comprehension: What is it? How do you teach it?* New Zealand Council for Educational Research.

Dymock, S., & Nicholson, T. (2010). "High 5!" strategies to enhance comprehension of expository text. *The Reading Teacher, 64*(3), 166–178. https://doi.org/10.1598/RT.64.3.2

EdWeek Research Center. (2020). *Early reading instruction: Results of a national survey.* Editorial Projects in Education. Accessed at https://epe.brightspotcdn.com/1b/80/706eba6246599174b0199ac1f3b5/ed-week-reading-instruction-survey-report-final-1.24.20.pdf on June 30, 2024.

Ehri, L. C. (1984). How orthography alters spoken language competencies in children learning to read and spell. In J. Downing & R. Valtin (Eds.), *Language awareness and learning to read* (pp. 119–147). Springer Verlag.

Ehri, L. C. (1987). Learning to read and spell words. *Journal of Reading Behavior, 19*(1), 5–31.

Ehri, L. C. (1989). The development of spelling knowledge and its role in reading acquisition and reading disability. *Journal of Learning Disabilities, 22*(6), 356–365. https://doi.org/10.1177/002221948902200606

Ehri, L. C. (1998). Grapheme-phoneme correspondence is essential for learning to read words in English. In J. L. Metsala & L. C. Ehri (Eds.), *Word recognition in beginning literacy* (pp. 3–40). Erlbaum.

Ehri, L. C. (2005). Learning to read words: Theory, findings, and issues. *Scientific Studies of Reading, 9*(2), 167–188.

Ehri, L. C. (2014). Orthographic mapping in the acquisition of sight word reading, spelling memory, and vocabulary learning. *Scientific Studies of Reading, 18*(1), 5–21. https://doi.org/10.1080/10888438.2013.819356

Ehri, L. C. (2020). The science of learning to read words: A case for systematic phonics instruction. *Reading Research Quarterly, 55*(S1), S45-S60.

Ehri, L. C. (2022). What teachers need to know and do to teach letter–sounds, phonemic awareness, word reading, and phonics. *The Reading Teacher, 76*(1), 53–61. https://doi.org/10.1002/trtr.2095

Ehri, L. C., Nunes, S. R., Stahl, S. A., & Willows, D. M. (2001). Systematic phonics instruction helps students learn to read: Evidence from the National Reading Panel's meta-analysis. *Review of Educational Research, 71*(3), 393–447. https://doi.org/10.3102/00346543071003393

Ehri, L. C., Nunes, S. R., Willows, D. M., Schuster, B. V., Yaghoub-Zadeh, Z., & Shanahan, T. (2001). Phonemic awareness instruction helps children learn to read: Evidence from the National Reading Panel's meta-analysis. *Reading Research Quarterly, 36*(3), 250–287. https://doi.org/10.1598/RRQ.36.3.2

Eldredge, J. L. (1988). Improving the reading comprehension skills of poor readers. *Reading Horizons, 29*(1), 35–42. Accessed at https://scholarworks.wmich.edu/reading_horizons/vol29/iss1/4 on October 17, 2024.

Eldredge, J. L. (1990). Increasing the performance of poor readers in the third grade with a group-assisted strategy. *The Journal of Educational Research, 84*(2), 69–77. https://doi.org/10.1080/00220671.1990.10885995

Eldredge, J. L., & Quinn, D. W. (1988). Increasing reading performance of low-achieving second graders with dyad reading groups. *The Journal of Educational Research, 82*(1), 40–46. https://doi.org/10.1080/00220671.1988.10885863

Elkonin, D. B. (1963). The psychology of mastering the elements of reading. In B. Simon & J. Simon (Eds.), *Educational psychology in the U.S.S.R.* (pp. 165–179). Routledge and Kegan Paul.

Elleman, A. M., Lindo, E. J., Morphy, P., & Compton, D. L. (2009). The impact of vocabulary instruction on passage-level comprehension of school-age children: A meta-analysis. *Journal of Research on Educational Effectiveness, 2*(1), 1–44. https://doi.org/10.1080/19345740802539200

Emberley, B. (1992). *One wide river to cross.* (E. Emberley, Illus.) Little Brown & Company.

Erbeli, F., Rice, M., Xu, Y., Bishop, M. E., & Goodrich, J. M. (2024). A meta-analysis on the optimal cumulative dosage of early phonemic awareness instruction. *Scientific Studies of Reading, 28*(4), 345–370.

Ferlazzo, L. (2017, November 29). Enriching academic vocabulary: Strategies for teaching tier two words to E.L.L. students. *The New York Times.* https://www.nytimes.com/2017/11/29/learning/lesson-plans/enriching-academic-vocabulary-strategies-for-teaching-tier-two-words-to-ell-students.html on April 20, 2024.

Figurelli, S. (2015, May 26). *The Matthew effect* [Blog post]. Accessed at https://stevefigurelli.blogspot.com/2015/05/the-matthew-effect.html on May 5, 2024.

Fisher, D. (2008). *Effective use of the gradual release of responsibility model* [Monograph]. McGraw Hill.

Fisher, D., Flood, J., Lapp, D., & Frey, N. (2004). Interactive read-alouds: Is there a common set of implementation practices? *The Reading Teacher, 58*(1), 8–17.

Fisher, D., & Frey, N. (2008). Releasing responsibility. *Educational Leadership, 66*(3), 32–37.

Fisher, D., & Frey, N. (2018). Raise reading volume through access, choice, discussion, and book talks. *The Reading Teacher, 72*(1), 89–97. https://doi.org/10.1002/trtr.1691

Fisher, D., & Frey, N. (2021). *Better learning through structured teaching: A framework for the gradual release of responsibility* (3rd ed.). ASCD.

Fisher, D., Frey, N., & Lapp, D. (2011). Coaching middle-level teachers to think aloud improves comprehension instruction and student reading achievement. *The Teacher Educator, 46*(3), 231–243.

Flesch, R. (1955). *Why Johnny can't read—And what you can do about it.* Harper & Brothers.

Fletcher, J. M., Lyon, G. R., Fuchs, L. S., & Barnes, M. A. (2019). *Learning disabilities: From identification to intervention* (2nd ed.). Guilford Press.

Fleischman, P. (2008). *Big talk: Poems for four voices* (B. Giacobbe, Illus.). Candlewick.

Florian, D. (2000). *Laugh-eteria: Poems and drawings.* Scholastic.

Fountas, I. C., & Pinnell, G. S. (1996). *Guided reading: Good first teaching for all children.* Heinemann.

Frasier, D. (2000). *Miss Alaineus: A vocabulary disaster.* Harcourt Brace.

Fry, E. (1980). The new instant word list. *The Reading Teacher, 34*(3), 284–289.

Fry, E. (2004). Phonics: A large phoneme-grapheme frequency count revisited. *Journal of Literacy Research, 36*(1), 85–98.

Fuchs, D., Fuchs, L. S., & Burish, P. (2000). Peer-assisted learning strategies: An evidence-based practice to promote reading achievement. *Learning Disabilities Research and Practice, 15*(2), 85–91.

Fuchs, D., Fuchs, L. S., Simmons, D. C., & Mathes, P. G. (2017). *Peer-assisted learning strategies: Reading methods for grades 2–6.* Vanderbilt University.

Furenes, M. I., Kucirkova, N., & Bus, A. G. (2021). A comparison of children's reading on paper versus screen: A meta-analysis. *Review of Educational Research, 91*(4), 483–517. https://doi.org/10.3102/0034654321998074

Gallagher, K. (2009). *Readicide: How schools are killing reading and what you can do about it.* Stenhouse.

Gambrell, L. B., Malloy, J. A., & Mazzoni, S. A. (2007). Evidence-based best practices for comprehensive literacy instruction. In L. B. Gambrell, L. M. Morrow, & M. Pressley (Eds.), *Best practices in literacy instruction* (3rd ed.) (pp. 11–29). Guilford Press.

Gamse, B. C., Bloom, H. S., Kemple, J. J., & Jacob, R. T. (2008). *Reading first impact study: Interim report* (NCEE 2008–4016). National Center for Education Evaluation and Regional Assistance, Institute of Education Sciences, U.S. Department of Education.

Gangi, J. M. (2008). The unbearable whiteness of literacy instruction: Realizing the implications of the proficient reader research. *Multicultural Review, 17*(1), 30–35.

Genishi, C., & Dyson, A. H. (2009). *Children, language, and literacy: Diverse learners in diverse times.* Teachers College Press.

Gersten, R., Baker, S. K., Shanahan, T, Linan-Thompson, S., Collins, P., & Scarcella, R. (2007). *Effective literacy and English language instruction for English learners in the elementary grades.* National Center for Education Evaluation and Regional Assistance. Accessed at https://ies.ed.gov/ncee/wwc/Docs/PracticeGuide/20074011.pdf on January 22, 2025.

Giles, R. M., & Morrison, K. (2023). An investigation of prekindergarten teachers' read aloud choices. *Literacy Practice and Research, 48*(2), Article 3. Accessed at https://digitalcommons.fiu.edu/lpr/vol48/iss2/3 on October 17, 2024.

Gillingham, A., & Stillman, B. W. (1960). *Remedial training for children with specific disability in reading, spelling, and penmanship* (6th ed.). Educators Publishing Service.

Ginkel, A. (2006). *I've got an elephant* (J. Bynum, Illus.). Peachtree.

Goldenberg, C. (2020). Reading wars, reading science, and English learners. *Reading Research Quarterly, 55*(S1), S131–S144. https://doi.org/10.1002/rrq.340

Goodman, K. S. (1967). Reading: A psycholinguistic guessing game. *Journal of the Reading Specialist, 6*(4), 126–135.

Goodman, K. (1986). *What's whole in whole language?* Heinemann.

Goodwin, A. P., & Ahn, S. (2013). A meta-analysis of morphological interventions in English: Effects on literacy outcomes for school-age children. *Scientific Studies of Reading, 17*(4), 257–285. https://doi.org/10.1080/10888438.2012.689791

Gough, P. B., & Tunmer, W. E. (1986). Decoding, reading, and reading disability. *Remedial and Special Education, 7*(1), 6–10. https://doi.org/10.1177/074193258600700104

Gordon, J. R. (1991). *Six sleepy sheep* (J. O'Brien, Illus.). Boyds Mill Press.

Graham, S., Liu, X., Aitken, A., Ng, C., Bartlett, B., Harris, K. R., et al. (2018). Effectiveness of literacy programs balancing reading and writing instruction: A meta-analysis. *Reading Research Quarterly, 53*(3), 279–304.

Graham, S., & Santangelo, T. (2014). Does spelling instruction make students better spellers, readers, and writers? A meta-analytic review. *Reading and Writing, 27*(9), 1703–1743.

Graves, M. F. (2000). A vocabulary program to complement and bolster a middle-grade comprehension program. In B. M. Taylor, M. F. Graves, & P. van den Broek (Eds.), *Reading for meaning: Fostering comprehension in the middle grades* (pp. 116–135). Teachers College Press.

Graves, M. F. (2016). *The vocabulary book: Learning and instruction* (2nd ed.). Teachers College Press.

Graves, M. F., Schneider, S., & Ringstaff, C. (2018). Empowering students with word-learning strategies: Teach a child to fish. *The Reading Teacher, 71*(5), 533–543. https://doi.org/10.1002/trtr.1644

Griffith, L. W., & Rasinski, T. V. (2004). A focus on fluency: How one teacher incorporated fluency with her reading curriculum. *The Reading Teacher, 58*(2), 126–137. https://doi.org/10.1598/RT.58.2.1

Grigg, W. S., Daane, M. C., Jin, Y., & Campbell, J. R. (2002). *The Nation's Report Card: Reading 2002.* National Center for Education Statistics. Accessed at https://nces.ed.gov/nationsreportcard/pdf/main2002/2003521.pdf on April 17, 2025.

Grimes, N. (1997). *Meet Danitra Brown* (F. Cooper, Illus.). HarperCollins.

Gunning, T. G. (1996). *Creating reading instruction for all children* (2nd ed.). Allyn & Bacon.

Guthrie, J. T., Wigfield, A., Metsala, J. L., & Cox, K. E. (1999). Motivational and cognitive predictors of text comprehension and reading amount. *Scientific Studies of Reading, 3*(3), 231–256. https:///doi.org/10.1207/s1532799xssr0303_3

Hancock, L. (2018, May 19). Coffee break with . . . Dr. Tim Rasinski. *Literacy Junkie.* Accessed at www.literacyjunkie.com/coffee-break/2018/5/18/coffee-break-with-dr-timothy-rasinski on October 17, 2024.

Hanford, E. (2018, September 10). Hard words: Why aren't kids being taught to read? *APM Reports.* Accessed at www.apmreports.org/episode/2018/09/10/hard-words-why-american-kids-arent-being-taught-to-read on October 17, 2024.

Hanford, E. (Host). (2022–present). *Sold a story: How teaching kids to read went so wrong* [Audio podcast]. *APM Reports.* Accessed at https://features.apmreports.org/sold-a-story on May 25, 2024.

Harris, T. L., & Hodges, R. E. (Eds.). (1995). *The literacy dictionary: The vocabulary of reading and writing.* International Reading Association.

Hart, B., & Risley, T. R. (2003). The early catastrophe: The 30 million word gap by age 3. *American Educator.* Accessed at www.aft.org/ae/spring2003/hart_risley on May 10, 2024.

Harvey, D. (2002). *Literature circles: Voice and choice in book clubs and reading groups.* Stenhouse.

Hasbrouck, J. E., & Tindal, G. (1992). Curriculum-based oral reading fluency norms for students in grades 2 through 5. *TEACHING Exceptional Children, 24*(3), 41–44.

Hasbrouck, J., & Tindal, G. (2006). Oral reading fluency norms: A valuable assessment tool for reading teachers. *The Reading Teacher, 59*(7), 636–644.

Hasbrouck, J., & Tindal, G. (2017). *An update to compiled ORF norms* (Technical Report No. 1702). Behavioral Research and Teaching, University of Oregon.

Hawkins, L. K. (2021). How to organize a classroom library to support inquiry: 4 systems that work. *The Reading Teacher, 75*(1), 107–111. https://doi.org/10.1002/trtr.2007

Heckelman, R. G. (1969). A neurological-impress method of remedial-reading instruction. *Intervention in School and Clinic, 4*(4), 277–282. https://doi.org/10.1177/105345126900400406

Heller, R. (1987–1998). *World of language* [Book series]. Grosset & Dunlap.

Henderson, J. W., Warren, K., Whitmore, K. F., Flint, A. S., Laman, T. T., & Jaggers, W. (2020). Take a close look: Inventorying your classroom library for diverse books. *The Reading Teacher, 73*(6), 747–755. https://doi.org/10.1002/trtr.1886

Henk, W. A. (1981). *Neurological-impress and reading. How and why?* [Conference paper]. Thirteenth Annual Three Rivers Reading Conference, Pittsburgh, PA.

Herold, B. (2022, April 14). How tech-driven teaching strategies have changed during the pandemic. *Education Week.* Accessed at www.edweek.org/technology/how-tech-driven-teaching-strategies-have-changed-during-the-pandemic/2022/04 on June 6, 2024.

Hiebert, E. H. (2013). Supporting students' movement up the staircase of text complexity. *The Reading Teacher, 66*(6), 459–468. https://doi.org/10.1002/TRTR.1149

Hiller, C. (2024). *Colossal words for kids: 75 tremendous words—Neatly defined to stick in the mind* (T. Freeman, Illus.). Frances Lincoln Children's Books.

Hoberman, M. A. (2006). *Very short stories to read together* (M. Emberley, Illus.). Little, Brown Books for Young Readers.

Hoberman, M. A. (2009). *Very short scary stories to read together* (M. Emberley, Illus.). Little, Brown Books for Young Readers.

Hoberman, M. A. (2012a). *Very short fairy tales to read together* (M. Emberley, Illus.). Little, Brown Books for Young Readers.

Hoberman, M. A. (2012b). *Very short Mother Goose tales to read together* (M. Emberley, Illus.). Little, Brown Books for Young Readers.

Hoberman, M. A. (2013). *Very short fables to read together* (M. Emberley, Illus.). Little, Brown Books for Young Readers.

Hoberman, M. A. (2019). *Very short tall tales to read together* (M. Emberley, Illus.). Little, Brown Books for Young Readers.

Hoffman, J. V., Sailors, M., Duffy, G. R., & Beretvas, S. N. (2004). The effective elementary classroom literacy environment: Examining the validity of the TEX-IN3 observation system. *Journal of Literacy Research*, *36*(3), 303 -334. https://doi.org/10.1207/s15548430jlr3603_3

Ho, J. (2023). *Say my name* (K. Le, Illus.). HarperCollins.

Holdaway, D. (1979). *The foundations of literacy*. Ashton Scholastic.

Hollenbeck, K. M. (2006). *Fluency practice read-aloud plays: Grades 1 -2*. Scholastic.

Hoover, W. A., & Gough, P. B. (1990). The simple view of reading. *Reading and Writing*, *2*(2), 127–160. https://doi.org/10.1007/BF00401799

Hopkins, L. B. (2000). *My America: A Poetry Atlas of the United States*. Simon & Schuster.

Hoyt, L. (2009). *Revisit, reflect, retell: Time-tested strategies for teaching reading comprehension* (Updated ed.). Heinemann.

Huck, C., & Zhang, J. (2021). Effects of the COVID-19 pandemic on K-12 education: A systematic literature review. *Educational Research and Development Journal*, *24*(1), 53–84.

Hudson, A. K., Moore, K. A., Han, B., Koh, P. W., Binks-Cantrell, E., & Joshi, R. M. (2021). Elementary teachers' knowledge of foundational literacy skills: A critical piece of the puzzle in the science of reading. *Reading Research Quarterly*, *56*(S1), S287–S315. https://doi.org/10.1002/rrq.408

Huey, E. B. (1968). *The psychology and pedagogy of reading; with a review of the history of reading and writing and of methods, texts, and hygiene in reading*. MIT Press. (Original work published 1908.)

Hurst, S., & Griffity, P. (2015). Examining the effect of teacher read-aloud on adolescent attitudes and learning. *Middle Grades Research Journal*, *10*(1), 31–47.

Ibrahim, E. H. E., Sarudin, I., & Muhamad, A. J. (2016). The relationship between vocabulary size and reading comprehension of ESL learners. *English Language Teaching*, *9*(2), 116–123. https://doi.org/10.5539/elt.v9n2p116

Idol, L. (1987). Group story mapping: A comprehension strategy for both skilled and unskilled readers. *Journal of Learning Disabilities*, *20*(4), 196–205. https://doi.org/10.1177/002221948702000401

Indiana Department of Education. (2023a). *Indiana academic standards*. Accessed at www.in.gov/doe/students/indiana-academic-standards on April 29, 2024.

Indiana Department of Education (2023b). *2023 Indiana academic standards: Grade 1 English/language arts*. Accessed at https://media.doe.in.gov/standards/indiana-academic-standards-grade-1-english_language-arts.pdf on October 18, 2024.

Indiana Department of Education (2023c). *2023 Indiana academic standards: Grade 3 mathematics*. Accessed at https://media.doe.in.gov/standards/indiana-academic-standards-grade-3-mathematics.pdf on October 18, 2024.

Indiana Department of Education (2023d). *2023 Indiana academic standards: Grade 5 science*. Accessed at https://media.doe.in.gov/standards/indiana-academic-standards-grade-5-science.pdf on October 18, 2024.

Institute of Education Sciences. (2007). *Effective literacy and English language instruction for English learners in the elementary grades* (NCEE Publication No. 2007–4011). National Center for Education Evaluation and Regional Assistance, U.S. Department of Education. https://ies.ed.gov/ncee/wwc/Docs/PracticeGuide/20074011.

Institute of Education Sciences. (2008). *Reading first impact study: Final report—Executive summary* (NCEE Publication No. 2009-4039). National Center for Education Evaluation and Regional Assistance, U.S. Department of Education. https://files.eric.ed.gov/fulltext/ED503345.pdf

Institute of Education Sciences. (2016). *Foundational skills to support reading for understanding in kindergarten through 3rd grade* (NCEE Publication No. 2016–4008). National Center for Education Evaluation and Regional Assistance, U.S. Department of Education. Accessed at http://whatworks.ed.gov on October 17, 2024.

International Literacy Association. (2000). *Providing books and other print materials for classroom and school libraries: A position statement of the International Reading Association* [Brochure] (ILA Publication No. 1039). Author. Accessed at www.literacyworldwide.org/docs/default-source/where-we-stand/providing-books-position-statement.pdf on April 10, 2024.

International Literacy Association. (2019). *Children's rights to excellent literacy instruction* [Position statement] (ILA Publication No. 9454). Accessed at www.literacyworldwide.org/docs/default-source/where-we-stand/ila-childrens-rights-to-excellent-literacy-instruction.pdf on October 18, 2024.

International Literacy Association. (2020). *Phonological awareness in early childhood literacy development* [Position statement and research brief] (ILA Publication No. 9457). Accessed at www.literacyworldwide.org/docs/default-source/where-we-stand/9457_Phonological_Awareness_1-2020_Final.pdf on October 18, 2024.

International Literacy Association. (2023a). *Children's rights to read*. Accessed at https://www.literacyworldwide.org/get-involved/childrens-rights-to-read on October 18, 2024.

International Literacy Association. (2023b). *Literacy glossary*. Accessed at www.literacyworldwide.org/get-resources/literacy-glossary on August 12, 2024.

Jay, M. (2023). *Ricky, the rock that just couldn't rhyme* (E. Wozniak, Illus.). New Paige Press.

Johnson, T., Cavendish, L. M., Waller, R., Hoch, M., Huggins, S., Gallagher, T., et al. (2024). Re-centering students and teachers: Voices from literacy clinics. *The Reading Teacher*, *78*(2), 98–105. https://doi.org/10.1002/trtr.2350

Johnston, R. S., & Watson, J. E. (2004). Accelerating the development of reading, spelling and phonemic awareness skills in initial readers. *Reading and Writing*, *17*(4), 327–357.

Johnston, R. S., McGeown, S., & Watson, J. E. (2012). Long-term effects of synthetic versus analytic phonics teaching on the reading and spelling ability of 10 year old boys and girls. *Reading and Writing*, *25*(6), 1365–1384.

Jones, C. D., & Reutzel, D. R. (2012). Enhanced alphabet knowledge instruction: Exploring a change of frequency, focus, and distributed cycles of review. *Reading Psychology*, *33*(5), 448–464. https://doi.org/10.1080/02702711.2010.545260

Justice, L. M., Pence, K., Bowles, R. B., & Wiggins, A. (2006). An investigation of four hypotheses concerning the order by which 4-year-old children learn the alphabet letters. *Early Childhood Research Quarterly*, *21*(3), 374–389. https://doi.org/10.1016/j.ecresq.2006.07.010

Kaefer, T. (2020). When did you learn it? How background knowledge impacts attention and comprehension in read-aloud activities. *Reading Research Quarterly*, *55*(S1), S173–S183.

Kaminski, R. A., & Good, R. H., III. (1996). Toward a technology for assessing basic early literacy skills. *School Psychology Review*, *25*(2), 215–227.

Kanik Uysal, P., & Duman, A. (2020). The effects of fluency-oriented reading instruction on reading skills. *Pegem Journal of Education and Instruction*, *10*(4), 1111–1146.

Keats, E. J. (1962). *The snowy day*. Viking Press.

Keene, E. O., & Zimmermann, S. (2007). *Mosaic of thought: The power of comprehension strategy instruction* (2nd ed.). Heinemann.

Keene, E. O., & Zimmermann, S. (2013). Years later, comprehension strategies still at work. *The Reading Teacher*, *66*(8), 601–606. https://doi.org/10.1002/trtr.1167

Khan, K. S., Purtell, K. M., Logan, J., Ansari, A., & Justice, L. M. (2017). Association between television viewing and parent-child reading in the early home environment. *Journal of Developmental and Behavioral Pediatrics*, *38*(7), 521–527.

Kilpatrick, D. A. (2015). *Essentials of assessing, preventing, and overcoming reading difficulties*. Wiley.

Kim, Y. S. G. (2017). Why the simple view of reading is not simplistic: Unpacking component skills of reading using a direct and indirect effect model of reading (DIER). *Scientific Studies of Reading, 21*(4), 310–333. https://doi.org/10.1080/10888438.2017.1291643

Kindle, K. (2011). Same book, different experience: A comparison of shared reading in preschool classrooms. *Journal of Language and Literacy Education, 7*(1), 13–34. Accessed from http://jolle.coe.uga.edu/wp-content/uploads/2013/03/7_1_2_kindle.pdf on August 12, 2024.

Klein, A. (2022, May 17). Case study: The hard transition to 1-to-1 computing continues. *Education Week*. Accessed at www.edweek.org/technology/case-study-the-hard-transition-to-1-to-1-computing-continues/2022/05 on April 30, 2024.

Klingner, J. K., & Vaughn, S. (1999). Promoting reading comprehension, content learning, and English acquisition through collaborative strategic reading (CSR). *The Reading Teacher, 52*(7), 738–747.

Klinner, L. (n.d.). *Phonemic awareness activities in the classroom: Phoneme isolation*. Libby Klinner Teaching. Accessed at https://libbyklinnerteaching.com/phonemic-awareness-activities-in-the-classroom-phoneme-isolation on June 16, 2024.

Klvacek, M. L. (2015). *Dyad reading experiences of second-grade English learners with fiction and nonfiction texts* [Unpublished doctoral dissertation]. Brigham Young University. Accessed at https://scholarsarchive.byu.edu/cgi/viewcontent.cgi?article=6527&context=etd on April 17, 2025.

Koss, M. D., & Paciga, K. A. (2022). Conducting a diversity audit: Who is represented in your classroom library? *The Reading Teacher, 76*(3), 261–268. https://doi.org/10.1002/trtr.2136

Kramer, S. V., & Schuhl, S. (2023). *Acceleration for all: A how-to guide for overcoming learning gaps*. Solution Tree Press.

Krashen, S. (2021, January 11). More books, not more phonics. *Education Week*. Accessed at www.edweek.org/teaching-learning/opinion-more-books-not-more-phonics/2021/01 on July 31, 2024.

Krashen, S. D. (1997). *Every person a reader: An alternative to the California Task Force report on reading*. Heinemann.

Krashen, S. D. (2004). *The power of reading: Insights from the research* (2nd ed.). Heinemann.

Kress, J. E., & Fry, E. B. (2016). *The reading teacher's book of lists* (6th ed.). Jossey-Bass.

Kristof, N. (2023, February 11). Two-thirds of kids struggle to read, and we know how to fix it. *The New York Times*. Accessed at www.nytimes.com/2023/02/11/opinion/reading-kids-phonics.html on August 17, 2024.

Kuhn, M. R., & Levy, L. (2015). *Developing fluent readers: Teaching fluency as a foundational skill*. Guilford Press.

Kuhn, M. R., Schwanenflugel, P. J., Morris, R. D., Morrow, L. M., Woo, D. G., Meisinger, E. B., et al. (2006). Teaching children to become fluent and automatic readers. *Journal of Literacy Research, 38*(4), 357–387. https://doi.org/10.1207/s15548430jlr3804_1

Kuhn, M. R., Schwanenflugel, P. J., & Meisinger, E. B. (2010). Aligning theory and assessment of reading fluency: Automaticity, prosody, and definitions of fluency. *Reading Research Quarterly, 45*(2), 230–251. https://doi.org/10.1598/RRQ.45.2.4

Kuhn, M. R., & Stahl, S. A. (2003). Fluency: A review of developmental and remedial practices. *Journal of Educational Psychology, 95*(1), 3–21. https://doi.org/10.1037/0022-0663.95.1.3

Kung, K. (2020). *Phonological awareness: A guidebook for parents*. Accessed at www.uwo.ca/fhs/lwm/teaching/dld2_2020_21/Kung_dld2.pdf on June 16, 2024.

LaBerge, D., & Samuels, S. J. (1974). Toward a theory of automatic information processing in reading. *Cognitive Psychology, 6*(2), 293–323.

Laminack, L. L., & Wadsworth, R. M. (2006). *Reading aloud across the curriculum: How to build bridges in language arts, math, science, and social studies*. Heinemann.

Lance, K. C., & Kachel, D. E. (2018, March 26). Why school librarians matter: What years of research tell us. *Kappan*. Accessed from https://kappanonline.org/lance-kachel-school-librarians-matter-years-research on July 31, 2024.

Langer, J. A. (1984). Examining background knowledge and text comprehension. *Reading Research Quarterly, 19*(4), 468–481. https://doi.org/10.2307/747918

Lapp, D., Fisher, D., & Grant, M. (2008). "You can read this text—I'll show you how": Interactive comprehension instruction. *Journal of Adolescent and Adult Literacy, 51*(5), 372–383. https://doi.org/10.1598/JAAL.51.5.1

Lee, J., & Yoon, S. Y. (2017). The effects of repeated reading on reading fluency for students with reading disabilities: A meta-analysis. *Journal of Learning Disabilities, 50*(2), 213–224. https://doi.org/10.1177/0022219415605194

Lee, S. H., & Tsai, S-F. (2017). Experimental intervention research on students with specific poor comprehension: A systematic review of treatment outcomes. *Reading and Writing, 30*(4), 917– 943. https://doi.org/10.1007/s11145-016-9697

Lesaux, N. K., & Siegel, L. S. (2003). The development of reading in children who speak English as a second language. *Developmental Psychology, 39*(6), 1005–1019. https://doi.org/10.1037/0012-1649.39.6.1005

Levitt, P. M., Burger, D. A., & Guralnick, E. S. (2009). *The weighty word book* (J. Stevens, Illus.). University of New Mexico Press.

Levy, B. A., Nicholls, A., & Kohen, D. (1993). Repeated readings: Process benefits for good and poor readers. *Journal of Experimental Child Psychology, 56*(3), 303–327. https://doi.org/10.1006/jecp.1993.1037

Lewis, J. P. (2012). *National geographic book of animal poetry: 200 poems with photographs that squeak, soar, and roar!* National Geographic Children's Books.

Lewis, J. P. (2014). *Everything is a poem: The best of J. Patrick Lewis* (M. C. Pritelli, Illus.). Creative Editions.

Liberman, I. Y., Shankweiler, D., Fischer, F. W., & Carter, B. (1974). Explicit syllable and phoneme segmentation in the young child. *Journal of Experimental Child Psychology, 18*(2), 201–212. https://doi.org/10.1016/0022-0965(74)90101-5

Literal Word. (n.d.). Matthew 25:29. *Crossway Bibles English Standard Version.* Accessed at https://esv.literalword.com/?q=Matthew+25%3A29 on January 24, 2024.

Locher, F., & Pfost, M. (2020). The relation between time spent reading and reading comprehension throughout the life course. *Journal of Research in Reading, 43*(1), 57–77. https://doi.org/10.1111/1467-9817.12289

Loftus, M., & Sappington, L. (Hosts). (2023, July 7). Science of reading beyond phonics: Fluency instruction and assessment with Jan Hasbrouck. In *Melissa & Lori Love Literacy* [Video podcast episode]. Accessed at www.youtube.com/watch?v=3HBElBysMUA&ab_channel=MelissaandLoriLoveLiteracyPodcast on October 18, 2024.

Logan, J. A. R., Justice, L. M., Yumuş, M., & Chaparro-Moreno, L. J. (2019). When children are not read to at home: The million word gap. *Journal of Developmental and Behavioral Pediatrics, 40*(5), 383–386. https://doi.org/10.1097/dbp.00000
00000000657

Loxterman, J. A., Beck, I. L., & McKeown, M. G. (1994). The effects of thinking aloud during reading on students' comprehension of more or less coherent text. *Reading Research Quarterly, 29*(4), 352–367. https://doi.org/10.2307/747784

Lundberg, I., Frost, J., & Petersen, O.-P. (1988). Effects of an extensive program for stimulating phonological awareness in preschool children. *Reading Research Quarterly, 23*(3), 263–284. https://doi.org/10.1598/RRQ.23.3.1

Lyster, S.-A. H., Lervåg, A. O., & Hulme, C. (2016). Preschool morphological training produces long-term improvements in reading comprehension. *Reading and Writing, 29*(6), 1269–1288. https://doi.org/10.1007/s11145-016-9636-x

MacDonald, C., & Figueredo, L. (2010). Closing the gap early: Implementing a literacy intervention for at-risk kindergartners in urban schools. *Reading Teacher, 63*(5), 404–419.

Madalyou, L. C. (2021). *Let's go, slow Moe!* Slugger International.

Maeker, P., & Heller, J. (2023). *Literacy in a PLC at Work: Guiding teams to get going and get better in grades K–6 reading.* Solution Tree Press.

Mahdavi, J. N., & Tensfeldt, L. (2013). Untangling reading comprehension strategy instruction: Assisting struggling readers in the primary grades. *Preventing School Failure: Alternative Education for Children and Youth, 57*(2), 77–92. https://doi.org/10.1080/1045988X.2012.668576

Manyak, P. C. (2007). A framework for robust literacy instruction for English learners. *The Reading Teacher, 61*(2), 197–199. https://doi.org/10.1598/RT.61.2.10

Manyak, P. C., & Bauer, E. B. (2008). Explicit code and comprehension instruction for English learners. *The Reading Teacher, 61*(5), 432–434. https://doi.org/10.1598/RT.61.5.9

Manzo, A. V. (1969). The ReQuest Procedure: Improving reading comprehension through reciprocal questioning. *Journal of Reading, 13*(2), 123–126.

Manzo, A. V., & Casale, U. P. (1985). Listen-read-discuss: A content reading heuristic. *Journal of Reading, 28*(8), 732–734.

Manzo, A. V., Manzo, U. C., & Thomas, M. M. (2006). Rationale for systematic vocabulary development: Antidote for state mandates. *Journal of Adolescent and Adult Literacy, 49*(7), 610–619.

Marcell, B. (2007). Traffic light reading: Fostering the independent usage of comprehension strategies with informational text. *The Reading Teacher, 60*(8), 778–781. https://doi.org/10.1598/RT.60.8.8

MacDonald, C., & Figueredo, L. (2010). Closing the gap early: Implementing a literacy intervention for at-risk kindergartners in urban schools. *The Reading Teacher, 63*(5), 404–419. https://doi.org/10.1598/RT.63.5.6

Martin, B., Jr. (2012). *Brown bear, brown bear, what do you see?* (E. Carle, Illus.). Henry Holt and Company.

Martinez, M., Roser, N. L., & Strecker, S. (1999). "I never thought I could be a star": A Readers Theatre ticket to fluency. *The Reading Teacher, 52*(4), 326–334.

Marzano, R. J. (2004). *Building background knowledge for academic achievement: Research on what works in schools.* ASCD.

Marzano, R. J. (2009). The art and science of teaching: Six steps to better vocabulary instruction. *Educational Leadership, 67*(1), 83–84.

Marzano, R. J. (2020). *Teaching basic, advanced, and academic vocabulary: A comprehensive framework for elementary instruction.* Solution Tree Press.

Marzano, R. J. (1984). A cluster approach to vocabulary instruction: A new direction from the research literature. *The Reading Teacher, 38*(2), 168–173.

Marzano, R. J., & Marzano, J. S. (1988). *A cluster approach to elementary vocabulary instruction.* International Reading Association.

Marzano, R. J., & Pickering, D. J. (2005). *Building academic vocabulary: Teacher's manual.* ASCD.

Marzano, R. J., Rogers, K., & Simms, J. A. (2015). *Vocabulary for the new science standards.* Marzano Resources.

Marzano, R. J., & Simms, J. A. (2013). *Vocabulary for the Common Core.* Marzano Resources.

Massey, D. D., & Heafner, T. L. (2004). Promoting reading comprehension in social studies. *Journal of Adolescent and Adult Literacy, 48*(1), 26–40. https://doi.org/10.1598/JAAL.48.1.3

Massey, S. L., Pence, K. L., Justice, L. M., & Bowles, R. P. (2008). Educators' use of cognitively challenging questions in economically disadvantaged preschool classroom contexts. *Early Education and Development, 19*(2), 340–360.

Mastrothanasis, K., Kladaki, M., & Andreou, A. (2023). A systematic review and meta-analysis of the Readers' Theatre impact on the development of reading skills. *International Journal of Educational Research Open, 4*, Article 100243. https://doi.org/10.1016/j.ijedro.2023.100243

Mattos, M., Buffum, A., Malone, J., Cruz, L. F., Dimich, N., & Schuhl, S. (2025). *Taking action: A handbook for RTI at Work* (2nd ed.). Solution Tree Press.

McBride-Chang, C. (1999). The ABCs of the ABCs: The development of letter-name and letter-sound knowledge. *Merrill-Palmer Quarterly, 45*(2), 285–308.

McCarthy, P. A. (2008). Using sound boxes systematically to develop phonemic awareness. *The Reading Teacher, 62*(4), 346–349. https://doi.org/10.1598/RT.62.4.7

McCormick, S., & Zutell, J. (2015). *Instructing students who have literacy problems* (7th ed.). Pearson.

McGregor, T. (2007). *Comprehension connections: Bridges to strategic reading.* Heinemann.

McGuire, L. (1996). *Big Frank's fire truck* (J. Mathieu, Illus.). Random House.

McQuillan, J. (1998). *The literacy crisis: False claims, real solutions.* Heinemann.

Melby-Lervåg, M., Lyster, S.-A. H., & Hulme, C. (2012). Phonological skills and their role in learning to read: A meta-analytic review. *Psychological Bulletin, 138*(2), 322–352. https://doi.org/10.1037/a0026744

Meltzer, J. (2001). *Supporting adolescent literacy across the content areas. Perspectives on policy and practice.* U.S. Department of Education, Office of Educational Research and Improvement, Educational Resources Information Center. Accessed at https://eric.ed.gov/?id=ED459442 on April 22, 2024.

Mesmer, H. A. (2005). Text decodability and the first-grade reader. *Reading and Writing Quarterly, 21*(1), 61–86. https://doi.org/10.1080/10573560590523667

Mesmer, H. A. (2019). *Letter lessons and first words: Phonics foundations that work, preK–2.* Heinemann.

Mesmer, H. A. (2020, January 23). There are four foundational reading skills. Why do we only talk about phonics? *Education Week.* Accessed at www.edweek.org/teaching-learning/opinion-there-are-four-foundational-reading-skills-why-do-we-only-talk-about-phonics/2020/01 on July 5, 2024.

Mesmer, H. A. (2024). Time in text: Differentiating instruction for intermediate students struggling with word recognition. *The Reading Teacher, 77*(6), 982–990. https://doi.org/10.1002/trtr.2332

Mesmer, H. A., & Griffith, P. L. (2005). Everybody's selling it—but just what is explicit, systematic phonics instruction? *The Reading Teacher, 59*(4), 366–376. https://doi.org/10.1598/RT.59.4.6

Mesmer, H. A., & Kambach, A. (2022). Beyond labels and agendas: Research teachers need to know about phonics and phonological awareness. *The Reading Teacher, 76*(1), 62–72. https://doi.org/10.1002/trtr.2102

Meyer, B. J. F. (1975). *The organization of prose and its effects on memory.* North-Holland.

Miles, K. P., Rubin, G. B., & Gonzalez-Frey, S. (2018). Rethinking sight words. *The Reading Teacher, 71*(6), 715–726. https://doi.org/10.1002/trtr.1658

Miller, D. (2009). *The book whisperer: Awakening the inner reader in every child.* Jossey-Bass.

Miller, D., & Sharp, C. (2018). *Game changer! Book access for all kids.* Scholastic.

Miller, D., & Sharp, C. (2022). *The commonsense guide to your classroom library: Building a collection that inspires, engages, and challenges readers.* Scholastic.

Moll, L. C., & Dworin, J. E. (1996). Biliteracy development in classrooms: Social dynamics and cultural possibilities. In D. Hicks (Ed.), *Discourse, learning, and schooling* (pp. 221–246). Cambridge University Press.

Morgan, A., Wilcox, B. R., & Eldredge, J. L. (2000). Effect of difficulty levels on second-grade delayed readers using dyad reading. *The Journal of Educational Research, 94*(2), 113–119. https://doi.org/10.1080/00220670009598749

Mosel, A. (2007). *Tikki Tikki Tembo* (B. Lent, Illus.). Square Fish.

Mulligan, T., & Landrigan, C. (2018). *It's all about the books: How to create bookrooms and classroom libraries that inspire readers.* Heinemann.

Nagy, W. E., Diakidoy, I.-A. N., & Anderson, R. C. (1993). The acquisition of morphology: Learning the contribution of suffixes to the meanings of derivatives. *Journal of Reading Behavior, 25*(2), 155–170.

Nagy, W. E., & Herman, P. A. (1987). Breadth and depth of vocabulary knowledge: Implications for acquisition and instruction. In M. G. McKeown & M. E. Curtis (Eds.), *The nature of vocabulary acquisition* (pp. 19–35). Erlbaum.

National Assessment of Educational Progress. (2005). *The nation's report card: Reading 2005.* Author. Accessed at https://nces.ed.gov/nationsreportcard/pdf/main2005/2006451.pdf on August 4, 2025.

National Center on Improving Literacy. (n.d.). *Learning literacy glossary.* Accessed at https://improvingliteracy.org/glossary on July 8, 2024.

National Council of Teachers of English. (2017, May 31). *Statement on classroom libraries* [Position statement]. Accessed from https://ncte.org/statement/classroom-libraries on June 3, 2024.

National Early Literacy Panel. (2008). *Developing early literacy: Report of the National Early Literacy Panel.* National Institute for Literacy.

National Governors Association Center for Best Practices & Council of Chief State School Officers. (2010). *Common Core State Standards for English language arts and literacy in history/social studies, science, and technical subjects.* Authors. Accessed at www.corestandards.org/assets/CCSSI_ELA%20Standards.pdf on January 24, 2025.

National Institute of Child Health and Human Development. (2000a). *Report of the National Reading Panel: Teaching children to read—An evidence-based assessment of the scientific research literature on reading and its implications for reading instruction* (NIH Publication No. 00–4769). U.S. Department of Health and Human Services, National Institutes of Health. Accessed at https://files.eric.ed.gov/fulltext/ED444126.pdf on January 22, 2025.

National Institute of Child Health and Human Development. (2000b). *Report of the National Reading Panel: Teaching children to read—An evidence-based assessment of the scientific research literature on reading and its implications for reading instruction: Reports of the subgroups* (NIH Publication No. 00-4754). U.S. Department of Health and Human Services, National Institutes of Health. Accessed at www.nichd.nih.gov/sites/default/files/publications/pubs/nrp/Documents/report.pdf on May 11, 2024.

National Institute of Child Health and Human Development. (2005). Pathways to reading: The role of oral language in the transition to reading. *Developmental Psychology, 41*(2), 428–442. https://doi.org/10.1037/0012-1649.41.2.428

Ness, M. (2011). Explicit reading comprehension instruction in elementary classrooms: Teacher use of reading comprehension strategies. *Journal of Research in Childhood Education, 25*(1), 98–117.

Ness, M. (2017). "Is that how I really sound?": Using iPads for fluency practice. *The Reading Teacher, 70*(5), 611–615. https://doi.org/10.1002/trtr.1554

Ness, M. (2023). *Read alouds for all learners: A comprehensive plan for every subject, every day, grades preK–8.* Solution Tree Press.

Ness, M., & Kenny, M. (2016). Improving the quality of think-alouds. *The Reading Teacher, 69*(4), 453–460. https://doi.org/10.1002/trtr.1397

Neuman, S. B. (1999). Books make a difference: A study of access to literacy. *Reading Research Quarterly, 34*(3), 286–311. https://doi.org/10.1598/RRQ.34.3.3

Newman, L. (2004). *The boy who cried fabulous.* Tricycle Press.

No Child Left Behind (NCLB) Act of 2001, Pub. L. No. 107-110, § 115, Stat. 1425 (2002).

O'Connor, R. E. (2011). Phoneme awareness and the alphabetic principle. In R. E. O'Connor & P. F. Vadasy (Eds.), *Handbook of reading interventions* (pp. 9–26). Guilford Press.

Okkinga, M., van Steensel, R., van Gelderen, A. J. S., van Schooten, E., Sleegers, P. J. C., & Arends, L. R. (2018). Effectiveness of reading-strategy interventions in whole classrooms: A meta-analysis. *Educational Psychology Review, 30,* 1215–1239. https://doi.org/10.1007/s10648-018-9445-7

Opitz, M. F., & Rasinski, T. V. (1998). *Good-bye round robin: 25 effective oral reading strategies.* Heinemann.

Ortlieb, E., & Norris, M. R. (2012). Preventing the development of struggling readers: Comprehension instruction in the science classroom. *Current Issues in Education, 15*(1). https://doaj.org/article/30bf59f5490e451fa05ad872df0f804e

Orton-Gillingham.com. (n.d.). *5 multi-sensory Orton-Gillingham activities to use in the classroom.* Institute for Multi-Sensory Education. Accessed at www.orton-gillingham.com/5-multisensory-orton-gillingham-activities-to-use-in-the-classroom on July 13, 2024.

Padak, N., & Rasinski, T. (2004). Fast Start: A promising practice for family literacy programs. *Family Literacy Forum, 3*(1), 3–9.

Padak, N., & Rasinski, T. (2005). *Fast Start for early readers.* Scholastic.

Padak, N., & Rasinski, T. (2006). School-home partnerships in literacy education: From rhetoric to reality. *The Reading Teacher, 60*(3), 292–296. https://doi.org/10.1598/RT.60.3.11

Padak, N., & Rasinski, T. (2008). The games children play. *The Reading Teacher, 62*(4), 363–365. https://doi.org/10.1598/RT.62.4.11

Paige, D. D. (2011). "That sounded good!": Using whole-class choral reading to improve fluency. *The Reading Teacher, 64*(6), 435–438. https://doi.org/10.1598/RT.64.6.5

Paivio, A. (1986). *Mental representations: A dual-coding approach.* Oxford University Press.

Palincsar, A. S., & Brown, A. L. (1984). Reciprocal teaching of comprehension-fostering and comprehension-monitoring activities. *Cognition and Instruction, 1*(2), 117–175. https://doi.org/10.1207/s1532690xci0102_1

Palmer, H. (1961). *A fish out of water* (P. D. Eastman, Illus.). Beginner Books.

Pardo, L. S. (2004). What every teacher needs to know about comprehension. *The Reading Teacher, 58*(3), 272–280. https://doi.org/10.1598/RT.58.3.5

Pearson, P. D., & Duke, N. K. (2002). Comprehension instruction in the primary grades. In C. C. Block & M. Pressley (Eds.)., *Comprehension instruction: Research-based best practices* (pp. 247–258). Guilford Press.

Pearson, P. D., & Gallagher, M. C. (1983). The instruction of reading comprehension. *Contemporary Educational Psychology, 8*(3), 317–344. https://doi.org/10.1016/0361-476X(83)90019-X

Peavler, J., & Rooney, T. (2019). *Orton Gillingham. Join the journey in support of reading. Teacher's manual.* M.A. Rooney Foundation. Accessed at https://or.dyslexiaida.org/wp-content/uploads/sites/20/2020/06/OG-Training-Manual-2019.pdf on February 22, 2025.

Peery, A. B. (2017). *Vocabulary in a SNAP: 100+ lessons for elementary instruction.* Solution Tree Press.

Peery, A. B. (2017). *Vocabulary in a SNAP: 100+ lessons for secondary instruction.* Solution Tree Press.

Pennell, A. E., Jordan, R. L. P., Nash, K. T., Elson, K., & Trathen, W. (2024), A healthy diet for beginning readers: Decodable texts as part of a comprehensive literacy program. *The Reading Teacher, 77*(5), 673–684. https://doi.org/10.1002/trtr.2287

Pfost, M., Hattie, J., Dörfler, T., & Artelt, C. (2014). Individual differences in reading development: A review of 25 years of empirical research on Matthew effects in reading. *Review of Educational Research, 84*(2), 203–244. https://doi.org/10.3102/0034654313509492

Piasta, S. B., & Hudson, A. K. (2022). Key knowledge to support phonological awareness and phonics instruction. *The Reading Teacher, 76*(2), 201–210. https://doi.org/10.1002/trtr.2093

Piasta, S. B., & Wagner, R. K. (2010). Developing early literacy skills: A meta-analysis of alphabet learning and instruction. *Reading Research Quarterly, 45*(1), 8–38. https://doi.org/10.1598/RRQ.45.1.2

Pico, D. L., Prahl, A. H., Biel, C. H., Peterson, A. K., Biel, E. J., Woods, C., et al. (2021). Interventions designed to improve narrative language in school-age children: A systematic review with meta-analyses. *Language, Speech, and Hearing Services in Schools, 52*(4), 1109–1126. https://doi.org/10.1044/2021_LSHSS-20-00160

Pikulski, J. J., & Chard, D. J. (2005). Fluency: Bridge between decoding and reading comprehension. *The Reading Teacher, 58*(6), 510–519. https://doi.org/10.1598/RT.58.6.2

Pressley, M. (2000). What should comprehension instruction be the instruction of? In M. L. Kamil, P. B. Mosenthal, P. D. Pearson, & R. Barr (Eds.), *Handbook of reading research* (Vol. 3, pp. 545–562). Erlbaum.

Pressley, M. (2002). Comprehension strategies instruction: A turn-of-the-century status report. In C. C. Block & M. Pressley (Eds.), *Comprehension instruction: Research-based best practices* (pp. 11–27). Guilford Press.

Pressley, M. (2006). *Reading instruction that works: The case for balanced teaching* (3rd ed.). Guilford Press.

Pressley, M., & Afflerbach, P. (1995). *Verbal protocols of reading: The nature of constructively responsive reading.* Erlbaum.

Pressley, M., Wharton-McDonald, R., Mistretta-Hampston, J., & Echevarria, M. (1998). Literacy instruction in 10 fourth and fifth-grade classrooms in upstate New York. *Scientific Studies of Reading, 2,* 159–194.

Pressley, M., Disney, L., & Anderson, K. (2007). Landmark vocabulary instructional research and the vocabulary instructional research that makes sense now. In R. K. Wagner, A. E. Muse, & K. R. Tannenbaum (Eds.), *Vocabulary acquisition: Implications for reading comprehension* (pp. 205–232). Guilford Press.

Pugliano-Martin, C. (1999). *Just right plays: 25 emergent reader plays around the year.* Scholastic.

Radice, L. M. (2024). *Leading a culture of reading: How to ignite and sustain a love of literacy in your school community.* Solution Tree Press.

Raphael, T. E. (1982). Question-answering strategies for children. *The Reading Teacher, 36*(2), 186–190.

Raphael, T. E., & Au, K. H. (2005). QAR: Enhancing comprehension and test taking across grades and content areas. *The Reading Teacher, 59*(3), 206–221. https://doi.org/10.1598/RT.59.3.1

Raphael, T. E., & McKinney, J. (1983). An examination of fifth- and eighth-grade children's question-answering behavior: An instructional study in metacognition. *Journal of Reading Behavior, 15*(3), 67–86.

Raphael, T. E., & Wonnacott, C. A. (1985). Heightening fourth-grade students' sensitivity to sources of information for answering comprehension questions. *Reading Research Quarterly, 20*(3), 282–296.

Rasiniski, T. (n.d.). *Fry instant phrases.* Accessed at https://timrasinski.com/presentations/dr_edward_fry_instant_phrases.pdf on January 23, 2025.

Rasinski, T. (1990). *The effects of cued phrase boundaries in texts: A review* [White paper] (ERIC Publication No. ED313689). Educational Resources and Information Center, U.S. Department of Education. Accessed at https://files.eric.ed.gov/fulltext/ED313689.pdf on January 24, 2025.

Rasinski, T. (1995). Fast Start: A parental involvement reading program for primary grade students. In W. M. Linek & E. G. Sturtevant (Eds.), *Generations of literacy: The seventeenth yearbook of the College Reading Association* (pp. 301–312). College Reading Association.

Rasinski, T. (2005a). *Daily word ladders: Grades 2–3.* Scholastic.

Rasinski, T. (2005b). *Daily word ladders: Grades 4–6.* Scholastic.

Rasinski, T. (2006). Reading fluency instruction: Moving beyond accuracy, automaticity, and prosody. *The Reading Teacher, 59*(7), 704–706. https://doi.org/10.1598/RT.59.7.10

Rasinski, T. (2010). *The fluent reader: Oral and silent reading strategies for building fluency, word recognition and comprehension* (2nd ed.). Scholastic.

Rasinski, T., & Cheesman Smith, M. C. (2018). *The megabook of fluency: Strategies and texts to engage all readers.* Scholastic.

Rasinski, T., & Griffith, L. (2005a). *Texts for fluency practice. Level A.* Shell Educational.

Rasinski, T., & Griffith, L. (2005b). *Texts for fluency practice. Level B.* Shell Educational.

Rasinski, T., & Griffith, L. (2005c). *Texts for fluency practice. Level C.* Shell Educational.

Rasinski, T., & Hoffman, J. V. (2003). Oral reading in the school literacy curriculum. *Reading Research Quarterly, 38*(4), 510–522.

Rasinski, T., & Padak, N. D. (2001). *From phonics to fluency: Effective teaching of decoding and reading fluency in the elementary school.* Longman.

Rasinski, T., Reutzel, D. R., Chard, D., & Linan-Thompson, S. (2011). Reading fluency. In M. L. Kamil, P. D. Pearson, E. B. Moje, & P. Afflerbach (Eds.), *Handbook of reading research* (Vol. 4, pp. 286–319). Routledge.

Rasinski, T., & Smith, M. S. (2018). *The megabook of fluency: Strategies and texts to engage all readers.* Scholastic.

Rasinski, T., & Stevenson, B. (2005). The effects of Fast Start reading: A fluency-based home involvement reading program, on the reading achievement of beginning readers. *Reading Psychology, 26*(2), 109–125. https://doi.org/10.1080/02702710590930483

Rasinski, T., Yildirim, K., & Nageldinger, J. (2011). Building fluency through the phrased text lesson. *The Reading Teacher, 65*(4), 252–255. https://doi.org/10.1002/TRTR.01036

Rasinski, T., & Young, C. (2024). *Build reading fluency: Practice and performance with Reader's Theater and more.* Shell Education.

Rasinski, T., & Zimmerman, B. S. (2001). *Phonics poetry: Teaching word families, K-3.* Allyn & Bacon.

Ray, K., Dally, K., Colyvas, K., & Lane, A. E. (2021). The effects of a whole-class kindergarten handwriting intervention on early reading skills. *Reading Research Quarterly, 56*(S1), S193–S207. https://doi.org/10.1002/rrq.395

Rayner, K., & Pollatsek, A. (1989). *The psychology of reading*. Prentice Hall.

Reed, J., & Lee, E. L. (2020). The importance of oral language development in young literacy learners: Children need to be seen and heard. *Dimensions*, *48*(3), 6–9. Accessed at https://files.eric.ed.gov/fulltext/EJ1293447.pdf on May 1, 2024.

Rehfeld, D. M., Kirkpatrick, M., O'Guinn, N., & Renbarger, R. (2022). A meta-analysis of phonemic awareness instruction provided to children suspected of having a reading disability. *Language, Speech, and Hearing Services in Schools*, *53*(4) 1177–1201. https://doi.org/10.1044/2022_lshss-21-00160

Reutzel, D. R. (2015). Early literacy research: Findings primary-grade teachers will want to know. *The Reading Teacher*, *69*(1), 14–24. https://doi.org/10.1002/trtr.1387

Reutzel, D. R., & Hollingsworth, P. M. (1993). Effects of fluency training on second graders' reading comprehension. *The Journal of Educational Research*, *86*(6), 325–331. https://doi.org/10.1080/00220671.1993.9941225

Riccomini, P. J., Smith, G. W., Hughes, E. M., & Fries, K. M. (2015). The language of mathematics: The importance of teaching and learning mathematical vocabulary. *Reading and Writing Quarterly*, *31*(3), 235–252. https://doi.org/10.1080/10573569.2015.1030995

Rice, M., Erbeli, F., Thompson, C. G., Sallese, M. R., & Fogarty, M. (2022). Phonemic awareness: A meta-analysis for planning effective instruction. *Reading Research Quarterly*, *57*(4), 1259–1289. https://doi.org/10.1002/rrq.473

Ricketts, J., Nation, K., & Bishop, D. V. M. (2007). Vocabulary is important for some, but not all reading skills. *Scientific Studies of Reading*, *11*(3), 235–257. https://doi.org/10.1080/10888430701344306

Roberts, T. A., Vadasy, P. F., & Sanders, E. A. (2019). Preschoolers' alphabet learning: Cognitive, teaching sequence, and English proficiency influences. *Reading Research Quarterly*, *54*(3), 413–437.

Roberts, T. A. (2021). Learning letters: Evidence and questions from a science of reading perspective. *Reading Research Quarterly*, *56*(S1), S171–S192.

Roehling, J. V., Hebert, M., Nelson, J. R., & Bohaty, J. J. (2017). Text structure strategies for improving expository reading comprehension. *The Reading Teacher*, *71*(1), 71–82.

Rosenblatt, L. M. (1938). *Literature as exploration*. Appleton-Century.

Rosenblatt, L. M. (1978). *The reader, the text, the poem: The transactional theory of the literary work*. Southern Illinois University Press.

Roth, F. P., Speece, D. L., & Cooper, D. H. (2002). A longitudinal analysis of the connection between oral language and early reading. *The Journal of Educational Research*, *95*(5), 259–272.

Routman, R. (2014). *Read, write, lead: Breakthrough strategies for schoolwide literacy success*. ASCD.

Rumelhart, D. E. (1975). Notes on a schema for stories. In D. G. Bobrow & A. M. Collins (Eds.), *Representation and understanding: Studies in cognitive science* (pp. 211–236). Academic Press.

Samuels, S. J. (1979). The method of repeated readings. *The Reading Teacher*, *32*(4), 403–408.

Saunders, W. M., Foorman, B. R., & Carlson, C. D. (2006). Is a separate block of time for oral English language development in programs for English learners needed? *The Elementary School Journal*, *107*(2), 181–198. https://doi.org/10.1086/510654

Saville-Troike, M. (1984). What really matters in second language learning for academic achievement? *tesol quarterly*, *18*(2), 199–219. https://doi.org/10.2307/3586690

Scarborough, H. S. (2001). Connecting early language and literacy to later reading (dis)abilities: Evidence, theory, and practice. In S. Neuman & D. Dickinson (Eds.), *Handbook for research in early literacy* (Vol. 1, pp. 97–110). Guilford Press.

Schatschneider, C., Fletcher, J. M., Francis, D. J., Carlson, C. D., & Foorman, B. R. (2004). Kindergarten prediction of reading skills: A longitudinal comparative analysis. *Journal of Educational Psychology*, *96*(2), 265–282. https://doi.org/10.1037/0022-0663.96.2.265

Schmoker, M. (2001, October 24). The 'crayola curriculum.' *Education Week*. Accessed at www.edweek.org/teaching-learning/opinion-the-crayola-curriculum/2001/10 on August 11, 2024.

Schnell, L. W. (lwschnell55). (2017, October 16). *Dyad reading: No more unsupported "read with a partner"* [Blog post]. Literacy Learner. Accessed at https://literacylearnerblog.wordpress.com/2017/10/16/dyad-reading-no-more-unsupported-read-with-a-partner/ on October 18, 2024.

Schotter, R. (2006). *The boy who loved words* (G. Potter, Illus.). Schwartz & Wade Books.

Schwartz, S. (2023, March 15). Kids understand more from books than screens, but that's not always the case. *Education Week*. Accessed at www.edweek.org/teaching-learning/kids-understand-more-from-books-than-screens-but-thats-not-always-the-case/2023/03 on April 30, 2024.

Schwartz, S. (2024a, February 27). Social studies and science get short shrift in elementary schools. Why that matters. *Education Week*. Accessed at www.edweek.org/teaching-learning/social-studies-and-science-get-short-shrift-in-elementary-schools-why-that-matters/2024/02 on August 17, 2024.

Schwartz, S. (2024b, October 11). Which states have passed 'science of reading' laws? What's in them? *Education Week*. Accessed at www.edweek.org/teaching-learning/which-states-have-passed-science-of-reading-laws-whats-in-them/2022/07 on July 1, 2024.

Sénéchal, M., & Young, L. (2008). The effect of family literacy interventions on children's acquisition of reading from kindergarten to grade 3: A meta-analytic review. *Review of Educational Research*, *78*(4), 880–907. https://doi.org/10.3102/0034654308320319

Serravallo, J. (Host). (2023a, September 18). John Walker and Dr. Jan Wascowicz—Speech to print approach to phonics and spelling instruction (No. 21) [Audio podcast episode]. In *To the classroom*. Accessed at www.jenniferserravallo.com/blog/walker-and-wasowicz on October 19, 2024.

Serravallo, J. (Host). (2023b, October 2). Dr. Tim Rasinski—Fluency instruction, and blending the art and science of reading (No. 20) [Audio podcast episode]. In *To the classroom*. Accessed at www.jenniferserravallo.com/blog/tim-rasinski at October 19, 2024.

Shanahan, T. (1984). Nature of the reading–writing relation: An exploratory multivariate analysis. *Journal of Educational Psychology*, *76*(3), 466–477. https://doi.org/10.1037/0022–0663.76.3.466

Shanahan, T. (2003). Research-based reading instruction: Myths about the National Reading Panel report. *The Reading Teacher*, *56*(7), 646–655.

Shanahan, T. (2005). *The National Reading Panel report: Practical advice for teachers*. Learning Point Associates.

Shanahan, T. (2008, November 10). *How do I select a phonemics awareness program?* [Blog post]. Accessed at www.shanahanonliteracy.com/blog/how-do-i-select-an-effective-phonemic-awareness-program on June 16, 2024.

Shanahan, T. (2011, March 10). *Early literacy questions and answers* [Blog post]. Accessed at www.shanahanonliteracy.com/blog/early-literacy-questions-and-answers on June 16, 2024.

Shanahan, T. (2015, May 7). *Should we teach spelling? Part II* [Blog post]. Accessed at www.shanahanonliteracy.com/blog/should-we-teach-spelling-part-ii on July 9, 2024.

Shanahan, T. (2016a, April 24). *Should I set reading purposes for my students?* [Blog post]. Accessed at www.shanahanonliteracy.com/blog/should-i-set-reading-purposes-for-my-students on July 29, 2024.

Shanahan, T. (2016b, July 2). *The slow path forward: We can—and do—learn from reading research* [Blog post]. Accessed at www.shanahanonliteracy.com/blog/the-slow-path-forward-we-can-and-do-learn-from-reading-research on August 3, 2024.

Shanahan, T. (2020). What constitutes a science of reading instruction? *Reading Research Quarterly*, *55*(S1), S235–S247. https://doi.org/10.1002/rrq.349

Shanahan, T. (2021, April 17). *Should we build a (word) wall or not?* [Blog post]. Accessed at www.shanahanonliteracy.com/blog/should-we-build-a-word-wall-or-not on August 15, 2024.

Shanahan, T. (2023, December 16). *Putting on your underwear first: Why instructional sequence doesn't always matter* [Blog post]. Accessed at www.shanahanonliteracy.com/blog/putting-on-your-underwear-first-why-instructional-sequence-doesnt-always-matter-1 on August 17, 2024.

Shanahan, T., & Beck, I. L. (2006). Effective literacy teaching for English-language learners. In D. August & T. Shanahan (Eds.), *Developing literacy in second-language learners: Report of the National Literacy Panel on language-minority children and youth* (pp. 415–488). Erlbaum.

Shanahan, T., Fisher, D., & Frey, N. (2012). The challenge of challenging text. *Educational Leadership, 69*(6), 58–62.

Shanahan, T., & Shanahan, C. (2008). Teaching disciplinary literacy to adolescents: Rethinking content-area literacy. *Harvard Educational Review, 78*(1), 40–59. https://doi.org/10.17763/haer.78.1.v62444321p602101

Share, D. L., Jorm, A. F., Maclean, R., & Matthews, R. (1984). Sources of individual differences in reading acquisition. *Journal of Educational Psychology, 76*(6), 1309–1324. https://doi.org/10.1037/0022-0663.76.6.1309

Sierschynski, J., Louie, B., & Pughe, B. (2014). Complexity in picture books. *The Reading Teacher, 68*(4), 287–295. https://doi.org/10.1002/trtr.1293

Silverstein, S. (2004). *Where the sidewalk ends: The poems and drawings of Shel Silverstein* (30th anniversary ed.). HarperCollins.

Smith, K. C., Young, C. A., & Yatzeck, J. C. (2022). What are teachers reading and why? An analysis of elementary read aloud titles and the rationales underlying teachers' selections. *Literacy Research and Instruction, 61*(4), 383–401.

Snow, C. E., & Kim, Y.-S. (2007). Large problem spaces: The challenge of vocabulary for English language learners. In R. K. Wagner, A. E. Muse, & K. R. Tannenbaum (Eds.), *Vocabulary acquisition: Implications for reading comprehension* (pp. 123–139). Guilford Press.

Snyder, L. S., & Downey, D. M. (1997). Developmental differences in the relationship between oral language deficits and reading. *Topics in Language Disorders, 17*(3), 27–40. https://doi.org/10.1097/00011363-199705000-00005

Spear-Swerling, L., Brucker, P. O., & Alfano, M. P. (2005). Teachers' literacy-related knowledge and self-perceptions in relation to preparation and experience. *Annals of Dyslexia, 55*(2), 266–296. https://doi.org/10.1007/s11881-005-0014-7

Stahl, S. A., Duffy-Hester, A. M., & Stahl, K. A. D. (1998). Everything you wanted to know about phonics (but were afraid to ask). *Reading Research Quarterly, 33*(3), 338–355. https://doi.org/10.1598/RRQ.33.3.5

Stahl, S. A., & Nagy, W. E. (2006). *Teaching word meanings*. Erlbaum.

Stalega, M. V., Kearns, D. M., Bourget, J., Bayer, N., & Hebert, M. (2024). Is phonological-only instruction helpful for reading?: A meta-analysis. *Scientific Studies of Reading, 28*(6), 614–635. https://psycnet.apa.org/doi/10.1080/10888438.2024.2340708

Stanovich, K. E. (1986). Matthew effects in reading: Some consequences of individual differences in the acquisition of literacy. *Reading Research Quarterly, 21*(4), 360–407.

Stanovich, K. E. (1991). Word recognition: Changing perspectives. In R. Barr, M. L. Kamil, P. Mosenthal, & P. D. Pearson (Eds.), *Handbook of reading research* (Vol. 2, pp. 418–452). Longman.

Stanovich, K. E. (2000). *Progress in understanding reading: Scientific foundations and new frontiers*. Guilford Press.

Stanovich, K. E., & West, R. F. (1989). Exposure to print and orthographic processing. *Reading Research Quarterly, 24*(4), 402–433. https://doi.org/10.2307/747605

Steig, W. (1998). *Pete's a pizza*. HarperCollins.

Sternberg, R. J. (2006). *Cognitive psychology* (4th ed.). Thomson/Wadsworth.

Stevens, E. A., Walker, M. A., & Vaughn, S. (2017). The effects of reading fluency interventions on the reading fluency and reading comprehension performance of elementary students with learning disabilities: A synthesis of the research from 2001 to 2014. *Journal of Learning Disabilities, 50*(5), 576–590. https://doi.org/10.1177/0022219416638028

Stevens, J. (1984). *The tortoise and the hare* (Illus. J. Stevens). Holiday House

Stevenson, B. L. (2001). *Efficacy of fast start parent tutoring program in the development of reading skills by first grade students* [Unpublished doctoral dissertation]. Ohio State University.

Stiggins, R. J., Arter, J. A., Chappuis, J., & Chappuis, S. (2004). *Classroom assessment for student learning: Doing it right, using it well.* Assessment Training Institute.

Suggate, S. P. (2016). A meta-analysis of the long-term effects of phonemic awareness, phonics, fluency, and reading comprehension interventions. *Journal of Learning Disabilities, 49*(1), 77–96. https://doi.org/10.1177/0022219414528540

Sweet, A. P., & Snow, C. E. (Eds.). (2003). *Rethinking reading comprehension.* Guilford Press.

Szabo, S. (2010). Older children need phonemic awareness instruction, too. *TESOL Journal, 1*(1), 130–141. https://doi.org/10.5054/TJ.2010.215246

Taba, H. (1967). *Teachers' handbook for elementary social studies.* Addison-Wesley.

Talbott, H. (2021). *A walk in the words.* Nancy Paulsen Books.

Taylor, B. M., Frye, B. J., & Maruyama, G. M. (1990). Time spent reading and reading growth. *American Educational Research Journal, 27*(2), 351–362.

Taylor, B. M., Pearson, P. D., Clark, K., & Walpole, S. (2000). Effective schools and accomplished teachers: Lessons about primary-grade reading instruction in low-income schools. *The Elementary School Journal, 101*(2), 121–165. Accessed at www.journals.uchicago.edu/doi/10.1086/499662 on July 26, 2024.

Teacher's Tech. (2022, September 25). *How to use Padlet: Beginner's tutorial* [Video file]. Accessed at https://www.youtube.com/watch?v=qqGhcWG6e2g on August 7, 2025.

Teale, W. H., & Gambrell, L. B. (2007). Raising urban students' literacy achievement by engaging in authentic, challenging work. *The Reading Teacher, 60*(8), 728–739. https://doi.org/10.1598/RT.60.8.3

Therrien, W. J. (2004). Fluency and comprehension gains as a result of repeated reading: A meta-analysis. *Remedial and Special Education, 25*(4), 252–261. https://doi.org/10.1177/07419325040250040801

Thorndyke, P. W. (1977). Cognitive structures in comprehension and memory of narrative discourse. *Cognitive Psychology, 9*(1), 77–110.

Tierney, R. J., & Readence, J. E. (2000). *Reading strategies and practices: A compendium* (5th ed.). Allyn & Bacon.

Tierney, R. J., & Readence, J. E. (2005). *Reading strategies and practices: A compendium* (6th ed.). Allyn & Bacon.

Tompkins, G. E. (2006). *Literacy for the 21st century: A balanced approach* (4th ed.). Pearson.

Topping, K. (1987). Aired reading: Powerful technique for parent use. *Reading Teacher, 40*(7), 608–614.

Torgesen, J. K., Alexander, A. W., Wagner, R. K., Rashotte, C. A., Voeller, K. K. S., & Conway T. (2001). Intensive remedial instruction for children with severe reading disabilities: Immediate and long-term outcomes from two instructional approaches. *Journal of Learning Disabilities, 34*(1), 33–58, 78. https://doi.org/10.1177/002221940103400104

Torgesen, J. K., Rashotte, C., Alexander, A., Alexander, J., & MacPhee, K. (2003). Progress toward understanding the instructional conditions necessary for remediating reading difficulties in older children. In B. R. Foorman (Ed.), *Preventing and remediating reading difficulties: Bringing science to scale* (pp. 275–298). York Press.

Torppa, M., Niemi, P., Vasalampi, K., Lerkkanen, M.-K., Tolvanen, A., & Poikkeus, A.-M. (2020). Leisure reading (but not any kind) and reading comprehension support each other–A longitudinal study across grades 1 and 9. *Child Development, 91*(3), 876–900. https://doi.org/10.1111/cdev.13241

Treiman, R., & Broderick, V. (1998). What's in a name: Children's knowledge about the letters in their own names. *Journal of Experimental Child Psychology, 70*(2), 97–116. https://doi.org/10.1006/jecp.1998.2448

Trelease, J. (2006). *The read-aloud handbook* (6th ed.). Penguin Books.

Troia, G. A. (2014). Phonological processing deficits and literacy learning: Current evidence and future directions. In C. A. Stone, E. R. Silliman, B. J. Ehren, & G. P. Wallach (Eds.), *Handbook of language and literacy: Development and disorders* (2nd ed., pp. 271-301). Guilford Press.

Tyson, K. A. (1993). *The efficacy of self-selected text-processing strategies on text marking and comprehension of more able and less able readers at the college level* (Publication No. KC-23-11-00) [Doctoral dissertation, University of Missouri–Kansas City]. University of Missouri–Kansas City University Libraries.

Tyson, K. A., & Peery, A. B. (2017). *Blended vocabulary for K–12 classrooms: Harnessing the power of digital tools and direct instruction*. Solution Tree Press.

Urquhart, V., & Frazee, D. (2012, December 20). Characteristics of literacy-rich content-area classrooms. *ASCD Express*, *8*(6).

Vacca, R. T., & Vacca, J. A. L. (2002). *Content area reading: Literacy and learning across the curriculum* (7th ed.). Allyn & Bacon.

van Bergen, E., Vasalampi, K., & Torppa, M. (2021). How are practice and performance related? Development of reading from age 5 to 15. *Reading Research Quarterly*, *56*(3), 415–434. https://doi.org/10.1002/rrq.309

Vaughn, S., Mathes, P. G., Linan-Thompson, S. L., & Francis, D. J. (2005). Teaching English language learners at risk for reading disabilities to read: Putting research into practice. *Learning Disabilities: Research and Practice, 20*(1), 58–67. https://doi.org/10.1111/j.1540-5826.2005.00121

Veenendaal, N. J., Groen, M. A., & Verhoeven, L. (2015). What oral text reading fluency can reveal about reading comprehension. *Journal of Research in Reading*, *38*(3), 213–225. https://doi.org/10.1111/1467-9817.12024

Verhoeven, L. T. (1994). Transfer in bilingual development: The linguistic interdependence hypothesis revisited. *Language Learning*, *44*(3), 381–415. https://doi.org/10.1111/j.1467-1770.1994.tb01112.x

Vygotsky, L. S. (1978). *Mind in society: The development of higher psychological processes*. Harvard University Press.

Waddell, M. (2003). *Hi, Harry! The moving story of how one slow tortoise slowly made a friend*. Walker Children's Paperbacks.

Wagner, R. K., Muse, A. E., & Tannenbaum, K. R. (Eds.). (2007). *Vocabulary acquisition: Implications for reading comprehension*. Guilford Press.

Wagner, R. K., Torgesen, J. K., & Rashotte, C. A. (1994). Development of reading-related phonological processing abilities: New evidence of bidirectional causality from a latent variable longitudinal study. *Developmental Psychology*, *30*(1), 73–87. https://doi.org/10.1037/0012-1649.30.1.73

Walther, M. (2019). *The ramped-up read aloud: What to notice as you turn the page*. Corwin Press.

Watts, J. L. D., & Gandy, K. J. (2024). Exploring children's varied responses to interactive read-alouds. *The Reading Teacher*, *78*(2), 131–139. https://doi.org/10.1002/trtr.2354

Wessels, S. (2011). Promoting vocabulary learning for English learners. *The Reading Teacher*, *65*(1), 46–50. https://doi.org/10.1598/RT.65.1.6

Wexler, N. (2019). *The knowledge gap: The hidden cause of America's broken education system—and how to fix it*. Avery.

White, K. (2017). *Softening the edges: Assessment practices that honor K–12 teachers and learners*. Solution Tree Press.

Whitehurst, G. J., Falco, F. L., Lonigan, C. J., Fischel, J. E., DeBaryshe, B. D., Valdez-Menchaca, M. C., et al. (1988). Accelerating language development through picture book reading. *Developmental Psychology*, *24*(4), 552–559. https://doi.org/10.1037/0012-1649.24.4.552

Williams, C., Phillips-Birdsong, C., Hufnagel, K., Hungler, D., & Lundstrom, R. P. (2009). Word study instruction in the K–2 classroom. *The Reading Teacher*, *62*(7), 570–578. https://doi.org/10.1598/RT.62.7.3

Wimmer, S. (2012). *The word collector* (J. Brokenbrow, Trans.). Cuento de Luz.

Winograd, P., & Hare, V. C. (1988). 8—Direction instruction of reading comprehension strategies: The nature of teacher explanation. In C. E. Weinstein, E. T. Goetz, & P. A. Alexander (Eds.), *Learning and study strategies: Issues in assessment, instruction, and evaluation* (pp. 121–139). Academic Press. https://doi.org/10.1016/B978-0-12-742460-6.50014-1

Wiseman, A. M. (2011). Interactive read alouds: Teachers and students constructing knowledge and literacy together. *Early Childhood Education Journal*, *38*(6), 431–438.

Worthy, J., & Roser, N. (2010). Productive sustained reading in a bilingual class. In E. H. Hiebert & D. R. Reutzel, (Eds.), *Revisiting silent reading: New directions for teachers and researchers* (pp. 241–257). International Reading Association.

Wright, T. S. (2019). Reading to learn from the start: The power of interactive read alouds. *American Educator*, *42*(4), 4-8, 40.

Wright, T. S., & Cervetti, G. N. (2017). A systematic review of the research on vocabulary instruction that impacts text comprehension. *Reading Research Quarterly, 52*(2), 203–226. https://doi.org /10.1002/rrq.163

Wyse, D., & Hacking, C. (2024). Decoding, reading and writing: The double helix theory of teaching. *Literacy, 58*(3), 256–266. https://doi.org/10.1111/lit.12367

Xue, Y., & Meisels, S. J. (2004). Early literacy instruction and learning in kindergarten: Evidence from the early childhood longitudinal study—Kindergarten class of 1998–1999. *American Educational Research Journal, 41*(1), 191–229. https://doi.org/10.3102/00028312041001191

Yashima, T. (1955). *Crow boy.* Viking Press.

Yopp, H. K., & Yopp, R. H. (2000). Supporting phonemic awareness development in the classroom. *The Reading Teacher, 54*(2), 130–143.

Young, C., Durham, P., & Rosenbaum-Martinez, C. (2018). A stacked approach to reading intervention: Increasing 2nd- and 3rd-graders' independent reading levels with an intervention program. *Journal of Research in Childhood Education, 32*(2), 181–189. https://doi.org/10.1080/02568543.2017.1418771

Young, C., Paige, D., & Rasinski, T. V. (2022). *Artfully teaching the science of reading.* Routledge.

Young, C., Rasinski, T., & Mohr, K. A. J. (2016). Read two impress: An intervention for disfluent readers. *The Reading Teacher, 69*(6), 633–636. https://doi.org/10.1002/trtr.1391

Young, C., Stokes, F., & Rasinski, T. (2017). Readers Theatre plus comprehension and word study. *The Reading Teacher, 71*(3), 351–355. https://doi.org/10.1002/trtr.1629

Young, T. A., Bryan, G., Jacobs, J. S., & Tunnell, M. O. (2020). *Children's literature, briefly* (7th ed.). Pearson.

Zaner-Bloser. (n.d.). *Spelling connections: A word study approach.* Accessed at https://www.zaner-bloser.com/spelling/spelling -connections/index on April 17, 2025.

Zaner-Bloser. (2022). *Spelling connections: A word-study approach.* Zaner-Bloser.

Zemelman, S., Daniels, H., & Hyde, A. (2005). *Best practice: Today's standards for teaching and learning in America's schools* (3rd ed.). Heinemann.

Zucker, T. A., Cabell, S. Q., & Pico, D. L. (2021). Going nuts for words: Recommendations for teaching young students academic vocabulary. *The Reading Teacher, 74*(5), 581–594. https://doi.org/10.1002/trtr.1967

Zucker, T. A., Ward, A. E., & Justice, L. M. (2009). Print referencing during read-alouds: A technique for increasing emergent readers' print knowledge. *The Reading Teacher, 63*(1), 62–72. https://doi.org/10.1598/RT.63.1.6

Zutell, J., & Rasinski, T. V. (1991). Training teachers to attend to their students' oral reading fluency. *Theory Into Practice, 30*(3), 211–217.

Index

E

F

G

H

I

L

Q

R

Read Alouds for All Learners
Molly Ness
In *Read Alouds for All Learners: A Comprehensive Plan for Every Subject, Every Day, Grades PreK–8*, Molly Ness provides a compelling case for the integration, or reintegration, of the read aloud in schools and a step-by-step resource for preK–8 educators in classrooms.
BKG116

Redesigning Small-Group Reading Instruction
Julie A. Taylor
Author Julie A. Taylor provides lesson plans containing the necessary skills and strategies to incorporate into small-group reading instruction. Teachers can create productive, positive, and equitable classrooms by ensuring all students are able to achieve the integral milestones of reading development.
BKG213

Literacy Triangle
LeAnn Nickelsen and Melissa Dickson
Accelerate learning with high-impact strategies. Beginning and veteran teachers alike will find insights and practices they can use immediately. No matter what content area you teach, this book will help you develop the strategic reader in every student.
BKF983

MTSS for Reading Improvement
Sarah Brown and Stephanie Stollar
Transform schoolwide reading achievement through systematic implementation of the science of reading within an MTSS framework. Brown and Stollar provide over fifty practical tools that help leaders engineer robust support systems and create lasting, system-level improvements for all students.
BKG251

Solving the Literacy Puzzle
Norene A. Bunt
Using graphic organizers, assessments, and reflection questions, educators can unpack five core components of literacy instruction within the science of reading framework. This comprehensive guide prepares teachers to confidently implement effective literacy instruction in their classrooms.
BKG158

Solution Tree | Press 

Visit SolutionTree.com or call 800.733.6786 to order.